The Growth of
Social Knowledge

The Growth of Social Knowledge

Theory, Simulation, and Empirical Research in Group Processes

Edited by Jacek Szmatka, Michael Lovaglia, and Kinga Wysienska

PRAEGER

Westport, Connecticut
London

Library of Congress Cataloging-in-Publication Data

The growth of social knowledge : theory, simulation, and empirical research in group processes / edited by Jacek Szmatka, Michael Lovaglia, and Kinga Wysienska.
    p. cm.
  Includes bibliographical references and index.
  ISBN 0–275–97213–5 (alk. paper)
    1. Social groups—Research. 2. Knowledge, Sociology of. I. Szmatka, Jacek. II. Lovaglia, Michael J. III. Wysienska, Kinga, 1976–
  HM716 .G78   2002
  305'.07'2—dc21   2001058046   4-16-03 dod

British Library Cataloguing in Publication Data is available.

Library of Congress Catalog Card Number: 2001058046
ISBN: 0–275–97213–5

First published in 2002

Praeger Publishers, 88 Post Road West, Westport, CT 06881
An imprint of Greenwood Publishing Group, Inc.
www.praeger.com

Printed in the United States of America

The paper used in this book complies with the Permanent Paper Standard issued by the National Information Standards Organization (Z39.48–1984).

10 9 8 7 6 5 4 3 2 1

We dedicate this book to Professor Jacek Szmatka who passed away on October 20, 2001, in Athens, Ohio. Polish and American sociology lost in him an outstanding scholar whose pro-science stance inspired many students and researchers. Jacek had rare intellectual leadership, creativity, and determination. He accomplished so much in a very short time as a researcher, as a teacher, and as a leader in Polish sociology. Describing a person like Jacek Szmatka and his contributions in just a few words is difficult to do. People who knew him and collaborated with him have lost not only an exceptional intellectual but also a wonderful friend. We will miss his innovative spirit, optimism, sense of humor, ambition, and charming old-world manners.

May his name and work remain in our memory.

Kinga Wysienska and Michael Lovaglia

Contents

PROLOGUE

Chapter 1

Developing Social Knowledge: The Group Processes Research Tradition

Jacek Szmatka, Michael J. Lovaglia, and Kinga Wysienska

Group processes researchers study society scientifically. They have used sociological theory to build cumulative, scientific knowledge about the social world. This conception of social theory as an explanatory tool contrasts with the widely held view of social theory as an interpretation of social reality. The classical works of Karl Marx, Max Weber, Emile Durkheim, and others can be studied and interpreted in varied ways depending on the perspective of the theorist. Although the interpretive approach has yielded much creative insight, cumulation of knowledge becomes problematic without a way to reconcile conflicting interpretations of different theorists (Cole 1994; Collins 1994; Davis 1994; Habermas 1988). Thus, sociological theory is often seen as social philosophy rather than as a component of the scientific method (Turner 1998:245).

Group processes research has self-consciously addressed itself, not only to conducting social research, but also to finding the best way to conduct it. The distinctive working style that characterizes group processes research dates to the 1970–1971 school year, when Joseph Berger was on fellowship at MIT. There he encountered the philosopher of science Imre Lakatos. Berger recognized that Lakatos's (1970) conception of a scientific research program could be adapted to social research. While Berger and his colleagues (Berger, Cohen, and Zelditch 1966, 1972; Berger, Zelditch, and Anderson 1972b) pursued their research program in status characteristics and expectations states, they also developed a distinctive recipe for the conduct of theoretical research programs in sociology (Cohen 1989; Wagner 1984; Wagner and Berger 1986, 1993; Berger and Zelditch 1997). At about the same time, David Willer, Thomas Fararo, and other group processes researchers worked independently, but just as self-consciously, to develop theoretical research programs in sociology (Fararo 1984; Fararo and Skvoretz 1987; Willer 1987; Willer and Anderson 1981).

Theoretical research programs coordinate theory and empirical research. Simply put, theory guides research, and research tests theory (Moore 1989). Research results provide insight that improves theories, which then require further tests. This reciprocal coordination of theory and research produces cumulative theory growth, the hallmark of science.

To build solid knowledge about social processes, theory cannot be separated from related empirical research that tests it. Group processes research has focused on experiment, although not to the exclusion of other social research methods. The control afforded by experiments makes them preeminently useful to test theories, the primary goal of group processes research. Not all research problems, in or out of sociology, lend themselves to experimental investigation, but the cumulative growth of verifiable knowledge can be readily observed in theoretical research programs that reciprocally develop theory and use experiments that both test it and suggest further theoretical development (Szmatka and Lovaglia 1996). Social processes need not be studied as a science, but group processes research shows that they can be.

Despite the success of theoretical research programs and the high regard in which sociologists hold theory-driven research, only a small, albeit growing, number of sociologists works within the confines of a theoretical research program. While undoubtedly effective, theoretical research programs are seen as constraining the way in which researchers work. Researchers may feel that to pursue a theoretical research program, they will have to spend much of their time away from the methods that attracted them to social research (Szmatka and Lovaglia 1996). Those who love to experiment may not wish to restrict themselves to a program of research mapped out by theorists, while theorists may feel hampered by the level of detail required to design an experiment to test a theory. Other researchers, fascinated by the observation of social phenomena, may not wish to devote the considerable effort necessary to fit their data to either developing theory or experimental test.

The goal, however, is not to force researchers away from the work they love, but rather to better coordinate the work of all researchers. Science progresses to the extent that earlier research is assimilated into the ongoing work. The more early research that can be brought to bear on a new question, the quicker an answer can be found. The division of scientific labor is the key to progress. Descriptions of theoretical research programs have focused on the close coordination of small groups of theorists and empirical researchers, usually experimentalists. Often, the same researchers in theoretical research programs developed theory and also designed and conducted its experimental tests (Szmatka and Lovaglia 1996). While certainly effective, such a strategy inevitably neglects the results of research unknown to workers in the theoretical research program. Coordinating the increasing division of labor among social researchers is the next step in the evolution of social science.

One fast-growing area of group processes research uses computer simulations to investigate the fundamental research problems addressed by theoretical research programs. For example, what sort of structural conditions gives some people power over others in a social network, or how can public works ever be successfully completed when people will benefit from them whether or not they contribute to the project? Computer simulators try to devise a simple social setting in which the phenomena in question will emerge. While interesting, the scientific usefulness of such demonstrations is unclear. How might theorists and experimenters use the results of computer simulations in their research programs? Michael J. Lovaglia and Robert R. Willer explore that question in the final chapter of this volume. Theoretical research programs have successfully synthesized the work of theorists and experimenters. A new synthesis is emerging that includes computer simulations as a basic component of theoretical research programs, which mediates between theory and experiment.

THEORETICAL RESEARCH PROGRAMS

This volume investigates how theoretical research programs coordinate theory and empirical research in sociology to produce scientific progress and how computer simulations have become an important component of theoretical research programs.[1] A theoretical research program is defined as interrelated theories or elaborations of a single theory, accompanied by theoretically guided research used to test, refine, extend, and apply them (Berger 1982 [1974]; Wagner and Berger 1985). Berger and Zelditch (1997) develop the latest formulation of the working of theoretical research programs to include the place of scientific models within them. Computer simulations are examples of scientific models. Meeker and Leik (1997) document the increasing use of computer simulations to develop theories within theoretical research programs. Lovaglia and Willer's chapter, "Theory, Simulation and Research: The New Synthesis," which concludes this volume, explores the various ways in which computer simulations as scientific models mediate between theory and research to advance scientific knowledge in theoretical research programs.

Scientific knowledge is conditional, which makes it a curious choice for an arbiter of truth in the modern world. The eternal verities of religion or the law's proof beyond a reasonable doubt would seem more likely candidates. Scientific knowledge about the real world is always partial, provisional, questionable, above all *hypothetical* (Sozanski 1995). Ironically, provisional scientific knowledge has produced facts as hard as the law of gravity, as well as the means to escape earth's gravitational pull.

The conditional nature of scientific knowledge necessitates the coordination of theory and research to produce it. Empirical research provides the means to assess the progress of theoretical development. Valid theory, then, is the first requirement of a theoretical research program. Group processes researchers have built on the long tradition of theory construction in sociology. Since the work of Marx, it has been clear that social theory, at least in the sense of an elaborated worldview, can have a huge impact on human affairs, although in unpredictable ways. Using theory to guide scientific inquiry, however, requires close attention to the conditions under which a social phenomenon occurs. Work in group processes, therefore, must simultaneously address ways to improve the coordination of theory and research and develop substantive theories that address the fundamental research questions concerning social phenomena and conduct research to test those theories.

IMPROVING SOCIAL THEORY

Theories are explanations. The theories used in theoretical research programs are explanations of social phenomena more precise than those usually associated with social theory. Sometimes called *unit theories*, to distinguish them from more general social theory (Berger and Zelditch 1997), these are sets of logically coherent and interrelated statements that are general, universal, abstract, and empirically testable. Some of these are definitions, whereas some are assumptions supplemented by scope conditions and logical rules of deriving one statement from another (Cohen 1989; Walker and Cohen 1985; Markovsky 1994; Szmatka 1997). In sum, a theory that is useful in a theoretical research program must be precise enough to suggest research capable of determining the validity of the theoretical explanation.

Crucial to the advance of theoretical research programs, then, are the development and dissemination of techniques for the construction of valid theories. Cohen's (1989) text on the development of sociological knowledge is the preferred starting point. The authors in the first section of this volume build on the tradition of theory construction in group processes.

Chapter 2, "Three Faces of Explanation: A Strategy for Building Cumulative Knowledge," by Henry A. Walker, exemplifies the project of constantly working to improve the quality of social theory. He examines the various conceptions of theory commonly used by sociologists: qualitative historical explanation, quantitative historical explanation, and general theoretical explanations. He then shows how the conceptions of theory are related. Identifying the relationships among disparate conceptions of theory leads him to insights capable of improving the way in which all sociologists build and use theories.

Chapter 3, "Formalization and Inference," by Geoffrey Tootell, Alison J. Bianchi, and Paul T. Munroe, focuses on a particular question of major importance to sociologists. How formal should a theory be? Formal theories are most useful for researchers in a theoretical research program because they pose the most precise hypotheses to be tested by empirical research. Formal theories, however, are less accessible to researchers outside the program that uses them than are discursive theories, which tell a more readily understood story. Thus, the compelling theoretical ideas in sociology that have attracted many researchers to the discipline have not commonly been pursued in theoretical research programs. Weber's theory of the Protestant ethic and rise of capitalism and Durkheim's theory of suicide are good examples. Tootell, Bianchi and Munroe describe the fundamental criteria needed to formalize a theory. They then show how a classic sociological theory, the Davis-Moore theory of social stratification, can be formalized, thus facilitating its use in a progressive research program.

Pidi Zhang addresses another fundamental question about theory construction in Chapter 4, "In Defense of Realistic Assumptions." How realistic should theoretical assumptions be? Introductory logic courses teach that assumptions used in logical proof can come from anywhere, whether rigorous observation of natural phenomenon or fanciful imagination. Assumptions are the starting point of theory. An unrealistic assumption is valuable if it helps to produce valid theory amenable to empirical test. Yet social theories are often criticized for using unrealistic assumptions. For example, rational choice theories face criticism for assuming that people calculate their maximum benefit before deciding among alternative courses of action. The assumption is unrealistic in that few people are capable of such calculation. Further, the information necessary to make the calculation is not usually available. Is the theory flawed if it uses an unrealistic assumption to make nontrivial predictions about social behavior that are repeatedly supported by empirical tests? Moreover, might theories that use unrealistic assumptions be more likely to produce interesting (that is, nontrivial) predictions?

In Chapter 5, "Positivism and Theory Construction in Group Processes," Kinga Wysienska and Jacek Szmatka argue that the history, development, and progress of sociological theories can be interpreted in terms of continuous attempts to make sociology a scientific discipline. According to them, sociological theory gradually advances methodologically. From the least methodologically developed theories (first genus), more methodologically advanced theories (second and third genera) evolve. The major criterion of this process is not the growth of empirical content, but the growth in terms of progressive ability in the application of scientific method by a given theory. Theories of the third genus accept methodological standards of the "hard sciences" and are specific to the group processes tradition. They are abstract, general, universal, and empirically testable. They maintain that there is one universal scientific method for all science. The idea of the unity of science was one of the rules that constituted positivism, which is why the question arises about the link between positivism and third genus theory construction in group processes. In this chapter, Wysienska and Szmatka examine these links to prove that positivist ideas have limited impact on scientific methods used in theory construction procedures. First, they explain their conception of positivism. They discern four stages of positivism: an early stage of positivism; logical positivism; a later stage, called *instrumental positivism*; and, finally, postpositivism. Then they show how positivism as a philosophy of science does not accord with the conception of theory testing and theory development that is widely used in third-genus theories in group processes. This conception is new in sociology, but it has long been used in natural theoretical sciences. The authors then examine the methodological link between postpositivism as a critique of neopositivism and third genus theory construction.

In Chapter 6, "Expectations, Need-States, and Emotional Arousal in Encounters," Jonathan H. Turner and David E. Boyns provide a glimpse into the process of theory construction as they wrestle with a fundamental aspect of social life that is extraordinarily difficult to explain: the role of emotions in social behavior. Their work shows the enormous range of knowledge necessary to open new research areas in sociology, as they draw on relevant sources in sociology, psychology, philosophy, neurology, and human evolution. They attempt to unite major research areas in sociology—expectations and identity—with the still germinal study of emotions as *social* feelings. The result is a number of propositions amenable to empirical test, which are necessary precursors of a new theoretical research program.

USING THEORY TO GUIDE RESEARCH

After developing theory, empirical research is the second requirement of a theoretical research program. What kinds of research qualify as legitimate tests of a theory? Most social theories fail to generate theoretical research programs because they have no guidelines for appropriate empirical tests. Without guidelines, research in the area founders.

Because scientific theoretical statements are always abstract and conditional, useful theories contain scope statements (Webster and Kervin 1971; Cohen 1989; Sell and Martin 1983). Scope statements are also abstract and conditional but provide guidelines for choosing the appropriate empirical situations in which to evaluate a theory. The vital link between theory and research provided by scope statements makes them an important area of analysis by group processes researchers engaged in theoretical research programs.

Status characteristics theory gives a clear example of the importance of scope statements. The theory proposes that people are awarded high status because they are expected to be highly competent. Moreover, status characteristics such as age, race, and education are associated with competence. The theory then predicts that people with the valued state of those characteristics, white men for example, are expected to be more competent than other people and will have more influence over others. Experimental tests of the theory measure the influence that people with different status characteristics have over each other. A problem, however, could arise in such an unrestricted research program. The theory could be valid and yet not be supported by experimental tests in all situations. Some experimental situations may fall outside the theory's scope, but which ones? Scope statements help researchers determine which empirical evidence is relevant to the validity of a theory.

If people have higher influence because they are considered competent, then competence must be relevant in the experimental situation. Any situation in which a person's competence is irrelevant would fall outside the scope of status characteristics theory. Thus, status characteristics theory includes scope statements limiting its predictions to situations in which group members work together on a task and care about its outcome. Scope statements allow researchers to test and refine a theory in a theoretical research program, but they also, necessarily, limit the theory's generality and explanatory power.

In Chapter 7, "How Scope and Initial Conditions Determine the Growth of Theory," Robert K. Shelly explores the role of scope conditions in the development of theoretical research programs. He presents a strategy that allows researchers to use scope conditions in ways that promote theory growth.

The use of standardized experimental settings has also increased the effectiveness of theoretical research programs. If most aspects of an experiment remain the same while only specific, theoretically relevant aspects are changed over time as studies progress, then the results of studies by different researchers at different times can be readily compared.

In Chapter 8, "The Relation between Experimental Standardization and Theoretical Development in Group Processes Research," Lisa Troyer reports on her research program, which seeks to determine both the benefits and the constraints of using a standardized experimental setting to test and refine theories. For theoretical knowledge to develop, the techniques of empirical research must grow as well. Experiments once conducted using paper-and-pencil measures and slide projectors are now conducted on computers. Where now participants come to the laboratory for a study, they soon will log on to a study Website from remote locations. Troyer's research compares the results of experiments in a standardized setting that has undergone a technological transformation.

Chapter 9, "Using Theory to Guide Empirical Research," by Joseph M. Whitmeyer, provides an overview of the ways in which theory can be used to guide research. He starts with Laudan's (1977) pragmatist approach to science: good science is practical. We value science because its results are useful. For Whitmeyer, theory is a way to organize knowledge and enhance its usefulness. He surveys how theory guides empirical research by dividing such research into four categories, based on the research's engagement with the natural world. The categories are "testing theory," "theory-based discovery," "demonstrating usefulness," and "being useful." Theory-guided research in each category can be useful, although different categories of research are useful in different ways. He then compares in greater depth the research programs focusing on expectation states and exchange networks to show how theory-guided research can be either more or less useful.

For a volume dedicated to the scientific study of social processes, there may seem to be little emphasis on data gathering here. This is partly due to the growing division-of-labor characteristic of modern science. If researchers are to concentrate their activities in areas that maximize their talents and interests, then not all researchers will gather data, nor will all edited volumes in the field be dedicated to reporting on it.

This does not imply that empirical research is a minor component of theoretical research programs. Whether theoretical development receives more emphasis than empirical research in any particular program varies, depending on the researchers involved, the subject of study and the stage of theoretical development. Regardless, theoretical research programs cannot be effective without ongoing empirical research.

The purpose of this volume is to show how that empirical research is produced, why it is effective, and how it can be improved. We would like to dispel any impression that empirical work is not as important in group processes as theory and its coordination with research. Most of the work produced by group processes researchers is careful empirical research that regularly appears in top sociology journals. A few recent examples will demonstrate the prominent role of empirical research in group processes as well as the coordination of theory and research:

- Shane Thye (2000) used experiments to test his theory of the relationship between power and status.
- Satoshi Kanazawa (2000) used data from a large-scale general social survey to validate an extended collective action theory, based in part on the computer simulation work of Michael Macy.
- Noah Friedkin's (1999) experiments supported his theory of group polarization.
- Linda Molm, Gretchen Peterson, and Nobuyuki Takahashi (1999) extended a long-established theoretical research program investigating negotiated and reciprocal exchange with a series of experiments.
- In a series of experiments, Cecilia Ridgeway, Elizabeth Boyle, Kathy Kuipers, and Dawn Robinson (1998) validated an extremely influential theory that explains how status characteristics can be constructed, thus laying the foundation for future beneficial social intervention.
- Building on the work of Ridgeway and her colleagues, Michael Lovaglia, Jeffrey Lucas, Jeffrey Houser, Shane Thye, and Barry Markovsky (1998) used status construction theory to validate an explanation for the racial differences found in mental ability test scores. Their experiments demonstrate that status processes can lower mental ability test scores, independent of individual mental ability.[2]
- Toshio Yamagishi, Karen Cook, and Motobi Watabe (1998) compared the results of experiments in the United States and Japan to support their theory explaining the role of uncertainty and trust in exchange behavior.
- Experiments by Lisa Troyer and C. Wesley Younts (1997) tested their theory that, although what others think of us is important for social behavior, what *we think* others think of us can sometimes be more important.

These examples of group processes research show the interplay of theory and research characteristic of theoretical research programs. The remaining chapters in this volume explore the increasingly important role of computer simulations as mediators between theory and research.

COMPUTER SIMULATIONS AS MEDIATORS BETWEEN
THEORY AND RESEARCH

Computer simulations can mediate between theory and research in two distinct ways. First, computer simulations can act as theoretical tools. With relatively few assumptions, a theory may be too complex for many of its implications to be apparent to researchers. Computer simulations that build in theoretical assumptions can be useful to explore their implications. Second, computer simulations can model data. Observed empirical generalizations can be built into simulations, which in turn can predict behavior and demonstrate relationships between variables in ways that further theoretical development. Most simulations embody elements of both functions, with some placing more emphasis on the theoretical functions of simulation and others, on the interpretation of data.

In Chapter 10, "Axiomatics and Generativity in Theoretical Sociology," Thomas J. Fararo describes in detail the use of assumptions (axioms) in building formal theoretical models of social processes. He demonstrates how the axiomatic method can produce models capable of generating the social phenomenon to be explained. It connects formal theory construction techniques in sociology to the models used to explore their implications. This approach has immediate application for sociologists interested in computer simulation to generate virtual representations of social phenomena.

Chapter 11, "Some Philosophy of Science Issues in the Use of Complex Computer Simulation Theories," by Barbara F. Meeker, also addresses the use of simulation in the development of theory. In particular she explores the nature of the output of simulations in terms of domain, measurement, and mathematical proof. She also examines questions such as what, exactly, do computer simulations demonstrate, and how are such demonstrations useful in developing and assessing social theories.

In Chapter 12, "Artificial Societies: Laboratories for Theoretical Research," Michael W. Macy and Walter Luke compare a traditional approach to theory construction—developing a mathematical model based on theoretical relationships, to an approach made possible by computer simulation—the agent-based computational model. A traditional theorist might try to discover the mathematical relationship between social variables. For example, some formula might predict a person's income based on age, race, gender, education, and other relevant variables. Given the number of relevant variables, such a formula would necessarily be complex, making problematic the job of developing the mathematics, measuring the variables with sufficient accuracy and testing the theory. Computer simulations offer the alternative approach of programming the assumptions of a theory into simplified agents, which are then set loose to create a virtual society.

Phillip Bonacich, in Chapter 13, "The Strength of Weak Power: A Simulation Study of Network Evolution," describes a comprehensive theoretical research program that includes traditional theoretical development, agent-based computer simulations of important social processes, and experimental research that validates his theory. While it is rare for any single researcher, or even for small groups of collaborating researchers, to possess all the skills necessary to produce such a comprehensive theoretical research program, Bonacich provides an accessible example of how theoretical research programs coordinate theory, simulation, and empirical research.

The norm in natural sciences and the trend in social sciences is for increased division of scientific labor. Specialists work with increasingly technical methods in narrowly defined research areas. Few specialists have sufficient grasp of others' specialties to use their work to further their own. A research career might comprise a series of increasingly refined experiments in one area of status characteristics theory. Alternately, a career might be spent on computer simulations of collective actions, or a theorist might develop a theory of either collective action or social status over the course of a career. Such specialization makes imperative the development of ever more efficient scientific communication. Perhaps a new scientific specialization will emerge to facilitate the transfer of specialized knowledge among researchers working in loosely related areas. For example, a researcher might specialize in the use of simulation output to develop theory, while another might design experiments based on theories that experimenters could then bring to fruition.

Together, the chapters in this volume describe the various aspects of theoretical research programs in group processes and provide a glimpse into the future of social science.

NOTES

1. See Berger and Zelditch (1997) for the most recent formulation of the methodology of theoretical research programs. See Meeker and Leik (1997) for the increasing use of computer simulations in theoretical research programs.

2. The theoretical work of Webster and Hysom (1998) also contributed to the creation of a status characteristic capable of demonstrating the role of status processes in mental ability test scores.

PART I

IMPROVING SOCIAL THEORY

Chapter 2 _____

Three Faces of Explanation: A Strategy for Building Cumulative Knowledge

Henry A. Walker[1]

A self-described "feminist philosopher" complained recently that "chauvinist male philosophers" accorded feminist philosophy low esteem. They did so by labeling the work "sociology" (Alcoff 2000). The philosopher's complaint spells double trouble for sociology and sociologists. First, sociologists ought to be concerned when others compare sociology with nonempirical fields of inquiry. Second, sociology and sociologists must be concerned with the low status that others attribute to our discipline. Problems of this sort plague disciplines in crisis.

Theoretical issues often play a central role in disciplinary crises.[2] Some indicators suggest that theoretical sociology enjoys good health. Many sociologists apply the term "theory-driven" to research described in conference papers, research proposals, and scholarly articles and books. The American Sociological Association devotes a journal (*Sociological Theory*) to theory matters and the association's theory section has a healthy membership. On the other hand, critics both inside and outside the discipline claim that sociology has failed to develop general theoretical explanations. The staunchest defenders of the theory construction enterprise admit that theory development lags behind the biological and physical sciences. Furthermore, the number of sociologists claiming theoretical status for their work surpasses liberal estimates of the number of theories in the sociological storehouse. Under the circumstances, it is not surprising that the broader intellectual community holds the discipline in low regard.

In this chapter, I analyze current discourse about the state of sociological theory. I claim that (1) some sociologists confuse metatheory with theory, (2) many fail to distinguish theoretical explanations from historical explanations, and (3) the discipline organizes status and rewards around historical analyses. These claims are the foundation for identifying three faces of explanation—the qualitative historical, quantitative historical, and theoretical. Each explanatory form answers a particular type of question and sociologists can take advantage of relationships among the three types to forge a high-consensus, rapid-discovery science (Collins 1994). Finally, I show how failure to distinguish the three forms of explanation can retard theory development.

ON THE CURRENT STATE OF SOCIOLOGICAL THEORY

Several recent developments illustrate the controversy that surrounds theoretical work in sociology. At an August 1990 conference at the University of Maryland, several distinguished panelists explored "causes for the 'death' of formal theory" (Hage 1994:1). In June 1994, *Sociological Forum* published a special issue on the topic, "What Is Wrong with Sociology?" Two years later, it published a second interchange concerning the death of the "theory construction movement." The controversy had not faded by millennium's end. A *New York Times* reporter panned the old century's last meeting of the American Sociological Association (Goodman 2000). The political and social commentator Ben Wattenberg (2000) attributed an antiscience orientation to the association's sitting president—an orientation he found all the more troubling because the president was *popularly elected*.

The most pessimistic critics take the position that sociological theory was stillborn. Cole (1994) asserts that sociology has no general theories and is incapable of producing them. Similarly, Zhao (1996) claims that sociologists tried to create general theory and failed. At the other end of the spectrum, I can find no one willing to claim that theoretical work in sociology compares favorably with theory development in the physical and biological sciences.[3] However, a number of others hold positions between the two extremes.

Many observers agree that an autopsy of the theory construction movement is premature. As an example, Collins (1994) admits the *possibility* of general theoretical arguments but claims that sociology will not become a high-consensus, rapid-discovery science. Willer (1996) offers the unique claim that there is more sociological theory than meets the disciplinary eye. That is, theory lives but remains essentially invisible to the discipline at large. Cohen (1994) offers an optimistic and conciliatory position and characterizes the "theory cup" as half-full.

Following Cohen, I describe the cup of theory as overflowing! That is the good news. The bad news is that the cup contains very little theory in the rigorous sense in which other sciences use the term. "Sociological theory" consists of ideas that motivate "theory-driven" research, long treatises on classical writers and their writings, and the familiar material that fills theory sections of journal articles and research monographs. In Davis's (1994) apt pronouncement, "[Theory is] a goopy mess of (deceptive) intellectual history, a healthy dollop of ideology, and a Chinese menu of 'schools,' 'approaches,' and buzzwords" (184).

Theory development in sociology is not dead but it needs critical care. There is less theory than many sociologists claim but, as Willer (1996) claims, theoretical work suffers from low visibility and low prestige. Its low visibility is due, in part, to the discipline's failure to train sociologists in theoretical methods. Consequently, many confuse theory with other forms of discourse that are neither theoretical nor explanatory. Having staked out this position, I restate the central question and offer a related one:

1. Why do we find the theory cup to contain so little theory when we boil the contents to its essence?
2. Why do sociologists have such difficulty evaluating the state of theory development?

In the next section, I look to the discipline's practice of science for answers. However, I will not engage in the public self-flagellation that all too often possesses members of the discipline. I agree with Cohen (1994), who describes such activity as counterproductive and poor public relations. Instead, I use the questions—and the conditions that motivate them—as a platform for reconstituting and redirecting the theory construction project.

CONFLICTING ASSESSMENTS: BACK TO THE SOURCE

Cohen (1994) offered two remarkable statements to the Maryland conference. They show keen insight into reasons for the underdevelopment of theoretical work in sociology and for the difficulty sociologists have in assessing the quantity and quality of theoretical work. Cohen claimed:

1. "A principal injunction of the methodology I am espousing [theory as problem solving] is that one counts successes and ignores failures" (Cohen 1994:78).
2. "There is considerable confusion between metatheory and theory and there is a widespread lack of understanding [among sociologists] of what a theory is, how a theory is constructed, how a theory is used, and so forth" (Cohen 1994:78).[4]

The first statement is sensible for those involved in creating, testing, and revising theories. We should judge scientific disciplines by the theories they produce rather than by unsuccessful attempts to create theory. I make clear my use of the term *unsuccessful attempts*. I apply it to putative theories that do not satisfy the criteria of a theory. I do not mean theories that have been found false or those that have been replaced by more powerful ones. Given this proviso, ignoring our failures is altogether proper. However, following Cohen's dictum under other circumstances can prove disastrous.

I agree with Cohen's second statement and argue that its applicability to sociology satisfies a prescription for disaster. Many sociologists confuse theory with metatheory, the writings of classical scholars and other work. No discipline can expect its members to identify theoretical successes and failures if they confuse theory with other intellectual products. I extend Cohen's claim and argue that our collective confusion is not limited to the distinction between theory and metatheory. Sociologists fail as well to distinguish theoretical explanations from other forms of explanation. Two implications follow from Cohen's line of argument. First, confusion retards theory development. Second, it also ensures that members of the discipline will offer contradictory assessments of the state of theory development.

Theory development suffers under the conditions Cohen describes because aspiring theorists are unlikely to create theories if they cannot distinguish them from other intellectual products. Myths of science aside, theory development is not accidental. (Compare stories involving Newton's serendipitous apple with those that describe an irascible scholar who worked for days and nights on end to develop theoretical understandings of physical phenomena.) The scholar may not know what the theory will look like until its completion, yet she will know that it is a theory when it is finished (Jasso 2000).

A discipline will count many failures (intellectual creations that are not theories) as successes if its practitioners confuse theory with metatheory and other types of explanations. This confusion also engenders conflicting assessments of the state of theory development. Confused colleagues will find many theories. On the other hand, those who can distinguish theory from other intellectual endeavors will lament the paucity of theory. Finally, those who fail to understand the nature of theory (e.g., those who presume that theories "hold" in all times and places) will find no theories at all.

RELATIVE PRESTIGE OF THEORY AND RESEARCH

Social and behavioral scientists disagree about definitions of theory and the possibility of creating social science theories. However, we generally agree that theories explain phenomena and that *theorists* devise explanations. So who, or what, is a theorist or theoretical sociologist? Lederman and Teresi (1993) offer a whimsical distinction between experimental and theoretical physicists. In their view, experimental physicists are physicists who conduct experiments whereas theoretical physicists are physicists who do not run experiments. Their remarks direct attention to a line that many sociologists draw between theory and research.

The Great Divide

For too much of its intellectual history, sociology (and sociologists) made distinctions that established a divide between theory and research. Whether the gulf persists is less important than the consequences that the idea of a gulf generated. Theorists, as Lederman and Teresi (1993) point out, get high marks—

and high status—for intellectual creativity. The discipline (and individual sociologists) endures debased status relative to fields that have vigorous and well-developed programs of theory and theory-driven research. Yet sociologists can garner high status within the discipline without ever producing work that passes theoretical muster. They can (and many do) label their work "theory" and themselves "theorists" and reap the status benefits that those labels imply. The result is not surprising if we grant plausibility to Cohen's claim that most sociologists can neither identify theories nor assess their worth. Our disciplinary history is strewn with classic examples of this phenomenon.

Many early sociologists and protosociologists developed grand theoretical schemes that proposed to explain everything as they acted quickly to supply the new discipline with substance and legitimacy.[5] In truth, however, such grand schemes rarely explained anything and sociologists found themselves without credible theories or the status that a science garners for its practitioners. Contemporary sociologists use developments in inferential statistics to bridge the status gap. We use modern statistical methods to "explain" variance and claim the best of two worlds. We conduct research and explain our findings (i.e., find reasonable values of R^2). It matters little that we rarely explain findings in the theoretical sense. Our statistical explanations permit us to legitimize our claims to being *explainers* (i.e., theorists), experts at formalization (read: use mathematics and statistics), and skilled researchers. Our capacity to explain findings statistically allows us to lay claim to being *real* scientists.[6] Many of us commit the offense because we do not understand fundamental differences between statistical and theoretical explanations. Furthermore, the small cadre that understands such differences ignores the problem or is powerless to correct it. As a result, the discipline has progressed quite nicely but without a real foundation. Today, many of our colleagues explain statistical variation in all sorts of social phenomena, receive high status for doing so and reap the rewards that exalted status brings. On the other hand, theoretical work suffers and nothing coheres (Davis 1994). I suggest that we can solve this problem by using our facility with other forms of explanation to enhance the prospects for making more rapid progress as a generalizing theoretical science.[7]

EXPLANATION AND THEORY

Sociological explanations abound but they are rarely powerful or general, even when the discipline's most skilled practitioners create them. Sociologists are most adept at creating *qualitative historical* and *quantitative historical* explanations. We are less proficient at developing theoretical explanations. Compared with historical explanations, theoretical explanations *are* statistically rare and less visible (Willer 1996) and their creators garner less prestige than their counterparts in more developed sciences.

The statistical rarity of theoretical explanations is due, in part, to the failure of sociologists to ask theoretical questions. The discipline trains sociologists to

pursue questions that produce either qualitative historical or quantitative historical explanations, but not those that motivate theoretical explanations. As Gibbs
(1994) suggests, some sociologists may actually resist doing theoretical work
because professional rewards and perquisites are organized around the creation
and dissemination of historical explanations. The next section describes historical and general theoretical explanations and the types of questions that motivate
them. Examples from the literature illustrate each explanatory form.

THREE FACES OF EXPLANATION

Sociologists characterize many intellectual inquiries as "theory-driven." I understand the term in two ways: First, theory-driven research includes inquiry
that pursues the goal of developing theoretical explanations. Second, the term
refers to activity that pursues the goals of testing or refining theoretical explanations. Most sociological research is *idea-driven*. Idea-driven research is fine
and we can use more of it; however, theories are more than ideas.

Sociologists apply the term *theory* to solitary "causal" statements or laws
(Stinchcombe 1968), mathematical models, and statistical analyses (Coleman
1990), the collected wisdom of classical writers, and almost everything between.[8] Wallace (1988, 1995) implores sociologists to adopt standardized terminology, and theory is one term on which we need to come to agreement—
and quickly. In the spirit of that assertion, I make clear what I mean by theory.[9]

Theories are deductive systems that explain statements about relationships
between phenomena. At a minimum, theories contain all the following:

1. A statement of universal form that claims a relationship between phenomena (i.e., an
   explanandum or thing to be explained).
2. Primitive terms.
3. Defined terms.
4. At least two nested theoretical propositions (arguments) of universal form that make
   claims about relationships between phenomena.
5. At least one statement of universal form that defines the scope of phenomena to which
   the theoretical propositions apply (Walker and Cohen 1985).
6. At least one new statement that can be derived from two or more of the theory's
   propositions (i.e., a statement different from the *explanandum*). Derived statements
   may be either universal or singular (i.e., statements that describe empirical phenomena).
7. The derivation of singular statements requires at least one statement of initial conditions that links theoretical terms (constructs) to empirical or observable terms.

Theories explain relationships between phenomena but they differ from other
forms of explanation in structure, content, and the questions that generate them.
I build on Berger, Zelditch, and Anderson's (1972a; see also Cohen 1989) dis-

tinction between historical and generalizing orientations to science to identify three distinct faces of explanation: the qualitative historical, quantitative historical, and general theoretical.

QUALITATIVE HISTORICAL EXPLANATION

Science begins with humankind's propensity for grouping and classifying phenomena. Our first questions often take the form: What is this? How is "this" different from "that" and the "other"? Most people stop at this stage. We are satisfied if we can classify a phenomenon as, say, an exchange of gifts, a prison riot, or a marriage. I classify as Type I all questions that ask for general descriptions or classification schemes. More curious persons go on to devise Type II questions.

Type II questions ask what one or more factors are related to the occurrence of an event, y, or members of an event class, Y?[10] Researchers answer Type II questions with either qualitative or quantitative historical explanations. Qualitative historical explanations fit most closely the ideas that Berger, Zelditch, and Anderson (1972a) use to describe a historical orientation to scientific work. Qualitative historical explanations take as their object a unique occurrence, which is explained by generating lists of empirical factors associated with the event. Consider the classic research of Gouldner (1954).[11]

Gouldner (1954) asked, "What factors account for (or explain) the wildcat strike at General Gypsum?" Gouldner's research showed that General Gypsum experienced three problems concurrently: (1) Management introduced new technology while, (2) the plant was experiencing high turnover, and (3) the administration was replacing several strategic middle managers. The chains of reasoning for historical explanations often become quite lengthy. For example, Gouldner offered the following ideas about the introduction of new technology:

1. The plant introduced new machinery for making gypsum board.
2. New machinery sped up the process.
3. The plant's new machines operated at unstable speeds, which led management to supervise more closely the technical aspects of production.
4. Technical problems distracted management from the supervision of the plant's *social* organization.

Gouldner offered similar elaborations of the other two problems.

Sociologists know this type of research as the qualitative case study. Qualitative historical explanations claim that some event, y, occurred because other concrete events $x_1, x_2, \ldots, x_n$, preceded y. Researchers may even claim that y would not have occurred if the xs had not occurred in a particular sequence. Of course, their speculations are fruitless because any particular array of xs with a particular y will never recur.

QUANTITATIVE HISTORICAL EXPLANATION

A variant of the basic Type II question motivates researchers to develop quantitative historical explanations. These questions take the form: What factors account for (explain) the occurrence of y-like events? Researchers develop such questions after they place y-like events in the general class, Y, and group various "explanatory events," x_i, in classes X_i. I offer two examples. Many sociologists would classify the first as "historical" although they might not characterize it as quantitative. The second is easily characterized as quantitative but not necessarily as historical.

Skocpol's (1979) *States and Social Revolutions* was intended to explain the occurrence of social revolutions. She identified revolutions in France (1789), Russia (1917), and China (1949) as events that satisfied her definition of social revolution. After detailed and painstaking analysis of historical data for the three cases, Skocpol concluded that several factors were common to the three social revolutions.

1. Each nation experienced military competition, intrusion from outside authorities, and political constraints imposed by their structures of class relations and political institutions.
2. Each nation experienced deteriorating military and administrative power.
3. Weakened state authority systems opened opportunities for internal political and class conflicts.
4. Contending groups overcame weakened state apparatuses.
5. Strong peasant and urban working-class movements undermined counterrevolutionary movements and restorative movements.
6. Without effective opposition (from either the state or counterrevolutionary or restoration movements), revolutionary leadership garnered popular support for their new regimes.
7. New regimes became stronger and more autonomous than former states and fought off intruders and domestic competitors.
8. New regimes altered class relations; the social revolutions were "successful."

Skocpol explained the emergence and stabilization of three successful social revolutions with this analysis. Skocpol's research exemplifies the pattern of historical explanation. She identified a class of events and connected the particular alignment of a class of concrete (i.e., empirical) "explainers" to events in the event class.[12] Furthermore, the work is quantitative in the sense that Skocpol analyzed multiple cases simultaneously. The method is isomorphic with standard multivariate analyses that have as their primary objective explaining variation in dependent measures.

AN EXCURSIS ON MULTIVARIATE ANALYSIS

Case studies raise several questions. Researchers must always consider alternatives to their explanations no matter how compelling the evidence. The problem is acute for solitary investigations because investigators never know whether the alignment of phenomena and factors that explain them reflects "real" relationships or is merely coincidental. Follow-up studies that involve multiple cases offer the opportunity to compile corroborative evidence of systematic relations. However, multiple-case investigations raise other problems. What can an investigator conclude if events in the classes of explainers, $X_1, X_2, \ldots, X_N$, occur in exactly that sequence in 31 of 100 instances of y-like events? What if the number were 76 of 100 instances? Furthermore, what would a researcher make of the finding that Y sometimes occurred with only some, but not all, X-events? None of these questions had clear answers before the development of inferential statistics.

The combination of multivariate analysis, inferential statistics, and the idea of statistical significance provides handy answers to all these questions. With these weapons in their analytic arsenals, researchers conduct multiple-case investigations and calculate the statistical significance of the joint occurrence of members of the classes Y and X_i. Sophisticated multivariate techniques permit them to extend this characterization to the entire set of explainers, X_n, about which they are concerned. More important, they can explain variation in Y and identify the most important "determinants" of variation in Y. Many investigators clothe such analyses in theoretical language but they retain their essential historical character.

Consider the research of Lichter, McLaughlin, and Ribar (1997), which studied determinants of female-headed families—a problem of both practical and substantive sociological concern. The investigators used county-level data from summary tape files of the 1980 and 1990 censuses to estimate a series of models. Their initial model estimates showed that thirteen of sixteen factors had statistically significant associations with the incidence of female-headed families (Lichter et al. 1997: 127). I summarize findings for the initial model only.

1. The number of female-headed families varied positively with combined welfare benefits, female earnings, percentage black, the natural logarithm of the population, and a dummy variable representing the year 1990.

2. The number of female-headed families varied negatively with the male-to-female sex ratio, male earnings, male employment, percentage aged 65 and older, percentage rural, percentage Catholic, percentage Mormon, and percentage conservative Protestant.

3. The number of female-headed households was unrelated to male education, female education, and percentage Hispanic.

This research shows quite convincingly that many factors are associated with the formation of female-headed families. The findings are important substantively and are clearly relevant to ongoing discussions of social policy. Furthermore, Lichter et al. explain much of the variation in their dependent measure ($R^2 = .834$). Their research is an excellent example of quantitative historical explanation. Membership in the event class, female-headed household, is the object of explanation and the investigators use a variety of empirical events to explain the likelihood of membership in the event class.

The research of Skocpol (1979) and Lichter et al. (1997) highlights two features of quantitative historical explanations. First, quantitative historical explanations focus on general classes of events (Y). Second, the structure of quantitative historical explanations is identical to that of qualitative historical explanations. The parallel forms permit us to understand that both types of historical explanation (1) use explanatory statements, or knowledge claims (Cohen 1989), that contain singular (or observable) terms and (2) offer assertions about relations between explanatory terms and the events they purport to explain. Qualitative and quantitative historical explanations are useful forms of explanation, and I suggest that they can be important components of theoretical research programs. However, historical explanations do not satisfy the first criterion I set for theoretical explanations. General theoretical explanations have as their objects relationships between phenomena and are made up of systems of nested knowledge claims or arguments.[13] The next section offers an example of a general theoretical explanation and shows how mixing explanatory types creates trouble for theorists and the theoretical enterprise.

GENERAL THEORETICAL EXPLANATION

Type III questions motivate theoretical explanations by asking: What one or more mechanisms explain the relationship between X_i and Y? Type III questions focus on the relationship *between* classes of events (X_i and Y) rather than on any given event or event class. They ask for arguments (i.e., descriptions of the mechanisms) that account for the focal relationship rather than an enumeration of factors associated with a given event or set of events (Kiser and Hechter 1991). The theory of status characteristics and expectation states proposed by Berger, Fisek, Norman, and Zelditch (1977) is an example of a general theoretical formulation.

Status characteristics theory focuses on the relationship between the socially determined status value of characteristics that actors possess and the positions of those actors in hierarchical structures of power and prestige. The theory applies only to situations that satisfy the theory's scope restrictions (see Berger, Fisek, Norman, and Zelditch, 1977 for a complete enumeration of restrictions on the theory's scope). It argues that several interrelated processes connect status characteristics to hierarchical patterns of interaction in task groups. These are the basic propositions concerning person, P, and other, O:

P1. If D is a social basis of discrimination (i.e., either P and O possess different states of D or D is connected to task outcome states), D is activated for P and O (Activation Process).

P2. If D is activated, P will believe that states of D are relevant (related) to states of an instrumental task characteristic, C* (Burden of Proof Process). Burden of proof processes operate if status characteristics are neither associated with, nor dissociated from, the task.

P3. If P believes that states of D are relevant to states of C*, P will assign performance expectation states for C* to the self and to O (Structure Completion Process). Emergent performance expectations carry the same sign or relative rank as states of salient status characteristics.

P3. If P assigns positive and negative expectations to the self and to O, P will assign *aggregated expectations* according to the principle of organized subsets (Aggregated Expectations Process).

P4. If P assigns performance expectation states for C* to the self and to O, P's behavior will be a direct function of the assigned performance expectation states (Basic Expectation Process).

The theory implies that actors (P and O) for whom coactors assign more positive expectations will hold a higher rank on emergent behavior and status orders than actors for whom performance expectations are less positive. Actors' standings on socially defined status characteristics are correlated with their task-related behavior, including their power and prestige rankings within the group.

What are the theory's important features? First, each proposition describes a relationship between two phenomena. Second, the phenomena are general; no proposition contains observable terms. Third, the propositions are nested. Each proposition contains at least one term found in a proposition that precedes or follows it. These features distinguish theoretical explanations from historical explanations.

RELATIONSHIPS AMONG TYPES OF EXPLANATIONS

The simplest theories are complex systems, and theory construction involves many elements of the research process (e.g., creating descriptions, definitions, classification schemes, etc.). Accordingly, building theoretical explanations is a daunting task, which may account for their statistical rarity.[14] I point out that the compound term "theoretical explanation" does not express a redundancy.[15] The widespread belief that every explanation, model, or simulation is a theory (or is based on one) is another source of misunderstanding about the theory-building enterprise.

Sociologists continuously devise and test explanations; however, most of the explanations we develop are not theoretical explanations. Instead, they are examples of either qualitative or quantitative historical explanations. Practicing

social scientists rarely identify these three faces of explanation, exploit the relationships between them, or recognize that each face can play a role in the
development of cumulative theoretical science. I offer a prescription for curing
this methodological malady.

Cohen (1989) noted that researchers often cast historical (or particularizing)
and generalizing strategies as opposing approaches to knowledge. They extol
the virtues of one approach while pointing to the other's vices. I advocate the
view that each explanatory form can serve a useful function as investigators
devise a coherent and systematic strategy for developing general theoretical explanations. Researchers commonly develop classification schemes to answer
Type I questions before advancing a Type II question. With classification
schemes in hand, a research team can launch either a qualitative or quantitative
historical analysis and develop a historical explanation. Once an investigator
identifies systematic relations between two or more phenomena (as in quantitative historical explanations), he or she can go on to develop Type III questions.

As an example, consider a researcher who uses Gouldner's (1954) investigation of a single wildcat strike as the basis for research that investigates factors
associated with strikes in general. She might emulate Franzosi (1995) who designed a multivariate study of Italian strikes over the period 1945–1980.[16] Assume that she finds a pattern of "strike waves," cyclical periods of labor unrest
followed by periods of relative peace, and learns that unions and employers
regularly undertake substantial reorganization at the end of a strike wave. She
can use this information to develop a general theoretical analysis as follows.
First, she can devise theoretical constructs of which particular strike waves (or
cycles of protest) and instances of institutional reorganization are empirical instances (Tarrow 1998). Call the constructs X and Y respectively. Next, she can
ask, "What accounts for the relationship between X and Y ($_xR_y$)?" The question
is a Type III question and only theories offer proper answers to such questions.

A theory of $_xR_y$ will describe the relationship between states of X (where X
may occur before Y) and states of other factors that influence, or determine, the
relationship between states of X and Y. My example shows how a researcher
can use Type I and Type II questions (and answers to them) to generate a Type
III question that permits her to develop a theory of $_xR_y$. In the process, the
investigator's focus shifts from a particular strike to strikes in general and eventually to the relationship between cycles of protest and institutional reorganization.

PROBLEMS AND PROSPECTS

I agree with critics who claim that our discipline has not lived up to its
expectations and the expectations others hold of sciences generally. Sociology
produces *less* general theoretical work than the sheer volume of research suggests. On the other hand, I strongly disagree with those who link the underdevelopment of sociological theory to characteristics of the subject matter (Cole

1994; Gergen 1973). Neither complex nor dynamic phenomena have stymied theoretical development in the physical and biological sciences.

I offer a different view: sociology, and sociologists, must look inwardly to solve this problem. The discipline must embark on a different path if it is to become a rapid-discovery, high-consensus science (Collins 1994). Sociology will create more general theory when more of its practitioners ask theoretical, or type III, questions.

The road to theoretical progress is neither straight nor free of hazards. Thousands of dedicated sociologists armed with an array of investigative and statistical techniques work diligently to explain social facts. They explain findings from hundreds of case studies and sophisticated quantitative analyses yearly. Despite the discipline's collective self-doubts, many sociological explanations exemplify the best that science—any science—has to offer. Therein lies the problem.

Most sociological explanations are historical. Historical explanations predominate because many sociologists hold a historical, rather than a generalizing, orientation to phenomena (Cohen 1989). Most training programs and the system of professional rewards sustain a historical approach to knowledge. It is not surprising that sociologists have become so proficient at developing historical explanations. After all, many prominent social scientists claim that social phenomena permit only historical explanation (Cole 1994; Gergen 1973).

Sociologists can become proficient at building general theoretical explanations. I describe ways of connecting historical and general theoretical explanations and show how sociologists can use their considerable skills and experiences with the former to further development of the latter. It will not be easy. Training programs must prepare more sociologists to do generalizing work in addition to (rather than instead of) historical work. While new training models are necessary, they will not be sufficient to produce change. The discipline must also develop new norms for presenting *and* criticizing scientific work. Some current practices retard theoretical development.

Many sociologists present "theoretical" work discursively. Consider Davis and Moore's (1945) theory of stratification or Becker's (1963) theory of labeling and deviant careers. Then compare either theory with Blau's (1970) theory of size and differentiation or the work of Berger, Fisiek, Norman, and Zelditch (1977) as previously described. Researchers who wish to use either Davis and Moore's or Becker's theories must first separate the theoretical wheat from its narrative chaff. Blau and Berger et al. clearly distinguish their arguments from the narratives that discuss theoretical processes. Sociologists-in-training can easily identify these writers' theoretical ideas, even if they are unsure about how to use them.

Sociologists must also distinguish form from substance. Some sociologists make clear the propositional structures of their "theories." However, close inspection often reveals hidden arguments that are crucial to understanding the relations under analysis. Fischer's (1975) subcultural theory of urbanism is an example. Fischer builds on the work of Wirth (1938), who argued that ecological characteristics of cities (size, density, and heterogeneity) ensure higher rates of unconventional behavior. Fischer introduces propositions that describe the effects of urbanism (measured as population size) on three factors, and claims that the set explains the relationship described by a fourth proposition.

P1. Urbanism increases subcultural variety.

P2. Urbanism increases subcultural intensity.

P3. Urbanism increases diffusion of subcultures.

P4. Urbanism increases rates of unconventionality.

Clearly, the first three propositions do not form a nested set and, consequently, proposition 4 cannot be deduced logically from them. Close inspection of his article shows that Fischer introduces additional arguments that spell out the connections among the first four propositions. As an example, Fischer argues that "the more variable and distinct subcultures there are, the more behavior there is that deviates from general norms" (1975:1328). He discusses other ideas that link subcultural intensity and subcultural diffusion to unconventional behavior. Only experienced theory hands can uncover the hidden assumptions and embed them in the propositional structure to complete the theoretical explanation. Knowledgeable critics—those trained in theoretical methods—must call attention to such problems and ask analysts to correct them *before* recommending publication.[17]

Some sociological work mixes explanatory types. Kingsley Davis, Wilbert Moore, and Melvin Tumin carried on one of the best-known public exchanges in the history of the discipline. (See the sample of papers compiled in Bendix and Lipset [1966].) Unfortunately, the exchange resulted in a mixing of explanatory types. Davis and Moore (1945) asked how *social positions* come to have different rewards attached to them—a Type III question. They offer a theory (written discursively) in response and state clearly that their theory does not apply to individuals (Davis and Moore 1945:242). Tumin (1953) criticized (among other issues) the theory's implications for the allocation of differential rewards to different groups (e.g., races or ethnic groups) and individuals. From that point on, Davis and Moore and Tumin debated factors that influenced the distribution of rewards to groups and individuals—an almost unending exercise in historical explanation. The debate added to the volume of published work but it distracted them and others from the principal issue of explaining the association between characteristics of social positions and the distribution of rewards.

Finally, I introduce an example of work improperly described as "theory." The work uses the propositional structure described here and clearly separates the "propositions" from the narrative discussion.[18]

The work under scrutiny begins with the statement that the paper will develop a theory that purports to explain the relationship between one construct (X) and another (Y). However, the narrative makes clear that the author or authors wish to understand how one predicts Y or $-Y$, given a particular value of X (i.e., under the given condition x_i). Additionally, the research is intended to predict the consequences of Y or $-Y$. At this point, the exercise in theory construction has already failed. The would-be theorist or theorists can only create a historical explanation. The next step is to develop the following core "propositions":

P1. Under condition x_i at time, t, Y varies inversely with F. (That is, if F, then $-Y$, and if $-F$, then Y.)

P2. P1 holds at $t_1, t_2, \ldots, t_n$. (Restatement of P1.)

P3. If Y at t, then either F or $-F$ at t_1. (That is, the occurrence or nonoccurrence of Y at t can affect the occurrence or nonoccurrence of F at t_1, but the relationship is indeterminate.)

P4. The last proposition describes criteria for evaluating, at t_1, the effect of Y's occurrence at t.

The work describes, in narrative form, a relationship between Y and F and a set of empirical outcomes that follow from the enactment of y compared with $-y$. In that regard, the work is not theoretical, or even explanatory in the historical sense. Unfortunately, the sociological literature contains many examples of such work, including theories comprised of "hypotheses" that merely restate abstract empirical generalizations. This state of affairs only adds to the collective confusion of sociologists regarding the nature of theoretical work.

SUMMARY

Sociologists misunderstand the nature of theory. Many confuse theory with metatheory, commentary on the classics, or historical explanations. The discipline affords greater visibility to historical explanations and offers greater rewards to those who create them. The current confusion ensures that members of the discipline make divergent assessments of the state of theory development. Most important, the confusion of historical and theoretical explanations contributes to the slow pace of theoretical development. As others have observed, the tremendous volume of research productivity does not cohere. However, theory is the glue that can hold such disparate findings together. I hold out hope despite my pessimistic assessment of the current state of theory development. Some sociologists have created viable and useful general theories. I argue that we can create more of them and do so more quickly than we have in the past. The methods I advocate illustrate the ancient aphorism: Questions *do* shape answers. Only theoretical questions will get theories as answers. Sociologists must learn to ask them.

NOTES

1. This chapter revises and extends a paper prepared for the Conference on Theory Development and Theory Testing in Group Processes held at the University of British Columbia, Vancouver, British Columbia on August 17–18, 1998. An earlier version is published in *Sociological Focus* (2000). I thank Dr. Martha Foschi for inviting me to present this work, and I am grateful to the anonymous reviewers and the editor of *Sociological Focus* for comments on earlier versions.

2. See Boutilier, Roed, and Svendsen's (1980) discussion of the connection between theoretical issues and the widely heralded crisis that afflicted sociological social psychology during the middle to late 1970s. (See also Archibald 1976; House 1977; McMahon 1984; Stryker 1977.) The main arguments apply to sociology as well.

3. I fail to uncover any logical or practical reason why disparate fields ought to have similar rates of theory development. On the other hand, the claim that sociology cannot create general theory is an important criticism (Cole 1994; Gergen 1973). Fortunately, it is demonstrably false.

4. Based on a practical reason, I reverse the order in which Cohen made the statements: the revised ordering fits the present discussion better than the original.

5. Parsons (1951; see also Parsons and Shils 1951) draws much attention as the high priest of "grand theory" in sociology. He is not alone, and has not been forgotten (see Crews 1986). Ironically, the grand theoretical schemes of Sigmund Freud, Alfred Adler, and others motivated Karl Popper's (1959) more constrained view, which informs my thinking on these issues.

6. I do not intend these statements as criticism of either mathematical sociologists or the use of mathematics to "formalize" general theoretical arguments. The translation of general theoretical arguments into systems of equations can be an important stage in the growth and maturation of a scientific discipline. However, systems of mathematical equations do not a general theory make.

7. I do not discuss differences between metatheory and theory in this chapter. Instead, I focus on differences between theoretical explanations and historical explanations— differences that are less frequently discussed. Many philosophers of science and sociologists offer extended discussions of the first issue. The interested reader may see, for example, the collections of papers in Lakatos and Musgrave (1970) or Suppe (1973). Berger, Zelditch, and Anderson (1972b), Chafetz (1978), Cohen (1989) and Wagner (1984) offer discussions of varied length that are accessible to the nontechnical reader.

8. Some adopt a catholic position with regard to theory and develop conceptions that admit everything but the proverbial kitchen sink. See Rule's (1997) definition for a recent example. In that regard, it is the mutability of "theory," not of social phenomena, that provides the moving target that some claim prohibits theory development in the social sciences (Gergen 1973; Cole 1994).

9. My description of an ideal-typical theory builds on ideas described by Cohen (1989). Critics will note that there exist alternative conceptions of theory and of deductive systems. (See the discussion in Suppe [1973].) I am willing to impose my conception on the discipline by fiat if doing so advances the development of sociological theory. We must begin somewhere.

10. I use lower-case symbols, such as x and y, throughout to represent singular events

(i.e., empirical instances) and upper-case symbols, such as X and Y, to characterize classes of events.

11. For the illustrations that follow, I chose either classic works or research published in the top journals in the field. I consider these works exemplary of the best the field has to offer.

12. Some of Skocpol's (1979) terms are general (e.g., "class relations," "social revolutions"). However, her inclusion of observable terms (see Willer and Webster 1970) and a focus on three concrete cases establishes the historical character of the explanation (see Cohen 1989:115).

13. More accurately, theoretical explanations contain *statements* about events or relationships between events (see Cohen 1989). I use the cryptic term "explanation of events" for ease of presentation.

14. The degree to which the costliness of creative work establishes barriers to its production should not be underestimated. For example, Miles Davis and Gil Evans produced a series of brilliant orchestral jazz recordings in the 1950s and early 1960s. However, Davis played these pieces only rarely afterward. After Davis agreed with producer Quincy Jones to perform some of the work at the 1991 Montreux Jazz Festival, he warned Jones that it would be expensive to produce. Jones remarked that a full orchestra would not cost much and pressed Davis on the issue. Davis growled, "It ain't that, man, it's just that this shit is hard to play" (Feather 1993).

15. I confess that I would not have made this statement two decades ago. I certainly did not believe it at that time. As a fledgling in the study of theoretical methods, I considered theories the only elements worthy of the appellation "explanation."

16. I recommend highly Franzosi's (1995) compelling, often brilliant, analysis of this subject. More important, the work serves as an exemplar of quantitative historical analysis.

17. Here, I am forced to violate my vow to avoid self-flagellation. Although I was trained to use the methods that I espouse, I have begun only recently to write manuscript reviews that raise objections such as those I describe.

18. In this instance, I use symbols to disguise the arguments and keep secret the identity of the writer or writers because revealing the article's title or authorship serves no useful didactic or practical purpose.

Chapter 3 _____

Formalization and Inference

Geoffrey Tootell, Alison J. Bianchi, and
Paul T. Munroe

"Yet it is an unfortunate matter of fact that human beings are inclined to give answers even when they do not have the means to find correct answers" (Reichenbach 1951:8). In formalizing a theory, the theorist uses logic or mathematics to constrain the theoretical argument, making it more amenable to empirical test. Sociology has spawned a variety of theories about the social world, most as yet unformalized. Some theories, not originally created using logic or mathematics, can benefit from formalization. As an example, we reexamine the debate over the Davis-Moore stratification theory. Once formalized, theories can then be refuted or developed progressively in theoretical research programs.

Most social theories are created and expressed in natural languages like English, and few social scientists are trained to work in any other medium. Yet these theories are not constructed so that they can be tested adequately by evidence gathered for that purpose. For example, Weber's explanation of the rise of modern rational capitalism is still contested (e.g., Goldstone 2000). We demonstrate the untrustworthiness of theories that lack *formal* representation, for they cannot be given a valid empirical test.

Theories that are intended to provide the grounds for making knowledge claims (Cohen 1989) must be structured so that those claims depend upon the rest of the theory in ways that are clear, unambiguous, and subject to proof and testing. Yet metaphysicians, epistemologists, logicians, and philosophers of science have found it difficult to agree exactly about how best to infer that a theory is adequate and about what foundations provide optimal theoretical growth (Hempel and Oppenheim 1953; Feigl and Brodbeck 1953; Feigl and Maxwell 1961; Nagel 1961; Popper 1963, 1969; Lakatos 1970, 1978; Feyerabend 1961,

1975, 1981; Laudan 1977, 1990, 1996; Suppes 1984). In most social sciences, it is not even clear what sort of language to use. The need of a formal language, although accepted by Galileo, is certainly not accepted by many social scientists.

Cohen (1989:178) defined a theory as a "set of interrelated universal statements, some of which are definitions and some of which are relationships assumed to be true, together with a syntax, a set of rules for manipulating the statements to arrive at new statements." Markovsky (1994) added that these statements should be abstract and able to explain or predict a general class of phenomena. An ordinary grammar could be used for a syntax *if and only if* it could be used to generate statements that guaranteed, following some carefully described observable beginnings, that some particular set of orderly processes will produce a specific set of predictions of observable outcomes (note Zetterberg 1965).

By *formalization* we mean the valid statement or restatement (translation) of a theory in a formal language, such as a branch of logic or mathematics. By *valid*, we mean the correct use of logic or mathematics to produce consistent consequences from the assumptions. Peirce (1925, quoted in Copi 1954:1) once described the central problem of logic as the classification of arguments so that the good (true) ones could be thrown into one category and the bad (false) ones into another. The same can be said for mathematics. A formal language requires a set of explicit rules that permit it to be used in ways that meet rigorous standards and which are accepted and applied by those who use it. For example, Aristotle, who invented Western logic, proposed three grounds of inference as ways to settle logical disputes: The principle of identity says that "X" always means X and must refer to the same objects or properties (definition) throughout the discussion. The prohibition of contradiction precludes something being described as X and not-X (~X) simultaneously (if one is true, the other must be false). And third, the principle of the excluded middle requires that an element be either X or ~X, not a bit of each or something in between. These formal languages are object languages: the language itself is an uninterpreted collection of signs and symbols—some of which represent constants, variables, or statements, while others stand for operations or rules of combination—which prescribe and/or constrain how these constants, variables, or statements may be joined. These rules (axioms) provide the syntax of the formal language. New statements (predictions) are deduced by applying these rules to the postulates of the system. A metalanguage is used to talk about the object language. Among other uses, metalanguage offers a means to interpret the formal theory so that it can be tested, applied, taught, or criticized. Formalization organizes theories strictly, requiring the use of rules of logic or mathematics to demonstrate consequences that can be deduced from their premises.

Formal theories have three desirable properties that theories may lack if they are expressed only in an ordinary (natural) language: (1) statements in formal theories are decidable; given minimal information, it is possible to decide whether a statement is formally true or false. (2) For a given system, it is often possible to prove that every statement of a certain kind is true, which means the system is complete. Although Kurt Gödel proved that these characterizations have limits, they do not affect the theories that interest us (Rosser 1939; Dawson 1997:37–81). (3) This suggests that skilled people working apart can use a formal theory to produce the same set of predictions, though this is not automatic, as formal reasoning disciplines imagination without binding it. Theories composed in ordinary natural languages can be understood fairly well by readers and writers, but not necessarily in the same way.

CLASSIFYING SOCIAL THEORIES BY THEIR STRUCTURAL TESTABILITY

Social theories that fit the concepts mentioned here can be divided into several categories:

Type A: Abstract, reproducible, valid formal theories.

Type B: Abstract, reproducible theories embedded in intuitively guided discussions that have been translated into valid formal theories.

Type C: Abstract theories embedded in intuitive discussions that have the potential to be translated into formal theories.

Type D: Other theories, which may or may not be abstract, but are not reproducible and cannot be formalized successfully.

We show that only formal theories are theoretically reproducible. A theory is theoretically reproducible if its syntax enables a well-prepared reader to reproduce exactly its theorems or consequences, including any predictions, from its primitive terms, assumptions, and definitions. A statement is abstract if its terms do not refer to any particular material objects or instances. Theories are intuitively guided if no equivalent version of the theory is expressed in a formal object language. Strictly speaking, potential for formalization is measured against a successful formalization, namely, a formal twin with the same assumptions and predictions that include the original ones. Although some intuitive theories can be formalized, others contain obvious contradictions or abdications of explanation.

Our principal objective is to show that, strictly speaking, only formalized theories (types A and B) can be refuted, and thus they are the only ones that can be supported logically by empirical evidence. They are also the only ones that can cumulate findings and extensions and establish a valid theoretical research tradition (see Cohen 1989, 1997). The cogency of an attempt to refute is diminished if informed readers cannot be assured of the relation of faulty predictions to the theory's postulates. Thus, only limited support can be gleaned for theories before formalization has been successfully completed. Nonformal theories that have been thoroughly researched, using careful research designs, are likely to belong to type C (cf. Cohen 1997). Though some distinctions are clear, the line between types C and D is fuzzy. A valid formalization of a theory once thought to be of either type can change it to type B.

Type D includes many varieties of theories; some contain no abstractions, whereas others do. Some include contradictions or unresolved ambiguities. Others do not generate consequences: some of these eschew explanation on principle; others simply never attempt it. When one of these signs is easily recognized, a theory clearly belongs to type D (as any of them would disqualify a theory from being type C).

Some Existing Formal Theories in Sociology and Social Psychology

Type A theories either originated in logical or mathematical form or their original form has been subducted by formal representations. Mathematics has become routine in economics. In sociology it has been used for a long time in demography and methodology. Much work has been done on mathematical measures (e.g., Lazarsfeld 1950; Festinger 1949; Luce and Perry 1949; Luce 1950; Hubbell 1965; Bonacich 1987; Friedkin 1998). Mathematicians and social theorists have been developing models over many years (see Bavelas 1948, 1950; Kemeny, Snell, and Thompson 1956; White 1963; Coleman 1964, 1990; Harary, Norman, and Cartwright 1965). Work on game theoretic applications shows new promise (see Luce and Raiffa 1957; Rapoport 1966; Shubik 1975; Bienenstock and Bonacich 1992; Bonacich and Bienenstock 1995; Bonacich 1998, 1999), as do developments in social influence theory (Friedkin 1998). Formal theory thrives on problems concerning superordination, subordination, flows of information or exchange, and networks (Granovetter 1973; Fararo and Skvoretz 1986; Markovsky, Willer, and Patton 1988; Lovaglia et al. 1995; Willer, Lovaglia, and Markovsky 1997; Willer and Skvoretz 1997). Arrow's impossibility theorem is a famous example of a logical theory (1951); among its many sociological implications is a fundamental dilemma within a theory of consensus.

Theories with Formal Twins

Type B theories, which were formalized after their original publication while their forms in natural languages survive and thrive, may be said to have a formal twin. At this point, those issues are unimportant if a theory has been formalized well and its formalized version is used. Status characteristics theory was formalized successfully by 1977 (Berger et al. 1977), almost twenty years after it had been proposed (Berger 1958). Affect control theory is another example (MacKinnon and Heise 1993). Balance theory (Heider 1958) was formalized by Harary, Norman and Cartwright (1965).

Unformalized Theories, Types C and D

Type C theories can be formalized. Hence, they are really identified with certainty only after they have a valid formal twin, whereupon they belong to type B. To guess which theories are type C is to bet on which will be formalized successfully. One indication is the application of the theory within elaborate, careful research designs (Cohen 1989, 1997; Szmatka and Lovaglia 1996). This suggests that theorists have used a logical approach to construct both. Examples include community power theory (Zelditch, Harris, Thomas, and Walker 1983) and the work of Zelditch and colleagues on legitimation and power (see Berger and Zelditch 1998:265–368). Ridgeway's work on status construction theory is another example (see Ridgeway et al. 1998).

Type D theories are familiar. Marx applied a materialistic version of Georg Hegel's dialectic to interpret economic and social history. Its ironic, even tragic, character often seems to fit historical chronicles, especially when applied selectively. It has been tied historically to moral instruction. But it does not work for prediction. Marx hoped that enlightened workers, recognizing their real material interests, would unite to replace capitalism by socialism and then welcome its evolution into communism. A less messianic use of his dialectic suggests that socialism would create a new class (bureaucrats), who would become the rulers and beneficiaries of a new society, supported by a working class. That would breed a new pair of competitive material interests and ultimately provoke new social changes. The dialectic is ambiguous with respect to the future, which is consistent with its dependence upon historical specificity, contraries, and contradictions (in contraries only one may be true but all may be false; in a contradictory pair, exactly one is true).

Many type D theories depend heavily on carefully placed observations, drawn conveniently from natural settings, to phrase an intuitively arranged string of "facts" that lead, whether gently or passionately, to a predicted "conclusion of fact." Often this pattern is then generalized without any reliance on sampling theory. In all too many cases, the "facts" have not been well evaluated empirically.

Some Recognized Sources of Problems of Testability in Theories Composed in Natural Languages

The typology just described addresses the problem that Gibbs (1972:58–60) noted: social theorists have established no common ground on what criteria one should use to judge good theory. He indicated that Talcott Parsons never specified what criteria he deemed right; C. Wright Mills's disciples wanted "significance" (defined to suit one's tastes, according to Gibbs; preaching to a chorus). Citing Frank (1956:13–35), Gibbs (1972:60) suggested these criteria: predictive power and accuracy, simplicity, logical consistency, plausibility, and fertility. The first was deemed most important, for it offered the best way to achieve a consensus among theorists, if they could agree on definition of an appropriate test and shed their ideological commitments.

Most would agree about logical consistency, though they may disagree about how to characterize it. Gibbs (1972:70) chose: "a necessary condition for predictive accuracy, . . . [as] contradictory predictions can only be derived from a logically inconsistent theory." Yet very few committed themselves to logical training and expression. Cohen observed that theorists typically embed a (theoretical) assertion in prose, make a claim about something, discuss its meaning, and justify its importance, as if in one gulp, leaving the reader to untangle the claim from the justification (1989:182).

With a formal theory, consequences are not independent of premises. Unless there has been a mistake, their formal truth or falsity depends explicitly upon the truth or falsity of the theory's assumptions (Zetterberg [1965: 20–28] suggested testing a theory's assumptions; if these are true and all consequences are derived correctly, the conclusions should be true, too). Relationships are validated by applying the appropriate rules of logic or mathematics. This should produce either contingent truths or tautologies.

Tautologies have a bad name in sociology; many sociologists think of them as repetitious efforts to convince, often using weak arguments. In logic and mathematics, as we use them here, they are formal truths, for example, given p; then $p \& \sim p$ is a contradiction, while $p \vee \sim p$ is a tautology. This is obvious, but that is not always so: suppose we prove that something is p if and only if it is also q $(p \Leftrightarrow q)$, so p and q are logically equivalent $(p \equiv q)$. The material equivalence of two statements is tautologous. A tautology like this can be especially strategic if it results from a proof that two propositions once thought to be unrelated can be defined by, or substituted for, each other. A classic example is Wiles's (1993) proof of Fermat's last theorem: he proved the Taniyama-Shimura conjecture by showing that every elliptical curve over the rational numbers is uniformized by a modular form. The mates in each pair (elliptical curve, modular form) are equivalent in this sense. (Ribet had already shown that proof of Taniyama-Shimura conjecture would imply Fermat's theorem [Aczel 1996:100–102, 119, 132–134; Singh 1997:199–203].)

An Early Instance of an Application of Logic

Some forty years ago Merton showed how to apply logic to existing theory (1967). He restated proposals by Durkheim to conform to a logical structure that would warrant their coherence. This implied that the data supported the theory as a whole, rather than just its conclusion.

1. Social cohesion provides psychic support to group members subjected to acute stresses and anxieties.

2. Suicide rates are functions of unrelieved anxieties and stresses to which persons are subjected.

3. Catholics have greater social cohesion than Protestants.

4. Therefore, lower suicide rates should be anticipated among Catholics than among Protestants (150–151).

Propositions 1 and 2 are major premises, proposition 3 is the minor premise (a singular proposition, or instantiation), and proposition 4 is the conclusion (see Copi 1954:66). This is a syllogism, a type of logical argument form, that is, if the premises are true, then the conclusion is valid. Merton recognized that a closer linkage of theory and research would offer more secure predictions than just extrapolating observed trends (1967:139–171, esp. 151–155). He also believed that theories would gain more precise expression, which would facilitate discrimination among alternative theories. When his essay was published, however, Merton could think of no example in social theory of a discussion of sociological laws ("statements of invariance that derive from theory") that offered an instance that fully met logical criteria (1967:151–153).

Some Inference Schemata

At this point, we should introduce four more inference schemata and a pair of fallacies. Let p, q, and r be sociological propositions. Relevant logical connectives are *not*, *and*, *or*, and *if . . . , then* and *therefore* (which are represented by ~, &, v, $\Rightarrow$, and $\therefore$).

Modus ponens is the most commonly expressed, and abused, of the logical schemata (valid argument forms) that appear in social science, though it is not used as often as it is mentioned: *if* p *and* p $\Rightarrow$ q are true, then one can infer that q is true. (Although theorists sometimes say *if . . . , then . . .* , usually they neither prove nor assume explicitly that p $\Rightarrow$ q.) Other valid argument forms include:

modus tollens, given that p $\Rightarrow$ q and ~ q $\therefore$ ~ p,

the *disjunctive syllogism*, given p v q and ~ p $\therefore$ q,

and the *hypothetical syllogism*, given p $\Rightarrow$ q and q $\Rightarrow$ r $\therefore$ p $\Rightarrow$ r.

(These are valid inference schemata but not syllogisms.) It is valid to substitute equivalents (if p $\equiv$ s & (t v u); replace this expression by p wherever it occurs in a true statement, and the statement remains true).

Fallacies (invalid inference schemata) include:

affirming the consequent, given that p $\Rightarrow$ q and q $\therefore$ p,[1]

and the *fallacy of denying the antecedent*, given p $\Rightarrow$ q and ~ p $\therefore$ ~ q.

APPLYING FORMAL METHODS TO EXAMINE PLAUSIBLE THEORIES IN ORDINARY LANGUAGES

Many theories written in ordinary English appear to have a logical framework. Some do have such a framework because their authors have used logic carefully as a subtext to see that their claims are indeed logically articulated. Most have not been constructed by using an actual logical framework, however. We consider five examples from a public dispute among a variety of leading theorists about how to explain stratification. Writing in natural languages, the authors made one position or another sound plausible. Their arguments still appear to be logical, and their writers seemed to believe that they were, as if they had checked before writing.

A Flawed Discussion: Davis-Moore, Tumin, and the Sources and Stability of Social Stratification

Between 1945 and 1963, Davis and Moore (1945), Tumin (1953), Wesolowski (1962), and Stinchcombe (1963) and many others (see Wesolowski 1962: 28 n. 2) offered an all-too-rare sequence of theoretical analyses of a single, interesting topic, in which a great deal of apparently solid critical thinking appeared in condensed statements. In an unpublished memorandum, Zelditch (1999) summarized the Davis-Moore proposal as follows: social stratification is universal. This is because recruiting talented people, training them well, and getting them to perform conscientiously depend on offering adequate rewards. Either the more important positions are assigned more rewards, or the particular society fails to survive. In fact, all societies are observed to have some positions that are more important than others, and some positions require more talent than others. Thus, all societies are stratified.

Davis and Moore

Superficially, Davis and Moore's argument appeared to be logical. No formal syntax was used in its written form, however. Few logical connectives appeared, nor was there mention of logical axioms or rules of inference that could help to show how an argument might be put into a logical form (1945). (For example, no "if, then" statements appeared on page 242; only three appeared on page 243; and there appeared to be no use of a pertinent "and," "or," or "not" on these pages.) The focus of their essay was substantive, relying on the credibility of their assumptions. Their argument may or may not be adequate, but we have no evidence that it was logically crafted.

Tumin

Tumin's main thrust at Davis and Moore was aimed at their assumptions (1953). He raised legitimate issues, but his argument rested on the assumption that his postulates differed enough that if they were true, the Davis and Moore argument should be false. But that requires that Tumin's premises were true, that they contradicted those of Davis and Moore, and, with regard to conclusions, that the logic applied in the Davis and Moore piece be correct. As these premises seem at worst to be contraries and there is no evidence that Davis and Moore used logic, this strategy is flawed. Neither party did much to show the empirical applicability or universality of their premises or conclusions.

Huaco's Logical Analysis of Davis and Moore

Huaco (1963:801–804) outlined four types of attempts made to justify the Davis-Moore argument logically. The first is a causal model with minimal assumptions. It can be represented as:

1. All societies have unequal rewards attached to various positions (the dependent variable or conclusion, which is a presumably correct, or lawful, empirical generalization).
2. Different positions are of unequal importance for the preservation of a society.
3. Adequate performance in these positions requires people with different and sometimes scarce skills (talent or training).
4. Greater rewards are attached to more important positions to secure incumbents with greater skills.
5. It follows from statements 2 through 4 that greater rewards will be attached to the positions that are of greatest functional importance, and hence (1), in all societies various positions have different rewards.

Huaco's reasoning looks sound, but he did not rely explicitly on any logical connectives, axioms, rules of inference, or theorems with proofs. The argument is reasonable; he cited correlational techniques and sprinkled comparative terms appropriately throughout his assumptions. Yet to claim that a work titled "Logical Analysis of the Davis-Moore Theory" is logical without obvious evidence of the use of logical or mathematical rules places the burden of proof on the author.

Huaco compared this "causal" or "unqualified" version with three others: the "consequential" or "functionalist," a qualified version, and a maximal one (1963: 802–803). His analysis attended to several critical issues, such as the need for useful definitions of terms such as survival, unequal functional importance, or necessity. He also pointed to the absence of critical argument or evidence of such things as whether the system of unequal rewards ensured the appointment (election) of the fittest or, generally, how one set of performances contributes to good performances of other sets of duties (1963:803).

Stinchcombe and Harris

Stinchcombe (1963:69–72) and Stinchcombe and Harris (1969:13–23) focused on some empirical consequences of Davis and Moore's (1945) theory that could be used to create valid tests of it. In his first effort, Stinchcombe picked conditions that would change the degree of importance of certain roles or identify groups in which particular roles would be (or become) more important. Next, he suggested measures of openness of recruitment and of degree of inequality of rewards (1963:70). If the changes in importance occurred as hypothesized and the measures were accurate, his results would be consequences of the theory and the truth of these predictions would support it.

His first test (1963) concerned the increase of the relative importance of generals in wartime. For example, assume that tycoons are constantly important. Then let p be, "We are at war," where q is, "Generals are more important than tycoons" and r is, "We shall promote generals based on their war-related achievements." Thus ~p v q is, "Either we are not at war, or generals are more important than tycoons," whereas ~q v r means, "Either generals are not more important than tycoons, or we shall promote generals based on their war-related achievements."

To prove that $p \Rightarrow r$ using the previous assumptions, definition, and De Morgan's axiom, $\sim p \lor q \equiv \sim(p \And \sim q) \equiv p \Rightarrow q$. Similarly, $q \Rightarrow r$. Then, by hypothetical syllogism, $p \Rightarrow r$. (See p. 78)

Any time that these assumptions are true, the conclusion will be valid. As with computer simulation, this yields predictions, not evidence. Both offer ways to check a model by comparing extrapolations to a standard, for they can reveal the existence of unexpected problems.

Stinchcombe recognized that a number of conditions could undermine the usefulness of his argument: (1) generals may not be recruited based on ability or performance in wartime (then the theory may be falsified), (2) they may not be more important in wartime, or (3) measures of openness, importance, ability, or relative reward mignt not work well (1963:70).

Interpretive research hypotheses should be theorems or corollaries that must be proven, using logic or mathematics, to be formally true. They may also be logical arguments, which include appropriate instantiations (e.g., Socrates fits the definition of a man in the syllogism beginning, "All men are mortal"). One must be sure: generals are soldiers, so if soldiers are more important in wartime, generals should be, too.

Thinking of likely alternatives is a quick way to check whether an assumption masks errors. Assume that generals are usually promoted on the basis of their performances (abilities being hidden), but in peacetime there are no relevant measures of wartime performance. As a result, decision makers may not know how to pick winners. Suppose that the officers are equally bad on both sides in a war, but the sergeants in one army are much better. That side wins, and its generals get promoted. The inequalities are not as predicted and the theory does not work as designed, yet it may pass muster unexamined.

A basic problem in examining the Davis-Moore dispute is to get independent measures of role importance. Stinchcombe and Harris (1969:13–23) created an example of how to devise a measure of functional importance as used here. They built formal models that would give correct predictions of role differentiation in both small and large groups, as the Davis-Moore hypothesis implies, specifically with respect to the effects of task structure on stratification structure (1969:13). If some roles are more important than others, then to ensure that they are performed adequately, it is rational to emphasize recruiting people with greater abilities and to train them to fill the more important roles better. It seems rational to pay more. Either method creates inequalities,

To get an independent measure of importance, Stinchcombe and Harris contrasted the problems of shaping steel while it is hot with those of cutting and grinding it after it cools (1969:14). Hot steel cannot be stored; cold steel can. In cutting or grinding operations, enough cold steel can be inventoried locally that if one machine breaks down, it does not affect the rest of the department before it is fixed. With hot steel, the failure of one operation causes a complicated and expensive process of shutting down the whole department. There operations are interdependent, whereas in the cold steel department, they are independent. Supervisors are charged with keeping all equipment working. It follows that supervision is much more important in the hot area, and a wise mill superintendent will get the best supervisors to oversee the hot operations.

Stinchcombe and Harris built models with which they could compare the marginal productivity of supervision by measuring the effects on group productivity of adding supervisors in each kind of operation (1969:15–20). Suppose there are n operators running n machines in each department. The probability of any machine breaking down is thought to be independent of another machine breaking. In the independent (cold) case, total productivity depends on the sum of the production of each machine (1969:15), or n multiplied by the mean production per machine, multiplied by b, a measure of the contribution of the supervisor. In the interdependent case, the average production per hour (week) is proportional to the product of the probabilities of each machine breaking down. Marginal productivity of a given amount of supervision is the partial derivative of total production with respect to the amount of supervision (1969:16), holding constant such factors as the abilities of supervisors and workers. Then the marginal productivity per supervisor in the hot case is almost n times that in the independent condition (1969:18).

This comparison lacks good, precise information concerning relative rewards. The ratio of supervisors' rewards to those of workers, for the same levels of abilities, should be the about the same in both departments (1969:22). However, no precise hypotheses join the measures of importance and of relative rewards. The models do not confirm that incumbents of one job must be paid more than those of the other. That requires assumptions about the labor market, including demand for, and availability of, good supervisors and good workers. The Stinchcombe-Harris models require a command of college-level mathematics; years after their creation, they remain sophisticated.

Zelditch's Formalization of the Davis-Moore Hypothesis

Zelditch (1999) attempts to reconstruct Davis and Moore's theory by explicitly stating what he believes to be the theory's domain, dependent variable (survival of a group or society), and scope conditions. He organizes the logic of the theory with definitions, assumptions, and their implications. While successfully formalizing the theory, Zelditch uncovers many of its basic weaknesses. He underlines that the domain of Davis-Moore's generalization is plainly universal. The theory's scope depends on a society being a system of interdependent positions filled by people whose choices and actions can be made independently. The importance of a position depends on some amount of dependence by others on the tasks expected of the person in that position. Scope conditions, if any, specify partial domains of other variables under which there exist observable interdependence and stratification (e.g., perhaps task difficulty and scarcity of rewards). Finally, the dependent variable is a function of the state of the system.

He grasps problems in Davis and Moore's analyses. For one, he recognizes that their theory depends on quantitative terms like "all," "none" (even if implied), or "greater," "more," "less," and so forth. Propositional logic is insufficient. Statements that should be conditional are not treated that way. For example, antecedents with variable terms (rather than constants) are conditional ("[If] some positions are . . . , then . . ."). The theory is based on the implicit assumption that it is desirable that each society survives ("Every society must . . ."). These are aesthetic or ethical as well as policy and empirical issues. Whether a society's survival is desirable or not ultimately involves questions of ethics and aesthetics. Whether survival strategies succeed depends on the truth of the assumptions underlying policy decisions, their implementation, and the empirical relation between them and a successful conclusion (survival). Unless pertinent discussions are carefully disciplined, conclusions and value statements may become entangled, confused, and yield unexpected or disappointing results. Metatheoretical statements are mixed with theoretical ones ("Difference[s] between one system . . . and another . . . [are] attributable to whatever factors affect . . .").

Then Zelditch constructs a more suitable version of the theory. The variable of interest is survival, and the theory is concerned with societies, which are thought of as systems of interdependent positions. Functions are actions, performed by incumbents of positions, which meet necessary conditions of a society's survival. Positions are characterized by how important they are to a society's functions, which is an important variable. Positions are filled by individuals, who are described by their talent, training, and the conscientiousness with which they do their position's duties.

Zelditch specifies a number of definitions, assumptions, and implications:

Definition 1. (Functional importance). One position is more important than another if it is the only position that performs a necessary function or if other positions are dependent on it for their own contribution to performance of the function, or both.

Assumption 1. (The functional axiom). The greater the chances that the most important positions are conscientiously filled by the most talented and trained persons, the greater the chances of the society's survival.

Implication 1. If functionally less important positions compete successfully with functionally more important positions for talent, the survival of society is endangered.

Assumption 2. (The motivational axiom.) The greater the rewards of a position, the greater its supply of talent and the more conscientiously its duties are performed.

Implication 2. Either (1) the greater the functional importance of a position, the greater its rewards, or (2) the less the chances of a society's survival. [If more important positions are rewarded well, they compete successfully with less important positions for talent. Similar arguments apply to inducing training and conscientious performance.]

Assumption 3. (The scarcity axiom.) With functional importance constant, the more scarce the supply of talent, the greater the rewards of the position.

Implication 3. With functional importance held constant, the greater the talent and/or training required by a position, the greater its rewards.

Assumption 4. The greater the talent and/or training required by a position the more scarce the supply of labor.

From these assumptions, and using his knowledge of mathematics, Zelditch derives several other critical implications. The most important implication, 4, follows from a concept of multivariate statistics plus the previous three statements. This assumes that rewards are a linear (mathematical) function of importance and scarcity.

Implication 4. The rewards of a position depend upon a linear combination of the independent effects of functional importance and [of] the labor supply. As one of these factors is held constant, rewards increase as a linear function of the other (factor), and their joint effect is additive. This reasoning was axiomatic in Zelditch's argument: implication 4 expressed the reasoning underlying assumptions 2 through 4, as well as implications 2 (part 1), 3, and 6. Implication 4, along with 2, can be used instead of the functional axiom.

Implication 5. If (any) function F is a necessary function in any society, then F is well rewarded in every society. This was a uniformity hypothesis, which Davis and Moore claimed they would explain.

Implication 6. In every society, prestige and economic rewards are correlated. Prestige and economic rewards are correlated with scarcity and functional importance.

Zelditch notes that these assumptions and implications do not explain universal stratification. He adds that usually it is possible to derive an empirical generalization from one or more general laws and another empirical generalization, but only if the antecedent is asserted (claimed to be true). Using this strategy, he concludes:

Implication 7. Every society is stratified or its survival is in danger. Zelditch says this is the only permissible result, as it is impossible to deduce that every society is stratified.

As a finishing touch, he suggests that his conclusion is supported by works of Inkeles (1950) and Feldmesser (1953) on the Soviet Union and of Spiro (1956), Talmon-Garber and Talmon-Garber (1956), Etzioni (1959), Vallier (1962), and others on the Israeli kibbutz. These works are important because they give evidence showing how societies with strong ideological commitments to equality responded to crises by enacting more stratified governance structures. Since sociologists have gathered scant empirical evidence to support functional explanations, Zelditch's interpretation of these studies' results presents interesting support for an appropriate version of Davis and Moore's use of structural functionalism. In the next section, we offer a model expressed in propositional logic. We can use Zelditch's work and our model to tell where to classify the Davis-Moore theory of stratification.

APPLYING LOGIC TO DAVIS-MOORE THEORY

The previous review of Davis-Moore theory introduced some of its supporters, detractors, and refiners. Their works included some attempts to formalize the work, in part or in whole. Zelditch's argument is close enough to guess this theory is type C. Yet unless someone can produce a formal model that has equivalent assumptions and consequences, it should be classified as type D. In this section we use propositional logic to construct a sample formalization. (P denotes a postulate, and T, a theorem or corollary.) Consider:

P1. Abilities and training are needed to perform roles well.

P2. Incentives above specific levels guarantee reliable role performances.

P3. Some roles are more important than others.

P4. People require added incentives to fill important roles.

P5. Society can survive in its current form.

P6. (Observation.) All societies have a form of stratification.

P7. (Definition.) There exists a positive correlation between the importance of roles in a society and the incentives awarded to each; we will call this correlation a stratification system.

As Davis and Moore made a "functional" argument, we should examine necessity rather than sufficiency (1945:242ff), stressing an effect rather than a cause. "Only if" or "if and only if" replaces "if, then." This suggests that "Society can survive only if (or if and only if) it is stratified." To deal with the imputed logic, we use $p \Leftarrow q$ rather than $p \Rightarrow q$. As a result, the truth table is slightly different.

p	q	$p \Rightarrow q$		p	q	$p \Leftarrow q$
T	T	T		T	T	T
F	T	T		F	T	F
T	F	F		T	F	T
F	F	T		F	F	T

As $\sim p \vee q = \sim(p \,\&\, \sim q) \equiv p \Rightarrow q$ (De Morgan, definition), then $p \vee \sim q = \sim(\sim p \,\&\, q) \equiv p \Leftarrow q$. Let us represent these propositions by p1, p2, ... p7. Assume:

P.8. (p1 & p2) v ~p7.
P.9. p5 v ~(p1 & p2).
P.10. (p3 & p4) v ~p5.
P.11. [p7 ⟺ (p3 & p4)] ≡ [p7 ≡ (p3 & p4)].
P.12. p1 v ~p2.
P.13. p7 v ~p6.

Theorems T.1 through T.6 can be derived from assumptions P.1 through P.13.

T.1. (p1 & p2) v ~p7 = ~(~(p1 & p2) & p7) (De Morgan's Law and P.8)
∴ (p1 & p2) ⟸ p6 (definition).

The three parts of T.2 are also proved using De Morgan's Law and the definition of implication.

T.2. (i) p5 ⟸ (p1 & p2); (P.9);
(ii) (p3 & p4) ⟸ p5; (P.10);
(iii) p1 ⟸ p2; (P.12).

Assume that the hypothetical syllogism applies for $p \Leftarrow q$, $q \Rightarrow r$ just as it does for $p \Rightarrow q$ and $q \Rightarrow r$.

T.3. p7 ≡ (p3 & p4) ⟸ p5 ⟸ p1 ⟸ p2 ⟸ p6.
T.4. p7 ⟺ p6 (application of definition).
T.5. p7 ⟺ (p3 & p4) ⟺ p5 ⟺ p1 ⟺ p2 ⟺ p6 (from T.3 and T.4).
T.6. p7 ≡ (p3 & p4) ≡ p5 ≡ p1 ≡ p2 ≡ p6 (substituting ≡ for ⟺).

Theorems 5 and 6 leave little doubt that the truth of one statement means they all are true; they hang together. If any assumption is untrue, all are untrue. Yet the dependent variable (p6) first appears here as an independent assumption, so the theories are not quite the same. As all statements are equivalent, we can easily rearrange them, moving p6 to the dependent variable position (commutativity holds for &, v, and equivalence). This model expresses the Davis-Moore assumptions slightly differently, but if we assume that these differences are not enough to alter the theory substantially, this appears to be a logically satisfactory rendition of Davis-Moore thinking in functional form. For anyone who accepts this argument as valid, it becomes a formal twin and Davis-Moore theory may be classed as type B. This implies that it was originally type C rather than type D.

Zelditch's results and our own show how logical models can be applied to this problem. As Zelditch's dependent variable is societal survival, his theory is not a formal twin of Davis-Moore theory; actually, it is better.

INFERENCE AND FORMALIZATION

In this section we prove a lemma and a corollary in support of our claims about what inferences can be drawn from formal versus nonformal theories. In particular, we demonstrate that if an author becomes careless and allows contradictions to appear improperly, absurd conclusions may appear. Often these may be in the guise of common beliefs, however, so their absurdity is not obvious. On the other hand, if the propositions in a theory are not tied together logically, the truth or falsity of any of them may not affect the truth or falsity of their predictions, and vice versa. The primary premise on which our argument is based is that if contradictions can be admitted into a theory, any conclusion is valid. Second, if no constraints, such as axioms or rules of inference, are imposed on an argument, all conclusions are independent of the premises. But to create a community of communication and common belief, scholars must apply logically valid rules or axioms uniformly throughout their arguments or disputes.

We treat theories as if they were logical arguments (see Copi 1954:3–5, 167–168, esp. 175–85). Arguments are ordered sets of statements, which include one or more conclusions that follow from a set of premises. We can divide arguments into those for which it is possible to determine whether the conclusions are actually derived from premises by some set of principles and those for which this is untrue. This means that some arguments refer to technical premises (e.g., from logic or mathematics) that authors and readers can use to infer whether a conclusion can be derived from the premises either by a method (schema) known to be valid or by a newly proven theorem.

Our argument is based on the following lemma, which is trivial but true.

Lemma 1: If propositions p1 and p2 can be derived from the same premises, and p2 = ~p1, then these premises imply that any proposition q is true.

Proof: Assume A1, . . . , Am, which imply both p1 and p2. By hypothesis, p2 = ~p1, thus, the assumptions exclude the principle of contradiction. Given that and the rule of conjunction, assert (p & ~p) and ~(p & ~p). Use the rule of addition and any arbitrarily chosen proposition q to form ~(p & ~p) v q, which is true whether q is true or not. This is equivalent to material implication (by definition). Then, applying modus ponens, given (p & ~p), (p & ~p) ⇒ q ∴ q; hence, q is true, as shown here.

Corollary 2. Given the conditions in lemma 1, all propositions used in the argument are logically independent of each other.

Proof: By permitting contradictions, any proposition can be added to an argument as true (lemma 1). If so, propositions can be added randomly. Let q, r, . . . , t and/or ~q, ~r, . . . , ~t be added in this manner. Now suppose the propositions u and v are added carefully; the results are the same, as any proposition or conclusion is valid. Hence the selection and state of each proposition added are independent of the proposition's predecessors and of its successors, as shown.

Immediate Results: Divergent consequences for evaluating type A and B theories versus type C and D theories.

Lemma 1 and corollary 2 imply that theories that are not formalized (types C or D) permit anyone to add any conclusion to a theory. For such theories, we must assume that any connection between assumptions and conclusions is accidental; the truth of one set gives no real information about the truth of the other. These also imply that theories of types C or D are not theoretically reproducible, as there are no principles that govern what will be added during this reproduction process. There is no guarantee that conclusions that are produced at one time by one person will be reproduced by others or that two or more experts, working from the same assumptions, would agree that each other's derivations were justifiable. This implies that theorists can repair, or dress up, a type D theory by replacing a false or unappealing statement with any proposition that better fits their agenda or taste.

These proofs, taken with what we know about formal theorizing, yield our central point: the truth of a theory is independent of the truth of its propositions unless conditions of that dependence are logically valid. Thus, if all testable statements in a type C or D theory have been found to be true, we remain unsure how, or even that, they reflect on the truth of the theory, as we do not know the conditions under which tests can refute the theory. For theories of types A and B, the interpreted formal theory specifies the conditions under which it is true. If they are met, the theory is credible. If they are not, it either cannot be applied or may be false. In short, a type C or D theory can never really be refuted, whereas, at least in principle, type A or B theories can be falsified by the results of even a single test.

CONCLUSIONS

While each of these theory types A, B, C, and D differs structurally from the others, the distinctions that are most significant are between the formalized theories, types A and B, and those without formalization. Indeed, their authors often address methodological problems differently (Szmatka and Lovaglia 1996). Unless all premises are empirical statements in which all semantic terms can be operationalized easily, not all propositions can be tested. The evaluation of a theory begins with its assumptions. With many theories, formal or not, many of their assumptions remain untested. A theory's premises include several kinds of assumptions: empirical generalizations, substantive theoretical assumptions containing theoretical constructs (e.g., function) or inferred entities (functional importance; see Bergmann 1953; MacCorquodale and Meehl 1953; Willer and Webster 1970), technical syntactic assumptions (logical or mathematical rules), and scope conditions (under which the theory can receive a valid test; see Berger 1982 [1974]; Cohen 1989; Foschi 1997; Tootell, Bianchi, and Munroe 1998). Syntactic assumptions are usually taken as given if they fit the data and do not contradict or depend on one another.

Some empirical generalizations may not be testable. For example, "No society survives without a stratification system." We might be able to show that every society observed by historians, anthropologists, and sociologists has been stratified. But these observations exclude many societies from the past and future. Another option is to intervene in an ongoing group by removing the stratification system. This can be done for small groups, although new hierarchies may emerge later. That can imply either that the group survived without a hierarchy or that the replacement of its hierarchy even helped it to survive. The same argument applies to a society. Does an absence of stratification (even a brief one) really prove that society can survive without it, or does this prove that survival depends on quickly installing a new hierarchy (as in many revolutions)?

To put this issue into perspective, compare tests of type C or D theories. Type C theories are more likely to be tested by nonexperimental methods (cf. Ridgeway et al. 1998). Authors writing type D theories may not even intend to create testable theories: they may believe their ideas to be vested in history or even to be obvious. Researchers need to catalogue the testable assertions of each theory by their test results. They may conclude by giving an estimate of the probability of finding an empirically sound statement in theory Ti versus Tj. As all statements are logically independent, the probability of all being true is the joint product of the probability that each is true. If the theory contains many sentences, this product will be low. Yet even if all statements appear to be true, there are no assurances that Ti, for example, is credible. By itself, a correlation among some or all variables explains nothing; it may be coincidental. Repeated observation helps us believe that it is not rare; yet it could be a result of a particular set of conditions, perhaps in the method. Thus, it is careless to generalize.

The choice of methods may mark a basic divide among theorists working with types A and B theories from those who work with types C and D (Szmatka and Lovaglia 1996). One reason why experiments can provide compelling evidence is that they can be constructed to mimic (represent) and compare the particular abstract conditions specified in a theory. The logical structure of a theory helps to identify tests of which assumptions or predictions (research hypotheses) will be most convincing. For instance, think of a bivariate theory that focuses on a sufficient condition. The theory will be false if $x = T$ and $y = F$. A formal theory can have a very large number of substantive interpretations (by a variety of theories). Interpretations of other models can also explain a variation in the dependent variable. Though many explanations may be contrary, or even contradictory, to the theory to be tested, rigorous theories and design create conditions in which apparently contrary theories are set in specific conditions in which their predictions prove contradictory. Terms and conditions can be operationalized and integrated best in experiments (cf. Kendall and Lazarsfeld 1950). Experiments can clarify precise issues with implications for theoretical decision making and development, which stimulate acceptance and growth of theory.

Laudan (1977) said that theory change and development occur through the solution of anomalies rather than the refutation of false knowledge claims. Among type D theories, ambiguity can cloak anomaly. But theoretical rigor helps to anticipate anomalies, as well as to discern them, frame them clearly, and resolve them, thus providing an engine for theory renovation and growth. The standard of selection among contrary theories should be to provide better solutions to selected problems (e.g., solutions that offer better empirical fit, are more fertile or ingenious, etc.).

Valid methods of empirical testing (and probability theory) must respond to an ancient problem of induction: it is impossible to deny that an item observed later may differ greatly from ones seen earlier. In the 1930s this was resolved for estimating population parameters from random samples by a betting strategy that depends on an optimization procedure, based on probability theory, to measure and minimize error; it became the foundation of statistical hypothesis testing (Neyman and Pearson 1933, 1936–1938; Ackoff 1953; see also Suppes 1984; cf. Cohen 1997). The argument resembles modus tollens. Even a very good experimenter cannot anticipate everything, and no empirically oriented knowledge is completely safe from this inductive problem.

The difficulty in eliminating all alternative explanations implies that building empirical evidence to support a theory (types A or B) occurs gradually and proceeds unevenly: some empirical results are more convincing than others, setbacks are not necessarily catastrophic, and resolving theoretical problems or anomalies can advance knowledge rapidly (Cohen 1997; Lakatos 1970, 1978; Laudan 1977; Kuhn 1970). We probably need a formal theory, perhaps statistical, to help optimize the growth of research programs. Already the careful coordination and accumulation of research and theorizing have led to the growth of scientific sociological knowledge in several A- and B-type theoretical-research traditions (Wagner and Berger 1985, 1986, 1993; Berger and Zelditch 1993c; Szmatka and Lovaglia 1996:401–407). Consider status characteristics theory (Berger et al. 1977; Wagner and Berger 1993), affect control theory (MacKinnon and Heise 1993), power dependence and exchange networks (Cook, Molm, and Yamagishi 1993), or network exchange theory (Willer and Markovsky 1993; Willer and Skvoretz 1997). As Szmatka and Lovaglia emphasized (1996:403), interplay between theory development and working strategies has produced these accumulations. Like other "real" scientists, sociologists can expand and enrich the knowledge in sociology's domain.

In sum, the testability of a theory depends on the existence and quality of its formalization. Unformalized theories cannot be tested or refuted clearly. Anomalies there may go unperceived. This benefits the reputations of authors of C or D theories, whose names and works can remain longer in public conversation. Yet absent proof and evidence, a theory is simply an opinion (and weak evidence offers fertile ground for projection).

Short Tests for Flaws

As noted, a faulty link, say p2 $\Rightarrow$ (p3 & p4), can flaw an entire formal theory. To examine large theories step by step can be exhausting. Logical tests may help, however. For example, a theorist-researcher can try to make all the premises true and the conclusion false. One way begins by listing the premises, with each variable they include. Assume the theory can be represented as modus ponens. To force the theory (P $\Rightarrow$ S) to be false, it must have a true premise and a false consequent (P is true; S is false). Working backward to achieve this, certain variables in each premise must be marked false. When enough are marked false to justify the falsity of the consequent, compare these assignments to their known truth values. If there is an inconsistency, the original argument can be declared valid.

Stinchcombe showed how model building can be structured by using graph theory (1968:130–148). Each variable, vector, or term in a model can be associated with a point (node, vertex) in a digraph (a directed graph). The arcs (arrows) that relate one point to another represent functions used to transform one variable by another. The path is the relevant function or proposition. A symbol of the operator is used as a label, for example, let y = f(x). Then:

$$x \xrightarrow{f(x)} y$$

At the next level, each point can stand for a proposition or operation, with the arc or linear operator being a matrix or linear transformation. Stinchcombe showed that different models can have very different graph structures. Suppose we graph the relations of variables and of the propositions or functions of a theory. As a theorist enlarges or extends a theory, this may generate sequences of graphs that are either supergraphs (theory construction) or subgraphs (predictions).

Robertson and Seymour (1983–1997, especially 1990) proved that "In every infinite set of graphs there are two such that one is a minor of the other" (Diestel 1997:249). This implies that, for a very wide range of applications, there exists a type of algorithm that determines whether certain types of complicated models can be used to order a set of relations that can be represented as a set of graphs meeting the conditions mentioned previously. This promises that algorithms can be constructed to solve a variety of unspecified problems. It can be used where Stinchcombe's ideas can be applied. Skill at this will become more useful as our theories become more complex.

Define *minor* (Diestel 1997:15–16): a graph X is a minor of another graph, Y, if and only if there is a class of graphs G, where G is a subgraph of Y, and X can be gotten from G by a series of graphs $G_0, \ldots, G_n$, where $G_0 = G$ with edges e_i as elements of G_i, such that $G_n \simeq X$, and $G_{i+1} = G_i / e_i$, for all i < n. This sequence is achieved by contracting any graph G_{i+1} by reducing an edge e (connecting v_x, v_y) to a vertex. The minor relation is reflexive, antisymmetric, and transitive and is a partial ordering on the class of finite graphs (Diestel 1997:15–17, 257–268). Graphs which cannot be embedded, for instance nonplanar graphs such as K^5 or $K_{3,3}$, are among those which have no minor and are called *forbidden* (or excluded). These classes of graphs are distinct from graphs that take minors, which are said to have a *hereditary* property (Diestel 1997: 257–268).

To ensure that a theory contains a sequence of relations that satisfies a solution algorithm generated by this method, we can represent each step by an appropriate digraph and exclude any sequence including a subgraph containing K^5 or $K_{3,3}$ (see Harary 1969). This affirms the organization of the argument. Rather than checking each step, researchers or theorists could first check their assumptions and then inspect the pattern of the argument.

The Davis-Moore Dispute and Its Lessons Regarding Advances in Sociological Knowledge

Can formalizing the Davis-Moore theory lead to its rejection after all these years? As first written, this debate might belong in type D. An accurate attempt to formalize a type D theory could show that it does not predict its previously presumed consequences, there exist contradictions among its assumptions or between them and a prediction, or it produces contrary or contradictory consequences. Indeed, the early pieces reflect serious flaws, which can abound in C or D theories (note Gibbs 1972:80–107). In particular, suppose $p \Rightarrow q$ was justified (in some fashion), p was assumed, and q was "observed." Where someone then concluded that p (one or more initial assumptions) was true, this affirmed the consequent (a fallacy). Although logic or evidence was scanty, at best, the flexible, spongy quality of nonformal theories makes them hard to refute. Other challenges intruded: moral or ideological issues often dominated scientific interests, as concepts such as social stratification are so central and so value burdened that they become the foci of strong, opposing opinions. Untested observations served as assumptions. Thus, despite disagreements, Davis-Moore theory has defied refutation for over half a century. Yet accepting our model as valid moves Davis-Moore to type B. (It was a mistake to think of it as type D.)

Formal theory can be rejected easily. Our model is severally vulnerable: the sequence of equivalences means that if one statement is false, all are false (though the theory is formally true). If some are true (empirically) while others are false, the theory is false. Propositional logic seems inadequate. The universal quantifier implied by the generalization that all societies have stratification systems requires only one exception to be false. Finally, the notion that the most important roles are rewarded generously seems vulnerable. A stratification system can be defined in many ways; think of it as a set of variables so related as to produce and maintain a set of ordered strata. Although inequalities can be universal, existence of a stratification system may not be. Davis and Moore stated (1945:243) that if the duties of each role in society were equally important and equally pleasant, then it would make no difference who filled any role. But, they added, this is false. How do we know that?

As an exception can disprove their ruling, consider a contrary proposition: regardless of perceived importance or relative reward, the performance of many "insignificant" roles make extremely vital (critical) differences to society's survival (note Huaco 1963:803; Stinchcombe and Harris 1969). Since 1800, better public health practices have probably extended life expectancies more than any other factor, followed, perhaps, by preventive inoculations (lowering infant mortality) and antibiotics. If so, those who maintain the quality of drinking water (especially in large river basins with big cities downstream) are probably much more important to society's survival (and welfare) than the highly regarded, and better paid, professional surgeons, athletes, or politicians. The abilities of sewage workers are rarely believed to be generalizable, unlike expectations based on gender, race, wealth, or status as a CEO. High-ability sewage workers would not be expected to have the talents (including the ability to learn) to fit positions in computer applications, universities, health services, or government; they lack the cachet needed for ready entry into the highly paid labor markets that would force up their pay at treatment plants. Will a civilization fail unless its saviors are paid like basketball stars (note Housman 1994:9–10)?

This example has many implications: It has potential practical effects on society. Its implications for stratification theory and perceptions of social importance are profound. Evidence above indicates that stratification may not be necessary for societal survival, while history suggests that it is probably not sufficient. As for metatheory, it asks what kind of construct is *functional importance*—an inferred entity, empirical construct, theoretical construct, or a false turn (Beck 1953; Bergmann 1953; MacCorquodale and Meehl 1953; Hempel 1965; Willer and Webster 1970)? Stinchcombe and Harris's work indicated that it is an inferred entity. Formalized Davis-Moore theory can be refuted by a few research findings. Still, the Davis-Moore debate illustrates that when a controversy gets enough attention, several people may take it seriously enough to create interesting and logically valid, testable theory.

Comments about How Type C and D Theories Reflect on Sociology

In sum, evidence favoring the truth of unformalized theories cannot be taken seriously. That does not imply that they are untrue. Some embarrass us; others are mines of valuable insights, perspectives, concepts, or hypotheses. They can inspire formal theorists and be sources of needed moral instruction (though those sources are much more valuable if their propositions are true, as interventions may work then). Of many sets of contrary ideas, some will be developed into valid formal theories. Of many contradictory ideas, half are true. Formal theorizing and careful research will help us determine which are worth keeping.

NOTE

1. "Proof through prediction"; see Merton 1967:152 n. 24.

Chapter 4

In Defense of Realistic Assumptions

Pidi Zhang

Social theorists differ as to whether a social theory's assumptions should be realistic. So far the debate has not proved productive because the exchange of ideas has been sporadic and intermittent. There has not been a deliberate dialog between the proponents and opponents of realistic assumptions. Theorists seem to be more occupied with the process of theory construction than with the *rules* involved. Moreover, they tend to believe what is important is, not whether an assumption is true or realistic, but rather whether it is useful. There has not been a collection of well defined terms on which social theorists can draw in their discourse of theory construction. It is generally *assumed* that a theory's assumptions should be realistic. At issue is what the term *realistic* means and why assumptions should or should not be realistic.

Sociologists sometimes criticize a social theory for its unrealistic assumptions, but the question of why assumptions should be realistic is often left unattended. Such criticism does not do justice to the theory. If we acknowledge that no assumption or assumption set can be perfectly realistic, an immediate next question is how unrealistic can an assumption be and still qualify as an assumption for a theory? Evidently, there is no consensus on the answer, and it is unlikely for sociologists or social scientists in general ever to come to agree on a set of guidelines. Acknowledging that assumptions do not have to be literal truths, this chapter discusses the preference for realistic assumptions and highlights some problems in unrealistic assumptions in constructing realist social theories. An inappropriate pursuit of unrealistic assumptions causes damage to the theory's structure. It is not the realism or generality of its assumptions that makes a theory elegant, but rather the appropriateness (in a sense that will be discussed later) of the connection between its assumptions and predictions.

ASSUMPTIONS

The term *assumption* has different meanings in different scientific contexts. This chapter recognizes three broad categories of assumptions. First, a researcher may *assume* that a certain entity or relationship exists and set out to verify its existence. How a researcher comes up with an "assumption" is irrelevant. It is the verification of the existence of the relationship or entity that is important. Making bold assumptions and testing them carefully is widely encouraged in scientific inquiries. A "bold" assumption is one that is not obvious and may even be counterintuitive. As such, bold assumptions may appear unrealistic. They may be more difficult to come up with, and thus seem more valuable. Although "assumptions" of this kind are efficient in expediting the discovery of new scientific knowledge, they do not constitute explanations of the relationships they portray. Instead, they contribute to knowledge development by begging explanations. Theories may be needed to explain such bold assumptions.

The second type of assumption consists of statements that help to constitute an explanatory theory. This kind of assumption, when used in theory construction, plays a role similar to that of the premise or antecedent in sentential logic. In a syllogism, the premises are necessary conditions for the conclusion. Similarly, the antecedent is a necessary condition for the consequent in an argument. The premises must be true and appropriately related to the conclusion. The same requirement is also applicable to the antecedent-consequent relationship. In theory construction, the requirement for the truthfulness of assumptions is by far less strict. Markovsky (1994:18) calls the antecedents in logical arguments "assumptions" because he "will *accept* [italics added] them as true." According to Cohen (1989:185), "assumptions are not literal truths, laws of nature, or immutable knowledge. They are assertions which, in form, can be true or false; which can be manipulated to generate other statements; and which do not depend on having the facts beforehand." Assumptions do not have to be literal truths, not because the truthfulness of them is not important at all, but because lack of truth in an assumption in some situations may not pose a problem for the theory constructed and because if only literal truths were accepted as assumptions, statements that could be used as such would be too scarce. As axioms and postulates are self-evident truths that may be used as assumptions in mathematical reasoning and theory construction, Cohen and Markovsky would agree that there should be some degree of truthfulness requirement for assumptions. However, it does not seem to them a worthy topic to evaluate the truthfulness of assumptions as long as there are good reasons for assuming them to be true. "Rather than argue about competing beliefs concerning the truth of an assumption, examining the use of the assumption and determining its usefulness is a more appropriate way to look at assumptions" (Cohen 1989:185). Although verification of the truthfulness of this type of assumptions is not usually productive, the verification is, nevertheless, generally possible and usually does not pose a great difficulty.

The third type of assumption is also called a presupposition. It is a special type of assumption that addresses the ontological question of "what is" and the epistemological question of "how to know what is." This type of assumption presupposes the nature of universe, actor, and the existence of certain relationships, and so on. Such presuppositions include what Kuhn (1970) calls "paradigms," the foundations of what Berger, Zelditch and others (1997) call "strategies," and even what students of sociology in general call perspectives, such as structural functionalism, conflict perspective, and interactionist perspective. Although a dominating paradigm in the natural sciences may last a long time and thus show substantial stability, in due course, old paradigms tend to be replaced by new ones over time. In the social sciences, the ontological and epistemological positions of the perspectives require that they look at different aspects of the social world for explanations of their subject matter. Although the ability to contain more empirical evidence serves as a criterion for the perceived importance, or even the life, of a perspective, evidence from one or a few studies does not falsify it. Therefore, one does not set out to test the perspectives. However, the influence of the perspectives does vary, alternate, and change, and it may even die out over time. The evaluation of the perspectives depends on the accumulation of unit theories and research findings as the results of a collective effort on the part of the social sciences community. The discussion of realistic and unrealistic assumptions in this chapter is mostly focused on the second type of assumption.

PROPONENTS OF UNREALISTIC ASSUMPTIONS

Due to the more or less self-evident presumption that assumptions should be realistic, critics of unrealistic assumptions do not feel an urgent need to justify their position. Supporters of realistic assumptions, therefore, do not have a well-developed apology for their standpoint. It is the proponents for unrealistic assumptions that have made efforts to construct metatheoretical justifications for their position. It is argued that a theory should never be judged by its assumptions. The test should focus on its predictions, because it is unlikely to be productive to examine a theory's assumptions (Jasso 1988). It is further argued that the more unrealistic the assumption the more productive the theory, because the more unrealistic an assumption, the smaller a slice of reality it describes or assumes and, in this sense, the more parsimonious the theory (Friedman 1953; Jasso 1988; Kanazawa 1998).

Friedman's Instrumentalism Misused in Realist Theory Construction

The most influential argument for unrealistic assumptions may be found in the works of Milton Friedman, who argues that the true test of a theory is whether its predictions are verifiable and not whether its assumptions have empirical correlates. "Truly important and significant hypotheses will be found to have 'assumptions' that are wildly inaccurate descriptive representations of reality, and, in general, the more significant the theory, the more unrealistic the assumptions" (1953:14). Friedman's argument reflects the instrumental nature of theories of economics, in which practical concerns take precedence over theoretical reasoning and accurate predictions are given priority over the inherent logical cohesiveness and truthfulness. For Friedman, the significant economic theories are those whose hypotheses are the result of unique insights obtained through abstractions from observations of events, and may not be immediately obvious to most economists. Similar to the first type of assumptions discussed here, the more unusual the insights, the more significant the hypotheses.

Friedman highlights the uniqueness of events, emphasizing the difficulty of specifying all the prerequisite conditions for the occurrence of an event. He would argue that each event has a unique set of conditions associated with it. Thus, it is impossible to specify general rules that apply to a broad array of events. The existence of unexpected outcomes tends to undermine the values of deductive rules. There may be nothing wrong with the rules—the problem is that one simply cannot determine all the "hidden" assumptions, so that in practice one cannot use the rules to make accurate predictions. In Friedman's view (1953), because of these unexpected outcomes and unspecified conditions, one cannot always be scientific in economics.

Friedman would not mind if a theory produced the right predictions for the wrong reason as long as the theory was useful producing them with reliability. His arguments do not support the construction of general explanatory economic theories. Friedman would argue that it would be even harder to build general explanatory social theories because, as he acknowledges (1953), unexpected events and unspecified conditions may be a greater problem for business and social life than for economics. Ironically, it is sociologists aiming to construct general social theories who use Friedman's arguments to justify their own work. These sociologists propose general theories that, they claim, are capable of explaining a broad array of sociological issues (see Jasso 1988; Kanazawa 1998). As Kanazawa has claimed, he, and probably Jasso as well, is following the realist philosophy, whereas Friedman belongs to the instrumentalist tradition. Unfortunately, the apology for unrealistic assumptions in the instrumentalist context is misused by Kanazawa and other bipartite theorists in their justification for unrealistic assumptions in the context of realist social theories.

The Logic of Bipartite Theories

A group of theorists who are trying to build what they call "bipartite theories" are defendants for unrealistic assumptions. According to Jasso (1988), the bipartite theory structure includes two parts: (a) postulates, which consist of abstract statements that are essentially untestable, and (b) empirically testable predictions "derived" from the postulates. Jasso avers that building "a theory begins with very general propositions about unobservables and ends with highly particular propositions about observables" (Jasso 1988:3). In presenting her distributive-justice force theory, Jasso cites a broad array of impressive sources in history (see Jasso 1988:11–12) that help to affirm the persistent usefulness of her axiom—an assertion of its historical realism. This effort seems to contradict her very argument against examining assumptions. The contradiction may be related to the bipartite theorists' confusion of abstraction and explanation.

Abstraction is the removal of any specificity from an idea. The abstraction of an idea may retain the structure of the idea and yet lack its content. A bipartite theory is an abstraction of a class of statements, or "predictions," as the bipartite theorists call them. The theory may either (a) *fit* these *statements* in structure, but not the *contents* of the statements, or (b) it may simply be a more abstract form of the statements. In the first situation, the theory may not be related to the statements in a substantive sense. In the second situation, the theory is not abstract to the degree that it loses all substantive meaning—the theory is only more abstract than the statements. However, although the theory and the statements may share some substantive interest, there is not any necessary or causal relationship between them. In the terms of category theory in mathematics, the relationship between the abstraction and illustrations may be expressed as a functor from category A to category B, as in Figure 4.1. (For more information about functor and categories, see Mac Lane's [1988] *Categories for the Working Mathematician*.)

The existence of a functor from the abstraction category, A, to the illustration category, B, implies that some (and maybe all) of the structure of category A is preserved in category B. If this functor is an equivalence of categories, then, as far as category theory is concerned, their structures are "essentially" identical. The substantive contents in categories A and B may not be related. In fact, A may be so abstract that it does not contain any substantive content but is nothing more than a structural relation in which an entity X (an object in the category A) is connected to another entity (object) Y in the same category by a one-way arrow from X to Y as specified by the axioms of a category. X and Y in A do not need to refer to anything specific. They may be anything that fits in the structural relationship of A. In category B, which is of a less abstract level than category A, Q may be a result or a function of P, P may be an explanation for Q, or Q may the result of a transformation of P. At a still less abstract level, P may be an independent condition that affects the benefit Q a person may receive.

Figure 4.1
Axioms and Illustrations Presented in Category Theory

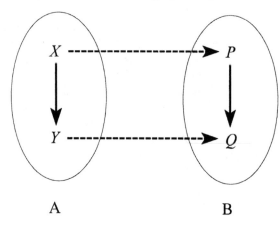

At a further less abstract level, P may be a person's educational attainment that affects his earnings Q. The functor between A and B preserves the composition of arrows: each arrow in the category A has a counterpart in the category B such that the composite of arrows in the category A corresponds to the composite of the corresponding arrows in the category B. Information may be lost in the correspondence between A and B: two arrows in A may correspond to one arrow in B, and vice versa. In our illustration in figure 4.1, A is the abstraction of B and, therefore, is more general than B.

There is a fundamental difference between the $X \rightarrow Y$ or $P \rightarrow Q$ relationship and the A–B relationship The confusion about the bipartite theories is in actuality a failure in distinguishing the two types of relationships. $X \rightarrow Y$ and $P \rightarrow Q$ may represent explanatory and predictive relations, whereas the relationship between A and B is their structural similarity. Most sociological theories address a $X \rightarrow Y$ or $P \rightarrow Q$ relationship, such as the relationship between family socioeconomic status and educational attainment. Family socioeconomic status is considered as an independent condition that in part predicts and explains educational attainment. The bipartite theory as proposed by Jasso does not address the explanatory and predictive relationship between X and Y or P and Q. In fact, it portrays the structural similarity of A and B, mistaking the more abstract A as the explanation of the less abstract B. The different parts of the theory are connected by different levels of abstraction, not explanation. For example,

$$Z = Z\,(A,\ C),\ \frac{\partial Z}{\partial A} > 0,\ \frac{\partial Z}{\partial C} < 0 \tag{1}$$

may be expressed in a less abstract form:

$$J = \ln (A/C) \tag{2.1}$$

or

$$J = \ln A - \ln C, \tag{2.2}$$

which is the comparison in a specific area—the justice evaluation function. To a still less abstract extent, the justice evaluation in social welfare may be expressed as

$$SW = \ln \frac{GM (A)}{GM (C)} \tag{3}$$

To an even less abstract extent, there are the "predictions" found in Jasso's 1988 article (for more details, see Jasso 1988). In the light of category theory, the axiom of comparison is not so abstract that it is devoid of any substantive content. Nevertheless, the different abstraction levels between the axiom, the theory, and "predictions" correspond to the abstraction levels implied in Figure 4.1.

WHY ASSUMPTIONS SHOULD BE REALISTIC

The closer an assumption is to the empirical world, the more confidence the theorist has about the derivations from the assumption. Assumptions are generally considered to be *axiomatic*, that is, self-evident statements about some part of the empirical world. In the history of science, if two different statements about the empirical world compete with one another as assumptions, if everything else is equal, the one that offers a less accurate description of reality must be abandoned or revised.

Philosopher of science Harold Brown (1977) discusses the slow, but steady, improvement of presuppositions, the third type of assumptions discussed previously, which provide systematic guidance for generating and testing theories about the empirical world. The Ptolemaic paradigm—the earth-centered universe presupposition—would not have been replaced by Nicolaus Copernicus's solar-centered paradigm if Copernicus had not questioned the Ptolemaic presupposition, and if Galileo Galilei and Johannes Kepler had not developed the physics that would empirically support Copernicus's theory (Kuhn 1957). The Newtonian explanation of universal gravitation would not have been rejected by Albert Einstein had he never questioned Sir Isaac Newton's presupposition. The succession of paradigms or presuppositions is determined by which paradigm or presupposition describes the empirical world more accurately (Brown 1977).

Whether an assumption should be allowed to be unrealistic depends on the nature and purpose of the inquiry. If predictions and calculations are needed rather than explanations, assumptions need not be realistic in any sense. Even in explanatory theories, if the purpose is to hold constant certain necessary relations or to hold off contingent interfering processes in concrete open systems, unrealistic assumptions may help to expose the theoretical claims more clearly. However, unrealistic assumptions may pose a serious problem when used for illuminating real objects. They may be interesting fictions which could never be made true in practice (Sayer 1994). Assumptions should never be made unrealistic intentionally because, all other things being equal, realistic assumptions offer a greater guarantee for valid hypotheses than unrealistic assumptions.

A deductive syllogism may illustrate the importance of truthfulness of assumptions as long as we agree that the first premise in a syllogism serves as an "assumption" as well as a "scope condition" and that the second premise and conclusion serve respectively as an "initial condition" and the "observation statement."[1] In a syllogism, not only must the premises be properly related to each other and to the conclusion, but both premises must be true as well if we are to derive a valid *and* true conclusion. It is often necessary to make use of assumptions that are only *probably* true. Take the following much-used syllogism, for instance:

Swans are white (first premise).

This bird is a swan (second premise).

This bird is white (conclusion).

This is a valid syllogism, but the first premise is not true because some swans, albeit very few, are black. Therefore, there is no guarantee that the conclusion is true. However, as overwhelmingly more swans are white, the conclusion that this swan is white has a greater probability of being true than the conclusion from a premise that says swans are black. Logically, the examples about white swans and back swans are equally problematic because the first premises in both cases are untrue. However, from a probabilistic approach, the white swan premise is more reliable, and the probability of truthfulness for the conclusion (prediction or observation statement) is therefore greater, due to the greater truthfulness of the premise (assumption). The greater the truthfulness of an assumption, the greater the probability of truthfulness for any conclusion derived from it.

SHOULD ASSUMPTIONS BE TESTED?

In general, theorists tend to agree that a theory is tested by subjecting its hypotheses to empirical evidence and that assumptions are not tested or falsified (Cohen 1989; Friedman 1953; Jasso 1988; Kanazawa 1998; Stinchcombe 1991). Certain conditions have to be assumed before one starts theorizing. In a valid deductive syllogism, only when the first premise or the general rule is true (and the second premise, a case covered by the rule, is also true and fits in the scope implied in the first premise) is it possible to guarantee a truthful conclusion. The first premise of the syllogism is true by *assumption*, not by evidence. The person using the syllogism must have enough reason to *assume* that the first premise is true. If the person needs to verify the truthfulness of the premise, it cannot be treated as such, and the person must rely on other antecedent information for the verification. The theorist is responsible for the truthfulness of the assumptions, at least to the degree required for the derivations to be valid and true.

Testing assumptions without discrimination is not only unproductive, it will also lead to an infinite regress, because logically, assumptions rest on other, antecedent assumptions. If assumptions were to be tested first, the theory itself could never be tested. Assumptions, by definition, are assumed to be true. However, in a different context, when necessary for whatever reason, the same assumptions may be treated as hypotheses, that is, not *assumed* to be true, and therefore should be tested. When an assumption serves as a starting point to derive hypotheses, it is not the focus of interest for the theorist, (the hypotheses are). However, when an assumption is tested in a different setting, it becomes the focus of interest in the new framework. Assumptions contain knowledge. All knowledge should be subject to empirical evidence, if possible. In fact, the business of science as a whole has the obligation to examine some assumptions, if not all, when necessary and decide whether they are consistent with the empirical world. If no assumptions had been questioned, Einsteinian, Newtonian, Copernican, and even Ptolemaic paradigms would never have emerged.

Testing assumptions, therefore, is not a transgression; it is a virtue of science under certain circumstances. This chapter does not encourage social scientists to engage in the largely unproductive work of testing all assumptions. Indeed, there is no point whatever in testing such assumptions as holding constant certain necessary relations. What is emphasized here is that statements used as assumptions do not have to be untestable, as the bipartite theorists tend to believe. Whether a statement is testable or should be tested depends, not on whether it is used as an assumption somewhere, but whether it is a primitive idea. Cohen (1989:183) avers that it is "desirable to keep the number of primitive terms in a theory to a minimum." The number of primitive ideas in a theory should also be kept to a minimum. To be sure, very few primitive statements have been used as assumptions in science compared with nonprimitive statements. Most assumptions that make knowledge claims in existing scientific theories are testable or tested already.

In the natural sciences, paradigms or presuppositions provide guidance for systematically generating and testing theories. According to Brown (1977), although a dominant paradigm may stifle ingenious ideas that challenge it, it guarantees the systematic development of scientific research and orderly accumulation of knowledge. Scientific revolution occurs only when an old paradigm or presupposition repeatedly contradicts new empirical evidence and new theories explaining that evidence. Due to the more perceptive nature of the paradigms in the social sciences, it may be more difficult for a new paradigm, presupposition, or research tradition to replace an old one than in the natural sciences. Paradigms and presuppositions in the social sciences tend to exist side by side rather than replacing one another (Kuhn 1970; Stinchcombe 1991). Nonetheless, social scientists bear the same burden of verifying the truthfulness of certain assumptions whenever necessary. Otherwise, there would be no fundamental development in the social sciences. The classical positivist assumption of an objective reality and objective knowledge, which were believed to be attainable through intersubjective testability, was challenged by the postmodernist "multiplicity, pluralism, variety, difference, contingency, ambiguity, interdeterminacy and ambivalence" assumptions; and the advent of "past-modern sociology" represents a sober confidence in the human observer's limited cognizance power—a major revision of the postmodernist (somewhat defeatist) epistemology (Stone 1996:61).

There have been many tests and improvements of assumptions in the practice of sociology. Three examples are discussed here as illustrations. Skvoretz and Zhang (1997) tested two of the assumed actor conditions of elementary theory (ET) in network exchange theories. The four actor conditions are assumptions about actor's responses to typical situations in exchange networks (Markovsky, Willer, and Patton 1988). ET theorists derive their theorems and hypotheses from these assumptions and from scope conditions they call position conditions. Skvoretz and Zhang tested actor conditions (2) and (3) by casting them into three hypotheses. An analysis of data from experiments supports the two actor conditions. The test increased the confidence in the theory by putting the two assumptions on a more solid ground, and the findings enhance the knowledge about two other studies in network exchange theories.[2]

An example of changing assumptions that dramatically improved the theory is the development of power-dependence theory (PD), also found in network exchange theories. Emerson (1972a:42) "provide[d] an explicit psychological underpinning as a basis for sociological theory construction." Emerson was developing "a theory of social exchange in which *social structure* [original italics] is taken as the dependent variable" (Emerson 1972b:58). Building on operant principles of psychology, Emerson assumes that repeated rewards of the same kind will cause a satiation in the actor, who will devalue the reward and become less dependent on it. Power develops from increasing satiation or decreasing dependence. Connecting the psychological principles to sociological model construction, he further assumes that the exchange relation has an effect on the development of social structures: Exchange relation is "the *smallest independently meaningful unit* [original italics] in terms of which larger structures will be developed" (Emerson 1972a:45).

The psychological assumptions of PD had to be abandoned when no empirical supporting evidence was found, and especially as evidence pointed to the effect of the social structure on social exchange. Social structure ceased to be a dependent variable when Cook and Emerson began to "manipulate network structures establishing power differentials" (Cook and Emerson 1978:725). The original assumption of social exchange shaping social structure is thus entirely abandoned by PD theorists. The major assumption for the improved PD is the structure's effect on behavior. The "rational actor," a concept probably originally developed by Max Weber and used as an assumption by George C. Homans (Cook and Emerson 1978; Homans 1961) remains an assumption for PD. The dramatic change of social structure from a dependent variable to an independent variable in the assumptions of PD has delivered PD out of a dead end and indicates a significant improvement for that theory.

Another example of changing assumptions for theory improvement is Kollock's (1993) modification of Axelrod's assumption in the study of cooperation. Kanazawa uses the same example in his apology for unrealistic assumptions, but this example should weaken his argument in every conceivable way rather than strengthening it. Axelrod's study is based on the results of two tournaments of the prisoner's dilemma game. (For a complete discussion of the prisoner's dilemma, see Axelrod's [1984] *The Evolution of Cooperation*.) Participants used computer programs designed to gain the most possible points from 200 rounds of the game. Each participating program was pitted against every one of the programs, including itself. Dozens of programs written by psychologists, economists, political scientists, mathematicians, and sociologists were entered in the two tournaments. The results showed that a strategy called Tit for Tat (TFT) was among the strategies that scored high. Although there were unfriendly strategies that beat TFT, these strategies did poorly against themselves and each other. TFT did well against itself and was the most efficient in promoting and maintaining cooperation. TFT is a strategy in which the actor initiates cooperation and then takes whatever move the other actor took in the previous round of the game in order to cooperate after the other actor cooperates and retaliate after the other actor defects. TFT is quick to forgive. In fact, the eight top-ranking entries are all "nice"—they are never the first to defect (Axelrod 1984).

Axelrod's rules for the prisoner's dilemma game imply the assumption that actors (programs in this case) understand each other's response in the previous round of the game and that an actor's behavior perfectly conveys that actor's intention. Axelrod's study assumes a "noise-free" environment. According to Kollock, this assumption is unrealistic because it leaves out the "noise"—all sources of uncertainty and distortion in the real world (Kollock 1993). TFT was the best strategy in part because of the noise-free assumption. After introducing noise into the environment, Kollock studied the benefits of strategies in which actors use different accounting systems to track ongoing exchanges. Kollock charted cooperation-promoting conditions in which actors can show degrees of cooperation even when mistakenly emitting a noncooperative move and in which actors' cooperative moves are misinterpreted. Results from computer simulations that permit degrees of cooperation provide evidence that under the assumption that takes noise into consideration, strategies employing a relaxed accounting system have many advantages. Under the relaxed assumption, TFT turned out to be a strict strategy that tended to result in actors punishing each other. A

Figure 4.2
The Three-Way Tug of War Between the Number of Assumptions, Appropriate Connections, and the Number of Predictions for an Assumption Set

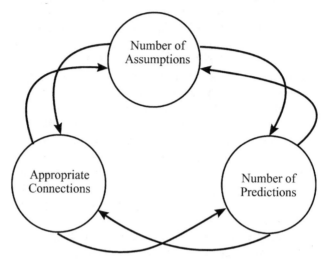

more lenient strategy was shown to be more effective in promoting and maintaining cooperation under the more realistic assumption, with noise taken into consideration (Kollock 1993). The three examples discussed here show that revising and improving assumptions in light of empirical evidence is a never-ending process present in science, a process in which scientific theories are improved and perfected.

ELEGANCE AND APPROPRIATE CONNECTIONS BETWEEN ASSUMPTIONS AND PREDICTIONS

Occam's razor, a rule that applies to both science and philosophy and has survived for several centuries, requires that the simplest of competing theories be preferred to the more complex and that explanations of unknown phenomena be sought first in terms of known quantities. Theorists are likely to emphasize simplicity and productivity and sometimes to ignore a most basic requirement, the proper connection of assumptions and predictions. In fact, theorists are faced with a three-way "tug-of-war" between the number of assumptions, the appropriate connection between the assumptions and the predictions, and the number of predictions (see Figure 4.2). The three-way tug-of-war reflects a challenge in building an elegant theory. Unfortunately, the three desirable characteristics of an assumption set do not help one another in adding to a theory's elegance. An attempt to improve any one characteristic tends to negatively affect at least one of the other two. Increasing the number of predictions tends to require more assumptions and thus cuts into fruitfulness. It would be a challenge to decrease the number of assumptions, on the other hand, without undermining the appropriate connections between the assumption set and predictions or decreasing the number of predictions.

Elegance in theory construction is a luxury that should not be pursued at the expense of validity and accuracy. The most conspicuous merit bipartite theories are claimed to have is the surprisingly small number of assumptions and large number of predictions. In fact, there is a tendency for bipartite theories to have one assumption only. Kanazawa argues that "there is a positive and monotonic relationship between the number of statements and the empirical complexities described," and that "one cannot describe *more* [original italics] of the empirical complexity with *fewer* [original italics] statements" (1998a:196). Many statements are mistaken as a more complete description of reality. He suggests increasing a theory's elegance by reducing the number of assumptions. In fact, the number of statements in an assumption set is not necessarily associated with the proportion of the described empirical world. A single, general statement may describe more than many statements of specificity. Although parsimony is a desired characteristic, what is more important is, not for an assumption or assumption set to describe as little or as much of the empirical world as possible, but to cover the appropriate aspects of the empirical world, such that the assumption set is sufficient and appropriate for formulating a theory and deriving hypotheses. Assuming too little does not allow for a proper construction of theory. On the other hand, unnecessary details may be a nuisance. Let us use an example of two assumption sets that Kanazawa used in his article (1998) as an illustration.

Assumption set A has only one assumption:

Given a set of alternative choices (A, B, . . . , N), actors will choose the one that will maximize their wealth in their subjective expectations. (Kanazawa 1998:196).

Assumption set B includes Assumption set A and eight other statements that address wealth, prestige, and so on. Kanazawa claims that "Assumption set B describes the state of the empirical world more accurately than Assumption set A" (1998:197). In fact Assumption set B is just as accurate as, but contains more details than, Assumption set A. Details have never been a requirement for assumptions. Even if a theory requires the assumed situations described in Assumption set B, the details would make it an awkward assumption set, because a simple but more general statement may serve the purpose better:

Assumption set C: Given a set of alternative choices (A, B, . . . , N), actors will choose the one that will maximize their gains in their subjective expectations.

This assumption contains the first few assumptions in Assumption set B and many other potential statements pertaining to the connotations and denotations of the term *gains*.

The detailed situations described by Assumption set B, or even those stated in the laconic form of Assumption set C, may not always be superior to the situation described by any one of the assumptions in Assumption set B, because different theories may require assumptions with different levels of generality. The appropriate connection discussed here does not indicate any superiority of more general assumptions to less general ones, or vice versa. This may be illustrated with the assumption of the "rational actor" for PD theory and ET theory. This assumption is superior to a list of statements that provide more specific behaviors that illustrate rationality. It is also superior to the "self-defense mechanism"—a more general statement about the behavior of biological beings, including plants, bacteria, and animals, as well as human beings. Therefore, the appropriateness of assumptions is not determined by the assumption set being complete, detailed, or incomplete. A theory may address a macro issue or a micro one, a general issue or a less general one. The appropriateness of assumptions is determined by their logical connections to the other parts of the theory. Realistic assumptions are generally true descriptions of the empirical world or descriptions that may be assumed to be true,[3] and that allow the theorist to derive theorems or hypotheses. A "parsimonious" and "fruitful" theory that purports explanation is not elegant if its assumptions are generally untrue, if the assumptions are so incomplete that they do not adequately allow for deductions of predictions, if the theory does not produce reliable predictions, or even if the theory produces reliable predictions for the wrong reason.

LACK OF DEDUCTIVE RELATIONSHIP IN BIPARTITE THEORIES

Deriving hypotheses from assumptions is a deductive process. The simplest deductive process is illustrated by a deductive syllogism. The conclusion is a natural derivation from the premises, and not vice versa. This is consistent with theorists' contention that assumptions are not derivable from any other part of the theory (Jasso 1988; Kanazawa 1998). However, theorists sometimes violate this rule. Friedman, Hechter and Kanazawa's (1994) theory of the value of children, which Kanazawa used as a commendable example for unrealistic assumptions, can serve as an instance of this kind of violation.

The uncertainty reduction assumption in Friedman et al. is:

Insofar as actors have it in their power to change an uncertain state to a certain (albeit risky) state, they will do so (Friedman et al. 1994:382);
or
Actors seek to reduce uncertainty (Kanazawa 1998:201).

One of the "predicted" hypotheses is:

The objective risk of divorce has a positive effect on the propensity to parenthood. (Friedman et al. 1994:384)

The rationale for this hypothesis is that divorce ushers in the unknown. Those who face the risk of divorce are more likely to seek parenthood in order to reduce uncertainty. However, uncertainty reduction is a purpose, not a specifiable precondition. It is not a premise from which conclusions can be drawn logically. The "assumption," therefore, is not the starting point of the inference that produces the hypothesis. The theory is not conditional in that it does not allow for any if-clause by asserting that all behavior has a purpose of certainty reduction behind it, even for behaviors that may actually increase uncertainty. The entire theory is assumed; nothing is deduced. For Friedman et al., the judgment of a behavior as having the purpose of reducing uncertainty does not depend on whether it literally reduces uncertainty—not even on whether the actor has the intention to reduce uncertainty—but on the interpretations or assumption of the bipartite theorist (Friedman et al. 1994:383). In addition to being unfalsifiable, the uncertainty reduction theory points to (a) a psychological explanation of behavior—a reductionist tendency of explaining sociological issues with untestable psychological reasons, and (b) a metaphysical explanation of behavior—a teleological explanation of phenomena by final causes—a characteristic that makes the theory nonscientific. The theory lacks a sociological or scientific dimension because it does not seek deductive explanations for social behavior or events from what is already known or verified, as required by Occam's razor, nor from the specifiable social, economic, historical, structural, or any other material context in which the behavior or event occurs.

DO EXCESSIVELY UNREALISTIC ASSUMPTIONS ASSUME ENOUGH?

There is one more reason why one should guard against pursuing elegance of theory only by assuming little and predicting more. One needs to ask whether one has assumed enough. Cohen, in a discussion of sociological theory construction, observes,

In order to operate with theories, our definition requires that what is the theory be clearly set off from what is a discussion of the theory. In other words, it must be possible to isolate theoretical statements from other text. This runs directly counter to much of current practice in sociology, where theoretical ideas are presented discursively. (1989: 182)

Indeed, it is far from uncommon practice for researchers to omit some assumptions or not to specify any assumptions at all in theory building and other research. But in so doing, they may imply their assumptions in the context. Sometimes other researchers may spell out the unspecified assumptions. That was what Kollock (1993) did when he specified the assumption of perfect information unambiguously implied in Axelrod's study. Theorists sometimes admittedly assume too little and, subsequently, have to rely heavily on other discourses and hidden assumptions in order to reach their hypotheses. Turner, in a comment on Jasso's "Principles of Theoretical Analysis," points out, "The 'derivations' Jasso provides rely very heavily on *added information* [original italics]" (Turner 1989:132). Kanazawa claims, as a merit, that the uncertainty reduction assumption "is one of the most unrealistic assumption sets in the social sciences precisely because it is so incomplete" (Kanazawa 1998:201). However, in "deriving" the hypotheses, Friedman et al. rely frequently on other, hidden assumptions, without which some of the hypotheses[4] would be untenable. The following hypothesis is quoted again for illustration:

The objective risk of divorce has a positive effect on the propensity to parenthood. (Friedman et al. 1994:384)

This hypothesis cannot be derived from the uncertainty reduction assumption without further assuming that divorce portends uncertainty and that parenthood contributes to uncertainty reduction. However, if these additional assumptions are present, the uncertainty reduction assumption will no longer be needed. The additional assumptions are more realistic than the uncertainty reduction assumption, in that they are empirically verifiable.

   Several other hypotheses show similar problems. One more hypothesis is examined for illustration:

Duration of marriage has a positive effect on the propensity to parenthood. (Friedman et al. 1994:386)

This hypothesis cannot be derived from the uncertainty reduction assumption without further assuming that the longer a couple is married, the less stable the marriage will be, and that parenthood contributes to uncertainty reduction. Again, when these assumptions are present, the uncertainty reduction assumption is not needed. Furthermore, the duration of a marriage may not indicate uncertainty. The hypothesis, therefore, is probably based on an implied false assumption.[5]

CONCLUSION

   This chapter argues that assumptions in social theories should be realistic to the extent that empirically testable hypotheses can be properly derived from them. In other words, there should be a logical relationship between a theory's assumptions and its predictions. A change or modification of a theory's assumptions should necessarily result in changes in the theory's predictions. Together with parsimony and fruitfulness, establishing the appropriate connection between the assumptions and predictions of a theory is crucial in evaluating the theory's elegance. Although parsimony and fruitfulness are important characters of elegant theories, it has been shown that a theory has a serious defect if its assumptions and predictions are poorly related and that a defective theory is not elegant. The structural parallelism and substantive separation between the more abstract postulates and less abstract "predictions" do not constitute an appropriate method of theory construction. All bipartite theories that fit the specifications made by Jasso (1988) and Kanazawa (1998) must appear "productive," because it is relatively easy to find illustrations for an abstract statement. If the "subsequent assumption" were not given in Friedman et al. (1994), how much more "productive" could the uncertainty reduction theory be? Nevertheless, the productivity is deceptive because there is no substantive relationship between the postulates and the "predictions." The number of so-called predictions made in this way is virtually infinite.

It has been shown that bipartite theories suffer from several defects. They are based on the misunderstanding of Friedman's defense of unrealistic assumptions for instrumental economic theories. Bipartite theories are abstractions from statements that take the form of hypotheses. The reasoning used in bipartite theory construction cannot be put in an antecedent-consequent format, because the "hypotheses" may have nothing to do with the abstraction or "axioms" except that they may share a similar logical structure. The abstractions are more general forms of their "predictions." It is shown that the "predictions" of bipartite theories are not real predictions, but illustrations of a more abstract idea that the bipartite theorists call a "postulate" or "assumption."

It has been demonstrated that examining the empirical validity of certain assumptions is not only justifiable, but also beneficial to theory construction and improvement. The practice was justified as early as the fourteenth century by the English philosopher William of Occam. The practice has been used successfully for a much longer period of time, as is shown by the succession of paradigms in the development of scientific knowledge. Assumptions of a theory should not be tested only in the framework of the theory itself, because they are already assumed true and because something has to be assumed to be true in the first place so as to derive testable hypotheses. However, the same assumptions may be tested in different settings, in which they are not assumed to be true.

This chapter argues that the number of details covered by an assumption or assumption set is unimportant. The appropriate connection between a theory's assumptions and its predictions should play the key role in theory construction. The appropriate connection is achieved through a logical structure similar to a deductive syllogism. This logical structure embodies the necessary relationship between assumptions and predictions. The assumptions of a theory are logically connected to its predictions via the same inference principle of a deductive syllogism.

This chapter does not criticize all kinds of unrealistic assumptions. Rather, it contends that the unrealistic assumption, as described by Jasso (1988) and Kanazawa (1998)—the more unrealistic the better—does not lead to the proper construction of realist theories, much less to elegant theories. The distinctions between the bipartite structure of their theories, as opposed to the conditional structure of scientific knowledge advocated by Popper and Cohen, deserve further investigation. But that should be the subject of a separate endeavor. That scrutiny should be expected to shed more light on the understanding of realistic and unrealistic assumptions, the characteristics of scientific and nonscientific theories, and subsequently contribute to the healthful development of social theories.

NOTES

1. It should be noted that the first premise of a syllogism is not exactly an assumption. It is more than an assumption. In essence, the first premise is a statement about a lawlike principle—similar to a *general principle*, a term used by Bernard P. Cohen (1989). In form, it is an assumption, the truthfulness of which is not verified in the syllogism itself. The first premise or assumption (in form) must be true in the first place in order to make meaningful inferences, because only true premises and valid formal inference can guarantee valid and true conclusions. Using a deductive syllogism is appropriate in this discussion to the extent that we realize that, in form, the first premise in a syllogism serves as an assumption as well as a scope condition and that the second premise and conclusion serve, respectively, as an initial condition and the observation statement—in Cohen's (1989) terms, again. Take the following syllogism as an example. First premise: All men are mortal. Second premise: Socrates is a man. Conclusion: Socrates is mortal. The first premise is, in essence, a law-like, general principle. In form, the first premise is the assumption (assuming all men are mortal) and the scope condition in form (applicable to all men). The second premise is an initial condition (a case covered by the scope condition), and the conclusion serves as the observation statement (an observable prediction by the general principle). Cohen (1989) used a similar syllogism as an example, but he did not spell out these correspondences, for which I assume responsibility.

2. The finding of extreme asymmetry response is consistent with the occurrence of bidding wars among peripherals in strong power networks in Willer (1987). The ways in which inexperienced actors act in weak power networks provide a more explicit basis for the Markovsky et al.'s (1993:205) hypothesis for the weak power networks that resource differentials will be greater for experienced subjects than for inexperienced subjects.

3. Cohen (1989) considers it too stringent a criterion for assumptions to represent universal statements not known to be false because many literally false statements are used as assumptions in geometry. Nevertheless, these statements are not unrealistic—they are true in very general terms. Cohen is consistent with the requirement of a syllogism for two premises in order to perform an inference when he observes that a theory must contain more than one assumption because it is impossible to derive consequences from a single statement (Cohen 1989:184). But this consistency would not make much sense if there were not a certain level of truth in the premises or assumptions, for the premises in a valid syllogism must be true in order to guarantee a valid and true conclusion.

4. Two hypotheses appear to be genuine hypotheses and consistent with the uncertainty reduction assumption: U-1.1: Exogamy and heterogamy have a positive effect on the propensity to parenthood. S-1: The multistranded quality of the relationship between

husbands and wives has a negative effect on the propensity to parenthood. Nonetheless, these hypotheses cannot be derived from the uncertainty reduction assumption. With some stretch, they can be considered statements obtained by reversing the abstraction of the uncertainty reduction assumption. In Turner's (1989) words, they are illustrations or confirming instances of an idea.

5. One would have to assume that the longer a couple is married the less stable the marriage will be in order to use the uncertainty reduction assumption and arrive at this hypothesis, because otherwise the hypothesis would state that duration of marriage has a *negative* effect on the propensity to parenthood. Therefore, although the Friedman et al. hypothesis seems plausible, it is plausible for the wrong reason. Friedman et al. use extensive verbal connections between the uncertainty reduction assumption and the hypotheses, from which some of the implied assumptions can be found. The verbal connections seem to be the authors's interpretations of certain social relationships. There are places where interpretations contradicting those of Friedman et al. may seem more plausible and would therefore lead to contrary hypotheses. An example of this is the observation in Friedman et al. that teenagers having children is an instance of uncertainty reduction behavior (Friedman et al. 1994:383).

Chapter 5

Positivism and Theory Construction in Group Processes

Kinga Wysienska and Jacek Szmatka[1]

The aim of this chapter is to show that theory construction in group processes can be pursued beyond the mainstream philosophy of science and that sociological theory can explain fundamental social processes, free from naturalistic or postmodern biases. Our goal is a thorough analysis of mutual relationships between the methodology of group processes theories and positivism. We demonstrate that accusations of positivist bias do not always hold true for these theories.

The problem is not unique to the social sciences. Controversial work in any discipline that is not exactly mainstream or is somehow new is very often accused of being nominalist, instrumentalist, positivist, and so forth. The difference between the social sciences and the hard sciences is that in the latter researchers do not devote much time to discuss these issues (Hawking 1993). In the former, however, to defend the applied methodology is a matter of "to be or not to be" in the field.

In social sciences the most pejorative and unclear term used to diminish someone's research is *positivism*. Evolutions within this current, antipositivist turns, positivist defenses (Turner 1985; Freese 1980b), and "decent burials" of positivism (Cohen 1997) show that this orientation is controversial. Discussions of positivism have ended with overwhelming aversion toward that current. Even in physics to call somebody a positivist has a negative connotation (Hawking 1993) and it usually means the negation of status of the discipline or a scientist's studies. The problem is that nobody is even able to state whether positivism refers to a philosophical, metatheoretical, or methodological position or what assumptions this position adopts. As Bernard Cohen proves, being positivist, antipositivist, and postpositivist simultaneously is possible and quite simple: "If Positivism means a commitment to using evidence, then this author is a Positivist; if it means that non-observable entities are inadmissible, then the present writer is an Anti-Positivist. If Post-Positivism represents a concern with the theoretical relevance of observables, then this analyst is a Post-Positivist; and so on" (Cohen 1989:44). Following this line of thought, Jonathan Turner asserts:

The result is that the term *positivism* [original italics] no longer has a clear referent, but it is evident that, for many, being a positivist is not a good thing. It is unlikely, then, that positivism will ever be an unambiguous and neutral term for sociological activity revolving around the formulation and testing of theory and the use of plausible theories for social engineering. (Turner 1992a:1511)

The basic methodological assumption about enforcing the same requirements and standards for building and testing theories in all sciences, which is held by group processes researchers, provokes associations with the most conspicuous positivist idea of the unity of science. For some critics it is enough to end the studies at this point and classify the group processes approach as positivist. In this chapter we examine different stages of positivism as a metatheoretical and methodological position. Next, we try to analyze whether there are any connections between theory construction in group processes and positivism. If there are any, should we be ashamed of this? First, however, we are going to present the idea of three theoretical genera. To do that, we try to debunk the persistent myths of what sociology should be as a science.

MYTHS AND THEIR CRITICISM

Sociology is full of mythical preconceptions about itself. These preconceptions create the greater disunity we find in sociology than in other sciences. Sociological research is carried out in various ways, at times so different from one another that the question arises of whether we are still dealing with one discipline. Sociology admits, as scientific products, narrative descriptions of social processes bordering on literature, as well as theory-driven laboratory experiments, analyses of taped telephone conversations, and reports on statistical distributions of responses to a set of questions given to a group of individuals. We do not intend to argue which variety of sociology is the best. We do, however, believe that some ways in which sociology is carried out and some assumptions about the form and content of sociological theory are based on persistent myths. We identify these myths and then analyze them critically.

Myth I: The Social World Has a Fundamentally Different Nature than the Physical World and, Because of Interpretiveness Sociological Investigations, Must Conform to Different Methodological Rules

This myth constitutes the metatheoretical validation of many broad theoretical orientations, such as the interactionist tradition, along with its offshoots (dramaturgic theory, ethnomethodology, etc.), humanistic sociology, and the theory of structuration. The assumption that the social world is fundamentally different from the physical world is, however, often seen as a metatheoretical foundation of all sociology, and not only of its particular theoretical orientations. Myth I rests on the thesis that the social world, in distinction from the natural world, is a product of human activity. As a consequence, the social world is more variable, fluid, and indeterminate than the natural world. This is so in virtue of the fact that, ultimately, almost every social process occurs at the intersection of two areas of social reality: the domain of structures and the domain of human activity. Even if we assume that, in the realm of social order, at least minimal stability exists, the same cannot be assumed a priori about the activities of individual people. The capacity for conscious, purposeful activity vested in the individual means that the amount of information that the sociologist must take into consideration in attempting to interpret or explain a given process is too great, and therefore impossible to enclose within the realms of a scientific model. The physicist is able to identify most important elements of a process under investigation and to build from them a closed model of this process that can subsequently be tested empirically. However, the sociologist can at best achieve an open model, that is, one in which not only not all minor factors are controlled and perhaps not but even all major factors are included, due to the inherent indeterminate character of the social world.

We regard this position as philosophical skepticism. Its adherents not only doubt the possibility of sociology as a science but attempt to justify its incapacity to be a science.

Interpretive sociology's assumptions about the nature of the social world are unrefutable, but also unprovable. We do not know, nor will we ever know (at least in the sense of having scientific, empirically tested knowledge about this issue) if the social world is fundamentally different from the natural world or if human subjectivity and agency radically limit the possibility of the scientific prediction of structurally constrained activities of people. We do not know, either, whether the symbolic character of interaction actually causes such immense fluidity and instability of the social world that scientific method (procedures considered in the physical sciences as the norm) cannot be applied to social processes. There can be no scientific evidence to support the claim that there is greater complexity in the social world than in the natural world. A proof of this thesis would show that sociologists know the properties of the world they research to the extent that they are capable of demonstrating its greater complexity. Scientific method, by its very nature, assumes the building of simple models for complex processes. The level of complexity of a given universe need not exclude the possibility of scientific investigation of the objects of this universe. The subject of life sciences also differs from the subject of physical sciences, but biology still applies the scientific method.

These assumptions could be validated only by showing that testable theories, which are based on this ontological image of the world, exist. The ontology assumed by interpretive sociology implies, however, that such theories cannot exist in principle because the possibility of applying scientific method to the social world is rejected. Furthermore, interpretive sociology has internal contradictions at the level of its assumptions. That is, in questioning the existence of permanent properties of the social universe, it assumes the existence of other invariants, such as the symbolic character of interaction.

In summary, we are not claiming that there are no problems whose solutions require the use of methods characteristic of interpretive sociology. We do argue, however, that it is possible to employ the scientific method to explain dynamic processes, social orders that emerge from social interactions, and actors' agency.

Myth II: Empirical Sociology Can Only Explore Concrete Social Phenomena Embedded in a Historical Context

The essence of this myth lies in the conviction that all empirical research in sociology, including that which has theoretical ambitions, must necessarily mean the exploration of some fragment of sociohistorical reality. Sociologists study phenomena that are located in space and time and always embedded in a concrete historical context. They are partially known to the researcher from experience (for example, the society in which he or she lives). Investigations only fill blank spots in our picture of the social world with increasing amounts of data. Explorative sociology is enthusiastic about any new information, especially if the data is methodically collected with the use of a large random sample. It is even better if the data reveal some regularity (i.e., some variables strongly correlate with each other) and, in addition, can be used to solve concrete social problems.

It goes without question that sociology is both an empirical and theoretical science and, therefore, its theories must be tested on the information coming from the world. Where the error lies and where this myth comes into play is in the fact that the data collection needed to test a theoretical hypothesis is too often falsely identified with the recording of events that occur in society (on their own or induced) in conditions that the researcher has neither control nor capacity to interpret with the aid of his or her theory. Besides, to generalize observable statements into general laws requires the method of induction. Hypotheses are believed to be true because of the data from which they have been induced. The reasoning, which assumes the validity of the general statement from the accuracy of specific observations, is false. The truth of the premises does not ensure the truth of the conclusion. We claim that data are meaningful only within a model and must be produced by the researcher in controlled conditions with the use of procedures that are an integral part of the theoretical system.

We do not intend to be extreme. Obviously, sociology describes the properties of concrete historical societies and carries out various diagnostic research (see Berger, Zelditch, and Anderson 1972a). But one should not deny or distort the fundamental difference between experimental testing of an abstract, general theory and the accumulation of information about some population, even if this information is processed with the help of the most advanced methods of data analysis. Such accumulation of information about concrete societies belongs to historical disciplines rather than to scientific endeavor.

Myth III: Grand Theory, for All Its Deficiencies, Gives Us a Proper Understanding of What a General Theory in Sociology Should Be

In the myth of the usefulness of general, all-embracing sociological theories, the affirmation of the theoretical goes together with an understanding of theory that is rather far from that of the exact sciences. This myth, which is rooted in the beginnings of sociology, has already ensured intellectual self-confidence for more than one generation of sociologists. Simultaneously, according to Turner, " 'theorists' in sociology rarely theorize, and as a result, we know embarrassingly little about the social universe. . . . and when theorists do make theoretical statements, they tend to develop empirical accounts of historical causes or they engage in flights of philosophical fancy into the realm of universal functions" (Turner 1985:24). Such an approach to sociological theory, which is generally regarded as the most prestigious and fruitful, usually goes hand-in-hand with the cult of the classics, which not only presents its own general theories but also imposes a certain style of scientific discourse about sociology. Consequently, sociology cannot effectively abandon the practices of philosophizing on the theme of social processes—and often in a pretentious manner—and building extremely general conceptions to "explain" social reality as a whole. Those in favor of this style of theorizing are usually convinced that "sociological theory, or at least a substantial portion of it, can be subsumed under a single overarching perspective" (Ritzer 1991:53). Moreover, they often "have a tendency to argue that they are offering the 'right' transcendent perspective and all other approaches, including those that argue that there can be no such overarching orientation, are wrong" (Ritzer 1991:53).

The third myth founders on the problem that an "overarching theory" is, in principle, devoid of verification procedures. Since it is untestable, it cannot be classified as a theory but should instead be considered a particular kind of social philosophy or orienting strategy. Such overarching theories have a heuristic utility only. For instance, some classical terms, despite their unclear connotation and undefined denotation, and some classical propositions, despite the imprecise area of their potential fulfillment and untestability, are useful sources of inspiration in the search for theoretical models and for adequate conceptualizations of social phenomena. But as theories, these grand conceptualizations fall short.

Sociology's ambition to produce scientific theories is only partially successful, as it tries to build general abstract theories but is rarely able to test them empirically. Second, sociology's ambition to be an empirical science is also only partially successful, as data are gathered but seldom interpreted in the context of a theory. In this context, the second and third myths reinforce each other and produce a strange division of labor among sociologists: it is considered normal that those who deal with sociological theory are those to whom empirical research is foreign, and vice versa. Such a state of affairs has strengthened and solidified in sociology, independent of geographical location.

THREE GENERA OF THEORY IN SOCIOLOGY

The myths described here have weighed heavily on the development of sociology. Freeing the sociological enterprise from them will allow its alteration (as a basic science endeavor) into a truly scientific discipline. The process of making the discipline more scientific will occur. We analyze this process into three phases of development corresponding to three families or genera of theory in sociology: the grand theory genus, the social theory genus, and the sociological theory genus. Not the chronological, but the methodological, criterion is decisive here (see Figure 5.1). Looking at three genera of theory gives an illustration how "antipositivist" myths influenced the development of the theory in sociology. The first and third myths described here led to theories of the first genus. Second-genus theories are the result of the second myth. However, although theories of the first and second genera are extremely important for understanding social processes, only theories of the third genus follow the widely accepted requirements of the scientific method. As these standards are shared with the exact sciences, their use in sociology has come under criticism. This is because in sociology, the postulate of the unity of a method, as with the positivist approach, was not accepted. Nevertheless, the existence of theories of the third genus shows that meeting criteria of the scientific method is not only possible in sociology, but fruitful as well.

Before we go further, let us define the theory in the way we understand it, following the standards of the scientific method. An empirical theory is defined by indicating its conceptual apparatus (the language of the theory), a set of accepted propositions (laws, principles), demonstration procedures (methods of proving certain propositions based on others), measurement procedures (methods of generating data), and the range of the theory, which refers to the class of systems whose behavior is explained by the theory (Wojcicki 1974:20).

The grand theory genus emerged with the classic systems of nineteenth century sociology. Theories in this genus have close links with social philosophy, so close that it is impossible to draw a line of demarcation between them. They are general conceptions about the social world that often contain elaborate conceptual schemes and sets of propositions. Usually these conceptions are presented in narrative form, in natural language without the articulation of a clear border between the theory's terms and common language expressions. Most of the notions in these theories have a vague meaning, and what they actually denote is not always clear. The internal structure of sets of propositions is also

Figure 5.1
Three Genera of Theory in Sociology

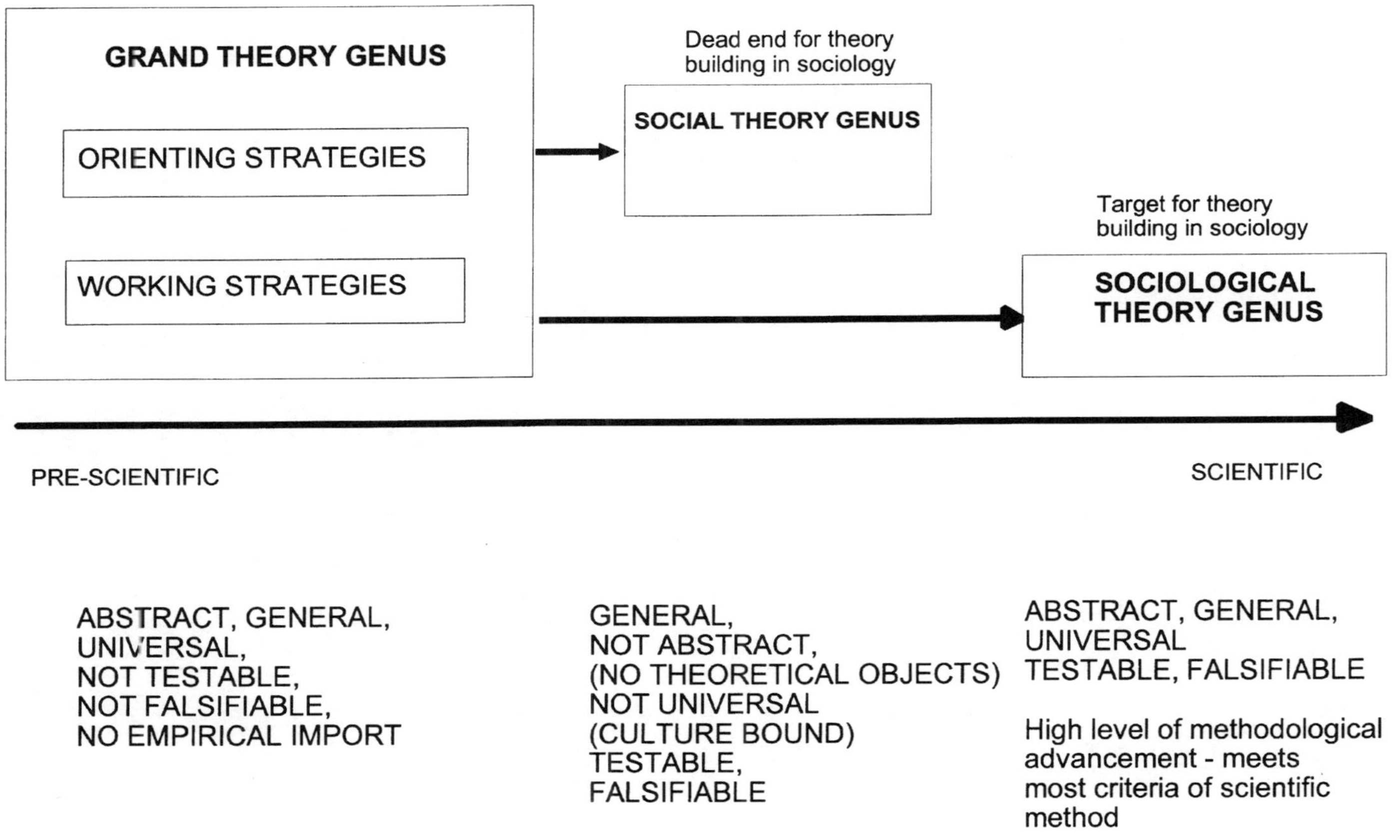

GRAND THEORY GENUS

ORIENTING STRATEGIES

WORKING STRATEGIES

Dead end for theory
building in sociology

SOCIAL THEORY GENUS

Target for theory
building in sociology

SOCIOLOGICAL
THEORY GENUS

SCIENTIFIC

PRE-SCIENTIFIC

ABSTRACT, GENERAL,
UNIVERSAL,
NOT TESTABLE,
NOT FALSIFIABLE,
NO EMPIRICAL IMPORT

GENERAL,
NOT ABSTRACT,
(NO THEORETICAL OBJECTS)
NOT UNIVERSAL
(CULTURE BOUND)
TESTABLE,
FALSIFIABLE

ABSTRACT, GENERAL,
UNIVERSAL
TESTABLE, FALSIFIABLE

High level of methodological
advancement - meets
most criteria of scientific
method

indeterminate. It is not known which are postulates, which are consequences, and which are accepted on empirical grounds. The theory's scope is also left unspecified. No stipulation is made about the domains to which the theory applies or in which its scope conditions can be potentially satisfied. Consequently, these theories are neither verifiable nor refutable and, therefore, either they do not satisfy the most fundamental scientific requirements or they are easy to disprove because their indeterminate scope and assumption of generality imply that cases can always be found that the theory is unable to explain.

Most classical sociology falls into this category, including contemporary conceptions of theorists such as Talcott Parsons, Niklas Luhmann, Lewis Coser, Jürgen Habermas, Herbert Blumer, Erving Goffmann, and Jeffrey C. Alexander. Even Merton's (1968) famous middle-range theories have a place here. Yielding to the charm of all-embracing theories, Merton held that these theories were sought simply to provide a stronger basis for attempts to build a grand theory, the final product of sociological theorizing. Grand theories can serve as orienting strategy, that is, a set of metatheoretical assumptions. They are best treated as a point of departure, not the final product.

Theories in the second category, that of social theory genus, differ from those in the first genus by two features. First, they have more or less precisely defined scope, given by the formulation of scope conditions that define the kinds of systems to which the given theory applies. Second, these theories are equipped with verification procedures (methods of generating relevant data). Having the given properties, they can thereby be tested. Furthermore, their terminology is much more precise than that of the first-genus theories.

Sociology has many theories of this genus. Presently, they seem to dominate numerically and somehow to determine the identity of the discipline. These theories differ from one another in terms of the scale, level (micro or macro), and nature of the phenomena researched. They have emerged in macrosociology, examples of which are institutional theory of stratification (Walder 1992), theories of meritocratic justice, theories of social structure in a comparative perspective (Kohn and Slomczynski 1990), and theories of social mobility (Wesolowski and Mach 1986), and in microsociology, for example, the organizational theory of collusion (Baker and Faulkner 1993), groupthink syndrome theory (Janis 1982), the contingency theory of leadership (Fiedler 1967), and the theory of differential social control (Heimer and Matsueda 1994).

These theories, despite their methodological advancement, do not, however, satisfy all conditions required of theories in nomothetic science. Theories of this genus define their object domains and problem areas by reference to concrete historical societies and their constitutive elements: individuals, social collectivities, and institutions. Usually, the aim of the researcher is to explain, with the help of a hypothetical causal structure of determinants, the intercorrelations in a set of variables. In theories of the second genus, it is the statistical criterion that usually determines which of those variables are identified as significant. Any factor such as gender, for instance, will be considered as a cause if a statistical test of its effect on the dependent variable gives a positive result, even if one cannot show how the given variable produced the difference. This situation is not exclusive to the social sciences. Often medical researchers find that some medication has a significant effect on a condition but cannot specify the mechanism by which it works. The statistical hypothesis about the effectiveness of the medication, even if confirmed with the help of a significance test showing a very small probability of type I error, is not considered a theoretical finding unless a model accounting for the action of the medication is proposed. If the factor working on the patient is difficult to identify and cannot be manipulated (as, for example, energy transmitted through healers), such purely statistical regularity is not even qualified as a scientific result. In social sciences such a position seems to be too rigorous, however.

Theories of the third, sociological theory genus have in common with theories of the grand theory genus the abstract character of their basic conceptual apparatus, and with theories of the second, social theory genus, the possession of verification procedures. The combination of both properties, which is often considered difficult to reconcile, is possible due to a qualitatively new conception of theory testing. It is new, of course, only to sociology, as it has long been used in the natural theoretical sciences. In this conception, theory does not refer directly to empirical reality, but to a theoretical universe containing idealized simple and complex objects.

The conception of the theoretical model is undoubtedly related to the method of ideal types, but there are differences. In speaking of the ideal type as a tool of interpreting social phenomena, Weber emphasized that this mental construct cannot be found empirically anywhere in reality (Weber 1949:90). Third genus theories are not so skeptical about the possibility of empirical interpretation of their abstract categories and the possibility of verifying their propositions. The role of the experiment is to create the initial conditions in which the laws will be given a chance to demonstrate how they work. If the laws of the theory are confirmed, they could then be used to study historical cases and to explain the functioning of real systems, similar to those created in the laboratory.

The examples of the third-genus theories involve the group processes tradition and other traditions as well. We have in mind, among other things, elementary theory (Willer 1992; Skvoretz and Lovaglia 1995; Lovaglia et al. 1995; Szmatka and Mazur 1998), expectation states theory (Berger, Fisek, Norman, and Zelditch 1977; Webster and Foschi 1988; Ridgeway 1997), distributive justice theory (Jasso 1978, 1980, 1997), rational choice theories (Hechter 1987; Coleman 1990), and the formal theory of macrostructure (Blau 1994). Each of these theories has its own problem area, specific terminology, hypotheses, and research procedures. The method of exact sciences links them together, but their naturalism ends there. The fundamental unit of analysis remains the actor in a situation. Yet the methods applied seem still controversial, and positivism is the most frequent connotation. Thus, more detailed elaboration of the meaning of positivism is needed.

THE MEANING OF POSITIVISM AND ITS VARIETIES

To provide a definition for the concept of *positivism* may not be a simple task. First, there are several different meanings of *positivism*, understood as methodology or as metatheory. Second, *positivism* has always meant somewhat different things to philosophers and to sociologists. Third, especially for social scientists, positivism is often associated with, and understood as, the philosophical doctrine developed by August Comte and his followers. In this section we will focus on positivism understood mainly as methodological conception, as only this aspect of a positivist standpoint is directly related to a theory construction process in sociology.

In its broadest sense, positivism refers to the theory of knowledge that asserts that the pursuit of causal explanation must be done by way of inductive generalization and that the only kind of sound knowledge available is that of science grounded on observation (Kolakowski 1972; Wacquant 1994). Thus,

in this point positivism is identical with traditional empiricism: positive (as opposed to theological and metaphysical) knowledge is empirical knowledge, which is the only sound (or scientific) knowledge because observation (or more generally experience) is the only sound source of knowledge. (Halfpenny 1982:115).

The core of the positivist doctrine in the social sciences constitutes three related principles:

- the ontological tenet of *phenomenalism* (knowledge can be founded on experience alone);
- the methodological tenet of the *unity of the scientific method* (procedures of natural science are directly applicable to the social world with the goal of establishing invariant laws or lawlike generalizations about social phenomena);
- the axiological tenet of *neutrality* (which denies normative statements the status of knowledge and maintains a rigid separation between facts and values) (Wacquant 1994: 495; Giedymin 1975:276).

We claim that as the core of the positivist doctrine, these three canons are present in all variants of positivism in the social sciences, although often in different forms. For example, for Jeffery C. Alexander, positivism in sociology is mainly a form of the principle of phenomenalism. He maintains that the central postulates of the positivist persuasion are (1) that a radical break exists between empirical observations and nonempirical statements, (2) that because of this break, more general intellectual issues—which he calls "philosophical" or "metaphysical"—have no significance for the practice of an empirically oriented discipline, (3) that the elimination of the nonempirical reference is a distinguishing feature of the natural sciences, and (4) in science, in which empirical observation is thoroughly unproblematic, questions of a theoretical or general nature can be correctly dealt with only in relation to such empirical observation (Alexander 1982:5–9).

Contrary to that, for A. Giddens, positivism in sociology is a form of the methodological tenet of the unity of science and the axiological tenet of neutrality, *but not* a form of phenomenalism. He claims that there are three suppositions specific for positivism in sociology. The first principle requires that the methodological procedures of natural science may be directly adapted to sociology. The second principle stipulates that the outcome of sociological investigations can, and must, be formulated in terms parallel to those of natural science (the goal of sociological analysis can, and must, be to formulate "laws" or "law-like" generalizations of the same kind as those established in relation to natural reality). The third principle asserts that sociology provides knowledge that is purely "instrumental" in form, that is, the findings of sociological research do not carry any logically given implications for practical policy or for the pursuit of values. Sociology, like natural science, is "neutral" in respect to values (Giddens 1974:4).

An Early Stage of Positivism

The characteristic point of view of the early stage of positivism can be seen in works of August Comte, particularly in those that address the issues of science, scientific inference, and scientific laws—namely those that refer to the tenet of phenomenalism. Although the ideas of the father of positivism are often labeled as "naive positivism" and have been a subject of criticism in many publications, the presentation of his conception seems relevant. Comte's ideas have influenced the way we in sociology perceive the relation theory—data and the problem of the unity of method. The thesis about the direct relationship between scientific laws and processes occurring in the phenomenal world is treated as valid even among postpositivists. Comte's ideas about the hierarchy of sciences (with the crowning position of sociology) have caused philosophers of science (positivists, too) to either attempt to create separate method for sociology or to limit their considerations to the exact sciences, especially to physics (for example, Karl Popper, Imre Lakatos).

August Comte's outlook is often presented in the following three claims:

- that facts were the bedrock of science;
- that they were based on pure observation; and
- that the connections between them—without benefit of abstract entities such as accrued in metaphysics—constitute scientific laws.

These both for three tenets are often presented as the core of positivist thinking and the expression of the essence of the positivist doctrine, particularly its early stage, and all refer to the principle of phenomenalism. Although Comte's exemplar for his advocacy for positivist sociology, with its goal to pursue an accurate discovery of laws, was Newton's law of gravitation, he seems unable to understand the role of abstraction in theorizing (Comte 1830). An early form of positivism is concerned not only with pronouncing the claims of experience as the ultimate foundation of human knowledge, but also with denying the possibility of knowledge of supersensible objects, whose very definition precludes their being given in sensory experience. As Hindess rightly asserts, for this form of positivism,

> there can be no essences lying beyond the realm of phenomena and no "ideal" objects corresponding to universal terms as square, circle, triangle, and so on; there are particular triangles but there is no essence of triangle of which each particular triangle is a phenomenal realization (Hindess 1977:14).

As can be seen, this principle of phenomenalism is not much different from that of positivism in contemporary sociology as described by Alexander.

Logical Positivism

Logical positivism represented important advance over early positivism because it recognized the importance of abstract theoretical objects in scientific method. Philosophers of the Vienna Circle, such as M. Schlick, E. Mach, R. Carnap, C. Hempel, and O. Neurath (see Neurath, Hahn, and Carnap 1973; Feigl 1969; Wartofsky 1982; Kolakowski 1972; Giedymin 1975) also have done much in the way of technical refinement of the Comte position. However, they were, for the most part, hardly less empiricist or inductivist than Comte was.

In this version of positivism, the principle of phenomenalism takes the form of the Verification Principle. The early formulation of this principle was based upon the thesis of Hume and Mach that the meaning of scientific concept can in principle always be reduced to empirical observations. As a result, the logical positivist view remained fundamentally ambiguous: while accepting the existence of "nonobservable entities" it also maintains that all theoretical statements can be verified by purely empirical procedures. The Verification Principle states that "scientific knowledge rests on the bedrock of facts formulated by way of 'protocol statements' (Mach) that provide an unadulterated immediate recording of sensory experience or elaborated via 'corresponding rules' (Carnap), forming a bridge between theoretical language and the language of observation" (Wacquant 1994:496).

The Verification Principle is closely linked to the Falsification Principle (Popper 1963), the idea that it takes only a single disconfirming instance to falsify a universal statement, and thus that instead of seeking confirmation or verification of a theory, the scientist attempts to refute it. The Falsification Principle holds that theories can be refuted, and therefore should be abandoned, in the light of "observations" thus conceived. The principle of phenomenalism was later substantially revised by logical positivism. In earlier versions, phenomenalism required "the reduction of science to statements about directly observable facts and the elimination as meaningless of any sentence that is neither analytic nor empirical" (Giedymin 1975:276). In later versions, it takes a form of a *moderate instrumentalism*, according to which theoretical sentences that are empirical, but not equivalent to observational statements, are allowed in scientific inquiry.

The principle of the *unity of the scientific method* has been altered by logical positivism as well. In logical positivism the principle of the unity of method takes a form of an assertion that scientific explanation in sociology or history follows the same "covering law" or "deductive-nomological" model as the natural sciences (Hempel 1965), in which an explanandum is deduced from a combination of initial conditions and universal law, and explanation is synonymous with prediction (Wacquant 1994). This model of explanation still rests on a conception of scientific laws as empirical generalizations, that is, statements about observable regularities that express a constant conjunction. Thus, scientific laws were still viewed as empirical statements for which the meaning was "verifiable" in some sense.

Postpositivism

Postpositivism is the latest and most sophisticated version of positivism in science, and in sociology as well, thinkers such as W.V.O. Quine (Quine 1960, 1963), Karl Popper (Popper 1957, 1959), Thomas Kuhn (Kuhn 1970), Paul Feyerabend (Feyerabend 1961), Imre Lakatos (Lakatos 1970), and Stephen Toulmin (Toulmin 1953) undermined the foundations of positivism (see also Giddens 1978; Alexander 1982; Turner 1992b). The internal ambiguity of logical positivism prompted critiques to such an extent that there emerged a consensus (even among those who often disagreed with one another) about the necessity for fundamentally reinterpreting the positivist perception of science.

First, even those involved in the Vienna group recognized that observation statements cannot be entirely "theory free." Popper, among others, has always denied the existence of an observation language in the strictly positivistic sense. Many authors have disputed the possibility of maintaining a rigorous distinction between theoretical and observational languages. As a result, postpositivism rejects the idea of correspondence rules: scientific theory does not involve two languages, language of observation and language of theoretical terms; rather, it involves two overlapping and intersecting uses of the same language.

According to the postpositivist perspective, all scientific development is a two-tiered process, propelled as much by theoretical, as by empirical, argument. This statement radically alters the old positivist principle of phenomenalism. Three principles of the postpositivist perspective represent alternatives to the old general positivist postulate of phenomenalism. These principles demonstrate that there is no such thing as theory-neutral observation (first principle) and that scientific theories neither are built inductively (second principle) nor tested individually (third principle). Next, we analyze all three principles more thoroughly.

1. All scientific data are theoretically informed (Lakatos 1970; Alexander 1982:30). This principle can be interpreted in the way offered, for example, by Keith Dixon, who says: "All data, whether in the natural or social sciences . . . must necessarily be viewed through the lenses of theory or accumulated together with a series of background assumptions which render the data less than neutral. . . . The possibility of treating data as hard almost always depends upon the prior existence of a *well-founded and established theoretical framework* [italics in original]" (Dixon 1973:10). Just as scientific theories are not tested inductively, there is no "observation" that is prior to "theory" in the form of protocol statements. All observations are "theory impregnated" and are interpretations of facts.

2. Empirical commitments are not based solely on experimental evidence (Lakatos 1970; Alexander 1982:30). The meaning of this principle can be traced to Imre Lakatos's assertion that determining whether an experiment is actually "crucial" for the refutation of the given empirical commitment is a matter that can be decided by scientific hindsight (Lakatos 1970:176–177; Alexander 1982: 31).

Major argument related to this principle can be reduced to the assertion that experimental or empirical evidence is insignificant in the genesis of the theory and that if the evidence remains in contradiction with the theory, it does not lead directly to theory rejection. Hence, as Popper asserts, science does not proceed through induction at all. However many tests we may make confirming a theoretical proposition, there is always a possibility that the next test will disconfirm it; hence, the validity of scientific laws and abstract propositions in science can never be conclusively verified.

Postpositivists such as Thomas S. Kuhn and Lakatos are concerned with the process by which scientific knowledge is being acquired. According to Kuhn: "We do not believe that there are rules for inducting correct theories from fact, or even that theories, correct or incorrect, are inducted at all. Instead, we view them as imaginative posits, invented in one piece for application to nature" (1970:12).

3. Fundamental shifts of scientific belief occur only when empirical changes are matched by the availability of alternative theoretical commitments (Alexander 1982:30). Lakatos offered "sophisticated methodological falsification," according to which: "Falsification in the sense of the naive falsification (corroborated counter-evidence) is not sufficient condition for eliminating a specific theory: in spite of hundreds of known anomalies we do not regard it as falsified (eliminated) until we have a better one" (Lakatos 1968:121). As Lakatos defines it, falsification is effective only when a better theory supersedes the existing one: "falsification is not simply a relation between a theory and the empirical basis, but a multiple relation between competing theories, the original

'empirical basis,' and the empirical growth resulting from the competition" (Lakatos and Musgrave 1970:120).

One should note that Kuhn, Lakatos, Paul K. Feyerabend, and other postpositivists (despite the differences between their conceptions) analyze and develop ideas of the structure and growth of all science, but not sociology in particular. They focus more on the mechanisms of growth and progress of science and less on the process and methods of theory construction, which is the main subject of our analysis.

CRITERIA FOR THIRD GENUS THEORIES IN SOCIOLOGY

The theory is a major result of any type of scientific activity and research. Its meaning and the criteria set for its construction stand for the level of development of the discipline. In this section we analyze seven criteria for third-genus theories in sociology. We do so to show that the conception of theory testing and theory development that is widely used in group processes is out of accordance with early positivism, logical positivism, and, sometimes, postpositivism as well. The analyses of the relationships between positivism and theory construction in group processes are not straightforward. All forms of positivism are more focused on the problem of demarcation in science than theory construction itself. The major postulate that we would like to prove in this chapter states that there is *no direct link* between positivism (whatever the version) in sociology and theory construction in group processes. We claim, then, that any accusations that the third genus theories are the straight result of positivist thinking and positivist bias are irrelevant (which does not mean that there are no similarities at all).

Abstractness

Each theory of the third generation is abstract, and so are each of its propositions. This feature has important consequences for the process of data collection and theory testing. It eliminates completely from the process of theory construction and theory testing the postulate of phenomenalism specific for all versions of positivism, including the postpositivist conception.

[Abstractness] is the quality of not being bound to specific objects, times, and places. Theories must be applicable to real events and phenomena, but they must not be wedded to a closed set of specific cases. They should be capable of transcending particular cases so that they remain applicable whenever and wherever the appropriate conditions arise. (Markovsky 1997:19)

From this it follows that the notion of abstraction "requires that knowledge claims be considered apart from application to any particular object" (Cohen 1989:76). Therefore, statements, and whole theories as well, do not refer to any aspect of the "real world." Rather, they refer to ideal objects, such as a "perfect gas," "rigid body," or "null connected exchange structure."

Abstractness as the major feature of the theories of the third genus makes the process of theory verification more complex than that implied by any version of the positivist tenet of phenomenalism, especially in the early stages of positivism. Logical positivism accepted the existence of nonobservable entities but also maintained that all theoretical statements can be verified by purely empirical procedures. Logical positivists' Verification Principle stated that scientific knowledge rests on the bedrock of facts formulated by way of "protocol statements," and that the only meaningful statements are those that can be tested by observation. None of these ideas can be accepted within the framework of the third-genus theories. Abstract statements cannot be verified by purely empirical procedures.

A major difference between postpositivist claim and our conception of abstractness and its role refers to the process of theory construction. In theories of the third genus, the theoretician begins with an abstract idea, develops this idea into an abstract model and a set of abstract laws, and finally tests it in the laboratory, setting up an abstract, experimental situation (Cohen 1989). Here, the theorist never leaves the abstract world of the theory. When testing theories of the third genus, our observations are not "theory impregnated"—they are "theory driven," as we do operate on abstract, theoretical objects. Contrary to that, Lakatos, for example, asserts that models forming a research program "emulate reality" (Lakatos 1970:136).

Generality

Another important characteristic of the theory is its generality. Generality refers to "the scope or domain of the theory . . . and indirectly to its scope conditions as well. The broader the scope (or domain) of a given theory, the higher its generality" (Szmatka 1997:91). As can be seen, generality is related to the method of induction. According to early positivism and logical positivism, the more observable statements we use to arrive to a conclusion, the more general will be the statement. In that way it relates (indirectly) to the first and second tenets of the postpositivist conception that scientific theories are not tested inductively, that there is no observation that is prior to theory in the form of protocol statements, and that no abstract and general proposition can ever be finally verified.

Universality

Universality means that the truth of the theory is independent of time, space, or historical circumstance. As opposed to abstraction and generality, universality surpasses "the world of theory" and refers to the relation of the theory to the "real world." The more universal the theory, the larger will be the number of different, real, time and space determined systems in which the theory has been empirically confirmed (Cohen 1989; Szmatka 1997). Because the theory cannot be universal if it is not abstract, our criticism of positivist claims in the relation to theory abstractness holds true, in this case, as well. For example, although Popper seems to have a definition of universality similar to ours, he asserts, simultaneously, that universal laws explain the regularity of events or facts (Popper 1972). However, theoretical laws state nothing about regularity of the empirical world (Willer 1987).

Testability

One of the most important claims about theories of the third genus is that empirical studies cannot falsify a theory. "In appraising the merits of theories, it is more important to ask whether they constitute adequate solutions to significant problems than it is to ask whether they are 'true,' 'corroborated,' [or] 'well-confirmed' " (Laudan 1977:14). Falsification may work as a criterion for demarcation, but it does not work as a method for *theory choice* (Cohen 1997; Wagner 2000). However, *theoretical statements* must be at least potentially testable. The following statement, "both formal and informal structure may emerge in a social organization," is unfalsifiable because it holds true if we observe both structures, just one of them, or none. Theoretical statements have to allow us to choose accurate empirical indicators. Testability also means that the theory itself must be equipped with the procedures of potential verification, scope, and initial conditions. Theories of the third genus reveal here characteristics that are radically inconsistent with any positivist postulate.

The Role of Theoretical Models

The process of theory verification and theory falsification involves several complex procedures and cannot be reduced to a simple empirical test. This goal can be achieved through the construction and use of theoretical models. As Skvoretz stresses:

Theories must be coordinated with data in scientific inquiry. Models are the devices by which such coordination is achieved. Through models, a theory's claims can be evaluated against relevant data. Models perform a bridging function between a discipline's theories and its data base of findings and observations. (Skvoretz 1998:238)

This is the process that goes far beyond any positivist postulate of theory verification, including postpositivist claims in this matter. Theoretical and methodological models describe the relations between the theory and data, and only the application of both models meets the conditions for third-genus theory testing.

In the logical positivist tradition, explanation is the deduction of statements about events or particular occurrences from more general statements. Let us remember that in logical positivism, the principle of the unity of science takes a form of an assertion that scientific explanation in sociology or history follows the same "covering law" or "deductive-nomological" model as in the natural sciences, in which an explanandum is deduced from a combination of initial conditions and universal law. Contrary to that, third-generation theory requires a model of a generative mechanism by which the regularities to be explained are produced.

As John Skvoretz points out, the real trick in scientific problem solving is the creation of models with interesting properties. Without the underpinnings of a theoretical model, the explanation of regularities by subsumption under more general statements appears to be merely a variablecentric analysis. Theory becomes a matter of informal guesswork about which variables affect which others and in what directions (Skvoretz 1998).

Conditionality

Scope conditions specify circumstances under which the relationship expressed in a hypothesis is expected to hold true. They are strictly related to such characteristics as abstractness, generality, and universality, and they do not make sense within a theory that does not meet these three criteria.

Because a scope condition constitutes the antecedent clause of a conditional statement, it follows that if this clause is not met, then nothing is being said about that relationship. In other words, by limiting the claim that is being made, scope conditions specify what can and what cannot be considered evidence relevant to the hypothesis. (Foschi 1997: 540)

Our criticism of positivist postulates related to abstractness, generality, and universality refers to scope conditions as well.

It is important to remember that

the significance of the idea of scope conditions is simply that *wherever scope conditions are met, a knowledge claim is applicable.* Nothing in either the scope statement or the knowledge claim guarantees that any particular situation will meet scope conditions, and this is the fundamental import of the requirement that knowledge claims be conditional. (Cohen 1989:83)

Cumulative Theory Growth

The conception of cumulative theory growth has been developed by Berger, Zelditch, and Wagner (Berger and Zelditch 1993a, 1993b, 1997; Wagner 1984) and then extended by Szmatka and Lovaglia (Szmatka and Lovaglia 1996). Berger and his colleagues developed their view of science from the philosophical programs of Toulmin (1953), Popper (1959), and Lakatos (1970), so one can claim that this conception is in a very close neighborhood to the postpositivist view. We will show that this claim is wrong.

Berger's model of theory growth comprises three levels of theoretical activity. The most abstract level is that of the *orienting strategy*, from which emanate *working strategies* that produce individual, *unit theories*. Orienting strategies are metatheoretical in nature. They contain the guiding assumptions that prompt scientific inquiry. They answer fundamental ontological questions and epistemological questions. They are often called *theory* in a shorthand way, and may in fact be what many sociologists consider theory. However, they are more abstract than the Popperian (Popper 1959) idea of a theory, and they do not qualify as theories in Popper's sense because they cannot be falsified. Metatheory, unlike theory, requires no test.

More concrete, but still metatheoretical, working strategies answer more specific kinds of questions: (1) *methodological working strategies* tell us how to construct a theory and how to formulate and assess an explanation, and (2) *substantive working strategies* tell us what kinds of concepts to use, what principles to formulate, and what theoretical questions to ask.

Unit theories describe specific empirical process. They are theories of the third generation; that is, they are abstract, general and universal. Unit theories do change, but attention to growth at this level focuses largely on theory-data relations. The other kinds of growth arise from theory-theory relations. Unit theories describe specific empirical processes. They relate concepts and principles that are abstract, general, and universal.

Theoretical research programs operate across working strategies and unit theories to produce theoretical growth. The *theoretical research program* is the level at which theory growth can be strategically manipulated. Such programs are made up of interrelated theories (or one theory that grows and changes) "together with a body of theoretical research testing, refining, and extending these theories and a body of applied research grounded in them" (Berger and Zelditch 1993b:1). Research programs encompass two levels in the model. It is the reciprocal interplay between working strategies, theories, and research testing of those theories that fosters theory growth and knowledge cumulation within a research program. Berger and Zelditch's (1993a, 1993b) theory growth model allows *intraprogrammatic* theory growth.

We claim that the *multidimensional model of growth* of Berger and others differs from both the *unidimensional, cumulative model of growth of positivism* (Hempel 1965; Nagel 1961; Popper 1959), and *models of discontinuous change by postpositivism* (Kuhn 1957, 1970). Furthermore, Berger's model has a different structure from Lakatos' postpositivist model of theory growth.

CONCLUSIONS

We can claim now that, methodologically, theories of the third genus form a third way that is directly compatible neither with positivism nor with postpositivism. Below we list the reasons.

1. Even if some individual positivist ideas (mostly postpositivist) have been incorporated by group processes tradition, neither positivism nor postpositivism as a whole were adapted for theory construction in the group processes tradition. Individual ideas, if incorporated, were always a subject of several, sometimes deep, modifications. For example, the idea of theoretical research programs, although taken from Lakatos, has been substantially revised and reworked.

2. Positivists, whether early positivists or postpositivists, never understood the role of abstraction in theory construction. According to early positivism, the theoretical world is to be inferred from a real, external world. To logical positivism, theoretical claims are to be tested in a real, phenomenal world (see the issue of protocol statements), and according to postpositivism, especially that of Lakatos and Toulmin, the theoretical world should be a mirror reflection of the external, phenomenal world. Under all versions of positivism, the process of empirical theory testing should always be conducted external to the theory world, that is, in external, phenomenal reality.

3. To most positivists, the relation between an empirical world and the theory is reversed and visualized as the relation from the empirical world to the theory, whereas in the third genus, this relation is from the theory to the empirical world (Skvoretz 1998).

4. The Similarity of several individual methodological ideas is understandable when one considers knowledge cumulatively. We claim that there is no foundation to accuse third-genus theories of positivism simply because one finds a resemblance between individual positivist ideas and individual methodological ideas about theory construction. When cumulative theory growth is at issue, there is no need to "reinvent the wheel." Quite the contrary, one should use existing, attainable knowledge.

Using individual positivist ideas and conceptions is not wrong if positivism (scientism) is considered as a method, or a set of ideas, serving to demarcate between science and metaphysics (Wolenski 1986) and regarding explanation and prediction as the main goal of science. As Freese claims: "Positivist methods serve a theoretical science whose aim is prediction. But quantitative methods in sociology, which are often taken to be positivist and sometimes aim at prediction, have produced a correlational science that is largely atheoretical" (Freese 1980b:4). If reaching the goal of explanation and prediction is possible only by the construction of simplifying theoretical models (Hawking 1993; Lakatos 1970), then positivism is not an unsuccessful child of the nineteenth-century sociology, but an underestimated and wasted idea of many scientific generations. Therefore, mythical preconceptions should not hamper the attempts to develop formal, testable, internally coherent theories in sociology.

NOTE

1. The first author acknowledges support from Fulbright Junior Research Grant, Polish National Committee for Scientific Research (KBN) Research Grant No. (1 H02E 008 19), and a Foundation for Polish Science (FNP) grant. The second author acknowledges support from a Kosciuszko Foundation Research Grant and research grant No. (1 H02E 001 14) from the Polish Committee for Scientific Research (KBN).

Chapter 6

Expectations, Need-States, and Emotional Arousal in Encounters

Jonathan H. Turner and David E. Boyns

In virtually all encounters involving face-to-face interaction, individuals come with expectations about what should occur, how others should act, how self should be treated, how needs are to be met, and how virtually all aspects of the interaction are to unfold. In this chapter, building on the large literature on expectation states (e.g., Berger 1958; Berger and Zelditch 1998; Berger, Rosenholtz, and Zelditch 1980; Berger, Fisek, Norman, and Zelditch 1977; Webster and Foschi 1988), we focus on the connection between the need states of individuals and expectations. Those need states that are always present during interaction are termed *transactional needs* (Turner 1987, 1988, 1994, 2000, 2002). A transactional need is a "desire" or "want" that drives the behaviors of individuals in all episodes of face-to-face interaction. When this need is met by a person's own actions and by the responses of others, people feel satisfied and experience positive emotions; conversely, when this need is not realized, individuals feel dissatisfied and experience negative emotions.

There is nothing new in this view of needs; the idea is implicit in many early theories of interaction, such as Mead (1934), Freud (1953 [1900]), Schutz (1967 [1932]), Cooley (1902), Durkheim (1954 [1912]) Marx (1964 [1932].), and Pareto (1935). Closer to the present, most theories of interaction posit some view of need-states. People are variously seen to have needs to confirm self and identity (e.g., Burke 1991, McCall and Simmons 1978; Stryker 1980), to experience balance, congruity, and consistency in cognitions and sentiments (Newcomb 1953; Heider 1946; Heise 1979), to realize profits in exchange relations (Homans 1961; Coleman 1990), to make roles (Turner 1962), to achieve a sense of a common reality (Garfinkel 1967), to present a face and line (Goffman 1967), to experience pride and avoid shame (Scheff 1988), to achieve prestige and power (Blau 1964), to experience trust and ontological security (Giddens 1984), or to augment cultural capital and emotional energy (Collins 1988, 1990). What we propose to do, therefore, is make more explicit this force of human interaction, while synthesizing various approaches with the key insight from expectation states theorizing.

TRANSACTIONAL NEEDS

In Table 6.1, we list the five basic transactional needs that drive interaction and establish expectations for how the self and others should behave. The most important need, we believe, is the need to confirm the self, which we conceptualize as a series of emotionally valenced images of oneself operating at three levels (Turner 2002): (1) core self feelings, (2) subidentities pertaining to general classes of situations, and (3) role identities tied to a particular encounter. These three levels of self set expectations for how a person should be treated and, as we will see, just which level of self is salient has powerful effects on the flow of interaction. Another important need is to receive profitable exchange payoffs, as measured against costs, investments, and standards of justice or fairness. This need follows from the "principle of reciprocity," which, we believe, is hard-wired in human neurology (Cosmides 1989; Fiske 1991). A third need is for group inclusion, in which individuals seek to feel a part of the ongoing flow of interaction. A fourth need is for trust, in which individuals need to sense that the actions of others are predictable, that the interaction reveals rhythmic synchronization, that others are sincere in their actions, and that others are respectful to the self. And the fifth transactional need is for facticity, as individuals desire to sense that the self and others are indeed experiencing the world in the same way, that the situation is as it appears, and that the reality of the situation has an obdurate character.

Each of these need-states generates expectations, and as a general law, individuals experience positive emotions—that is, variants of satisfaction-happiness such as liking and pride—when these five need-states are realized; and as a result, the interaction is more likely to proceed smoothly and, thereby, to avoid breaches and strains. Conversely, when one or more of these needs is not met, individuals will experience variants and combinations of negative emotions— anger, fear, sadness, shame, and guilt. As these negative emotions are aroused, strains in the flow of the interaction develop and potentially breach the encounter. And when individuals consistently fail to realize their transactional needs, they will seek to change or leave the encounter; but if they cannot do so, the negative emotions will increase in intensity. As we will see, however, these straightforward relations are mediated by additional forces. One is the nature of the expectations generated by these needs; another is the activation of defensive strategies and defense mechanisms, in particular attribution processes.

Table 6.1
Transactional Needs

1. *Verification of Self*	Humans have emotionally valenced and generally implicit cognitions of themselves as certain kinds of persons deserving of particular responses from others. These emotionally valenced cognitions exist at three levels: (a) trans-situational core self-feelings about who one is, (b) sub-identities about who one is in general classes or types of situations, and (c) role identities about who one is in a particular encounter. People seek to have all levels of self confirmed by the responses of others, although the salience of any one level can vary.
2. *Profitable Exchange Payoffs*	Humans assess all situations for the available resources and symbols, extrinsic and intrinsic, that can allow them to experience gratification or utility. These assessments implicitly calculate (a) the rewards potentially available, (b) less the costs (expenditures of energy and alternatives forgone) and (c) investments (accumulated costs and commitments) that are measured against (d) a standard of justice or fairness. People seek to gain some profit—rewards less costs and investments measured against a standard of justice—in all situations.
3. *Group Inclusion*	Humans examine all situations for signs from others of their inclusion in the ongoing flow of interaction. People seek to feel that they are part of the interpersonal flow.
4. *Trust*	Humans assess all situations for signs that the responses of others are (a) predictable, that others are in (b) rhythmic synchronization, that others are (c) sincere, and that others are (d) respectful of self. People seek confirming responses from others along all of these dimensions.
5. *Facticity*	Humans assess all situations for signs indicating that (a) self and others are experiencing a common world, that (b) the situation is as it appears, and that (c) reality has, for the purposes of this encounter, an obdurate character.

NEED TO VERIFY SELF

As noted, our view is that self operates at three levels (Turner 2002). First is a *core self*, composed of images and emotions about the nature and worth of a person in all situations. This aspect of self is thus transsituational; and when salient, the emotional stakes of an interaction are dramatically raised. Our notion of self follows Cooley's (1902) insight by suggesting that the core self is composed of the most fundamental feelings about a person; and these generate expectations for a person's own behavior and for how others should respond to this behavior. A second level of self is what we will term *subidentities*, which represent applications of elements of core self to particular institutional spheres, such as family, work, politics, religion, community, education, and other major domains of social life. This level of self involves individuals' conceptions and feelings about how they should behave and be treated in a domain of activity. A third level of self is *role identities*, which are applications of elements of core self and subidentities to role making efforts in a particular encounter.

While individuals seek to sustain consistency among these three levels of self, a certain amount of slippage is inevitable and, indeed, functional for the person. When every role identity is a marker of core self, for example, problems in role making become a crisis of a person's most powerful feelings about him- or herself; and as a result, the individual is always emotionally charged, making it difficult for others to interact with this person. As Peter Burke (1991) emphasizes, a "tightly structured" self almost assures that a person will fail to confirm all aspects of core self, whereas when core feelings are of less salience, the failure to make a role successfully does not cause an emotional crisis for the individual.

Let us draw out in more detail these relations between expectations and self. When any level of self is confirmed by a person's own perceptions or by the responses of others, the individual will experience at least satisfaction (low-level happiness); and the more core self feelings are salient, the greater will be the sense of happiness. If a person had some fear that he or she could not confirm any or all levels of self in a situation, this person will experience pride when successful; and the more salient is core self, the greater will be this sense of pride. An interesting twist occurs when expectations are exceeded. When people's expectations are exceeded and they perceive their success to be the result of their own actions, they will experience more intense forms of happiness; and, if they had some fears about achieving any success, they will experience even greater levels of pride. When, however, individuals see their success in exceeding expectations as the result of the actions of others, their level of self esteem intervenes. Persons with a high level of self-esteem who exceed expectations for self-confirmation will still experience high levels of happiness towards self and express positive emotions for those who are seen as responsible for their good fortune, whereas people with low self esteem will experience incongruity that must be resolved by maintaining a low evaluation of themselves through an even higher evaluation of others who are perceived to have allowed them to exceed expectations.

Turning to the negative side of emotions, individuals will experience negative emotions when any level of self is not confirmed; and the more salient is the core self, the more powerful will be the negative emotions experienced. But which combinations of negative emotions will people experience? Attribution processes intervene, especially for expectations that have not been realized. If a person blames him- or herself for the failure to confirm expectations for self, this person will experience anger towards self; and if this failure continues across iterated encounters, the individual will also exhibit fear and sadness, especially for low self esteem individuals. Increasingly, these negative emotions will combine to produce shame (Turner 1999, 2000), and if individuals begin to evaluate their failures by reference to moral codes, they will experience guilt as well. In contrast, when individuals blame others for the failure to meet expectations for self, they will experience—and, if they can, express—anger toward these others. There will be, however, a tendency for external attributions to shift toward self blame across iterated encounters as individuals must continuously confront the failure to confirm self. Moreover, anger expressed toward others will invite negative sanctioning from these others, thereby decreasing the possibility that self can be confirmed. If only a role identity is being disconfirmed, a new role identity can be attempted, perhaps increasing the likelihood of self confirmation at this level. But the more salient are core self feelings and the less the individual can leave the encounter or iterated encounters, the more likely that the blame will shift from others to self, or, if the individual persists in expressing anger toward others, this individual will increasingly be marginalized, thereby violating other transactional needs, such as those for group inclusion, trust, and positive exchange payoffs. As blame shifts towards self, a person will increasingly experience sadness about failure, fear about the consequences of this failure, and anger toward self; when these are experienced simultaneously, the combination of these negative emotions will arouse shame and, if expectations from moral standards are invoked in self evaluation, guilt as well.

Attribution processes are a kind of defense mechanism, because when others are blamed for the failure to confirm self, this external attribution becomes a way of protecting one person from negative self-evaluation. Other defense mechanisms can also be employed. A person can project anger at self onto others, but this defense mechanism is likely to invite negative sanctioning from others, thus decreasing the likelihood that self will ever be confirmed. Displacement can also be used, but this only makes others aggressive in return, unless those who are the targets of displaced anger cannot fight back. Repression is also possible, but repressed anger, fear, and sadness, especially when these are combined to generate shame and guilt, incur a heavy toll on individuals' emotional energy as they try to control these negative emotions. The likely outcome is that these individuals will reveal low levels of emotional energy, as well as sadness, punctuated by high-intensity spikes of negative emotional energy, which, in turn, require even more active and costly repression. Thus, the use of defense mechanisms is almost always counterproductive in sustaining self in an encounter because it invites negative responses from others or imposes energy-draining costs on individuals.

Short of these more pathological uses of defense mechanisms are what we term *defensive strategies*, in which individuals can avoid some of the inconsistency between their expectations for self and the nonconfirming responses of others. These strategies work best for role identities or even subidentities that have failed to be confirmed, but they become less viable as core self feelings become salient. One strategy is the selective perception of responses from others so that self is confirmed; a related strategy is the selective interpretation of these responses. Another strategy is to draw on what McCall and Simmons (1978) term *short-term credit*, in which memories of positive confirmations of self in the past are invoked to ride out an episode of disconfirmation of self. Another strategy is to shift role identities. Still another is to disavow a particular presentation of self as not representing one's true self; and relatedly, one can display role distance to an identity that is not being confirmed. And finally, a person can simply disavow the audience who has failed to confirm an identity. These kinds of defensive strategies can work in the short run or in onetime encounters, but their habitual use in iterated encounters will invite negative sanctions from others. Moreover, these strategies are less viable when core self-feelings are salient in role making.

When self is disconfirmed, then, encounters become less viable because negative emotions are aroused. Moreover, these emotions become convoluted because of attribution processes, defense mechanisms, and defensive strategies. The end result is that, over iterated encounters, the flow of negative emotions makes the encounter strained, if not breached; and, equally important, other transactional needs are not likely to be met. Thus, in our view self is a master need, which determines whether other transactional needs are likely to be realized.

NEED FOR POSITIVE EXCHANGE PAYOFFS

All exchange theories emphasize that actors are "rational" to this extent: they seek to receive rewards in excess of costs (rewards forgone and energy expended) and investments (accumulated costs previously incurred). Whether humans actually seek to maximize their payoffs is a debatable, but not an essential, assumption to the basic argument that people attempt to achieve profitable exchange payoffs in interactions with others. Most of the time, the rewards in interaction are symbolic and frequently intrinsic. In particular, individuals pay close attention to the symbols and resources allowing them to confirm other transactional needs for self-confirmation, group inclusion, trust, and facticity. Indeed, the things that are defined as valuable in an interaction are often the symbols marking self-confirmation, trust, inclusion, and facticity. Individuals initially scan an encounter for all the available resources, in the following sequence: (1) an assessment of relevant resources and a general expectation for which resources can potentially be claimed and in what quantity; (2) a search for symbols confirming self; and (3) a scan for the symbols marking group inclusion, trust, and facticity. At each stage, expectations are revised. In the end, a kind of meta-expectation emerges, based upon perceptions of costs and investments compared to those of others, measured against a standard of justice; possibilities for self confirmation at the level of roles, subidentities, or core self feelings, and judgments on the costs and investments incurred in achieving a sense of group inclusion, trust, and facticity.

As this meta-expectation emerges, it guides the behaviors of individuals. Because these expectations almost always contain standards of fairness, exchange payoffs typically become a moral issue, thereby raising the stakes when payoffs do not meet expectations. When costs and investments are high, expectations for payoffs increase and become a moral issue, and doubly so when core self feelings are salient in calculations of payoffs. And so, the higher are the expectations, the more emotions will be aroused and the more likely are these emotions to be embellished in terms of morals, ethics, and other evaluative symbols.

Individuals will experience variants and combinations of satisfaction and happiness when expectations for payoffs are realized or exceeded, while experiencing negative emotions when they go unrealized. As with all emotional reactions, especially when invoking moral standards, attribution processes are critical to the flow of interaction. When individuals see the realization of expected payoffs as coming from their own actions, they will experience positive emotions toward self, and they will experience pride if they had some doubts or fears that their payoffs would meet expectations. When individuals meet or exceed expectations and attribute this success to the actions of others, they will experience positive sentiments towards these others and remain committed to interaction with them now and in future encounters.

It is the negative side of exchange payoffs that is the more interesting, because when expectations are not realized, there are three negative emotions that can be aroused singularly, or in combination. Again, attribution processes help untangle the emotional dynamics involved. If individuals blame themselves for their failure to meet expectations for payoffs, they will experience sadness; and if this sadness is also accompanied by anger at self and fear about the consequences to self of this failure, a person will also experience shame; and since payoffs are almost always moral issues involving standards of justice, persons will also experience guilt for not having lived up to moral standards. In contrast, if individuals blame others for their failure to meet expectations, they will be angry, seeing others as unfair and as acting unjustly. Others may resent this anger, becoming angry themselves; and this cycle of anger only highlights the inability to meet expectations. Oftentimes, in order to avoid these negative reactions from specific others, particularly if they are powerful, individuals will blame categories of others or the structure in which the encounter occurs, or they may displace their anger on those who cannot fight back.

As individuals experience negative emotions towards self, others, categories or structures, definitions of costs, investments, and standards of justice are recalibrated (typically downward, so that expectations are lowered). As a result, if an interaction must be iterated, the readjustment of expectations downward can lower the potential for negative emotional arousal; and if a person has engaged in realistic readjustments of expectations in light of what has occurred, he or she may experience relatively little anger as the responses of others now correspond to lowered expectations. Yet if an individual lowers expectations but still sees him- or herself as incurring high costs and investments and not receiving justice, then the anger will increase in intensity. As a result, this individual will seek to leave the encounter or, if exiting is not possible, he or she may repress the anger, causing this person to lose emotional energy and become chronically sad (although this sadness may be punctuated by sporadic episodes of intense anger and resentment).

On the more positive side of emotions, when individuals receive positive rewards, and especially when they receive rewards exceeding expectations, they (ironically) become more vulnerable to failure in subsequent interactions because they may have raised their expectations, and when these escalated expectations are not realized, they will become angry, having evaluated their payoffs relative to these escalated expectations. And the more core self is salient, the more intense these negative reactions will be.

Defensive strategies can, at times, mitigate against extreme emotional gyrations. People can selectively perceive and interpret in order to sustain the myth that their expectations for payoffs have been met; and they can draw upon credits of positive outcomes in the past to ride out failures in the present so as to meet expectations. But these strategies can work in the short term only, and if individuals try to employ defense mechanisms, these usually backfire because projection, external attribution, and displacement invite counteranger, which only assures that expectations will not be met. People can, of course, lower their expectations, but a residue of resentment from the first time expectations were not met will generally remain. Under these conditions, repression is often the best option for individuals in iterated encounters where they habitually do not realize past or present expectations for payoffs. However, repression is costly and generally lowers emotional energy and generates sadness, which may lower expectations at the conscious level but only aggravate the anger being held in at a subconscious level. Indeed, such individuals often have outbursts of anger when the neo-cortical sensors that control emotions are not at full strength.

NEED FOR GROUP INCLUSION

Individuals need to feel part of the ongoing flow of interaction. This need for group inclusion is not, however, a drive for high solidarity with others; too much solidarity is tiring and constraining, with the result that people are highly selective in entering situations where inclusion means high degrees of social solidarity. But individuals always want to sense that they are minimally included in encounters; to be an outcast, however subtly, is highly distressing for people, and humans have powerful needs to avoid experiencing such deprivation.

When individuals do not feel included, it becomes ever more difficult to verify self or receive positive payoffs in exchanges with others. As a result, individuals will withdraw self or, if they cannot, they will present role distance and feign disinterest. And they will lower their costs by reducing the modal level of energy put into roles (but not their anger) and by cutting back on their investments in such roles (while seeing their previous investments as a waste of time).

When individuals' expectations for group inclusion are realized, they experience satisfaction, and when a role identity presented is a marker of core self feelings, more intense forms of happiness will ensue. Moreover, if a person had doubts about being included, he or she may also experience pride. But again, it is the negative side of emotions that is the more interesting and complicated. When individuals do not meet expectations for inclusion, they may experience hurt (a variant of sadness); at other times, they may feel angry; and at still other moments, they may be afraid. How, then, are we to explain these different reactions?

Attribution processes are one critical force. When individuals blame themselves for the failure to meet expectations for inclusion, they experience sadness; and when they also experience anger at themselves and fear about the consequences to self of exclusion, they are likely to experience shame. The more core self feelings are salient under these conditions, the more intense will be the experience of shame; and when individuals also evaluate their failure to meet expectations for inclusion from the perspective of moral codes, they will feel guilt as well. When others are blamed for the failure to meet expectations, anger is the most likely reaction, and the more salient is self, the greater will be the anger that is felt and, in all likelihood, expressed. Fear may also be experienced, especially if those who are blamed have high authority and prestige.

Defensive strategies can allow an individual to temporarily avoid the sense of exclusion, but if the encounter is iterated or persists for a long period, it becomes ever more difficult to use selective perception, selective interpretation, short term credits, or disavowal. If the person can, he or she will leave; and if this individual must stay in the encounter, he or she will feel trapped, reducing emotional energy and investments in roles but still holding onto negative emotions. External attributions, projection, and the displacement of negative emotions are, however, likely to cause counteranger from others, thus assuring that a person will be rejected. Repression can operate successfully, but this defense mechanism will accentuate the arousal of sadness as emotional energy is drained away in order to keep a person from facing the fact that his or her expectations for inclusion have not been realized.

NEED FOR TRUST

People need to sense that the behaviors of others are predictable, that the give and take of gestures is in rhythmic synchronization (Collins 1988), that others are being sincere (Habermas 1988), and that others are respecting one's own dignity. Humans thus role-take along these dimensions of trust, and an interaction will not flow smoothly unless these dimensions are realized. When individuals experience trust, they will experience and display positive emotions, usually at the low-intensity end of the satisfaction-happiness spectrum. When core self feelings are salient, especially if a person was somewhat fearful or uncertain about an encounter, their emotions will be more complex, ranging from relief and gratitude to pride. If people attribute the success to achieve trust to others, particularly under conditions of some fear about whether their expectations could be met, they will reveal gratitude towards these others; whereas, if they attribute their success to their own actions, they will feel pride.

When expectations for trust are not realized, individuals will almost always blame others, and they will generally reveal low-key anger toward these others, unless salient core self feelings push up the emotional thermostat. If these others also have power or authority, a person's anger will be tempered by fear. While individuals typically blame others in cases where trust is not achieved, they can, at times, see their own actions as at fault, and under these conditions, they will be sad. If self is salient, they will also experience anger at themselves, and if others in the encounter are powerful, they will reveal fear about the consequences of violating trust. Moreover, when these three negative emotions are experienced simultaneously and moral codes are invoked a person will feel shame and guilt as well.

NEED FOR FACTICITY

People need to sense that they share a common world with others during an interaction, that the situation is as it appears, and that reality has an obdurate or inflexible character for the duration of the interaction. When individuals realize this sense of facticity, they experience calm and a low-key satisfaction that is hardly noticeable, but when they do not realize expectations for facticity, they become highly irritated, particularly if core self is salient. Subjects in Harold Garfinkel's (1967) breaching experiments revealed surprising levels of anger which, on the surface, seemed disproportionate to the nature of the breach. What, then, accounts for the anger?

One element is that when individuals do not feel a sense of facticity, other transactional needs are difficult to realize. Expectations for self confirmation are not fully realized; exchange payoffs are uncertain; group inclusion is difficult, and trust is tenuous, at best. When so much is at stake, then, emotions can run high, and anger is the most typical response from those who have not had their expectations for facticity realized. It is rare for individuals to make attributions to self for failures to achieve facticity; so the anger is directed toward others. If, however, no specific person or persons can be blamed, mild to moderate fear, such as anxiety or distress, will be experienced. People will sense that something is wrong, but if they cannot target others, they will feel concern and, generally, redouble their efforts to achieve facticity through highly visible and ritualized gesturing (Goffman 1974; Turner 2000). Defensive strategies can be employed to hide the failure to meet expectations for facticity, but these are, once again, only a short-term solution. Defense mechanisms are rarely employed, we believe, over the failure to meet expectations for facticity. People respond immediately to a failure to realize expectations for facticity; they rarely repress this failure because they are too quick to blame others or use anxiety to redouble their efforts to realize these expectations.

CONCLUSION

In this chapter, we have sought to outline a theory of motivation in face-to-face interaction in encounters. There are many forces mobilizing humans' motivational energy, but among the most important sociologically are what we have termed transactional needs, which individuals seek to realize in each and every encounter, no matter how short term or seemingly trivial. These need-states work through humans' cognitive capacities to create expectations about what should transpire in an encounter, and, in turn, the realization or failure at realization of these expectations arouses emotions. People respond emotionally to these expectations because they are tied to the most basic social needs guiding the flow of interaction among humans. Indeed, all other expectation states—from status, norms, or social structure—are, to a very great extent, guided by these need-driven expectations.

A more robust theory, of course, would address the connections among other sources of expectations, emotional arousal, and the dynamics of micro encounters (see Turner 2002, for one such effort). Our goal has been much more limited: to argue that expectations are formed and driven by motivational need states among humans in face-to-face encounters. With this more limited theory, efforts can be made to integrate the theory into other theories that examine expectations in face-to-face human interaction. For the present, let us summarize the theory in somewhat more formal terms.

I. Human beings seek to satisfy basic transactional needs in social encounters. These include needs for self-verification, profitable exchange payoffs, group inclusion, trust, and facticity. When these needs are realized, individuals will experience variants and combinations of positive emotions like satisfaction or happiness and will be more committed to the encounter. When these needs are unrealized, individuals will experience variants and combinations of more negative emotions such as anger, fear, and sadness, and as a result, they will seek to change or leave the encounter.

II. Individuals seek to confirm and verify self. The self operates at three levels: the transsituational core self, institutionally oriented subidentities, and the role identities that emerge in specific encounters. The more salient are core self feelings to a subidentity or role identity, the more powerful will be the emotions that are aroused in an encounter, and visa versa.

   A. The more salient are core self feelings to identities, the more intense will be the satisfaction or happiness experienced.

1. The greater was the fear about confirmation of self, the greater will be the pride experienced when successful confirmation of self occurs.

2. The more self-confirmation is seen by individuals as the result of their own actions, the more intense will be their positive emotions.

3. The more self-confirmation is seen by individuals as the result of the actions of others, then:

   a. the higher the level of an individual's self-esteem (core self feelings are positive), the more positive are the emotions toward self and others.

   b. the lower the level of an individual's self-esteem (core self feelings are negative), the more positive are the emotions toward others.

B. The more expectations for self are not confirmed, the more an individual will experience variants and combinations of negative emotions—sadness, fear, or anger—and the more salient are core self feelings, the more intense will be the negative emotions experienced.

1. The more individuals attribute the failure to confirm expectations for self to themselves, the more likely they are to experience:

   a. sadness about self.

   b. anger at self.

   c. fear about the consequences of self.

   d. shame, when sadness, anger, and fear are experienced simultaneously.

   e. guilt, when sadness, anger, and fear are experienced simultaneously and moral codes are salient.

2. The more individuals attribute to others the failure to meet expectations for self, the more intense will be their anger toward these others.

3. The more anger is expressed toward others, the more likely are these others to sanction the individual's self negatively.

4. The more interaction with others over iterated encounters fails to confirm an identity, the more likely are external attributions to be supplemented by self-attributions.

5. The more an identity fails to be confirmed and the less this identity is tied to core self feelings, the more likely are some of the following defensive strategies to be activated:

   a. selective perception of the responses of others.

   b. selective interpretation of the responses of others.

   c. invocation of memories of positive confirmations in the past as short term credit to obviate the disconfirmation in the present.

   d. changes in role identities.

   e. distance of self from a particular role identity.

   f. disavowal of the audience.

   g. exiting the encounter.

6. The more an identity fails to be confirmed and the more this identity is tied

to core self feelings, the more likely are some of the following defense mechanisms to be activated:

a. projection of negative emotions onto others.

b. displacement of negative emotions onto others.

c. repression of negative emotions, thereby reducing the modal level of emotional energy and increasing the likelihood of sudden and disproportionate spikes of negative emotions.

III. Individuals seek to acquire positive resource payoffs in encounters. When needs for profitable exchange payoffs are realized, individuals will experience and express positive emotions, whereas when they are not realized, individuals will experience and express negative emotions.

A. Individuals will initially scan encounters for available resources and symbols that allow them to meet other transactional needs.

1. The more needs for self are salient, the more individuals will seek symbols and resources for the confirmation of self, and the more these expectations for self are met, the more intense will be their positive emotions.

2. The less needs for self are salient, the more individuals will seek the resources and symbols necessary for meeting other transactional needs, and the more these expectations are met, the more they will experience positive emotions, but not to the same degree as when self is highly salient.

3. The more individuals attribute successes in realizing expected payoffs to their own actions, the more positive are the emotions towards self, and the greater was the fear about realizing these expected payoffs, the greater will be the sense of pride.

4. The more individuals experience positive emotions in realizing expected payoffs and attribute this success to others, the more likely they are to express positive sentiments and commitments toward others, both now and in future encounters.

5. The more expectations have been realized or exceeded in exchange payoffs, the higher will subsequent expectations for exchange payoffs become; and the higher the expectations become, the more vulnerable are individuals to failure in meeting these expectations in subsequent interactions.

B. The more expectations for exchange payoffs fail to be realized in an encounter, the more likely are negative emotions to be aroused.

1. The more core self feelings are salient and the less expectations for exchange payoffs are realized, the more intense will be the negative emotions.

2. The more individuals blame themselves for the failure to meet their expectations for exchange payoffs, the more likely they are to experience sadness.

a. If this sadness is accompanied by anger and fear, individuals will also experience shame.

b. If this sadness is accompanied by anger and fear in reference to moral standards, individuals are likely to experience guilt.

3. The more individuals attribute the failure to meet expectations for exchange

payoffs to others, the greater will be their anger and resentment toward these others.

4. The more expectations for exchange payoffs go unrealized in iterated encounters, the more likely are expectations to be lowered and the greater will be the anger expressed.

5. The more anger over the failure to realize expectations for exchange payoffs cannot be expressed by individuals for fear of negative sanctions from (powerful) others, the more likely is repression to reduce modal levels of emotional energy and the more likely are episodic spikes of negative emotions.

IV. Individuals seek to feel a part of the flow of interaction. When needs for group inclusion are realized, individuals will experience and express positive emotions, whereas when needs for group inclusion go unrealized, individuals will experience and express negative emotions.

A. The more group inclusion is necessary for the confirmation of core self feelings, the stronger will be needs for group inclusion and the more intense will be the positive emotions experienced when these needs are realized, whereas the more intense will be the negative emotions experienced when these needs are not realized.

B. The more the failure to realize needs for group inclusion is attributed to the self, the more individuals will experience sadness; and when this sadness is accompanied by anger at the self and fear about the consequences of group exclusion, the more individuals will experience shame and, if moral codes are salient, guilt as well.

C. The more the failure to realize needs for group inclusion is attributed to others, the more likely are the individuals to experience and express anger toward these others, and when others are powerful, individuals will also experience fear.

V. Individuals seek a sense of stability, sincerity, respect, rhythm, and predictability in encounters. When these needs for trust are realized, individuals will experience and express positive emotions (usually low-level satisfaction-happiness), whereas when needs for trust are not realized, individuals will experience and express negative emotions (usually low-level sadness, anger, or fear).

A. The more individuals attribute success in realizing expectations for trust to their own actions, the greater will be the positive feelings experienced towards self, and if they had some fear about achieving trust, they will also experience pride.

B. The more individuals attribute success in realizing expectations for trust to the actions of others, especially in situations with a degree of uncertainty, the more they will experience and express gratitude toward these others.

C. The more individuals attribute the failure to realize expectations for trust to themselves, the more they will experience sadness, and the more salient are core self feelings, the more individuals will also experience anger at themselves and fear about the consequences of their failure, thereby increasing the likelihood that they will also experience shame and, if moral codes are relevant, guilt as well.

D. The more individuals attribute the expectations for trust to the actions of others, the greater will be their anger toward these others, and this anger will increase as the salience of the core self feelings in the encounter increases.

VI. Individuals seek to sense that they are experiencing a common and obdurate reality. When expectations for facticity are realized, individuals will experience low-intensity positive emotions, whereas when their expectations are not realized, they will experience and express low-intensity negative emotions.

    A. The more needs for facticity go unrealized, the more likely are individuals to blame others for this failure and the more likely are negative emotions toward these other to be experienced and expressed.

    B. The more needs for facticity go unrealized and the less specific others can be blamed, the more likely are individuals to experience a diffuse sense of low-intensity fear.

PART II

USING THEORY TO GUIDE RESEARCH

Chapter 7

How Scope and Initial Conditions Determine the Growth of Theory

Robert K. Shelly[1]

Sociologists often discuss how to accumulate knowledge and promote the growth of theory. Problems of substantive knowledge growth, improvements in predictive accuracy of theories, and refinement of knowledge claims are issues explored in these discussions. Concerns include problems of precision in prediction, the falsifiability of theoretical claims, prediction of future data from past data, and forecasting real-world outcomes. One area of interest that has received little attention is the relationship between a theoretical working strategy, the logical extension of the theory, and its models; the methodological working strategy, the design of research, and collection of evidence employed to test theories; and the substantive working strategy, the focus of the research problems addressed by a theory. This chapter describes how relationships between these elements of orienting strategies promote the growth of theory. I explore the role of boundary conditions, specified by the domain and range of theoretical research programs. For particular theories, these boundary conditions are specified by *scope conditions*, which abstractly define the situation of application, and *initial conditions*, which provide concrete situations for a test of a theory. The relationship between the domain and range of the theoretical research program and the scope and initial conditions for a particular theory provide systematic guidance in growing theories.

I identify issues in the development of empirically based theories in an attempt to establish a set of criteria for the evaluation of tests. These include fundamental assumptions about how to explain human behavior, criteria for evidence reflected in epistemology, and ways in which various sources of evidence are brought to bear in testing explanatory extensions. The chapter concludes with an illustration based on an effort to expand the domain of expectation states theory to integrative as well as differentiating social structures. This expansion of the explanatory domain takes advantage of a working strategy in which theory, model, and method are linked to evidentiary sources defined by particular boundary conditions.

ISSUES IN THEORY GROWTH

Questions about promoting the growth of theories to explain observable phenomena have a long history in philosophy of science. Enlightenment philosophers such as John Locke and David Hume asked questions about how observation could improve our understanding of the world around us. Their answers provided two important tenets of epistemology. One is the importance of experience as a source of information and the associated importance of being able to communicate about this experience in systematic ways to others, due primarily to Locke (1964 [1690]). The second is the importance of association or the linking of concepts as an organizer of knowledge, due primarily to Hume (1962 [1748]). Observation and association are fundamental tenets of science. Contemporary philosophers, particularly Carl Hempel (1965) and Karl Popper (1959), have extended this to include theories, which capture the organized association of observations.

Hempel (1965) and Popper (1959) develop the requirement that theories contain specific properties to be considered proper theories. Theories contain concepts, a logical structure, and correspondence rules to link observations to concepts. Popper added the idea that theories can never be demonstrated to be true, but rather must be subject to falsification. This insight provides background for two important developments of epistemological interest in theory growth in recent intellectual history.

Popper (1969) and Imre Lakatos (1976) highlight feedback processes in the development of explanatory principles in their work on conjecture and refutation. Their approach proposes that knowledge increases as challenges arise to existing theories in the form of new theories (conjectures) or new data (refutations). As the process of investigation proceeds and challenges are resolved, knowledge increases and theories grow while the domain and range of explanation expand to accommodate new theories or data. The standard for a knowledge claim remains how well the theory organizes our knowledge of observables. For instance, Popper (1972) provides the example of how Albert Einstein's theory of relativity replaced Sir Isaac Newton's theory by subsuming it and explaining more data from new observations that had been thought to be inconsistent with Newton's theory. In accomplishing this, Einstein also expanded the domain of application of the theory.

Sociological interest in this approach has been developed by Berger, Wagner, Zelditch, and Cohen in their work on how sociological theories change and grow within theoretical research programs. A *theoretical research program* is composed of core theoretical ideas that govern empirical investigation, together with a set of criteria that may be applied to new information to determine whether it is to be included as a part of the program (Berger, Wagner, and Zelditch 1985, 1989, 1992; Berger and Zelditch 1993c, 1997; Cohen 1989, 1997; Wagner 1984; Wagner and Berger 1985, 1986, 1993; Zelditch 1991, 1992). This core of ideas is fundamental to a family of theories that share the same domain but may have different ranges of application. Scope statements, which define the situation of application, and initial conditions, which define the starting point for the process under consideration, govern the range of application.

Berger and his collaborators recognize several ways in which theories change and evolve in their explanatory sophistication and application as a research program develops over time. According to this analysis, five different consequences of theory growth are possible.

Elaboration occurs when a theory becomes more comprehensive in its scope and ability to explain phenomena and, as a consequence, has greater power. Popper's example of Einstein's development of relativity theory and its relation to Newton's theory of planetary motion is an example of this type of growth (Popper 1972).

Proliferation enlarges the range of application by expanding the domain or scope of the theory to new situations. An example of this type of growth is Jasso's (1978, 1983) development of the theory of justice evaluations based on a new scope of explanation for justice situations.

Variants of a theory are closely related to the base theory but posit different mechanisms for the process under investigation. The various branches of exchange research programs developed by Molm (1997) and Willer and his associates (e.g., Willer 1999) are examples of this form of theory growth.

Competitors employ different concepts and principles to explain the same range and scope of phenomena as the original theory. The two-process theory of status and dominance developed by Lee and Ofshe (1981) and the single process theory of Ridgeway (1987) are examples.

Integrations consolidate two or more theories by identifying relationships between two or more theories with the same range and domain of application (Berger and Zelditch 1993a, 1997).

These processes of theory growth are governed by intellectual strategies that organize concepts, delineate rules of evidence, and specify the content of the theory. Statements that govern epistemological and ontological claims are part of this fundamental set of ideas. Such strategies are subject to changes as theories evolve and grow. Berger and Zelditch (1993a, 1997) assert that *orienting strategies* are very stable, as they provide the basic framework for the organized effort to develop knowledge. The foci of such strategies are fundamental claims about epistemology and ontology that govern theoretically motivated investigations. *Working strategies* are more malleable and include three general classes. One class is focused on theoretical issues, such as the nature of theory, the logic of explanation, and criteria for theory growth. Another class addresses substantive issues in the theory and focuses on the "what," rather than the "how" issues of the theory. Observation statements, evidentiary criteria, and issues of domain and range of explanation constitute this second class. Applications and situations of investigation constitute the third class, which is focused on substance.

Little has been done to take advantage of this classification of theories to provide direction for substantive efforts to grow theory. Berger and Zelditch discuss how the comparison of several proliferations of expectations states theories lead to the identification of a new and important concept for the research program, the *social framework* (1997:39). Social frameworks, which are fundamental for any state-organizing process, are distinguished from the situation of action. A social framework is the broad set of cultural elements such as "norms, values, beliefs and social categories; formal, [such as] institutionalized and formalized role and authority positions; or interpersonal, as enduring networks of sentiments, influence, and communication" (Wagner and Berger 1993: 56). A situation of action occurs within the broader social framework.

The identification of this key concept and recognition of its importance occurred only after theorists examined efforts to identify what was common to several theoretical approaches in the context of the methodological strategies employed in the research program. An integration of diverse theories of status processes now makes logical as well as substantive sense, as the theories apply to the same general social setting rather than a variety of settings, as implied by their various initial conditions. The identification of covering concepts in the domain of a theory, as exemplified in this case, was accomplished by expanding the range of the theory. Such an expansion of initial conditions is one way to extend a theory's explanatory power.

Berger and his collaborators do not elaborate criteria for how to grow a theory. In the example cited here, additional concepts were found by attempting to integrate several theories. It is just as reasonable to think that the identification of tests between competitors would produce additional information, as is suggested by the experience with the dominance-cues debate. The challenge initiated by Lee and Ofshe (1981) with their two-process theory provoked research by Ridgeway (1987) and others to determine whether interaction style alone was sufficient to establish status advantages. An identification of the distinction between status cues and dominance behaviors resulted from this challenge. Whether one of these strategies is more desirable than another is an open question for philosophers of science. Apparently no epistemological rules govern which elements of either scope or initial condition to include in efforts to grow theories (cf. Laudan 1996).

One approach to this problem is to recognize that theories apply only to certain kinds of phenomena under certain conditions (Walker and Cohen 1985; Cohen 1989; Foschi 1997). These scope conditions delimit the abstractly defined situations appropriate for a particular theory. Initial conditions delimit specific instantiations by defining particular circumstances under which a test is carried out (Walker and Cohen 1985; Cohen 1989). Varying scope conditions require that a new theory be constructed as an elaboration or proliferation. Varying initial conditions for a theory test may lead to the development of variants or competitors. Efforts to integrate two or more theories require the union of two sets of scope conditions. This approach represents one *growth strategy* for the expansion of a theory through organizing the development of elaboration, pro-liferation, and variation of formally developed theories. It also enhances our understanding of the role that competitors and integrations play in theory growth.

I propose a strategy, inherent in the logic of theoretical research programs, to organize theory growth based on expanding boundary conditions of theories within a research program. This strategy allows for an explication of links be-tween theoretical working strategies, which include rules for what constitutes a theory and the logic of explanation; methodological working strategies, which provide rules for what constitutes evidence for a test of a theory; and substantive working strategies, which identify a theory's substantive foci. These linkages may then be employed to identify an epistemological warrant for strategies of theory growth.

Alterations of the substantive strategy involve two classes of changes. The first is based on changes in the strategy itself and focuses on an idea expressed in the form, "What would happen if . . . ?" The dependent clause in this state-ment suggests a concrete change in an instantiation without an abstract reference in either the scope conditions or initial conditions. Often, the consequence of this approach is a piecemeal advance in knowledge based on being able to identify one effect at a time. No generalization strategy is in place to move new information gained from this exercise into the abstract base provided by the methodological and theoretical strategies.

The second class of changes is based on altering concrete statements and observations based on a systematic change in scope and initial conditions. This allows investigators to pursue, as part of a research program, new instantiations that lead to theoretical growth. These new instantiations are added to the meth-odological and theoretical bases of the research program to provide an expanded domain and range of explanation. This second class of changes in the substantive strategy is entailed when scope statements and initial conditions are deliberately manipulated.

I develop a systematic program to rigorously develop elaborations, variants, and proliferations of theories. This is pursued by focusing on how methodolog-ical working strategies can be manipulated by amending scope and initial con-ditions in substantive situations to identify new phenomena to investigate and new theoretical patterns. Theoretical strategies suggested by Berger and his col-laborators provide the framework for developing new, rigorous explanations.

METHODOLOGICAL WORKING STRATEGIES

Methodological working strategies include the practical, everyday activities of the scientific enterprise, as defined in analytic terms. These include the implementation of observation activities, decisions about how to store and analyze data, and decision-making criteria applied to tests of theories. These activities define the nature of evidence, namely, what types of behavior to observe, aggregation rules for accumulating information, and how information is to be compared to theoretical predictions.

The scope of application of a theoretical idea abstractly defines situations that are to be investigated (Walker and Cohen 1985; Cohen 1989). For instance, expectation states theories apply in situations in which actors are engaged in a task, with a collective orientation, that has differentially valued outcomes. Exchange theories apply in situations where actors are engaged in an interaction that involves the exchange of valued rewards.

Abstract treatments of initial conditions have received limited attention (Cohen 1989:80). Initial conditionals are often confused with scope conditions or elements of the substantive working strategy. When confused with scope statements, situationally defined initial conditions needlessly restrict the domain of application of a theory by adding unnecessary constraints. For instance, exchange theory might benefit from a systematic review of issues of network structure, reward patterns, rules of the game, and other elements that vary across situations. Such a review might lead to the reclassification of some or more of these boundary conditions from scope to initial conditions. When confused with the substantive working strategy, initial conditions restrict knowledge growth by concretizing statements that should be abstract.

Foschi (1997) suggests that varying scope conditions allow investigators to systematically alter environments for investigations. While advocating altering the environment of investigation, Foschi does not specify how this is to be accomplished. Tootell, Bianchi, and Munroe (1998) also developed an attempt to manipulate scope conditions and increase the domains of application for theories. However, the systematic alteration of boundary conditions has not been examined as a generalization strategy in this work.

One approach to these abstract principles to providing elaboration and variation in a theoretical research program is to treat them as distinct elements in the set of ideas that govern investigation within the program. It is reasonable to consider scope conditions and initial conditions as two sources of variation in theoretical ideas that are part of a methodological strategy within a theoretical research program. With this approach, scope conditions and initial conditions can be treated as variables and manipulated as such. It is important to note here that scope statements are not varied for a particular theory, but may vary across theories within a program.

Altering scope statements and initial conditions has substantial effects on evidentiary claims and observation statements because a change in either of these boundary conditions changes the nature of situations in which data is collected. For instance, changing data collection situations often constrains whether data is collected based on observed behaviors or self-reports of internal states. Altering data collection processes may also affect a theory test, since models of data must be respecified for particular conditions in which data are collected. Such alterations will not affect the theoretical strategy, as it is determined by epistemological, rather than substantive, concerns. However, the changes do affect the substantive strategy, as they alter statements about concrete situations observed during an investigation.

There are four possible ways in which boundary conditions may be varied in combination with one another. These are detailed next.

In the first case, scope conditions of the theory may be made less restrictive by changing their status to that of an initial condition. Such a change then allows the investigator to apply a new theory to a broader range of situations. This is the exchange theory example cited earlier. A set of scope statements may be manipulated in one of two ways.

Foschi (1997) observes that a narrowly defined scope of explanation is desirable early in the theory development process in order to clarify the role of boundary conditions. Scope statements explicitly made to define the range of a theory are systematically relaxed in order to enlarge the number of situations to which a theory is applied. However, Foschi does not specify how this expansion is to take place. For example, expectation states theories were initially formulated with a scope statement that specified (1) collectively oriented (2) task groups solving problems that had (3) both good and bad solutions. Each one of these conditions is a candidate for alteration in order to expand the scope of the theory. Each condition could be changed by simply treating it as one of two, mutually exclusive categories so that an expansion of the theory might include (1) individually oriented (2) task groups solving (3) differentially valued tasks. Similar changes could be introduced for each condition.

The second case is simply the reverse of the first. The investigator alters the scope conditions to include what was previously defined as an initial condition. In such a case, a new theory may apply to a narrower range of situations than its earlier sibling.

This is the reverse of the exchange theory example. For instance, in addition to specifying that exchange theory applies to actors engaged in an interaction in which rewards are transferred between them, the investigator might add conditions that specify that this exchange occurs within a particular structure or set of structures. It is also possible to consider altering such scope conditions so that schedules of reward are varied; only one value of a reward is transmitted—either positive or negative. Such conditions restrict the range of application of a theory to only certain structures, reward schedules, or values of rewards, which may nonetheless have value for the investigator interested in a narrow band of phenomena.

The third case involves changing the scope of the theory but maintaining the initial conditions. This, in effect, requires a new theory of the phenomenon of interest. An example here is the work on rewards and social justice developed by Jasso (1978, 1983).

This alternative for expanding the scope of a theory involves constructing a new set of conditions that must be satisfied if a test is to be conducted. Such a set of conditions might be identified based on efforts to integrate two theories. For instance, efforts to join elements of exchange theory and expectations theory must include scope statements from both theories about collective task orientation and reward distribution, in order to adequately test any propositions from the integrated theory. Such integration is intuitively obvious, but other means of adding new scope statements to an existing theory are less apparent. Investigators have usually not considered how to do this analytically, but rather have proceeded on an ad-hoc basis or worked with a substantively based strategy to expand scope.

The fourth case involves maintaining the scope conditions and altering the initial conditions of application of the theory. This approach broadens the range of explanation and has an initial impact on the substantive strategy for the theory. An example of this is Shelly's 1993 extension of expectations theory to cover social structures defined by sentiments.

Investigators generally do not systematically expand the range of initial conditions for theory tests. Frequently, such expansions are discovered as a result of efforts to implement a new, substantive working strategy. It is useful to carefully consider how one might expand such conditionals. One strategy is to examine scope conditions to discover other, similar situations entailed by the type of situation to which an explanation is applied. Once a catalog is developed, abstraction from specific instances can identify one or more principles that guide the identification of conditionals. For instance, expectation states theories apply to general classes of situations in which evaluative processes are embedded. Such situations involve a large and diverse number of initial conditions. Some of these conditions initially rank order actors in the situation, whereas others begin with initially undifferentiated actors. The variety of ways in which rank orders can arise, as well as the equalitarian situation, constitutes different sets of initial conditions that may be examined.

One may also examine initial conditions to identify situations that complement those that have already been investigated. Such an approach requires the investigator to catalog initial conditions and then ask what situations are not covered by such a list. This strategy is distinguished from the previous one in that it relies on identifying the differences rather than similarities of characteristics in the conditions being investigated. For instance, the focus of expectations theory on evaluative processes has recently been expanded to include situations in which social structures based on social similarity rather than evaluative differences have become the foci of investigation.

To summarize progress thus far, four strategies have been identified for expanding boundaries of theoretical explanation for scope conditions and initial conditions as elements of the methodological working strategy of a theory. Each of these strategies involves creating a new situation of action and an associated theory about behavior in the situation. The first strategy to expand the scope of explanation is to relax initial constraints by treating specified scope conditions as variables with two or more categories. The second strategy varies scope conditions to create potential environments for new theories. The third strategy adds new constraints to the scope of the theory. Finally, the fourth strategy is to attempt an integration with another theory that requires integrating scope conditions unique to theory 2 to the set for theory 1.

Expanding the range of initial conditions is possible if one searches the scope conditions for clues as to general traits of the scope of the theory and exploits them to arrive at covering concepts that lead to new sets of initial conditions. A second approach in the expansion of initial conditions employs complementary situations to those in which existing tests have been carried out. These complements become candidates for new instantiations and, by extension, new theoretical explanations as a consequence of careful analysis of how these new situations may or may not fit the existing evidence and explanation. For example, in expectation states theories, collective orientation is a key scope condition whose complimentary condition is individual orientation. Expanding expectation theories by altering this scope condition provides an opportunity to test the robustness of the theory in competitive, as well as cooperative, situations.

Scope and initial conditions are inextricably linked elements of methodological strategies. Exploiting these links extends the domain and range of explanation of a theory by applying systematic search schemes to boundary conditions of a theory. In fact, this strategy can be detected in post-hoc consideration of how the expectations program evolved over time. Initially, the theories were applied only to task-oriented groups collectively engaged in solving a problem. Subsequent effort expanded the theory by developing explanations for new processes such as reward allocation and its consequences, the identification of additional status characteristics and of structures such as legitimate authority and sentiment, and so forth.

EXTENDING BOUNDARIES: AN EXAMPLE

The ideas developed in this chapter identify how variants and elaborations of theories emerge from manipulating boundary conditions. This is illustrated with an example from the expectation states research program. First, the scope statements that have traditionally defined social situations in which expectations theories are applied are examined. One of these statements is identified for modification, and the implications of this change in the boundary conditions are considered. Second, initial conditions commonly employed in expectations research are identified. These initial conditions are then modified, and implications of these changes in the expectation formation process are developed.

Expectation states theories initially employed three boundary conditions as scope statements. First, actors are engaged in a collectively valued task. This collective orientation guides group behavior toward the production of an outcome to which all members contribute. An important element of a collective orientation is that all members of the group are interested in the group's success and will subordinate their individual interests to this collective goal.

The second boundary condition treated as a scope statement is that the group task has differentially valued outcomes, which are characterized as success or failure. It is possible to think of actors having rank-order preferences for these outcomes. Such preferences could lead either to a circumstance in which all members of a group share an interest in an outcome with no differential value except success preferred by all actors in the group or one in which each actor prefers a different outcome.

The third boundary condition specifies that groups must be engaged in task activity to provide a suitable social environment for the operation of state-organizing processes. This condition distinguishes groups that form for purely social reasons from those that form for instrumental reasons. Groups of actors may meet this condition at one time and not at another. Some groups may always be task focused, whereas others may never meet the condition.

A likely scope condition to alter is the first, which specifies a collective orientation for group activity. Altering this condition creates situations in which actors attempt to maximize their own task success without regard to the possible success of the group. The domain of the theoretical research program that is focused on evaluation processes is not altered. Such situations have been created from time to time in expectations theory research to examine whether actors form expectations independent of group task settings (cf. Balkwell et al., 1992; Shelly 1998).

Initial conditions explored in the expectation states program have included two broad classes of situations. In one case, groups are not initially differentiated, and members of the group interact with one another. State-organizing processes embedded in interaction sequences lead to the formation of expectations by each actor that organize subsequent behavior. In the other case, received structures activate expectations for behavior of the self and other as a result of direct instantiations of status orders—in the case of specific status structures—or through a status generalization process—in the case of diffuse status structures (Fisek, Berger, and Norman 1991; Wagner and Berger 1993). Expectations are also formed when actors are differentiated by rewards received or legitimated social structures of authority through the burden-of-proof process (Berger, Ridgeway, Fisek, and Norman 1998).

A straightforward approach to altering these initial conditions is to change how received social structures are defined. For instance, nonevaluative structures defined by social ties, such as sentiments, provide patterned environments for emergent state-organizing processes (Shelly 1993). An important question when altering received structures is whether expectation formation occurs in sentiment

Figure 7.1
The relationship between theoretical strategy, methodological strategy, and substantive strategy

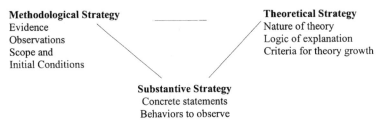

structures in the same way as in status structures. That is, do sentiments lead to the formation of expectations? The device of expanding boundary conditions by altering scope and initial conditions provides a systematic approach to find an answer to this new question.

Figure 7.1 contains a representation of the changes in boundary conditions described previously. This figure highlights how variation in the orientation and type of structure informs theory development. The upper row of Table 7.1 is based on the scope condition of expectations theory that emphasizes collective orientation. The upper-left cell includes traditional instantiations of expectation states theories that emphasize received structures in social situations with collective orientations. Received structures in this cell include diffuse and specific status characteristics, legitimated authority structures, and reward systems. Each structure is treated as unique. Legitimated authority structures are not evolved from a status order if imposed on a group at the beginning of its activity together. The upper-right cell presumes that collective orientation is present in a group with a received social structure based on patterns that do not involve evaluative elements. Such structures might be based on similarities of interest, attitudes, or sentiments. Each structure is unique and does not emerge from other structures such as status structures, authority structures, or reward structures.

The lower row of the table is based on an altered scope condition that emphasizes individualistic orientation. Actors are interested only in their own outcomes and are not interested in collective success or failure. Situations included in this row of the table occur when actors confront individually competitive environments in group contexts, namely, members in a group compete for an outcome that is available individually, but not collectively. The lower-left cell instantiates situations in which actors are in received structures based on specific and diffuse status characteristics, authority structures, and reward structures with outcomes that are individually available. The lower-right cell of the table involves situations in which actors are differentiated from each other by their degree of similarity of interests, attitudes, or sentiments and individualistic orientations toward outcomes are emphasized. Such situations have recently re-

Table 7.1.

The Relationship of Scope Conditions and Initial Conditions in Expanding Theory

Orientation of actor	Initial Conditions: Type of Social Structure	
	Status Structures	Non-Status Structures
Collective Orientation	Expectation State Theories: Reward expectations, diffuse and specific status, etc.	Evolution of status from sentiment structures
Individual Orientation	Expectation formation in individualistic situations	Expectation formation from sentiments in individual situations

ceived attention by investigators in the expectation states research programs. However, theoretical developments are not yet robust in this area.

A systematic variation of boundary conditions in the manner described here leads to the identification of areas where theory growth is possible and points to possible areas of investigation to govern the direction of growth. For instance, the relative lack of studies exploring individual orientation suggests that theoretical knowledge of expectation formation in these situations is an area for possible attention. Similarly, the relative lack of theoretical growth in situations instantiated by such structures is an area of potential growth for expectation states theories.

EXPLOITING VARIATIONS IN BOUNDARY CONDITIONS

Recent studies have attempted to develop new areas of research by exploiting variations in boundary conditions. Each has taken a different approach to the instantiation of nonstatus structures in groups and has examined a slightly different version of the expectation formation process. All three studies examined here developed their research within the traditional scope of expectations states theory, each has retained the collective orientation scope condition.

The first example of this research examined sentiment structures in three person discussion groups. Shelly (1993) used similarity of attitude to create structures in which one person was well liked in a group. Members discussed a problem for a brief period of time. The dependent variable was the number of acts initiated by each member of the group. Actors who fill high status positions in such groups initiated the most activity. Well-liked actors filled the first or second most active role in the majority of groups in this study; the best-liked actor was the most active in a plurality of groups. This outcome suggests that sentiment and status structures organize emergent power and prestige orders in a similar way.

In the second example, Lovaglia and Houser (1996) reported a series of studies in which status structures were combined with various nonstatus structures based on emotional responses to other actors in the situation. They were able to show that actors adjust their behavior depending on their emotional reaction to others in the group. Actors who dislike a partner, whether the partner is of higher or lower relative status, are more likely to resist influence than if they like the partner. They conclude that emotions combine with status characteristics according to the combining rule for status characteristics.

The last example of this research is a recent study by Driskell and Webster (1997). They instantiated status and sentiment structures in dyads in a collectively oriented decision-making situation. Their results show that actors adjust the rate at which they accept influence based on whether they like or dislike their partner in the study. The researchers also asserted that they could discriminate between sequences in the information-processing steps that link status and sentiment information, the formation of expectations, and the translation of expectations into behavior. They concluded that actors form relative performance expectations based on status information and employ sentiment information when translating expectations to behavior. This outcome suggests a two-process model to information processing when sentiments and status are included in the study. This two-process approach raises fundamental questions about basic assumptions of expectation states theory.

Only a few studies examine expectation formation in individually oriented situations. Such situations require that actors gather status information about the self and others, use this information to form expectations, and translate these expectations into action that serves only their own interests. One example of this type of situation is a study that asked respondents to pick advisors in a social dilemma in which potential advisors varied on status attributes that suggested relative success or failure at an upcoming classroom assessment task[2] (Balkwell et al. 1992). Respondents chose advisors in ways confirming that they formed expectations consistent with expectation states theory. High-status advisors were chosen more often than low-status advisors, and advisors with multiple, mixed high- and low-status characteristics were chosen according to the combining rules of the theory.

A recent study has employed vignettes to determine whether respondents process status information as if it had dichotomous or continuous attributes. Shelly (1998) asked respondents how they viewed potential advisors who had different levels of one of three different status attributes. Each attribute had an ordered pattern of status value, with continuous gradations of expertise or status position for each characteristic. In addition, each attribute varied in its degree of task relevance, with a diffuse status characteristic, specific status characteristic, and performance characteristic. The results show that respondents treated status information as if it had a threshold effect, producing two-step, graduated levels of expectation. The cut-off points for the steps varied depending on the nature of the status information. An actor either has or does not have high status on diffuse attributes. Data for the specific and performance-based characteristics show a step function quality of graded expectation states. It is as if an actor has to cross over a performance threshold to be assigned the high state of the characteristic.

The lack of research examining how actors form expectations in individually oriented nonstatus structures is starkly apparent when applying the classification system described here. This area of research has substantial potential in a variety of ways. First, some theoretical ideas have already been developed that can be employed to develop this area of investigation. Ridgeway's (1991) work on how social categories acquire status value is an example. She has been able to demonstrate how group membership in categories such as "a minority group" or "female" by itself is often sufficient to entail the assignment of low status. Her work expands the set of initial conditions; however, it does not exploit the distinction made here in which scope conditions are treated as variable.

The second point is that no efforts have been developed to exploit social structures defined by social similarity, interests, or attitudes and individual orientation. This area remains ripe for investigation. Findings from the research cited here suggest several possibilities for a program of research in this area. For example, an attempt to determine if actors form graduated expectations based on degrees of similarity is one possible research question; the alternative is that actors form dichotomous expectations. Another question to pursue includes the role of multiple structures that include both sentiment and status information. Research could determine whether sentiments are constitutive of expectations or have an impact only when expectations formed from status information are translated to behavior.

CONCLUSION

I began with the question of whether, when working in a research program, it is possible to grow a theory with planned variations. Philosophers of science have generally agreed that this is not possible. Adherents of systematic philosophy of science have not exploited the idea of a process of conjecture and refutation, as based on the work of Popper and Lakatos. This approach requires falsifiable theory with well-defined concepts, a syntax, and derived observation statements. Such theories grow through tests of conjectures. Refutations of parts of such a theory lead to its reformulation, the development of new conjectures, new efforts at refutation, and so forth. Whether any particular test refutes or fails to refute a particular conjecture, the theory gains in explanatory power with each effort to falsify it. Such research traditions are scientific research programs.

The role of scientific research programs as generators of multiple theories and theory-driven research has provided important concepts by which to organize the variation of research programs. First, there is a recognition that empirical programs are evidence driven, with tests of derived hypotheses providing opportunities for the refutation of a theory. Second, it is possible to identify a variety of ways in which such programs grow. Growth can be categorized into five types: elaboration, proliferation, variation, competition, and integration. Each type has a characteristic pattern in a strategic approach to theory growth. These strategies, in turn, provide governing frameworks.

An important part of the working strategy of any theory program is the set of boundary conditions that describe situations in which the theory is applied. Two types of boundaries are identified. Scope conditions have been explored by several authors, and we have some sense of how varying them will lead to theoretical advances. The second type, initial conditions, has not been examined in any detail. This set of conditions defines the starting point of an investigation by defining what a system must look like at the beginning of an observation sequence. The systematic variation of boundary conditions provides for a systematic exploration of ways to generate elaborations, variations, and proliferations of theories in a research program.

An example from expectation states research was developed that varied one scope condition and one initial condition to arrive at a cross-classified table, with status and nonstatus social structures on one axis and individual and collective orientations on the other. Status and nonstatus social structures refer to differences in sets of initial conditions that provide evaluative and nonevaluative criteria for the characterization of structures. Individual and collective orientations refer to the interest of the actor in a group-based outcome. This example leads to the conclusion that current work on sentiments has solved some problems but not others. For instance, emotions apparently combine with status in the same way as multiple status elements. Other research finds that sentiments impact status structures only as they affect the translation of expectations to behavior. Juxtaposing these findings suggests a two-process theory of information processing, which is inconsistent with fundamental assumptions of expectation states theory.

Another result of varying scope conditions is the recognition that expectation processes govern behavior in group and individual settings. This opens the way for studies of how actors form expectations independent of group action. This should allow for the explicit identification of how actors form expectations and how expectations change when new information is introduced into a situation. These questions broaden the range of applied evidence and require that we develop new models of behavior to test theoretical conjectures.

Finally, by varying scope and initial conditions, we identify a new area of research. How sentiments lead to the formation and enactment of expectations in individually oriented situations is an unexplored area. Recognizing that it falls within the domain of an established research program provides an important source of new research ideas. This leads to the formulation of new ideas about how to relate concepts in the theory and develop models to explore new situations, as well as how models influence the choice of theoretically interesting social structures.

NOTES

1. Prepared for presentation at the Conference on Theory Development and Theory Testing in Group Processes, Vancouver, British Columbia, Canada, August 18, 1998. I wish to express my gratitude for the comments of Ann Converse Shelly as I prepared this chapter.

2. An interesting issue arises in this situation. The actor is making the choice of whom to seek advice from as an individually oriented action, that is, to maximize success on the classroom exercise. The possibility exists that the actor and advisor(s) engage in a collectively oriented task to ensure this outcome. Determining which of these scope conditions applies in this situation is not a straightforward process.

Chapter 8 _____

The Relation between Experimental Standardization and Theoretical Development in Group Processes Research

Lisa Troyer[1]

My goal in this chapter is to examine how a standardized research protocol contributes to theoretical growth. To accomplish this, I draw on examples from the standardized experimental setting (SES) for research on status characteristics theory. I begin with an overview of the relation between experimental research and theoretical development. Next, I describe status characteristics theory and discuss how the SES has been used in research related to the theory. I suggest that inconsistencies between the SES characterizing earlier and more recent research may have affected recent results related to how status-organizing processes affect influence. A theoretical examination of these inconsistencies (and their possible effects on results) suggests interesting new theoretical avenues to explore.

EXPERIMENTATION AND THEORETICAL DEVELOPMENT

The virtues of experimental methods are well recognized: they increase control, the isolation of key theoretical variables, the possibility of testing causal inference, and the potential for replicability (e.g., Aronson et al. 1990; Blalock and Blalock 1968; Christensen 1997). Perhaps less well recognized, however, is the role of standardization in experimental protocols within theoretical research programs (TRPs) (e.g., Wagner and Berger 1985). As Wagner and Berger note, "Theoretical context as well as empirical context is vital to the search for evidence of theoretical development" (1985:698). TRPs are characterized by core theoretical concepts and relations, and likewise, a standardized experimental setting is characterized by core procedures that correspond to core theoretical elements. An important contribution of a standardized protocol is the efficiency it lends to research that advances a TRP. The efficiency arises from practicality and commensurability. First, using a standardized experimental protocol is practical, since it provides researchers with a preestablished stock of operationalizations. Second, the results of research based on a standardized protocol are more readily compared to prior research. This comparability makes empirical results more theoretically interpretable. In the next section, I summarize status characteristics theory (hereafter SCT), one branch of the theoretical research program on expectation states. This will serve as a case for discussing the contribution that a standardized research protocol can make to theoretical growth. I describe a standardized protocol, the standardized experimental setting, that characterizes much of the SCT research. Next, I describe interesting theoretical implications of these variations in the SES.

STANDARDIZATION IN SCT RESEARCH

Status characteristics theory (e.g., Berger, Cohen, and Zelditch 1966; Berger, Cohen, and Zelditch 1972; Berger and Fisek 1970; Berger, Fisek, and Freese 1976; Berger, Fisek, Norman, and Zelditch 1977) describes the processes whereby social attributes (such as sex, age, or race) become sources of influence in groups. According to Berger and his colleagues, attributes that differentiate group members are invested with social value, creating a status hierarchy in the group. An actor's position in the hierarchy corresponds to expectations that the actor and others have for his or her competence relative to others. Actors who are higher in the status hierarchy are expected to be more competent than actors lower in the hierarchy. Competency expectations are manifested in interaction patterns in the group, which lead higher status actors to exercise more influence in the group. Status (and, hence, expectations and influence) arises from attributes that (1) differentiate group members, and (2) have not been explicitly dissociated from the group's task. This second condition, referred to as "burden of proof," implies that any differentiating characteristic in a group may become the basis of a status hierarchy as long as it is not overtly demonstrated to be irrelevant to the group's work. The link between a differentiating attribute and influence holds for groups that are task-oriented and collectively oriented. These latter conditions represent the scope conditions of the theory; they specify the conditions under which we expect the theory's claims to be true (e.g., Cohen 1989; Walker and Cohen 1985). Groups working on tasks that have valued outcomes (i.e., there is a preferred or "successful" outcome) are task oriented; and groups whose members believe it is appropriate to consider the input of one another are collectively oriented. Researchers have found that variety of social attributes operate as status characteristics, including sex (e.g., Lockheed and Hall 1976), race (e.g., Cohen 1971), beauty (e.g., Webster and Driskell 1983), educational affiliation (e.g., Moore 1968), and physical disability (e.g., Houser 1997).

The Standardized Experimental Setting

Over several years, adherence to a standardized experimental setting has contributed to systematic theoretical growth, facilitating the comparison of results across different studies and development of formal models of status-organizing processes.[2] The SES, as detailed in Cook, Cronkite, and Wagner (1974) and summarized in Berger and Zelditch (1977) and in Moore (1968), represents a set of standardized procedures through which researchers operationalize key independent and dependent theoretical variables while instituting manipulations to ensure that the theory's scope conditions are also met. Of course, it is neither possible nor desirable to hold every detail of the experimental setting constant across all studies. Such rigidity would not permit the testing of new variables or processes arising from theoretical elaborations.

Results are more interpretable, however, if comparisons can be made across experiments. Such comparisons are only possible, however, to the extent that the experiments employ consistent procedures, varying only in terms of the theoretical variables of interest. This is the motivation behind the SES. The SES protocol involves (1) standardized instructions to subjects regarding the rationale behind the experiment, (2) directions for completing the experimental task, (3) experimental procedures dictating how and when manipulations are introduced (including manipulations establishing scope conditions and introducing status characteristics), (4) a type of task (i.e., binary-choice task) that provides a context in which influence can be operationalized, and (5) debriefing procedures.

The SES instructions begin by informing subjects that they are participating in research designed to test a "newly discovered skill" (most commonly, "Contrast Sensitivity Ability," "Meaning Insight Ability," or "Spatial Judgment Ability") that is purportedly unrelated to known abilities such as mathematical competence or artistic ability. This instruction is important because it reduces the likelihood that the subjects will have prior beliefs about the skill and increases the likelihood that their behavior in that setting will reflect expectation states arising from experimental manipulations.

Next, the subjects are informed that they will be working with a partner on a task related to the skill. They are then introduced to the "partner." The methods through which the partner has been introduced bear mention, as they may have important effects on the extent to which the scope conditions of the theory are realized. In early versions of the SES (e.g., Moore 1968), subjects participate jointly in the study. Although they do not see one another (an important control for visual factors that may affect status), they are present in the same room (separated by partitions) and are led to believe that they will be working together as partners on a task. Both subjects in this version of the SES are actually equal on the status variable of interest. For example, if the status variable of interest is educational attainment, then both subjects will be at the same grade level. Using this example, the experimenter might state, "I see we have a female first-year undergraduate and a female first-year graduate student." Because, in this example, both students are first-year undergraduate students, they would assume that the other person (ostensibly their partner) is of higher status (i.e., a first-year graduate student).

Later experiments introduced the partner through a video system, in which the subject views the partner on a video monitor (e.g., Wagner, Ford, and Ford 1986). In reality, the partner is a videotaped confederate. In the video setting, when the partner is introduced, the subject receives information about the partner (via the audio/video system) that manipulates his or her status. Again, using the example of educational attainment as a status characteristic, if subjects are first-year college students, then the partner might introduce him- or herself as a first-year graduate student.

Recent experiments have employed a computer-mediated interaction system. In some of these experiments, the partner is introduced by sending the subject information in text form over a computer system that describes that partner (e.g., Troyer 1999). In this setting, the first-year undergraduate subject might receive textual information describing the partner as a (higher-status) first-year graduate student. In the computer-mediated system, text instructions direct the subjects to enter information about themselves on one screen. Then, a few seconds later, they view on a computer screen information that they entered about themselves along with information about their partner, which their partner ostensibly entered. In reality, the computer software for the experiment is programmed to adjust the status level of the partner, as the study hypotheses require. All three of these variations of the SES involve similar status manipulations. Yet, the medium through which they are delivered varies (e.g., in-person, via an audio/video system, or in a text format, via a computer system). Later, I will discuss the implications of these subtle differences for the realization of the theory's scope conditions.

Next in the protocol, the task is described to subjects. The task is a binary-choice task involving a series of trials, with each trial representing a decision that the subject must make between one of two alternatives. Two tasks are used in many of the SCT experiments: "Contrast Sensitivity Task" or "Meaning Insight Task" In the Contrast Sensitivity Task, subjects are asked to choose which of two arrays of black-and-white rectangles has the most white. In reality, the arrays have nearly equal amounts of black and white. In the Meaning Insight Task, subjects are asked to choose which of two words from a purportedly primitive language is closest in meaning to an English word (e.g., Webster 1977). In all tasks, subjects are led to believe that one alternative is correct and the other is incorrect. This instruction is important, because it operationalizes task orientation, one of the scope conditions of SCT. The subjects are advised that they will begin each problem by making an initial choice regarding the correct alternative, independent of their partner. Then, they are told that the initial choice will be communicated to their partner and they will be told their partner's initial choice. The subjects are then asked to make a final choice. No feedback is provided about the partner's final choice, and the subjects are not advised whether the choices are correct.

In the in-person and video-mediated settings, the subjects communicate their choices by pressing buttons on a console corresponding to the alternative they have selected. They then receive feedback regarding their own and their partner's initial choice through lights on the console. In the computer-mediated setting, subjects communicate their choices by either typing a number corresponding to an alternative or clicking a mouse on a button on the computer screen corresponding to the alternative they have chosen. They receive feedback regarding their partner's initial choice (and their own) through text displayed on their computer screen. It is important to note, however, that there are two variants of the computer-mediated setting that convey feedback in different ways. In one variant (e.g., Foschi 1996), subjects are advised which choice their partner made along with the statement that the partner "Disagrees" or "Agrees" with the subject. In the other variant (e.g., Troyer 1999), subjects are only advised which choice their partner made. As I will later describe, this difference may affect the realization of scope conditions and results.

The feedback represents a manipulation that allows researchers to operationalize influence. Since the subject is not actually working with a partner, the experimenter manipulates the feedback to reflect that the partner has made either the same initial choice as the subject or a different initial choice. Generally, the percentage of trials in which the subject's initial choice is different than the partner's is high (usually about 80 percent). The trials involving different initial choices are "critical trials" because they allow influence behavior to be operationalized. If subjects stay with their initial choices, this is recorded as a "stay" response, a rejection of the other's influence. Altering one's initial choice corresponds to acceptance of the other's influence. The proportion of critical trials for which subjects issue a stay response, P(s), operationalizes influence.

Task and collective orientation are also manipulated by reporting the scores of individuals and groups, ostensibly from prior studies of the task. The scores are accompanied by a label indicating that varying performance levels correspond to different scores obtained over the trials of the task. For instance, in Moore (1968), a score of 32–40 (out of 40 trials) by an individual is designated as "Superior," 22–30 is designated as "Good," 12–20 is designated as "Fair," and 0–10 is designated as "Poor." This reminds the subjects that there are successful and unsuccessful outcomes and that success is more valued than failure. Thus, it reinforces task orientation. In addition, the scores are used to manipulate collective orientation. For instance, in Moore's study, subjects were advised that, "individuals whose performances are fair or good when they do *not* have additional time and information are frequently capable of attaining *superior* performance when they *do* have this additional time and information" (Moore 1968: 54; emphasis in the original). The "additional information" is feedback regarding the partner's initial choice. The subjects are told that they should not hesitate to make a different final choice if the information they receive from their partner helps them choose correctly. These instructions reinforce collective orientation.

Like other manipulations that may bear on the scope conditions, the manner in which the scores are conveyed has varied across forms of the SES. In Moore's (1968) study, the scores for individual performance were displayed on a chart in the room in which the experiment was conducted. In Wagner, Ford, and Ford (1986), the subjects viewed charts with the scores and received the commentary describing different scores through an audio/video system. Furthermore, in Wagner, Ford, and Ford (1986), subjects were not only shown individual scores. They were also shown "group" scores that clearly indicated higher performance levels by groups than individuals. In Troyer and Younts (1997) and Lovaglia and Houser (1996), subjects viewed individual scores on the computer screen, along with text briefly describing the fact that groups outperform individuals. As with other protocol differences, these variations may affect study results.

The comparability benefits of the SES may be even greater if baseline conditions are included. In a baseline condition, correspondence to the SES protocol should be high, with no new manipulations. For instance, in the example involving educational attainment, a condition involving peer interaction (i.e., no differentiation with respect to educational attainment) represents a baseline condition. The baseline condition allows researchers to "calibrate" results to the results of previous research (and formal models, described later). Such a comparison will assist the researcher in fine-tuning the procedures or signal any discrepancies that may threaten the integrity of the experiment and analysis and interpretation of results. Thus, each study in which a new variable of conceptual interest is explored can ideally incorporate a baseline condition that allows the researchers to test the effects of the setting, independent of new manipulations. If each study adheres to the procedures of the SES and includes a baseline condition, then the researcher is provided with a benchmark against which the setting itself can be examined and the effects of the new variable can be more systematically interpreted. In the following section, I discuss two important developments in SCT that facilitate cross-study comparisons.

Two Key Advances in SCT Research

Two developments in SCT are particularly worthy of note: (1) the graph-theoretic representation of status-organizing processes (leading to a formal model of status-organizing processes), and (2) meta-analysis leading to the estimation of parameters in the formal model. First, Berger, Fisek, and Norman (1977) developed a graph-theoretic representation of the status-organizing processes described in SCT. This representation links actors, status characteristics, competency expectations, and task expectations to task outcomes (i.e., performance on a task). In this representation, each relation (i.e., link) between an actor and a component of the graph structure is valenced (i.e., positive or negative). There are three relations in the graph-theoretic representation: possession, rele-

Figure 8.1
Graph-Theoretic Representation of Two Actors of Different States of Educational Attainment Working on a Collective Math Problem

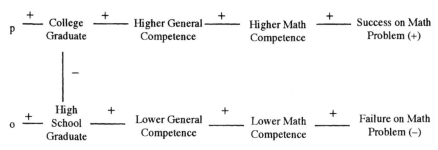

vance, and dimensionality. Possession (indicated by a positive valence) indicates a relation between an actor and the state of a characteristic. Consider a scenario involving two actors working on a mathematics problem, one of whom, p, is a college graduate, and the other, o, a high school graduate. In this example, the actor p is positively linked to the "college graduate" state of the characteristic, educational attainment. Relevance (also indicated by a positive valence) indicates that one component of the graph is expected to imply another component. For instance, the college graduate state of the characteristic educational attainment is linked to a general expectation of higher competence (compared to the state of high school graduate). Dimensionality (indicated by a negative valence) refers to oppositely evaluated states of the same characteristic possessed by actors. As such, the state, of college graduate, held by p of the characteristic educational attainment is negatively linked to the high school graduate state of educational attainment held by o. The sign of a path linking an actor through components to a task outcome is determined by taking the product of the lines linking the components. A positive path corresponds to expectations of achieving success on a task; a negative path corresponds to expectations of not achieving success. Figure 8.1 indicates these relations for this example.

In this example, p has two positive paths to task success, while o has two negative paths to task success (for each there is a direct horizontal path to the outcome, and a path through the dimensionality relation linking college graduate to high school graduate). A second important attribute of a path (aside from its sign) is its length. The length of a path is the number of links between an actor and the task outcome in the path, (represented as $f(i)$), where i represents the path length. In Figure 8.1, p has a horizontal positive path of length four, and a positive path through the dimensionality relation of length five. In contrast, o has a negative horizontal path of length four and a negative path through the dimensionality relation of length five.

Path length corresponds to the strength of an expectation; shorter paths represent stronger expectations, compared to longer paths. In Figure 8.1, p's paths would be represented as $f(4)$ and $f(5)$. We also see that o has two negative paths, which would be represented as $f(4)$ and $f(5)$. Berger, Fisek, and Norman (1977) propose that paths of the same sign be combined in a set, with each additional path added to a set contributing in a decreasing manner (referred to as the "attenuation principle" in SCT). A positive set is referenced as e_x^+, while a negative set is indicated by e_x^- (where x represents the actor). The functional form for e_x^+ and e_x^- is:

$$e_x^+ = [1 - (1 - f(i)) \ldots (1 - f(n))]$$
$$e_x^- = - [1 - (1 - f(i)) \ldots (1 - f(n))]$$

Once each set is calculated for each actor, the two sets are additively aggregated (i.e., e_x; eq $e_x^+ + e_x^-$). The resulting value represents the actor (x's) aggregate expectation for the task situation. The difference between two actors' aggregate expectations for the task situation, $e_p - e_o$, represents the expectation advantage of actor p compared to actor o. The expectation advantage, in turn, directly determines p's power and prestige position in the situation relative to o. Since influence behavior is directly linked to an actor's power and prestige position, the likelihood that p will exercise influence over o corresponds to p's position in the power and prestige order. In a case where two actors, p and o, disagree, the likelihood that p will hold fast to her own position (i.e., "stay") is given by the following function:

$$P(s) = m + q(e_p - e_o)$$

The graph-theoretic representation is amenable to mathematical calculations. If the function corresponding to the path values (i.e., $f(i)$) is specified and m and q are also specified, then researchers can precisely predict the theoretical likelihood that an actor will maintain his or her position after disagreeing with another actor. As noted by Berger, Fisek, and Norman (1977), the parameter m corresponds to status-equal interaction within a particular subpopulation, whereas q captures particular effects of experimental manipulations (e.g., the degree of collective orientation of interactants). This leads to the second important development in SCT, the specification of these model parameters.

Status characteristics researchers (e.g., Berger, Fisek, and Norman 1977; Fisek, Norman, and Nelson-Kilger 1992; Fox and Moore 1979) have conducted meta-analyses of studies that followed the SES protocol. From these analyses, the parameters of the formal model of status and influence (described previously) have been examined. First, Berger, Fisek, and Norman (1977) provide empirical estimates of $f(i)$ for path lengths between two and six.[3] Second, Fisek, Norman, and Nelson-Kilger (1992) use these estimates to generate a functional form for $f(i)$:

$$f(i) = 1 - e^{-2.618(2-i)}$$

Fisek et al. (1992) fit the model to cases from 24 experiments involving 127 experimental conditions that employed the SES to estimate m and q. Their results fit the existing data well and provide an estimate of $m = .637$ for undergraduate subjects in setting where 80 percent of the trials are critical trials. In other words, the likelihood that an actor will stay with his or her own position when faced with a disagreement from another actor of the same status is .637 among college undergraduates. Fisek et al. also found that $q = .106$ for males, and $q = .130$ for females.

Using Parameter Estimates to Explore Recent Results in SCT Research

The Fisek et al. (1992) estimates allow researchers to generate a priori estimates for experimental studies using the SES. The sytematic use of the estimates, however, has not been common in published results of SCT experiments using the SES. An examination of recent research indicates lower P(s) values than those predicted by the Fisek et al. model, as shown in Table 8.1.

Each condition generated lower P(s) values than the Fisek et al. (1992) model predicts, and each varied in how it represented components of the SES protocol. For example, Foschi (1996) provided all instructions for the experiment face-to-face (experimenter and subject). Lovaglia and Houser (1996) as well as Troyer and Younts (1997) issued instructions to the subjects via computer (i.e., they read the instructions on a computer monitor). Houser (1997) provided some instructions via a videotape and some instructions via computer. Furthermore, the actual instructions varied. Foschi, who explored the effects of status variables on standards for performance, could not include the information on prior performance standards without confounding her test of the effects of status on standards. Prior performance standards, however, evoke task orientation and collective orientation. Lovaglia and Houser (1996), Houser (1997), and Troyer and Younts (1997) included information on performance standards, but in the abbreviated text-based form corresponding to the verbal instructions in Moore's (1968) protocol. The studies in Table 8.1 also relied on representing feedback regarding the partner's initial choice on critical trials as "disagreements."

Thus, there are two differences in the protocols described here and those of other research in SCT that may explain the lower-than-predicted P(s) values: (1) the medium through which the experiments were conducted, and (2) the instructions or feedback provided to the subjects. A third interesting source of variation is that these studies correspond to recent research on the effects of status variables, whereas the other studies through which parameters were estimated are older studies. The effects of status characteristics may shift over time, which represents a potentially important theoretical factor in the study of status-organizing processes. I turn now to a discussion of the theoretical implications of these three sources of variation.

Table 8.1

Observed and Estimated P(s) Values for Selected Conditions from Five Recent Experiments Involving SCT Research

Study	Status Characteristic	Peer Interaction	High - Low[a] (p - o)	Low - High[b] (p - o)
		P(S) Values (Flsek et al. (1992) Estimates in Parentheses)		
Foschi (1996)	Gender	.55[c] (.64)	.66 (.68)	.47 (.59)
Lovaglia & Houser (1996)	Year in School	.55[c] (.64)	.59 (.68)	.51 (.59)
Houser A (1997)	Disability	.43 (.64)	.56 (.68)	----[d] (.59)
Houser B (1997)	Disability	.48 (.64)	.58 (.68)	----[d] (.59)
Troyer & Younts (1997)	Year in School	.54[c] (.64)	.60 (.68)	.48 (.59)

Note: Houser A (1997) and Houser B (1997) are two separate experiments reported in Houser (1997). In all studies except Foschi, subjects were female undergraduates. Subjects in Foschi (1996) were male (in the High-Low interaction condition) or female (in the Low-High interaction condition).
[a]High-Low indicates study manipulations led subject to perceive self as higher status than partner.
[b]Low-High indicates study manipulations led subject to perceive self as lower status than partner.
[c]Peer interaction condition was not included; value is estimated from mirror-image conditions.
[d]Condition was not included in study.

MEDIUM, PROTOCOL, TRENDS: THREE SOURCES OF VARIATION

Media and Variation in Recent SCT Research

The potential for media effects should not be taken as a call to abandon the use of computer technologies in experimentation. As noted by Cohen (1988), computers can offer several advantages in experiments. For instance, a computer-mediated experimental setting can reduce experimenter effects by delivering instructions to subjects in a standardized text format. Additionally, subject suspicion regarding the presence of a partner in the SES may be reduced, because the fact that the subject cannot see another actor becomes more plausible in a computer-mediated communication setting. Also, computers can efficiently store data (e.g., the subject's initial and-final choices on a binary-choice task). Moreover, retrieval and analysis of the data is more efficient, as the computer can be programmed to generate data that is readable by statistical analysis programs. Also, human error in the recording and retrieval of subject transactions is reduced, since the computer directly records subject input. In the video-mediated SES, the experimenter manually records the subject's choices on the task and manually designates feedback information for the subject, thus increasing the potential for error.

These advantages suggest why researchers increasingly rely on computers in SCT experiments. To exploit these advantages, Foschi (1996) developed software to administer the binary-choice task in the SES. This software, which was employed in the experiments noted in Table 8.1, has become a technological cornerstone of recent studies. However, the administration of the SES through this alternative medium may affect status-organizing processes.

Theoretical Relevance of Differences in Medium

The medium of administration may affect four factors relevant to status-organizing processes: (1) salience of characteristics, (2) status cues, (3) the collective orientation of actors, and (4) the actors' task orientation. First, actors communicating via computers may be deprived of visual stimuli with respect to one another. Visual cues related to appearance may reinforce a status characteristic (such as sex, age, or race). As such, it is possible that the lack of visual cues in computer-mediated interaction may reduce the salience of a status characteristic that corresponds to observable differences between actors. The traditional video-based context of the SES provides a brief visual introduction of the subject's partner. Although brief, the visual stimulus may increase the salience (and perhaps endurance) of the status differences, particularly when the status characteristic is one that is linked to appearances (e.g., age, sex, race).

Thus, one candidate explanation for the finding of lower $P(s)$ in computer-mediated studies may reflect the effect of the medium on the salience of status characteristics. As a result, the effect of status differences may be lessened. Also, visual cues may operate as status cues. Berger, Webster, Ridgeway, and Rosenholtz (1986) propose that visual nonverbal behaviors (such as eye contact and maintenance of gaze) and paraverbal behaviors (such as voice volume, tone of voice, and frequency of interruptions) operate as cues that provide information regarding an actor's task performance.[4] If status cues are reduced in computer-mediated interaction, we might expect a further reduction in the salience and effect of status differences. If the effect of status differences is lessened, we might expect an interaction that more resembles status-equal interaction. This would suggest that both actors would move toward a $P(s)$ of 0.64, the Fisek et al. (1992) estimate for peer interaction. That is, the $P(s)$ for lower-status actors would increase while the $P(s)$ for higher-status actors would decrease. This logic cannot fully explain the results in Table 8.1, however, since these results indicate that both higher- and lower-status actors' $P(s)$ are lower than the formal model predicts. Nonetheless, the study of how the medium affects the salience of status differences represents a potentially important theoretical and empirical area of research.

The lack of visual representation of a partner in the computer settings may also affect the extent to which actors consider a partner's input (i.e., their collective orientation). Although researchers using both computer-mediated and video-mediated settings commonly assess whether an actor considered the input of a partner (i.e., a scope manipulation check), I am unaware of any systematic assessment of whether the extent of collective orientation is equal across different media. Even though the introduction of the partner is brief in video-based settings, that brief introduction may increase an actor's orientation toward the other.

We might expect that reduced collective orientation would generate an increased propensity to stay with one's own initial response, generating a higher P(s); however, this is inconsistent with the pattern of results in Table 8.1. Both lower- and higher status actors had lower P(s) values than the Fisek et al. (1992) model predicts. The effects of collective orientation may be more complex than simply an intuitive sense that another person's input is important. Instead, collective orientation may provide actors with a point of reference from which they gauge their own behavior. In the absence of that orientation, the sense of the other as a point of reference may be reduced, resulting in a more randomized pattern of response, and hence P(s) values that regress toward .50, for both higher- and lower-status actors.

Task orientation may also be affected by the particular medium. Working via a computer on tasks common to the SES (i.e., contrast sensitivity or meaning insight) may correspond to subjects' experiences with tasks in video games. Therefore, we might expect heightened task orientation in a computer-mediated SES. Task orientation should lead actors to pay closer attention to any information they receive (about the self, partner, or task). This suggests that task orientation might increase the impact of status differentiating information, leading to a larger effect of status on influence outcomes in computer-mediated settings compared to video-based settings. The evidence in Table 8.1 is not consistent with this prediction, however, in that both higher- and lower-status actors had lower P(s) values. Even so, the effects of medium on task orientation represent an important area of theoretical inquiry. My point is that it is both theoretically and empirically important to understand how the interaction medium affects each of these facets of status-organizing processes.

Protocol and Variation in Recent SCT Research

In addition to media differences, the instructions provided to subjects in the computer-mediated studies in Table 8.1 differ from earlier SCT studies (e.g., Moore 1968; Wagner, Ford, and Ford 1986). Earlier studies provided more extensive evidence on the difference between individual and collective task performance. For instance, in Moore's (1968) study, a chart depicting the relation between individual scores and levels of performance provided a constant reminder of the task-related nature of the setting (promoting task orientation). In the video-mediated setting used by Wagner, Ford, and Ford (1986), the depiction of individual scores was followed by a detailed depiction of group scores. These instructions indicated that the groups outperformed the individuals (promoting collective orientation). In contrast, the recent studies noted earlier in this chapter provided briefer summaries of prior scores.

Additionally, the presentation of the contrast sensitivity stimuli is different in the recent computer-mediated studies compare to earlier studies. The Foschi program (e.g., Foschi 1996), used in the studies in Table 8.1, presents the two contrast sensitivity patterns as a configuration of red-and-black squares (video-mediated studies use white-and-black squares). There is little theoretical reason to believe that the squares' color may affect the study results, however. Perhaps a more theoretically relevant feature of these settings is the feedback that the subjects receive. On critical trials, subjects receive a message on their computer indicating that their partner "disagrees" with them. Since the partner presumably makes an initial choice without knowledge of the subject's initial choice, however, the partner cannot "disagree"; the partner can only have a *similar* or *different* initial choice. In the earlier studies, subjects only receive information indicating the partner's initial choice, with no reference to agreement. Consequently, a second candidate explanation for the differences between observed and predicted results in the more recent studies corresponds to differences in the content of instructions or presentation of stimuli.

Theoretical Relevance of Differences in Protocol

Variations in the protocol may affect theoretical components of status-organizing processes. In particular, the protocol components related to individual versus group scores and task feedback may affect both task and collective orientation among subjects. First, the lack of an extended discussion of scores and performance levels in recent, compared to prior, studies may reduce subjects' task orientation, leading then to pay less attention to cues that may enhance performance, including status differences between the subjects and their partners. That is, status differences would become less salient in studies reflecting less discussion on scores and performance. When status differences are less salient, we might expect more peer-like interaction, in which P(s) values regress toward 0.64 for both higher- and lower-status actors. Thus, the reduced evidence regarding the relation between scores and performance in recent experiments may explain depressed P(s) values for higher-, but not lower-, status subjects.

Second, we might also expect an effect of an explicit and detailed comparison between individual and group scores (as in Wagner, Ford, and Ford 1986) on collective orientation. This protocol feature shows that the consideration of another's input improves performance, which should lead subjects to attend more closely to their partner. In the absence of such emphasis (as in more recent studies), collective orientation may be reduced. Following the arguments I offered in the prior section regarding the effects of reduced collective orientation, we would might expect a regression of P(s) values toward more random (0.50) behavior.

Third, the feedback regarding the partner's initial choice may affect the task and collective orientation of subjects. Recent research relied on feedback that informs the subject that the partner "disagrees" on critical trials. It may be that the term "disagree" evokes a strong reaction in subjects, perhaps acting as a status cue and leading both higher- and lower-status subjects to view their partner as more competent than they would in the absence of the feedback. As a result, subjects may alter their initial choice more often than they would otherwise, leading to lower P(s) values.

To summarize, variations in the presentation of performance standards in the SES may affect task and collective orientation. Effects of variation in these scope conditions, in turn, may affect the salience of status differences. Also, the form of feedback regarding a partner's initial choices may have direct effects on status perceptions. The combination of these different variations in the protocol may be complex. Elsewhere, I describe an experiment (95 subjects per condition) designed to examine the effects of each of these variations (Troyer 2001). The results indicated that abbreviating the presentation of performance standards lowers task orientation for both higher- and lower-status actors. However, neither collective orientation nor P(s) were affected. Compared to a condition in which the initial choices of partners were indicated without commentary, conditions in which a "disagreement" statement was added generated lower P(s) values for lower-status actors (but not for higher-status actors). Interestingly, the inclusion of this statement also led to elevated levels of collective orientation for higher-status actors (but it had no effect on task orientation for higher- or lower-status actors). This statement may prime higher-status actors to search for information (thus increasing collective orientation), while also providing a reinforcing status cue for lower-status actors. Indeed, these results suggest that the combination of these factors may be complex, pointing to the value of further research on, and careful attention, to features of the SES.

Attitude Trends and Variation in Recent SCT Research

Finally, it is important to point out that the studies in Table 8.1 were conducted in 1994 or later, whereas the studies from which the Fisek et al. (1992) estimates were derived were conducted in 1987 or earlier and did not include all studies that used the SES protocol. Social attitudes regarding the attributes on which status differences are based may change over time. For instance, a greater proportion of adults in the United States favored equal economic and political rights for women in 1993 compared to 1977 (e.g., Davis and Smith 1993). Thus, sex may have less of an effect as status characteristic. Likewise, social attitudes regarding disability may have undergone change concomitant with legislation regarding disability (i.e., the Americans with Disabilities Act), and as a result, the disability may have less of an effect as a status characteristic.

Attitudinal shifts related to status characteristics can be examined in terms of Berger, Ridgeway, Fisek, and Norman's (1998) theory of legitimation. These researchers argue that the cultural beliefs and reactions of others generate a collectively constructed local reality that determines deference behaviors. If cultural beliefs regarding the status value of a characteristic have changed and there is no mechanism in the setting to reinforce the value of one state of a characteristic compared to another state, then the legitimacy of a power and prestige order based on that characteristic may decline. Under such circumstances, we would expect actors to view the situation as one involving greater status equality.

For the SES, this argument suggests that actors' $P(s)$ values should approach 0.64 (i.e., the formal model's predicted value for peer interaction). As indicated in Table 8.1, however, lower $P(s)$ values resulted for both higher- and lower-status actors. Perhaps, when attitudes shift higher status actors are the first to adjust. It may be less risky for higher-status actors to attempt to debunk a power and prestige order than for lower status actors to engage in behavior that potentially violates norms. In fact, lower-status actors unexpectedly encountering deference from higher-status actors may increase their own deference behaviors. This line of reasoning would begin to address why the downward trend in $P(s)$ values in recent research has occurred for both higher- and lower-status actors but has been greater among higher-status than lower-status actors. It is also consistent with work by Guttentag and Secord (1983), who argue that shifts in sex ratios in the population generate shifts in attitudes and behavior related to gender equality. Although not emphasized by Guttentag and Secord, their logic suggests that men's attitudes and behaviors shift towards equality prior to women's. A generalization of this logic could explain reduced influence behaviors among status-advantaged and -disadvantaged populations whose numbers undergo a shift. Ideally, these arguments could be linked to the legitimacy processes described by Berger et al. (1998).

In summary, there are three candidate explanations that might account for reduced $P(s)$ findings in contemporary research relative to model estimates based on prior research. Differences in the protocol and/or medium through which the SES is administered may represent two sources of the variation. Cultural shifts in status value represents a third candidate explanation. As I have proposed, identifying the source or sources of this variation represents an important contribution to theory and research on status-organizing processes.

CONCLUSION

The arguments in this chapter highlight the contribution that a standardized research protocol lends to theoretical development. Indeed, a standardized experimental setting offers both practicality and efficiency regarding theoretical growth. Yet it is not always possible, nor desirable, to maintain the existing features of a standardized research protocol nor to limit new research to it. Doing so would inhibit theoretical growth. A good example of this is the work I described by Foschi on performance standards (e.g., Foschi and Foddy 1988; Foschi 1996), which requires that a key component of the SES, information on performance standards, be omitted. Thus, features of a standardized research protocol corresponding to a theoretical research program are not unchanging. Yet theoretical development will be more efficient if protocol changes are made incrementally and with attention to existing features of the research protocol (and the rationale behind their inclusion). Moreover, pilot testing of alterations to the protocol and the inclusion of baseline conditions wherever possible will also facilitate the interpretation of results, thereby promoting theoretical growth.

Another suggestion that I have made in this chapter is that researchers attend to the effect that seemingly subtle protocol changes have for the scope conditions of the theory (and resulting effects on outcome variables of interest). Results of the experiment I briefly described (Troyer 2001) suggest that small changes to the protocol may elicit significant and complex effects on social influence and the realization of scope conditions. This has two implications. First, as argued by Foschi (1997), an important theoretical and methodological function of scope conditions is to allow researchers to hold a set of relevant variables constant, while assessing the effect of variables of interest on established processes. If these variables are not held constant, then there may be effects on outcome variables of interest, net of manipulated variables, thereby potentially confounding results. Second, as also argued by Foschi, scope conditions themselves may represent variables of theoretical interest. Therefore, the exploration of factors that impact scope conditions and the effect of scope conditions on outcome variables in SCT research represents an important area for further study.

Finally, my discussion in this chapter points to the importance of exploring how different interaction media may affect status-organizing processes. As new technologies populate both the social landscape and our research methodologies, we can expect to observe new patterns in social interaction. Careful observation of these patterns along with conscientious attention to the development of theory to account for these processes will generate an enhanced understanding of the impact of these technologies. The knowledge gained in understanding how computer technologies might affect social processes serves a dual purpose. First, it informs our interpretation of results of research employing these technologies. Second, it helps us extend our theories to the interpretation of how the social processes are effected by these technologies. As a starting point for exploring these effects, it is important to conscientiously incorporate components of the existing standardized protocol with the use of computer-mediated interaction settings (for an example, see Troyer 2000).

In conclusion, the combination of systematic research, relying on a core set of standardized procedures, and careful, programmatic theorizing together facilitate efficient theoretical development. This combination has long been evident within the expectation states theoretical research program. And it is this combination that has already paved the way for the adoption of new research technologies, such as computer-mediated interaction settings. An incrementally accumulated body of research provides a standard against which each new set of results can be compared. When deviations become apparent, a theory that has been constructed and tested with vigilance provides the machinery for interpreting deviations. The complementary relation between theory growth and a standardized research protocol represents an important key to the advance of social scientific knowledge.

NOTES

1. This chapter is based on a paper presented at the Conference on Theory Development and Theory Testing in Group Processes, Vancouver, British Columbia, Canada, August 1998. Martha Foschi and Jane Sell provided useful comments on the paper, for which I am grateful.

2. The summary of the standardized experimental setting (SES) presented here is drawn primarily from Berger and Zelditch (1977); Cook, Cronkite, and Wagner (1974); and Moore (1968); as well as discussions with Joseph Berger, David G. Wagner, and Murray Webster, Jr. I am grateful for their insights and advice. Of course, any errors or oversights in the presentation are my own.

3. Paths of less than one are not possible since an actor is not herself directly linked to a task outcome, but rather, is linked through possession and relevance to an outcome. Berger, Fisek, and Norman (1977) argue that paths of lengths greater than six do not contribute significant additional information, given the attenuation principle.

4. Research on computer-mediated interaction suggests that there may be proxies for status cues. The fluency and rapidity of text-based communication may indicate the actor's task ability. Also, emoticons (symbolic representations of expression; e.g., MacKinnon 1992) may be status cues. Newer sophisticated computer-mediated interaction systems that permit real-time, nonsequential interaction allow for interruptions. As computer-mediated communication develops, more proxies for status may evolve, suggesting the theoretical importance of studying this medium.

Chapter 9

Using Theory to Guide Empirical Research

Joseph M. Whitmeyer[1]

I begin with the metatheoretical assumption that the philosophy that best characterizes and guides the scientific enterprise is pragmatism (Laudan 1977). Crudely put, it means that the sine qua non of science is usefulness: we evaluate everything according to usefulness and keep what is most useful. Indeed, we practice science itself and the scientific method because they have proved the most useful ways of understanding our world.

"Theory" is our name for the organization of scientific knowledge. We have theory because knowledge is more useful organized than unorganized. I will not go into all the ways theory is useful, but one is relevant here. Namely, having theory enables us to expand scientific knowledge more quickly and effectively. Theory guides empirical research; it tells us what research to do, and what to look for in research we are doing.

This chapter is a look at how that happens, in particular in the area of group processes. Usefulness is its guiding theme. I begin with the necessary preliminary of defining and describing theory. I then group the ways in which theory guides research, or should guide research, into four different categories, in order of increasing engagement with the natural world. I then go more deeply into implications of trying to maximize usefulness by comparing some aspects of theory-guided empirical research in two of the most active research programs in group processes, expectations states and exchange networks.

ON THEORY

Definition and Method

A scientific theory is a body of knowledge concerning a particular set of phenomena that is logically coherent. Often much of the theory follows deductively from a set of core assumptions. Other assumptions, sometimes called the "scope conditions" of the theory (Foschi 1997; Walker and Cohen 1985), state conditions under which the theory holds.

The logical component of a scientific theory is formal and mathematical, or can be made so. Before the advent of computers, logical deduction in science was almost always closed form, meaning that it could be written in the form of a mathematical proof. Computers have made an alternative form of deduction possible, namely through simulation. Being a new technique, there has been some confusion as to the status of simulations and their results—whether they count as theoretical deduction, empirical research and data, or something halfway between. At this point, however, it seems clear they are the former: they are theoretical, mathematical deduction. As physicist Per Bak (1996) says, they are an alternative way of deriving conclusions from assumptions, with some advantages and some disadvantages compared with closed-form mathematical derivation.

In science generally, and in social science in particular, it is useful to construct theory at different levels, according to the size of the unit acting at that level— for example, atom, protein, cell, organ, individual, or collective actor. Theory at a given level is based on models of the units acting at that level. Assumptions going into these *unit models* ultimately must be justifiable, meaning explainable by lower-level, more micro-level models. More generally, theory at different levels must be compatible. However, at a given level it is primarily unit models that are deducible from lower levels. Much else at that level is not; there is emergence (Whitmeyer 1994).

Thus, much sociological theory, and all theory in the area of group processes, is based on models of human actors; that is, assumptions about human individuals. The graph theoretic model in expectation states theory (see Berger et al. 1977), rational choice assumptions underlying theories concerning exchange networks (see, e.g., Bonacich 1998; Lovaglia 1999), extensions of rational choice into the area of trust (see, e.g., Kollock 1993; Yamagishi 1998), Jasso's justice function (see Jasso and Webster 1999), models underlying identity theory (see Stryker and Burke 2000), the control model of affect control theory (see Smith-Lovin and Heise 1988), and models of social influence (see Friedkin and Johnsen 1999) are all conceptions of how individuals produce (usually) behavior, but also beliefs and emotions. Theory development and research, then, are devoted to investigating the consequences and emergent effects of these models in social settings.

Concepts

Although the logical structure of theory is important, its concepts also are crucial. To be useful, concepts must be defined, explicitly or implicitly, and, in fact, should be measurable if possible. Group process theories have been successful in part because they have used precisely defined measurable concepts. Expectation states, network structures, power, social influence, and identity salience, for example, can each be specified numerically in their respective theories, which has facilitated theory development, testing, and further theory development. It may be noted that concepts need not be directly observable or measurable. An example is the concept of "expectation advantage" in expectation states theory, which is numerically specified yet not directly measurable.

It should be noted also that hand-in-hand with a pragmatist approach to science goes a nominalist rather than essentialist approach to concepts. In other words, the name we give to a concept is not very important. What *is* important is the definition, especially the measure for the concept. Concepts will survive and flourish or languish and perish according to how useful they are, irrespective of the name. Definitions and measures can be refined or even replaced when more useful ones are found. Names of concepts are useful as labels, but arguments as to whether some definition is really the right one for some concept are pointless.

THEORY-GUIDED EMPIRICAL RESEARCH

Next I will discuss research guided by theory. Once again, the bottom line is usefulness. When we want to develop theory, we need empirical research that is most useful for theory development. However, we want to develop theory ultimately useful for application to the natural world (Turner 1998), which then leads to empirical research of a different sort—research to evaluate success of the application. To highlight such distinctions, I divide theory-guided empirical research into four categories, according to the degree of involvement in the natural world. They are research testing theory, which tests with as much control as possible theory that is abstracted from the natural world; theory-based discovery, which is research based on theoretical ideas and concepts that leads to new theory; research demonstrating usefulness, which describes, explains, or predicts naturally occurring phenomena; and research being useful, which changes the natural world.

Testing Theory

Testing theory is the archetype of theory-guided empirical research. It is a key element of the Popperian version of theory development, in which falsifiable propositions are deduced, tests are devised for those propositions, and then theory is either rejected, modified, or provisionally accepted, depending whether the tests contradict, partially support, or completely support the predictions (Popper 1935). One especially useful empirical test is a "critical test" in which different theories or versions of a theory make different, empirically distinguishable predictions. If predictions generated by one theory come closer to empirical outcomes than those generated by the others, then usually we will find that theory superior and preferable to the others.

By now, we know from the work of Thomas Kuhn (1970), and many successors that the Popperian picture of science is not complete, at least in the stark terms in which I have presented it. For one thing, no test can be completely definitive and no test can be executed perfectly. Nevertheless, over time if a theory fails repeated empirical tests we lose confidence in it. If another theory repeatedly proves better at prediction of important observations we tend to accept that other theory, at least provisionally.

Another reason why theory testing, and especially theory competition, can be murky and confusing and, ultimately, take many years to resolve is that science is a human social activity, with ample amounts of intrigue, self-interested behavior, alliances, antagonisms, stubbornness, and the like. Thus "critical tests" in fact may be biased, other important test results may be ignored for years, the publication of important results may be suppressed or forced to journals with low visibility, and so forth. Nevertheless, in the long run, the theories and the concepts that do best on empirical tests survive, and the others disappear. In the long run, it is in almost everybody's interest to go with what works best.

Controlled laboratory experiments are the ideal method for testing theory, as situational factors can be controlled to a great extent and other factors can be controlled through the randomization of subjects. The development of most group process theories has involved laboratory experiments, as many of the phenomena that are the subject of group process theories can be studied in the laboratory. For some purposes, where controlled laboratory studies are not as feasible, quasi-experimental methods have been used, such as vignette studies and discussion groups.

Let me give an example. Within the expectation-states research program, Murray Webster and I (Webster and Whitmeyer 1999) took up the theoretical problem of second-order expectations, the effects of what a person (p) believes an interaction partner (o) thinks about p's and o's abilities. A statement such as, "I know you think I'm better at this job than you," expresses second-order expectations. This phenomenon had been investigated previously by Moore (1985) and Troyer and Younts (1997), but our goal was to treat it formally within expectation states theory, adding as few assumptions as possible. Webster and Whitmeyer constructed a mathematical model for the effect of second-order expectations using the graph-theoretic model originally introduced by Berger, Fisek, and Norman (1977), adapting Fisek, Berger, and Norman's (1995) model for evaluations from outside sources (itself based on Webster and Sobieszek's [1974] research on sources), and finally hypothesizing parameter values using a technique suggested by Balkwell (1991). The Webster and Whitmeyer model generates values for expectation states and status advantage, given second-order expectation information and other status characteristics of p and o. Those values are predictions that can be tested, but only indirectly, as expectation states are not directly observable.

The usual testing method for predictions concerning expectation states values is the "standard experiment." After appropriate manipulation, each subject (p) works on a binary task, first making a decision, and then, after hearing that their partner (o) made the opposite decision, choosing between changing, or sticking with, the original decision. On the theoretical, deductive side, researchers use another simple model to turn predictions for p's status advantage into predictions for P(s), the proportion of time the subject p will reject the influence of partner o in the task.

In fact, currently Murray Webster, Lisa Rashotte, and I are running a laboratory study, using the standard experiment, to test the Webster and Whitmeyer (1999) model's predictions. As many factors as possible are controlled. The subjects, all female, are isolated, working in cubicles. They do not meet or interact with their partner but only see her on a closed circuit TV, which actually is a videotape, so that each subject sees the same partner. Before the subjects perform the binary task, status differences are created through the results of a test for a phony ability, "meaning insight." Our study will do more than test our models predictions for P(s) against empirical P(s) values. We have constructed different conditions such that the Fisek, Berger, and Norman (1995) source model generates P(s) predictions differing ordinally from ours. Troyer and Younts's (1997) earlier study of second-order expectations suggests still another ordering of conditions by P(s). Thus, our study will see which model does best at predicting effects of second-order expectations.

Theory-Based Discovery

Some research, accidentally or by design, suggests new theory. It suggests relationships between concepts that we did not suspect, that we vaguely suspected, or that we guessed but did not have solid enough theory to deduce. Many times this occurs through failure or partial failure of a prediction from theory. Sometimes we are actively looking for unknown relationships, using as a guiding premise a statement that variable X is related to variable Y without specifying more about the manner in which they are related. An example might be, "Social class is related to trusting behavior." We can call such research "theory-based discovery"—discovery because we are finding out new, unpredicted empirical relationships, theory-based because theory guides our discovery by giving us the concepts, the factors, that we find are related.

In science generally, perhaps the most common way for theory to advance is through theory-based discovery stemming from the failure or partial failure of predictions. Instances of this have occurred in the study of exchange networks. For example, many theories have predicted that in certain networks, weak actors would receive essentially no reward at all. That does not occur in laboratory exchange networks, which has necessitated modifying the underlying actor model, or at least the recognition that some modification is necessary. Recently, researchers in one of those theories, network exchange theory, have noted that some modification of their theory may be necessary because it does not predict accurate outcomes for some large networks (Walker et al. 2000).

Yamagishi's (1998) research program on trust provides many examples of theory-based discovery due to the failure of predictions. Yamagishi has developed his theory through an extensive series of laboratory experiments, along with some survey research. Frequently, theoretical work has alternated with experimental work in testing new theoretical predictions or ideas, which in turn frequently are the result of failures or unexpected findings in previous experiments. Another common route of theory-based discovery is to probe somewhat vaguely conjectured relationships. For example, the impetus behind Yamagishi's research program on trust was an initial discovery that subjects' level of general trust—measured through a simple questionnaire—was an unexpectedly powerful predictor of the collective outcome in some experimental social dilemmas (Yamagishi and Cook 1993).

This type of theoretically guided empirical research is probably far more prevalent than a survey of published literature would show, for publishing norms give the highest value to research that is presented as theory testing. Therefore when theory-based exploration uncovers a relationship, researchers have an incentive to come up with a post-hoc deductive derivation of the finding and to present the research as a test of deductive theory.

One last example worth mentioning is the fairly recent attempt to combine elements of the expectation states and exchange network research programs. One underlying theoretical idea has been that we know that rewards can affect status (Berger, Fisek, et al. 1985), possibly in the context of exchange networks (Lovaglia 1995). A complementary conjecture, which now has empirical support, is that status affects the value of rewards (Thye 2000). This work suggests an overlap of the domains of the two research programs and the possibility of their fruitful combination.

However, it is worth noting that in science the most useful combination of theories typically involves a *union* of the theories, by going to deeper theoretical principles that imply both theories as well as their intersection (Kaku and Thompson 1995). Thus the scope of the new theory is broader than the scope of its predecessors. So far, theory and research combining expectation states and exchange network theories have concerned the *intersection* of the theories, and thus a narrowing of their scope. I suspect that ultimately we will unite the theories in a broad scope theory that will be able to account for most of the facts explained by the older, separate theories. Nevertheless, that unifying theory also will have to be compatible with current theory-based discovery in the area where those separate theories intersect.

Demonstrating Usefulness

At least three different types of research demonstrate the usefulness of theory. One is collecting data and using them to construct mathematical models of naturally occurring processes. Theory dictates the elements of the model and, often, the basic mathematical structure of both the elements and the model as a whole. Data are then used to estimate the model, that is, determine values of its parameters, and to test the model, against either other models or some sort of null or random model.

The model may be estimated from data collected from natural situations. Often, however, this modeling is easiest if the data used are collected not from natural processes themselves but from abstracted and controlled re-creations of natural processes, such as through vignettes or in the laboratory. An example of such vignette research is Jasso and Webster's (1999) modeling of mechanisms of just earnings based on theoretical work in justice theory (Jasso and Wegener 1997). Two examples of laboratory re-creations of natural occurring processes for modeling purposes are Friedkin and Johnsen's (1999) use of experiments to evaluate their model of network effects on social influence and research, in which I have participated (Skvoretz, Webster, and Whitmeyer 1999), to evaluate the Skvoretz and Fararo (1996b) model of hierarchy formation in task-focused discussion groups.

The artificiality of situations from which data are collected is an asset to modeling, because of the increased control thus provided, and thus the increased precision possible in the model. However, it is important to keep in mind that such models are *descriptive*; their usefulness comes from being descriptive of naturally occurring situations. As a result, they will not be useful unless the artificial research conditions are sufficiently similar to naturally occurring situations. The success of such models at describing the collected data and, ultimately, at describing naturally occurring instances of the phenomena in question demonstrates the usefulness of the theory involved in constructing the models.

Two other types of research that demonstrate the usefulness of theory are research using theory to *explain known outcomes* in natural phenomena and research using theory to *predict unknown outcomes* in natural phenomena. In Murray Webster's and my (Webster and Whitmeyer 2001) recent article on applications of group process theories, the first corresponds to a type 1 application and the second to a type 3 application of theory. Our type 2 is rather an auxiliary to the other types, for it consists of demonstrating that certain features of natural situations indeed correspond to certain theoretical concepts. This justifies and raises our confidence in application to those situations of theories involving those concepts either to explain or predict.

The Webster and Whitmeyer (2001) article on applications describes many examples of type 1 and 3 applications of group process theories. Rather than repeat those examples here, I refer the reader to that article. I should note that we found more type 1 applications than type 3. Clearly, however, type 3 applications—predicting unknown outcomes in natural situations—demonstrate the usefulness of a theory more than type 1 applications—explaining known outcomes. Consequently, ceteris paribus, type 3 applications, are preferable. Another reason to pursue type 3 applications is that when we use theory to predict outcomes in natural situations and then evaluate those predictions we are testing the theory, as in the first category of theory-guided empirical research.

For testing theory, predicting unknown outcomes in natural situations is inferior to methods that offer more control, such as laboratory experiments, when they are possible. Moreover, for group process theories, methods that offer more control typically *are* possible. However, eventually it is probably best to have a mix of controlled tests of theory and type 3 applications, since tests involving prediction of outcomes in natural situations offer the additional benefit of demonstrating usefulness. For example, Cast, Stets, and Burke's (1999) results broadly conform to predictions of our (Webster and Whitmeyer 1999) second-order expectations model. Cast et al. hypothesize and show that self-views of both members of married couples is more heavily influenced by the higher-status person than by the lower-status person. With such research it would be difficult to develop or evaluate a model as precise as ours. However, the Cast et al. study has the advantage of demonstrating the usefulness of work in this area, for it suggests that second-order expectations do matter in natural phenomena.

Moreover, the more established and empirically supported a theory is, the less testing of it in natural situations has to do with actually testing the theory and the more to do with demonstrating its usefulness, that is, showing its applicability to natural situations. In a sense, we need to show that a laboratory setting is not a scope condition for the theory. Ultimately, if a theory is sufficiently well-established and supported, using it to explain or predict some natural phenomenon and then evaluating your success will have little import for either testing or demonstrating the usefulness of the theory. Such use of theory and research is likely only as a step prior to some sort of intervention (discussed in the next subsection). Thus, when Pat the service person uses theory concerning electricity to troubleshoot your dishwasher's problem, Pat is not really testing that theory nor demonstrating its usefulness, for both of those will stand unmarred, even by a total failure on Pat's part. Pat simply hopes—as do you!—that Pat's theoretically based explanation and empirical research to confirm it will help Pat figure out how to fix it.

Being Useful

The last category of theory-guided empirical research is research connected with application of theory that enables the user to get more desired results in natural situations. It is true that being able to predict successfully already is useful. If you can predict outcomes, you can take steps to prepare for those outcomes and take advantage of them. Here, however, I am referring to the proactive use of theory and accompanying research.

This category can be subdivided into two or three types in order of increasing manipulation of natural situations. The first is Webster and Whitmeyer's (2001) fourth type of application, what we call "intervention." The researcher uses theory to design an intervention or alteration of a natural situation and then tests that intervention in an artificial, controlled setting. One practical reason for this research is to ensure that the proposed action has a strong probability of producing the desired affects before it is implemented where it can affect people and lives.

The next type fits under Webster and Whitmeyer's (2001) fifth type of application, called "full engineering," following Turner (1998). Full engineering entails changing a natural situation in order to affect results in some desired way predicted by theory. The research end of this application consists of an evaluation of the degree to which the intervention changed results as predicted. To the degree that desired and designed results are produced, the evaluation demonstrates the theory's usefulness.

Webster and Whitmeyer (2001) found few examples of these kinds of applications and corresponding research. The clearest example was Cohen's use of intervention outside of classrooms (e.g., Cohen 1972), and then full engineering within classrooms (e.g., Cohen, Katz, and Loman 1976; Cohen, Lotan and Leechor 1989), to overcome status inequalities between children.

If the full engineering type of application is carried out on a massive enough scale, it perhaps should be considered yet another type of application, called "social invention" following Whyte (1982). Here, social scientists use theory to design or redesign so many aspects of the social situation that implementation means reconstructing entire social institutions or constructing them for the first time. Thus far, there probably has been no such application of group process theories. This is probably a good thing. Technical difficulties aside, the theoretical hurdles also are considerable. Because, in most natural social settings, a variety of group processes occur, successful social invention will need to use theory that integrates our understanding of all important group processes. I suspect such integration is possible through integration of actor models underlying currently separate theories, but it certainly has not occurred yet.

In any event, once we can and do carry out social invention, its effects will need to be evaluated. Such research will show where the invention—and perhaps the underlying theory—needs improvement. Plus, where the invention proves successful, it will demonstrate the usefulness of the underlying theory.

ON MAXIMIZING USEFULNESS: A COMPARISON OF TWO RESEARCH PROGRAMS

To illustrate and emphasize the importance of the criterion of usefulness in undertaking theory-guided empirical research, I turn now to a deeper comparison of the two group process research programs I know best, expectation states and exchange networks. Over the past few decades, these have been two of the most active research programs as well, making comparison easy and potentially of use.

My comparison centers on how research relates to natural situations. Both research programs have involved extensive laboratory research in plainly artificial settings. For some time, we have known the fallacy of the argument that our experimental settings should resemble situations in the outside, natural world (see Webster and Kervin 1971). The purpose of laboratory studies is to test *theory*, and supported theory is what should be applied to natural situations. The demand that experimental situations look like natural ones is essentially lazy, a demand that we be able to predict or explain by analogy rather than having to learn theory then apply it in order to predict and explain.

However, the legitimate element of that demand is the implicit demand for usefulness. In fact, I suggest that in designing our empirical research, we should try to maximize its usefulness. One implication is that we should test theory in as simple and controlled a situation as possible. That is likely to be most informative about the theory, and thus most useful. Therefore, if we are testing something about individuals, then we should control social aspects of the situation, especially social interaction.

Expectation States

The expectation states research program has primarily used two basic research designs, the "standard experiment" and discussion groups. In the standard experiment, the focus is on individual subjects, ultimately on how much a subject accepts influence, with the social aspect of the setting tightly controlled. The theory tested concerns the expectation states model of the human actor. On the surface, the experimental setting has little resemblance to natural situations. For example, tasks performed in the experimental setting are deliberately unlike any that subjects would have performed before. However, results are likely to be useful, because the situation is simple and the basic features of the phenomenon studied—typically, status differences, with influence possible—are common, in fact ubiquitous, in natural social situations. It is useful to know how humans respond to those features, which is the concern of the theory being tested.

The focus of discussion group research is not individual behavior, but emergent group phenomena such as hierarchy and relative or proportional amounts of performances such as speech acts, interruptions, and so forth. Many different factors, including status characteristics, verbal behaviors, nonverbal behaviors, and bystander observations (Skvoretz and Fararo 1996b; Rashotte and Smith-Lovin 1997), may affect how individuals contribute to creating these emergent phenomena. Moreover they do so in a stochastic, complicated fashion (Skvoretz, Webster, and Whitmeyer 1999). As a result, there is no simpler, more controlled situation in which we could study those phenomena. On the other hand, discussion group research is less appropriate for testing the expectations states model of the individual human actor, simply because more is going on, much of it uncontrolled, and measurement of key variables such as influence is more difficult.

In short, the standard experiment and discussion groups are each appropriate—that is, maximally useful—for constructing theoretical models at their respective levels. Theory at the individual level, predicting acceptance of influence and so forth, is tested most effectively under the controlled conditions of the standard experiment. The *theory* is quite applicable and useful in more natural situations—including discussion groups! The social setting is artificial, but theory being tested only represents the social setting quite abstractly. In discussion group research, theory is concerned with group-level, emergent outcomes. Theory here also is applicable in natural situations, although in a smaller subset of them since scope conditions are less general than for just the actor model.

In fact, it is important to note that models of laboratory discussion groups are useful only because such discussion groups resemble naturally occurring social phenomena. That is, they incorporate the key features, as identified by theory, of those phenomena. A laboratory discussion group is a group of people, previously strangers to each other, focused on a making a collective decision concerning some unfamiliar problem. That is a common occurrence in the natural world. Examples are work groups, committees, task forces, and juries. Thus, theory that we develop concerning laboratory discussion groups is likely to be useful. Suppose, however, we studied some "unnatural" situation—say, how a group of two-year olds (incapable of much collective orientation) accomplishes a collective task such as washing a car or dirty dishes or clothes. Surely, something emergent would happen, which perhaps we *could* model. However, we *would not* model it because such theory would not be useful; this is because the situation resembles no naturally occurring phenomenon.

Exchange Networks

By way of contrast, let us consider the study of exchange networks. This differs from the study of hierarchy formation in discussion groups in two critical ways: the nature of the model of the actor and the nature of the social situation. Let us take the actor model first. Like all group process theories, every recent theory of exchange networks is based on a model of the actor (see Bonacich 1998; Burke 1997; Friedkin 1992; Lovaglia 1999; Molm 1997; Yamaguchi 1996). Different approaches model the actor differently, and to a different degree of formality. However, all models have two features in common. First, they all assume that actors attempt to maximize gain; that is an explicit scope condition for the work. In empirical research, material gain almost always is the primary incentive for subjects to participate. Second, actors follow strategies. Strategies become important when actors are pursuing something and others can affect whether or not they get it. Thus, strategies are likely to be important in exchange theories or possibly control model theories, but less so in expectation states theory or social influence theory.

These two features of actor models underlying exchange network theories have crucial implications. One implication is that, by using the actor models, it is possible to deduce network results without empirical research. Network results are specifically the distribution of gain among network members, or "power," as it typically is labeled. Deduction of results without empirical research is possible because models are simple. A member of an exchange network tries to get the best possible offer—using a very limited number of strategies—and accepts it. There are not several processes to combine nor any uncertainty as to how to combine them. Deduction of results can be done in closed form (e.g., Bonacich 1998; Whitmeyer 2001) or computationally through simulation (Markovsky 1987; Whitmeyer 1999b).

A related implication is that when results from such deduction are tested against empirical results from exchange networks, the crucial part of the theory being tested is the actor model, assumptions made about how the actor produces behavior. Deductions cannot be falsified, for they are logical, inevitably true unless some mistake in logic has been made. For evidence of this point, look at research on exchange networks when predictions do not match empirical outcomes. The explanation is always given in terms of individuals deviating from assumptions. Thus, Molm (1997) notes that her subjects use punishment less than they could, which she explains in part by a desire to avoid retaliation. Others have noted that subjects often prefer no exchange to an exchange lopsided in their partner's favor.

Contrast this to research on discussion groups. In discussion groups, there is too much going on to deduce results without empirical research. One reflection of this is that actor models for discussion groups are complicated (e.g., Skvoretz and Fararo 1996a) and empirical research is necessary to determine the values of key parameters. Moreover, the failure of empirical results to match theoretical predictions may be due to a problem with the actor model but alternatively could be due to underappreciation of some social process.

The maximize-through-strategy actor model has another crucial implication. Unlike actors in many group process theories, actors can do better and worse. The importance of strategy means that skill and thus experience, training, and basic ability can matter. Moreover, theory can be prescriptive as well as descriptive.

For maximizing usefulness of research, this feature of theory is both hindrance and opportunity. It will hinder application of research on exchange networks to natural situations until level of skill, or experience and training, of network members is a variable incorporated in theory or at least in experimental results. This is because application of research findings to natural situations probably requires that both be matched on that variable. The opportunity is that we can use theory backed by empirical research to determine optimal or at least improved strategies, and advise people in natural situations on applying them.

For example, I have suggested an improved strategy for weak actors in strong power networks. In strong power networks, there are large power differences between actors; that is, some actors earn considerably more than others (see Lovaglia 1999). I have suggested that weak actors may maximize their results through abstention strategies, that is, refusing to participate in exchange at regular intervals (Whitmeyer 1997). Experimental results show some signs of partial use of such abstention strategies (see Whitmeyer 1999a). However, whether training or even experience can get weak actors to use them fully when there is no explicit coordination is unknown, since empirical research has yet to be carried out on the question. If training works, then we can apply this knowledge.

Turning to the nature of the social situation, the key point is that scope conditions of experimental exchange networks are matched in few if any natural situations. In experimental exchange networks, subjects cannot leave the network, other subjects cannot join the network, and subjects have no alternative rewarding activity to participating in exchange. These conditions must be considered scope conditions on current theory; they almost certainly affect network outcomes. Yet they rarely, if ever, characterize naturally occurring exchange networks. If we look at subjects themselves, in experimental exchange networks, they never acquire much experience in the experimental exchange network situation and they always are completely untrained. Since there is reason to believe such things matter, this essentially functions as a scope condition on most current theory. Again, it probably is not met in most naturally occurring exchange networks. One last point, not concerning scope conditions, is that for the most commonly studied kind of exchange networks, called "negatively connected" or "exclusionary," it is difficult to find naturally occurring large exchange networks—in fact, exchange networks with more than four actors. Yet negatively connected or exclusionary large networks are a common focus of research.

Therefore, we are left with only two ways in which experimental research on exchange networks can be of much use. First, for small networks, it is an effective way of testing the actor model. Second, in a sort of doubting Thomas effect, experiments show the results that mathematics or logic predicted but that we did not truly believe until we saw it happen.

SUMMARY

Let me sum up by comparing research programs somewhat differently. In the expectation-states research program, the standard experiment, while it appears artificial, in fact is useful. This is because that research is about the model of the human actor—fundamentally about mental states and their conversion into accepting or rejecting influence—and there is no reason to suppose that in that regard, humans would behave differently in the standard experiment than in more natural situations.

By comparison, discussion groups involve a variety of interaction processes. Thus, there is reason to believe that the format and conditions of the situation will affect the outcome. However, here the laboratory situation in fact resembles many natural situations in all scope conditions we think are important. Members are initially strangers to each other; they are task focused—committed to reaching a decision on a given task; they are collectively oriented—trying to reach that decision together. Group members may or may not differ on status characteristics such as race, gender, and credentials, as well as on demonstrated abilities. The task in question does not lie obviously within any group member's area of expertise. Beyond that condition on the task, we have no reason to think the specific task will affect formation of the power and prestige hierarchy. Thus, that artificial characteristic of laboratory discussion groups should not affect their usefulness.

In short, although the standard experiment and discussion groups seem to differ in their artificiality, in fact both strongly resemble natural situations at the level of theory that they are testing. At least they resemble natural situations sufficiently that the burden of proof is on those would claim otherwise. The skeptic needs to prove that people in the natural world process status characteristics differently, or that task-focused discussion groups created in the natural world form hierarchies differently.

Compare this now to research on exchange networks. Once again, when research is testing a model of the human actor—here fundamentally about a preference for gain and strategies for pursuing that preference—there is no reason to suppose that humans would behave in laboratory exchange networks differently than humans in more natural situations. However, when research is testing models of network outcome—the distribution of gain, or "power"—then to ascertain usefulness we have to ask whether important scope conditions of experimental exchange networks sufficiently resemble those found in natural situations. If not, then except for testing the actor model, we must ask how useful exchange network research can be. Even when testing the actor model, we ought to ask whether the experimental exchange network is an optimal design.

CONCLUSION

In this chapter, I have looked at how theory may be, and is, used to guide empirical research, assuming "usefulness" as our fundamental objective. Ultimately, what matters for science and scientific theory is how useful it is at the explanation of, prediction of, and, ultimately, intervention in natural phenomena. Its usefulness in dealing with the natural world justifies our time, the time we make our students spend, and financial support we receive.

Consequently, I looked at four categories of theory-guided empirical research, based on how much the research engages the natural world. The first, testing theories, is often most useful done in a controlled setting detached from the natural world. Ultimately, it will be useful for application if the theory being developed is useful. The second, empirical discovery based on theory, is useful because it advances our knowledge and our development of useful theory. The third category, demonstrating usefulness of theory, begins to make a strong case to skeptical outsiders that our theory is worthwhile, that it can help us—and them. Finally, the fourth category consists of evaluations of proactive uses of theory. Our research confirms (we hope) that theory has been a useful tool for affecting the natural world.

Finally, I also took a deeper, comparative look at empirical research in two research programs, expectation states and exchange networks. I did so for two reasons. Substantively, it sheds light on why the first of those programs has proved more useful in application to the natural world. On the more abstract subject of this chapter—using theory to guide empirical research—the comparison helps clarify how we should choose research to develop theory best, that is, most usefully.

Categorizations such as the one I have presented are not "right" or "wrong," they are only more or less useful. Likely, ultimately the usefulness of theory or empirical research—in the expectation states program, the exchange networks program, or any other—will not be decided by arguments but by whether or not it gets used. However, I believe that we are likely to do better at developing and using theory if we are conscious of how we do it (Opp 1999). I have chosen this way of examining how theory guides empirical research because I think it may be helpful if we are conscious of how our work ultimately is or is not likely to be useful.

NOTE

1. I am grateful to Murray Webster for his helpful comments. This work was supported in part by funds provided by The University of North Carolina at Charlotte and by a grant from the National Science Foundation, #SES-9911135. Direct all correspondence to Joseph M. Whitmeyer, Department of Sociology, UNC–Charlotte, Charlotte, NC 28223. E-mail: jwhitmey@email.uncc.edu.

PART III _____

COMPUTER SIMULATIONS AS MEDIATORS BETWEEN THEORY AND RESEARCH

Axiomatics and Generativity in Theoretical Sociology

Thomas J. Fararo

The aim of this chapter is to show how the axiomatic method may be employed in the construction of theoretical models of social processes. One viewpoint on axiomatization is that it is only a "cleaning up" operation performed on an already existing theory. To be sure, one use of this method does involve clarifying the logical structure of a less formal theory. Such a deployment of the method can give rise to extensive new results through constructive and deductive operations that were absent in the original formulation.[1] But a wider role exists for the axiomatic method, and it is one purpose of this chapter to show, through examples, how the method can be, and has been, used in the context of setting out models for the analysis of social processes.

The first part of the chapter is an introduction to the axiomatic method in sociology, whereas in the second part the aim is to show how this method is used in connection with two types of formal model building. The first type involves the construction of a generating process that accounts for the changes over time in some observables through the postulation of an underlying dynamic process. The second type of model involves the construction of a generative rule system that combines grammatical and process elements, the former as representing the cultural aspect of an institution and the latter as representing the action processes that presuppose this common culture. Both types exhibit the property here termed *generativity*, the capacity of enabling the derivation of instances of a phenomenon to be explained.

AXIOMATICS

Sociological theory consists of a very heterogeneous body of writings created with diverse aims and employing diverse methods. The axiomatic method, within sociology, is a formal means sometimes employed to fulfill the aim to create theories that are scientific in structure and function.[2] However, even among those theorists who are committed to creating scientific theories, the axiomatic method is not usually the preferred means. Rather, theories are stated in a more-or-less formal manner. Hence, *formal theory* is a term sometimes used to denote a type of theorizing in which assumptions and definitions are clearly stated and some effort is made to draw out their logical implications. Sociologists tend to use the term *formal* whenever ideas are set out in some explicit way, especially with defined terms. But this alone does not constitute formal *theory*. For instance, Max Weber's "conceptual exposition" of the action foundations of sociology (Weber 1978 [1921]) is formal in terms of setting out a sequence of definitions, but it is not a formal theory because he is not concerned to derive the logical implications of a set of specified assumptions.

The axiomatic method may be regarded as a rigorous mode of presentation of a formal theory, although the degree of rigor may vary. The basic requirements may be set out as follows (see Fararo 1973, Sect. 4.18).

First, one must clearly specify undefined terms. These are called *primitive terms* of the theory. Second, one must clearly specify a set of unproven statements—in the sense of deductive logic—that employ only the primitive terms (plus any presupposed purely logicomathematical terms, such as *and* and *three*). These unproved or assumed statements may be called the *primitive statements* of the theory, or the *axioms*. The primitive basis of the axiomatic theory consists of the primitive terms and the primitive statements.

The axiomatic system is then a logical elaboration of this primitive basis using two procedures: definition and deduction. First, *defined terms* are formulated by reference only to the primitive terms and, recursively, to previously defined terms. Second, *proved statements* are obtained by deduction from the axioms and the defined terms. Some sort of formal logic is presupposed, providing the rules of inference for the deductive elaboration. For instance, the tautology "Q if P, and P, then Q" will be used but not mentioned, functioning as a logical rule of inference. Again, "x + y = y + x," where x and y are any real numbers, will be used but not mentioned, essentially functioning as a rule of inference. These requirements as to the primitive basis, the logical elaboration in terms of definition and deduction using presupposed rules of inference may be called *syntactical*.

By contrast, the intended meaning of the terms and the axioms and the intended uses of the system as a theory pertain to the *semantics* and *pragmatics* of the axiomatic system, respectively.

First, the axiomatic system is a theory when there is some semantic reference supplied for it, called the *intended interpretation*. For instance, the relational symbol aDb may be said to refer to a social relation of dominance between a and b. Second, the axiomatic system can be regarded as a scientific theory if it functions in the context of fulfilling some goal expected of theories in science, especially explanation, but also the conceptual clarification of ideas.

In the context of theoretical sociology, we are mainly concerned with axiomatic systems that have reference to recognizably sociological entities (including processes) and have some scientific function expected of theories. Thus, an axiomatic theory in sociology has the syntactical form of an axiomatic system supplied with an intended sociological interpretation and addressing some problem requiring a theoretical formulation.

For instance, in syntactical terms, a theorem is *any* logical consequence of the axioms. But in practice—now invoking the semantics and pragmatics of axiomatics—only the most important or useful logical consequences of the axioms are called theorems. Thus, in practice, a *theorem* is a logically derived consequence of the axioms that functions as a theoretical answer to a scientific problem. In fact, a similar informal conception of theorems was widely used in economic theory long before it was subjected to axiomatization (see, for instance, Menger 1996 [1883]). In this informal usage, a theorem is a statement that compactly summarizes the main idea thought be demonstrated by some relatively informal logical argument. Parsons employed this usage of the term in sociological theory, for instance. What Parsons (1968 [1937]) calls the "sociologistic theorem" is the idea that a necessary condition for social action system equilibrium (social order) is a common value system. The "fundamental dynamic theorem of sociology" (Parsons 1951:42) links this idea to a psychological mechanism, namely internalization of those values that are institutionalized in role definitions. If social action systems theory were reconstructed along the lines of axiomatic theory, it might aim to formulate the necessary primitive basis such that these statements might then become theorems in the formal sense. Such an axiomatization of the informal theory would tend to (a) clarify terminology through the necessity of stating primitive and defined terms, (b) explicitly formulate the assumptions of the theory as axioms, and (c) logically derive the Parsonian theorems and perhaps others.

By contrast with the Parsonian or functionalist tradition in sociological theory, its anti-tradition—rational choice theory—has a heritage of theoretical work done in the axiomatic style. For example, the mathematical theory of games— a multiperson form of rational choice theory—produced by von Neumann and Morgenstern (1947) is an axiomatic theory. First, in syntactical terms, the theory takes the form of an axiomatic system. For instance, its primitive terms include *player*, *move*, and *outcome*. Second, in semantic terms, the axiomatic system is supplied with an intended interpretation. It is a theory of the strategic interaction of rational actors. Third, in pragmatic terms, the deductive elaboration is governed by the aim to produce theoretical answers to important problems, for example, theorems deal with the question of the existence of optimal strategies for certain classes of games.

It is useful to regard the axioms of an axiomatic theory as defining an *exact concept*. Thus, *game* is an exact concept defined by the axioms of game theory. Such an exact concept is not a mere replica of the intuitive ideas antecedent to the theory because the axiomatic theory abstracts from the totality of prior usage, retaining what is thought to be useful for its scientific purposes. For instance, the play of a game is included in game theory but its "playfulness," if any, and its enjoyment are excluded. It intends only a rigorous expression of ideas connected with strategic interaction. In this aspect of abstraction, axiomatic theory is not different from scientific theory as a whole.

There is a particular mode of axiomatization that has proved most useful in the social and behavioral sciences because it is linked to the notion of a mathematical model. Logician Patrick Suppes (1957) calls it *axiomatization within set theory*.[3] Logicians have shown that set theory—a set is a collection of elements, called its members—can be taken as the foundation of mathematics, in the sense that any mathematical object can be defined within this theory. Through axiomatization within set theory all prior pure mathematics is available for use in stating the axioms. In addition, the usual rules of inference, as routinely employed in mathematics, may be used as needed. The procedure has two steps. In the first step, we specify the primitive entities as set-theoretical entities. In other words, primitive terms are given an interpretation in terms of set theory and hence mathematics. This means that one can employ such entities as matrices, functions, and the like, all of which are abstract set-theoretic entities. In the second step, the axioms are regarded as constraints on the interrelations of these entities. The axioms are construed as defining a new "set-theoretical predicate." For instance, a collection of mathematical objects (set-theoretical entities) "is a game" if the axioms defining the exact concept of game are satisfied. Thus, "is a game" is a set-theoretical predicate. This procedure or something very much like it, has been used in a variety of theoretical contexts in the social and behavioral sciences, including formal language theory in linguistics, general equilibrium theory in economics, learning theory in psychology and balance theory in social psychology.

Note that, in the pragmatic context of science, either or both definitions and axioms may be modified in adjusting a formal theory to the contexts in which it is employed in science. For instance, balance theory is a body of scientific theory that includes a number of distinct axiomatic systems dealing with signed graphs and their interpersonal interpretation (Cartwright and Harary 1956; Davis 1967).

In *Mathematical Sociology* (Fararo 1973), I explicated an axiomatic approach to theoretical sociology based on synthesizing certain key ideas drawn from the postpositivist literature in the philosophy of science. The viewpoint taken there and in this chapter is that the axiomatic method can function as a working method for creating theoretical models. It is not just a mode of organizing preexisting generalizations or principles. In particular, we can combine the notion that a theory specifies a generative mechanism with the procedure of formulating the description of the mechanism in an axiomatic manner.

GENERATIVITY

There are two basic types of theoretical models that incorporate generativity into their structure. One type has its historical antecedents in classical physics. The focus is on aspects of events in the world, seen as dynamically generated by some underlying process derived within a theoretical framework. The other type has its antecedents in modern theoretical linguistics. It starts with the special character of human action systems relative to other phenomena in the world: the existence of cultural meanings embodied in systems of symbols. The focus is on symbol structures and their constitutive interrelations and on formal models that show how such structures are generated from primitive symbols based on rules. The common element is *generativity*, defined here as the exhibition of instances of the phenomenon to be accounted for by explicit derivation from mechanisms or rules formulated in a model. The following discussion will employ research-based examples to convey the intuitive meaning and significance of this important idea.

The first or "physics" type incorporates generativity in the form I have called *generating processes* (Fararo 1969a, 1969b) and, in another context, "the state space approach" (Fararo 1973: Ch. 8). Observable phenomena are accounted for by treating them as the behavior or "outputs" of a system characterized in terms of various underlying states. These states are changing over time as characterized by model rules, such as a system of differential equations or a transition matrix.

The other type of model incorporates generativity in the form of what I will call *generative rule systems*. Formally, one thinks of a set of explicit rules for combining primitive symbols into symbol structures or strings. These observable symbolic expressions are assigned a structural description in terms of the underlying derivation from the rules.

It is reasonable to think of the second type of generativity as potentially appropriate to the characterization of cultural patterns. Indeed, "structuralism" in at least one of its meanings has exactly this premise as it investigates language, myth, music, art, literature, and so forth (Lane 1970).

Institutions, perhaps the core of social reality from a phenomenological point of view (Berger and Luckmann 1966) are cultural, but also social. In this usage (in agreement with Parsons 1951) an institution is not identified with a collectivity as such. Rather it is the sort of entity that can be embodied in numerous collectivities. For instance, tenure is an institution in the American university system and as such is embodied in numerous universities. It is cultural in that it consists of a kind of design or template. It is social in that it is a design for social action. So understood, institutions include a kind of constant potentiality for process, as stressed elsewhere (Axten and Fararo 1977; Skvoretz, Fararo, and Axten 1980; Fararo and Skvoretz 1984), where it has been proposed that a more "active" representation of them is required, shifting the mode of representation from the type employed in linguistics toward the dynamic type while preserving the symbolic element. An institutionalized design for social action is realized by recurrent processes of social action in the same sense that a symphony is not just a written-down musical score—it is realized in performances as streams of collaboratively generated sounds satisfying certain cultural standards. This is the variant of the second type—which is really a "hybrid" mode of generative model—that will be discussed in this chapter.

In what follows, the two types of generative models will be illustrated from work done with my colleagues, primarily John Skvoretz.

Generating Processes

Scientific explanation is closely connected with the use of dynamic theoretical models. Scientifically accepted dynamic models have the property that necessary consequences within the model, taking the system from its description at any given time (the so-called initial conditions) to its description at a later time, match the corresponding empirical phenomena. But would we not expect different pasts to lead to different futures?

The application of dynamic systems analysis to social systems is complicated by strong historical dependencies that usually exist. These dependencies appear to nullify the idea that from a given initial condition the model's derivation of future conditions will agree with observations. How is this aspect of processes to be dealt with?

The general answer is that the problem is not unique to social systems and that a generic methodology for treating it is available. General theories of the type exhibited in physics usually involve a strategy that builds the property of "state-determination" into the meaning of its theoretical concepts. This idea of *state-determination* is that from an initial state and parametric conditions a unique future state logically follows from model rules. (For a clear exposition of this idea, under the terminology "state-determined system," see Hall and Fagen 1968.) What this means is that theoretical constructs are stipulated by *meaning postulate* (Fararo 1973:422) to satisfy the state-determination property.[4] The observables are distinguished from the state description in terms of such constructs and treated as "outputs" of the system as it responds to various conditions, its "inputs." This involves the formulation of a generating process, specified in terms of the state description, for the observable process. The same state-determination idea holds for probabilistic processes, where the principle of state-determination means that the process of state transitions is *Markovian*.

Note that because the observables are displayed as functions of the state, the process involving the derivation of the over-time behavior of the state of the system also yields the behavior over time of the observables. In this sense, this dynamic state description provides a generating process for the observables. One general interpretation of the function of this sort of construct is that it is positing a memory as part of the structure of the category of systems under investigation. The past leaves its trace in the ever-changing contents of memory. (For a related discussion, see Ashby [1963:115]). Margenau (1950) provides a philosophically and mathematically sophisticated exposition of how theoretical physics uses this approach to formulate its fundamental theoretical models. One important point that he makes is that the principle of causality is closely connected with the introduction of state descriptions. The intuition of an entire complex of conditions—a state description—as the causal background for a later state or aspect of that state is built into this idea. It is reflected in the typical mathematical formalism in theoretical physics: a system of partial or ordinary differential equations.

It should be noted that more is involved than generating over-time paths. The analytical techniques include the study of attractors (generalized equilibrium states), comparative statics, comparative dynamics, and structural stability and catastrophe analysis (Fararo 1989: Ch. 2). The important point is that state description is very much a matter of understanding the dynamics of a system.

I have discussed some aspects of the idea of dynamic models in relation to the concept of state variables as constructs with special reference to the problem of the historical character of observable processes. I use the term *generating process* to summarize this approach. A generating process is a process formulated in terms of states as constructs that are stipulated to satisfy the principle of state-determination. This includes both deterministic and stochastic processes. It is one of two modes of incorporating generativity into theoretical model building. Expectation states theory currently provides some of the best sociological examples of the general logic of generating processes derived within a theoretical framework. The formulations involve dual representation: unobservable expectation states and observable actions.

In the generalized theoretical method that we have termed "E-state structuralism" (Fararo and Skvoretz 1986), the aim is to bridge the two levels of actor/ situation and social system. Logically, the approach combines the expectation state (E-state) construct from expectation states theory and the structure concept employed in social network analysis. The initial application was to the problem of deriving emergent hierarchy in small groups of animals who are initially unacquainted. Put another way, we begin with a form of regularity and ask for a theoretical model that accounts for it. An axiomatic description of a general process is given in which the key mechanism is the "bystander effect," that is, the formation of E-states by a third party based on observation of the encounter of another pair of animals.[5]

In this model the system state is a matrix of relations among all pairs, in which each relation is defined in terms of a conjunction of E-states. This shift to a structural state description, while preserving and generalizing the logic of the expectation states construct, is what justifies calling this procedure "E-state structuralism."

In this sort of theoretical model, the construct "E-state" is a primitive term, as is the behavioral output, which is interpreted as an "attack." The key axioms describe the probability of the formation of E-states, given an attack event, both for the immediate parties to the attack and the bystanders. Another axiom sets out a constraint on attack events, given the current structure of E-states. For instance, if animal A has a deferential E-state toward animal B, then A will never attack B, although B may attack A. Basic parameters are introduced in the axioms, as is typical in probabilistic model building. For example, the by-stander effect is a parameter that is interpretable as the probability that organism C will switch to a dominant E-state with respect to organism B if C observes some organism A successfully attack B.

In this model, it proves useful to first define a key term and then employ it directly in the axioms. Namely, with aE_Hb as a relation interpreted as "animal a in the high expectation state toward b (ready to dominate)" and aE_Lb interpreted as "a is in the low expectation state toward b (ready to defer)," we define:

aDb if and only if aE_Hb and bE_La

and interpret D as the dominance relationship between a pair of animals. This step is taken because, in this first model, the transition to the formation of a dominance relationship where none existed earlier is treated as the event of interest. That is, the event of interest is characterized by the condition: whenever the high state forms for one animal, the corresponding deferential state forms in the other animal as a consequence of some encounter. (This constraint is relaxed in later work reported in Fararo, Skvoretz, and Kosaka [1994].)

Formally, the axioms in the original and simplest dominance structure for-mation model (Fararo and Skvoretz 1986) are:

Axiom 1 (Initial Condition). At t = 0, every pair is in state not = D.

Axiom 2 (E-state Formation). At any t, if a pair is in state not-D and if one member a attacks another b, then aDb forms with probability π.

Axiom 3 (E-state Stability). Once D forms, it is retained: for any a, b and time t, if aDb at t, then aDb at t + 1, no matter what attack event occurs at t.

Axiom 4 (Deference). At any t, if aDb, then b does not attack a at t.

Axiom 5 (Bystander). At any t, given an attack event in which some a attacks some b, then their relationships to any third animal c, called a bystander, may change as follows:

  (i) if a(not-D)c at t, then aDc at t+1 with probability θ

  (ii) if c(not-D)b at t, then cDb at t+1 with probability θ

and events (i) and (ii) are independent and also independent of the event in Axiom 2.

Axiom 6 (Attack Events). At any t, given the constraint of Axiom 4, all potential attacks have the same probability of occurrence.

From these axioms, using tree diagrams, it is shown how, from the dominance relationship matrix at time t, attack events yield a set of possible new matrices, each with a certain probability. The process is a Markov-generating process. (In particular, it is an absorbing Markov chain.) The system states are constructs. The observable attack actions are probabilistically dependent on the system state. But the state changes, depending on whether or not (with certain probability parameters) E-states form in the aftermath of the particular pairwise attack action. In equilibrium, the E-states so constrain which attack actions will take place at all, and those that occur so validate the existing E-states, that no further change occurs. Note that this is exactly the sort of consequence one wants from a construct that functions as if it were an expectation state.

In terms of logical consequences, for most parametric conditions, the probability is nearly unity that the equilibrium is a hierarchy, corresponding to the data on chicken groups. However, the particular model does less well in the generation of the time path to equilibrium, as compared with the data (Fararo and Skvoretz 1988). Additional elaborations of E-state structuralism in application to the formation of dominance structures in animal interactions have been undertaken (Fararo, Skvoretz, and Kosaka 1994). More recently, E-state structuralism has been integrated with other expectation states theoretic developments to treat status and participation in small group interaction (Skvoretz and Fararo 1996b).

In regard to the earlier discussion of axiomatics, it may be noticed that the axiom system, as given above, is not presented as defining a set-theoretical predicate. However, with a little further formalism, this could readily be done (but this is unnecessary for present purposes.) Then we could say that the axioms define a family of models in terms of the exact concept or set-theoretical predicate, "is a simple dominance formation process." The word "simple" points toward the later developments in which the model is made much more complex in order to analyze human groups. In fact, the model is generalized in the sense that it becomes a special case of a far more general axiom system. Hence, there is clear continuity between the simple "animal" model-family and the later "human" model-family. For instance, the first two axioms remain the same and the two parameters π and θ are retained with reference to the same mechanisms, even as additional mechanisms and hence parameters are introduced. In particular, the interaction process is treated in terms of the quantitative notion of expectation advantage now standard in expectation states theory.

In sum, E-state structuralism is a theoretical method involving a combination of the two fundamental features of theoretical method being discussed in this chapter: axiomatics and generativity. The mode of generativity has been the first type, involving state-transitions in time, generating observable events from a postulated generating process on a state space.

Generative Rule Systems

The second mode of generativity involves the idea of generation but within a rather different conceptual framework. The idea here is that the empirical entities treated are essentially symbol structures that are to be logically derived or generated from a finite set of rules specifying legitimate combinations of certain basic symbols.

The basic examples of the pure type of generative rule system model come from formal language theory. A finite set of rules, called a grammar, is such that the rules "generate" an infinite set of symbol strings that count as a particular language. When the language is formal—for example, a computer language—the grammar comes first and the language second in the experience of the model builder. Indeed, in this case the "model builder" is a designer of a language. When the language is natural—for example, English—it comes first and the grammar second in the experience of the model builder. Then there is a theoretical problem with an empirical aspect: account for the language as an infinite totality that is to be generated by a postulated finite set of rules, a grammar. The rules include grammatical constructs as part of a hypothetical generative basis, where such constructs do not occur in the actual linguistic expressions to be generated. And the generation means, "derived from the grammatical rules." Hence, the final steps in the derivation end up replacing all the "unobservable" grammatical constructs with "terminal" symbols, namely, observable symbols employed by the actors who communicate with such symbol strings. The underlying grammatical forms are structural descriptions of the terminal sentences. Sentences that are interrogative forms of declarative sentences are obtained from the structural descriptions of the latter through transformation rules, which map one structural description into another. A similarity to, and a difference from, this type of structuralism and E-state structuralism should be noticed. The common element is the interest in the specification of structures and in the study of transformations of structures. The differentiating element is that E-state structuralism treats transformations as dynamic transitions; grammatical structuralism treats transformations as timeless relations among symbolic structures.

The theoretical focus of the generative rule system approach is given by working within an axiomatic characterization of the entire class of grammatical models (as stated, for instance, by Chomsky and Miller [1963]). The research program is informed by many kinds of philosophical, methodological, and substantive considerations (see, for instance, Chomsky [1965]).

The actor is conceived to have an internalized cultural structure, a grammar, which constitutes a competence held in common with other members of the linguistic community. What the grammatical model explains is not why the actor says *this* rather than *that*, as between various expressions in the language, but rather that the actor *can* say any number—an infinite number—of things. The actor *can* because the actor has the finite basis. As a system in the world, the actor could not literally possess all the sentences of the language, because this infinite set could not be stored in a finite brain. But by holding a generative rule system the actor has the capacity to produce or generate any member of the infinite set. If the grammatical model cannot generate what the actors do in fact say as a regular and accepted practice (subject to idealization), then it fails on empirical grounds in the same way that a dynamic model can fail in terms of empirical predictions. There is a sense, too, in which the path dependency problem is involved in these generative rule systems. In his pioneering work on the subject, *Syntactic Structures* (1957), Chomsky shows that the elementary "Markov type" linguistic model in which the next symbol (e.g., word) in an expression depends only on the current word must be rejected on empirical grounds. In English, for instance, sentences of the forms "if . . . then" and "either . . . or" illustrate the point. Thus, embedding is occurring. The next word depends on words before the current word.

It is such considerations that led to a development within the generative rule system methodology analogous to the shift from the observable to the unobservable construct in the definition of state spaces in the generating process methodology. The key idea is that of recursion involving nonterminal symbols. To specify the language, one uses a recursive procedure to enumerate the infinite set. Thus, a grammar is a finite set of rules that recursively specifies the expressions of the language and assigns a nonterminal structural description to each terminal expression.

It is important to realize that the generative rule system methodology just discussed does not include any model of process. The generativity is with respect to a symbol system conceived as given in the empirical system and to be accounted for in the sense of a hypothesis as to its grammar, which forms its rule basis. What sort of entity can embody both symbolism and process? One of the great intellectual discoveries of this century is the answer to this question in terms of the concept of a program. A program is a system of symbols; it performs a control function, and programs are constructed within formal languages.

A program is a certain type of symbol structure. I will follow Newell and Simon (1972) here in my definitions. A *symbol structure* consists of a set of tokens (or instances or occurrences) of symbols connected by a set of relations. A memory is a component of an information processing system that can store symbol structures. An *information process* is a process that has symbol structures for some of its inputs and outputs. A symbol structure *designates* or *means* an "object"—whatever the type—if there exist information processes that admit the symbol structure as input and either directly affect the object in some way or produce symbol structures as outputs that depend on the object. A *program* is a symbol structure that designates an information process.

Given a set of expressions involving symbol structures that designate events and objects for the given information processing system, it has *knowledge states*. The totality of relevant knowledge states may be termed a knowledge base.

A *production rule* is an "if-then" rule that operates on a knowledge base to produce some new element of the base. A system of production rules functions as a dynamic generator in a space of knowledge states in the same sense that a differential equation system is a dynamic generator in a numerical space. Indeed, in both cases we can speak of a state space. For production systems, the state space is a space of possible knowledge states and the system moves in the space in a goal-oriented way, as in cognitive problem solving. This production system idea exhibits the explicit representation of symbol strings that are employed in the control of the behavior of a system, a kind of symbolic computation. The philosopher Margaret Boden (1980) has interpreted the family of developments in artificial intelligence and cognitive psychology that employ this type of control system approach to be a second type of cybernetics, conceptually distinguished from the "first cybernetics." The key feature of the latter is the negative feedback loop in the context of continuous signals. The application of the first cybernetics in social science reached its analytical high point in the work of Powers (1973). Subsequently, in sociology, Heise (1979) initiated a formal symbolic interactionist research program on its basis.

The second cybernetics involves the "computational" model of mind, a matter of some dispute among philosophers who follow work in artificial intelligence (Searle 1984; Haugeland 1985).

Whatever the merits of this model of mind, from the perspective of the topic of this chapter, what is involved is the treatment of systems that interpret symbol systems as the essence of their processes. In a sense, "positivistic" dynamic analysis (the first mode of generativity) and "idealistic" symbolic analysis (the second mode of generativity) are linked, however inadequately at the present time. The key idea is to take knowledge seriously: real languages are not understood without world knowledge and situational features. The absence of any treatment of knowledge and situation is notable in the generative-transformational models of linguistics. However, at the same time, dynamic processes involving intelligent systems are not understandable without treating their competence with respect to symbolic systems.

This leads us to our next topic, the application of this dynamic variant of generative rule system model building to the key objects found in social reality, institutions. The question is: how will such an application be related to axiomatics?

Earlier it was noted that we follow Berger and Luckmann (1966) in regarding institutions as the hallmark of social reality. Also, we take note of anthropologist Nadel's (1951) point that an institution is a standardized coactivity involving "if" situations. That is, the standardized conduct is contingent upon situational conditions. Building on ideas such as these (see Fararo and Skvoretz [1984] for an extended discussion), a formal approach to institutions was developed that employs the production system approach sketched in what follows.

In analogy to the concept of "unit-act" (Parsons 1968 [1937]) as the foundation unit for discussion of the structure of social action, we have introduced the notion of "unit-institution." It is the most elementary form of social structure realizing the concept of institution. Any actual institution is treated as a complex of interrelated unit-institutions, by hypothesis. The working definition of "institution" is "stable design for social action." This involves typified actors, typified acts, and typified situations, where the typifications are based upon the first-order constructs of the actors (Schutz 1973). For instance, the design relating a bus driver to passengers on a public bus is a unit-institution, a basic unit of a public transportation system in modern societies.

We attempt to model unit-institutions in terms of generative rule systems, where the rules are of two types. One type is analogous to the grammatical type in linguistic theory and a collection of them serves to define a space within which process takes place. For instance, the space will contain types of physical objects, social objects and cultural objects in the institutional setting. For example, the social objects in the typical bus situation are of two types, passenger and driver.

The other type are those that call for an action contingent upon a situation, they are if-then rules. These are the production rules in their institutional interpretation. That is, unlike the corresponding rules in cognitive problem-solving models, which vary with individuals, these are thought to be general rules shared in a given social system. The two types of rules, those defining the entities and those calling for contingent actions, are two types of "social culture," the former "inert" and generative of symbolic structures only, the latter "active" and generative of action in the sense of events. But the two are intertwined in the conception of a unit-institution.

A rough sketch of an axiomatic concept—a set-theoretical predicate—that incorporates these ideas (but only to some extent, to avoid complexity) follows. Again, for the sake of clarity, the intended interpretation is written into the axioms: that is, the set-theoretic or mathematical object is specified, along with its interpretation for institution theory.

Definition. A set-theoretic structure (X, V, A, P, R) is a *unit-institution generator* if and only if:

Axiom 1 (Terminal Symbols). X is a set of terminal symbol structures (types of physical, social and cultural objects in the institutional setting).

Axiom 2 (Nonterminal Symbols). V is a set of nonterminal or variable symbols (whose values are terminal symbols, e.g., <social object> is nonterminal, but <driver> is terminal).

Axiom 3 (Situated Actions). A is a set of actions (that are the typified acts performed in the institutional setting).

Axiom 4 (Production Rules). P is a set of production rules (hence, internally, each such rule maps a symbolic expression denoting a type of situation into an action).

Axiom 5 (Roles). R is a partition of P and an ordering of each part (so that the generative rule system is distributed among acting units in particular embodiments of the institution, e.g., particular organizations, and where the ordering establishes priority among rules).

Particular unit-institution models are constructed entities, comprised of a particular space of symbol structures and a corresponding partitioned and distributed production system, intended to be generative of an observable corpus of activity in an institutional setting. For example, Skvoretz and Fararo (1996a) construct and test such a model for a restaurant setting with its two basic parts, customer and waitperson. The latter's detailed observable activity, in particular, is compared with generated action sequences in an empirical test of the model. The activity is dynamic: a whole series of contingent actions are taken, some repeatedly, some not, but each depending upon the particulars of the immediate situation. Just as in the grammatical models, the actual instances of sentences are generated, so in the restaurant case, the production system generates representations of actual sequences of actions in context, for example, taking of customer orders, delivering orders to the kitchen, serving and the like. Each of these is contingent on situational conditions—involving multiple customers simultaneously—over time. The obvious constraints we recognize in everyday life have to be generated by the production rules (e.g., a bill must not be presented to a customer before an order is taken). When role differentiation is introduced—for instance, between waitperson and cashier—the production system is repartitioned with suitable new productions so that the contingent actions of the differentiated roles are coordinated.

Despite this enormous contingent aspect, a general waitperson production system provides a reasonably good account of this dynamic activity. The point is that the model involves a generative rule system of the "hybrid" type in which what is generated is based on knowledge states that are changing over time, and such that the observed activity is a function of such changing knowledge states.

Having made the point that in theoretical science there have been two types of generative models, the dynamic and the grammatical, I have then focused on a variant of the latter that is very much an example also of the former. It differs from the E-state structuralist models in its enormous detail as to the underlying information processes of institutional actors as they recognize and respond to typified features of their situations. By contrast, the E-state approach is focussed on a subinstitutional level of information processing, as in the determination of expectation advantages of each actor vis-à-vis others. The E-states are not expressed as production rules, although it may be that at some point in the further development of E-state structuralism and of institution theory in its production system form, some convergence of formalisms might occur.

CONCLUSION

This chapter has discussed two central ideas in the contemporary methodology of theoretical science: axiomatics and generativity. The conception of axiomatics set out here stresses it as a working method for the construction and study of theoretical models. And the particular types of models that are strong in explanatory significance possess the property of generativity. Two major types of generative models—dynamic (generative processes) and grammatical (generative rule systems)—were discussed, with a special focus on a hybrid type of model that incorporates a dynamic analysis into a generative rule system approach. Both types can be specified by a set of axioms, thereby making explicit their logical structure and their intended interpretation, as well as opening the way to formal derivations of consequences of the processes specified in the axioms.

NOTES

1. For example, this happened with respect to the development of formal macrostructural theory by John Skvoretz and myself. The initial step included an axiomatic component although the major deductive tool was biased net theory. See Fararo (1989: Part 4) for an overview and references.

2. See Freese and Sell (1980) for an historical and critical discussion of the use of axiomatic method in sociology. Freese (1980a) critically discusses the wider category of formal theorizing, within which axiomatic theories are treated as one type. For more recent analyses of formal theory in sociology, see the papers in Hage (1994). Markovsky (1994) provides a lucid elementary introduction to the structure of formalized theories.

3. See Suppes (1957: Ch. 12) for a convenient early statement of the approach and for an application to stimulus sampling theory see Suppes and Atkinson (1960) and Berger et al. (1962).

4. A complex concept in use may be explicated by setting out postulated conditions that must be satisfied as part of the meaning of that concept. This is what is meant by a meaning postulate. For details, see Fararo (1973: Sect. 4.4) as well as the cited reference to page 422, where a more extended discussion of the Markov property as a meaning postulate for the concept "state of system" is provided.

5. The empirical evidence that this effect is real and is explanatory of the higher than chance probability of hierarchy in chicken groups is to be found in the work of Ivan Chase, who first suggested the mechanism but framed it at the level of observables rather than in the theoretical construct mode adopted here. See, for instance, Chase (1980).

Chapter 11

Some Philosophy of Science Issues in the Use of Complex Computer Simulation Theories

Barbara F. Meeker

In this chapter, I discuss several philosophy of science issues that I have encountered while working on a complex computer simulation theory. By a complex computer simulation theory I mean a research program that uses computer simulations to model processes that may be unobservable and makes mathematical assumptions the consequences of which may be impossible to derive without using computer simulation. Such simulations are increasingly an important part of theory development in sociological research programs (for several examples, see Meeker and Leik 1997). Although they can be extremely useful they present problems of interpretation on which the users do not always agree. The philosophical issues they raise are only beginning to be discussed (see, e.g., Hegselmann, Mueller, and Troitzch 1996). I believe that explicitly recognizing and discussing such issues can be of value to research programs that use complex computer simulation theories, and possibly to other theoretical research programs as well.

First, I will describe some of the results from a research program involving complex computer simulation theory. Then, I will use these results to illustrate some of the dilemmas confronting researchers who use them. I will discuss three categories of philosophical questions, which I have classified as involving domain, measurement, and the nature of mathematical proof.

A COMPUTER SIMULATION EXAMPLE

The computer simulation project from which I take an example began as a joint project with Robert Leik (Leik and Meeker 1995; Meeker and Leik 1997).

This project used computer simulation to explore variants of two models from quite different empirical areas: we developed an additive model based on Richardson's international arms race model (Richardson 1960; see also Huckfeldt, Kohfeld, and Likens 1982) and a model of species competition from population ecology widely known as the Lotka-Voltera model (e.g., Voltera 1931; Lotka 1932). The population ecology model of species competition describes a competition for resources within a space; two species must occupy the same ecological niche, and compete for food. The larger the population of a species, the more it can reproduce, but also, the more it uses up food. Using up food reduces the resources available for the species itself and also for the other species. Thus, being "successful" is self-limiting. A good reference for the basic mathematics of these models is Boyce and Diprima (1986) or other introductory level textbooks on differential equations. These models were quite influential in theory and research in population ecology (Scudo and Zeigler 1978). To adapt this model to human interaction, we assume that human beings monitor and adjust their behavioral output throughout an interaction, using social comparison and seeking equity. I return to a discussion of the assumptions of this model later.

A variety of interesting social phenomena can be theoretically described as interactions within a space with limited resources. In the original Leik and Meeker publications, the simulation is used deductively; that is, different assumptions about the actors, the resources, and the importance of social comparison are incorporated into the simulation, which then predicts the consequences. No comparison was made with actual data. In the present chapter, I move to an inductive use of the simulation, that is, I try to find assumptions to incorporate in the simulation that make it describe a particular observed phenomena.

The Problem: Differentiation of Amount of Talking in Discussion Groups

A feature of social interaction that has been well documented in small group research is that in a face-to-face, task-oriented discussion group, there is almost always an unequal distribution of acts. Beginning in the 1950s with observations of group interaction by Bales and his colleagues (Bales 1950; Bales et al. 1951), this inequality has been shown to have certain regularities. These include:

- The most active group member talks much more than the next most active, with the differences declining more slowly for the third and then fourth most active member, and so on;

- The difference between the most and least active members is greater for larger discussion groups;

- The most talkative person also produces a "profile" of behavior that exceeds the rest of the group in amount of group-directed, organizational behavior; and

- The most talkative person has more influence and prestige and is seen as a group leader (see Bales 1965).

The dominance of interaction by the most active participant holds for a variety of ways of measuring participation. Bales (1950) observed "unit acts," namely, the shortest meaningful act (usually a sentence or short phrase, although the pattern also describes activity measured by number of seconds of talking, by interruptions, by turn taking, and by other ways of defining a unit of activity). Other, more recent research using act-by-act coding systems derived from Bales includes Smith-Lovin and Brody (1989); Robinson and Balkwell (1995); and Johnson (1993).

This pattern of development of a hierarchy of inequality of interaction is not only quite regular, it is also theoretically important, as it has been shown to be associated with hierarchy of influence and leadership within small groups, factors that reflect and reinforce larger societal bases of stratification. These have been extensively investigated by the expectation states and status generalization programs of research (Fisek 1974; see also Berger, Rosenholtz, and Zelditch 1980; Ridgeway and Walker 1995; Meeker 1981).

Mathematical Models of Differentiation

The existence of a regular pattern that is robust under different techniques of measurement and in different settings has intrigued mathematical modelers for many years, and many models have been proposed; one of the earliest appeared in 1952 (Stephan and Mishler 1952) and some of the most recent appeared in 1995 (Robinson and Balkwell) and 1996 (Skvoretz and Fararo 1996a). In the more than forty intervening years, models of this phenomenon have come to include Bales (1965); Chase (1980); Fararo and Skvoretz (1988); Fisek (1974), Fisek, Berger, and Norman (1991); Goetsch and McFarland (1980); Horvath (1964); Kadane and Lewis (1969); Leik (1967); Leik and Meeker (1975:38–52); Skvoretz (1988); Smith-Lovin, Skvoretz, and Hudson (1986).

All of these models have assumed a stochastic process, in which the probability of an individual's initiating or receiving an act changes as the interaction proceeds. The models proposed by Fisek (1974) are based on the assumption that the underlying process involves the differentiation of task performance expectations; that is, that group members come to think some members have more to contribute to the task, and hence grant them more control over talking time. Fararo and Skvoretz (1988) and Skvoretz (1988) focus on the resolution of disagreements between actors and the development of consensus by third parties as to which of two disagreeing actors legitimately should prevail. These models assume (consistent with the expectation states theoretical approach) that differentiation of task performance expectations is contingent on the resolution of disagreements. There are two "competitions"; one of time (only one person can talk at once) and one of influence (only one person's directive task act can prevail at once). When a group is "collectively" oriented, all members are motivated to accept the contribution of the more competent member and reject the contribution of the less competent. Because the collective orientation is crucial to allocation of talking time and directive behavior, norms of "fairness" must be seen to prevail in order to motivate members to continue in the process. The forty years' worth of models mentioned here have had varying success in replicating the observed distributions of inequality and incorporating theoretical propositions about the underlying process.

Differential Equation Models of Competition, Convergence, and Divergence

This project takes a different mathematical approach; this model is *not* stochastic, that is, it assumes no operation of probability in the development of differentiation.

Although the models were originally continuous differential equations models, they have been modified to be discrete time, difference equations models. The simulation is written in the PASCAL programming language and runs on IBM PCs (Leik and Meeker 1995; Meeker and Leik 1997).

The model involves the following basic elements:

- two actors, #1 and #2,
- a series of time points, t = 0, 1, . . . t,
- each actor's "output" at each time point, and
- the assumption that each actor's output is a function of three things: the other actor's previous output; the actor's own previous output; and factors specific to the situation but independent of either one's own or the other's previous level of output.

In a discussion group, the scarce resources are time for talking and limitations on the number of directive acts that can prevail, whereas the self-limiting factor occurs because talkers require responses from listeners. Thus, the more Actor 1 talks, the less Actor 2 can talk in that particular moment. Furthermore, the more Actor 1 has talked, the more he or she is allowed, and motivated, to talk more as the expectations for amount of talking differentiate, thus reducing the time available for Actor 2. However, if one actor does *all* the talking, the group process breaks down, so even a talkative actor must occasionally stop to receive a response. Typically, groups develop norms about sharing the floor, turn taking, and deference (e.g., Manzo 1996).

In words, the output (amount of talking) for each actor at each time point is the sum of the previous output, plus an increment based on the previous output, weighted by the actor's reactivity to the other's output, the actor's self-response to his or her own previous output, and a parameter characteristic of each actor independently, of his or her own or the other's past output. This relationship is expressed in Equations 1.1 and 1.2, which show that each actor's ability to act is decreased by more acts from the other (interference) as well as by his or her own past level.

$$O_{1,t+1} = O_{1,t} + O_{1,t}[- R_1{}^* O_{2,t} - S_1{}^* O_{1,t} + C_1]$$
Eq 1.1

$$O_{2,t+1} = O_{2,t} + O_{2,t} [-R_2 {}^* O_{1,t} - S_2{}^* O_{2,t} + C_2]$$
Eq 1.2

This kind of mathematical system is well known to be very sensitive to the values of the parameters; parameters in one range produce output in which both actors converge on a stable result at asymptote, whereas parameters in another range result in a divergence of the output of the two actors (the Richardson arm's race model has the same feature). In the species competition application, this means that when there is divergence, over time, one species wipes the other out and the stable state is extinction for the losing species.

These ranges are shown in Equations 2.1 and 2.2.

$$R_1 {}^* R_2 < S_1 {}^* S_2$$
Eq 2.1: Convergence

$$R_1 {}^* R_2 > S_1 {}^* S_2$$
Eq 2.2: Divergence

The parameter R expresses the actor's reaction to the past behavior of the other. The parameter S expresses the effect on the actor of the self's past output. The parameter C is a constant; it expresses features of the actor's behavior that are not directly reactive to the other's or his or her own behavior, and can be conceptualized as incorporating individual (personality) differences, role behavior, or situational factors not directly related to own or other's past output.

To adapt this model to human interaction, we take into account that human beings monitor and adjust their behavioral output throughout an interaction. Social comparison and equity are among the most important monitoring and adjusting processes. In the allocation of talking and listening time, norms of fairness must be seen to prevail. In initially homogeneous groups, the standard for fairness is equality. Thus, we assume that in initially homogeneous groups, when rates of participation depart from equality, some change in rate of participation or response will occur. In contrast, in groups that begin with status differences among the members, the standard for fairness is unequal participation; those with more competence or higher status are expected, by the self and others, to talk more. When differences in output are legitimate, we assume that they produce no change in rate of participation or response. This introduces an additional assumption to the model, that the parameters describing response to one's own past output (S) or other's (R), or to individual differences (C), may vary depending on how unequal the rates of contribution have become. They may change with each "round" or time point, as actors constantly compare own output with the output of others.

Calculation of Parameters

To calculate the Reactivity parameter, R, first calculate the proportion of total output coming from #1; this is referred to as "REL," for "relative output of the two actors" (Equation 3).

$$Rel_{i,t} = O_{i,t} / (O_{1,t} + O_{2,t})$$ Eq 3

Then, for the conditions: fixed, up, down, and equal, use the following equations to compute the value of reactivity for the next cycle:

$$R_{i\,t+1} = R_{i,t}$$ Eq 4.1: Fixed

$$R_{i\,t+1} = R_{i,t} + (Rel_{i,t} - 0.5)$$ Eq 4.2: Up

$$R_{i,\,t+1} = R_{i,t} + (0.5 - Rel_{i,t})$$ Eq 4.3: Down

$$R_{i\,t+1} = R_{i,t} + (abs\ [rel_i - rel_j])$$ Eq 4.4: Equal

Equal is the inverse of up when i is ahead of j, and the inverse of down when i is behind. The parameters for self-response and continuity also have possible functions of up, down, and equal. If the parameters do not change, the value is fixed.

Note that reactivity governs the extent to which the *other* actor's output *decreases* this actor's output. If reactivity is 1, one's own output is reduced by exactly the amount of the other's output, whereas if it is 0, the other's output has no effect on one's own output. Thus, an actor trying to maintain equal output should increase reactivity when getting ahead of the other, and decrease it when getting behind. In our model, reactivity would be up. For self-response, denoted S, the parameter governs the extent to which the actor's *own* output *decreases* his or her own output. If self-response is 1, the actor's output is reduced by exactly the amount of his or her own output, whereas if it is 0, one's own previous output has no effect on current output. An actor whose act requires a response (for example, a direction to others, or a question) would increase self-response, as would an actor who wishes to defer to or include others in the discussion.

When all three parameters are fixed, the model is the same as the Lotka-Volterra model. No computer simulation is required to produce predicted outcomes in this case; however, when the assumption that the parameters themselves change as a result of processes during the interaction, no analytic solutions exist and computer simulation is the only way to produce predictions.

To model data from a small task-oriented discussion group that is not initially differentiated, we need a model that predicts an initial phase in which the "lead" in talking alternates between the two actors, followed by a gradual differentiation into stable unequal output, but in which both actors continue to contribute something (that is, neither drops to zero).

Model Applied to Data

This example uses results from a small data set collected a number of years ago as part of a student research project. These data are from a laboratory study of leaderless, four-person problem-solving groups; the subjects were second-semester freshmen, who were initially strangers to each other. The data shown here are from twelve such groups. Their "task" was to solve a series of short problems, such as definitions of words, questions of general knowledge (e.g. "Where is Brazil?"), and explaining analogies (e.g., "What is similar about wood and alcohol?"). The task lasted nineteen minutes and was videotaped.

The dependent variable is number of "organization acts" per person per minute. These are task-oriented statements, questions, or comments that are procedural in nature; for example, "Do we all have the same questions?" or "Shall we all write down the answers?," one subject reading the problems aloud to the others, and suggestions of ways of resolving disagreements ("Let's just put down South America" or "We can't agree; let's go on to the next one"). Task-oriented acts addressed the content of the problems; for example, statements such as "Brazil is in South America" or simple agreements and disagreements were not coded as organization acts. The coding was done by a pair of student assistants, who viewed each tape together and discussed each act until they reached consensus about whether it was an organization act and which group member had produced it.

The data are aggregated so that the person who dominated the number of organization acts is "Person 1" or "top actor" and the other three are aggregated together as "Person 2" or "others." Eight of the twelve groups were all male. One of these eight was differentiated from the beginning; the most active member produced more organization acts than the other three combined in the first minute of interaction and in the following eighteen minutes; the other seven all-male groups became differentiated gradually. Figure 11.1 shows the results.

The pattern shown is a familiar one; initially it is not clear which "actor" is in the lead, and there is a gradual differentiation into a stable pattern of inequality. The question I ask now is: is there a set of assumptions for the more general Leik-Meeker model that will produce a pattern like this? Since these are initially homogeneous groups, I wish to assume that the two actors begin with identical parameters, identical initial output, and the same equations for changes in parameters.

For comparison, the same analysis for the other four groups, which were either all female or mixed gender (two of each), is shown in Figure 11.2. These groups are not so highly differentiated as the all-male groups. For these groups, the top actor did not produce more than the three others combined. However,

Figure 11.1
Average Number of Directive Acts, Eight All-Male Four-Person Groups

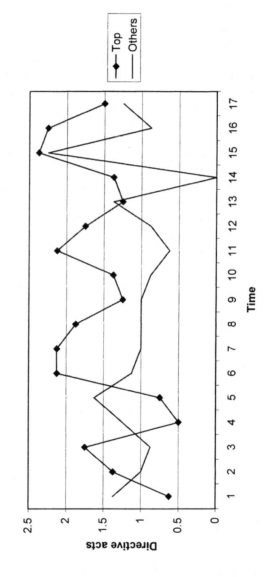

Figure 11.2
Average Number of Directive Acts, Four All-Female or Mixed Sex Four-Person Groups

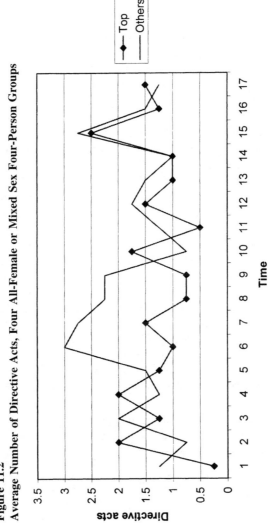

if we consider the "others" as the dominant actor and the "top" actor as producing less, the pattern looks rather similar.

The first step in applying the simulation is to ask whether there is some combination of assumptions for the ways the parameters change (up, down, or equal) that can produce a pattern of initial lack of differentiation followed by gradual stable differentiation, but with both actors continuing to contribute. With three parameters (R, S and C) and four possible assumptions for each (fixed, up, down, and equal), there are a total of 64 combinations. I first tried running all 64 combinations, with initial parameters in a range that would produce divergence if all were left fixed. Only one combination produced what I was looking for; most of the rest either predicted that one actor drops to zero or both escalate rapidly to infinity. A few produce interesting but bizarre patterns that do not look like gradual differentiation. The combination UPUP-DNDN-EQEQ (reactivity up for both actors, self-response down for both, and continuity equal for both) works well; the output of the two actors begins to become differentiated after several trials, and after some instability settles into a stable pattern of differentiated, but nonzero, output.

My initial assumption had been that the third parameter, C, or continuity, would remain fixed. This is because I conceptualized this parameter as reflecting the actor's propensity to contribute, namely, as an individual difference parameter. However, this assumption turned out to produce results that did not look much like the data from actual problem-solving discussion groups. After the systematic comparison of parameter settings just described, I concluded that the protocol equal for the parameter C is appropriate. Unlike the assumptions for the parameters R and S, this is not a theoretically based assumption, rather it should be considered a "result" that requires theoretical interpretation. Such an interpretation might be that as the distribution participation gets farther from equality, the tendency for individual contribution increases.

The second step is to see if initial values of the parameters R, S, and C can be estimated from the data. Parameters were estimated for the eight all-male groups as follows:

First, the equations for calculating output (Eq 1.1 and 1.2) were revised to have the parameters as values to be estimated, and the output as data. This produces the regression equation:

$$Y = R(X_1) + S(X_2) + C,$$

where

X and Y are data calculated from number of organization acts in a two-minute time segment;

$Y_{1, t} = (\text{Output}_{1, t} - \text{Output}_{1, t - 1})/\text{Output}_{1, t}$

$X_1 = \text{Output}_{2,\,t}$

$X_2 = \text{Output}_{1,\,t}.$

An SPSS linear regression program produced estimates of R, S, and C for the eight groups for the first eight minutes. These are aggregated into two-minute time segments. Data are defined as "missing" when there are no organization acts in a particular two-minute time segment; there are 26 nonzero data points (out of 32 possible). This produces estimates of:

$R1 = R2 = .21$

$S1 = S2 = .02$

$C1 = C2 = -.38$

These values are next put into the simulation, along with the assumptions of R being up, S being down, and C being equal. The results are shown in Figures 11.3 and 11.4. Figure 11.3 shows the simulation compared to the eight all-male groups (from Figure 11.1), and Figure 11.4 shows the four other groups (from Figure 11.2). For the four other groups, the positions of "top" and "others" are reversed, that is, I compare the simulated top actor with the other group members and the simulated second actor with the top.

The simulation shows actors beginning equally, dropping slightly, and then beginning to differentiate, with the "top actor" increasing output substantially, but then dropping off but to a higher level than the "other" actors. The real data show this same pattern for the "top," although not so extreme. Before running the simulation it was tempting to attribute this rise and fall in output of the top real actor to changes in the task that required reorganization. However, it seems this may be part of the differentiation process without reference to changes in task demands. This may be considered another possible "result" of the analysis. For a longer time, the simulation predicts that the system will reach an equilibrium in which the top actor produces about 1.4 organization acts per two-minute time segment and the other 3 group members about .58 organization acts per two-minute time segment.

An additional result of the longer simulation is that at equilibrium, the value of reciprocity for the leader is near 1.0, whereas the value for the rest of the group is near 0, suggesting that the emergent leader is paying very close attention to relative contributions, while the rest of the group pays very little.

In addition to a "qualitative" fit, we can assess the "quantitative" fit of the model by calculating a chi-square value for what is expected (the simulation) compared to what was observed (the data). A chi-square comparison of real top actors for the eight all male groups with simulated top actors is 7.7. For the all-male groups, "real others" compared to "simulated second actor" has a chi square of 14. For the other four groups, chi square comparing real others with simulated top is 22.9, and chi square comparing real others with simulated top is 4.7. With 17 degrees of freedom, for three out the four comparisons, the

Figure 11.3
Simulated and Real Actors, Eight All-Male Groups

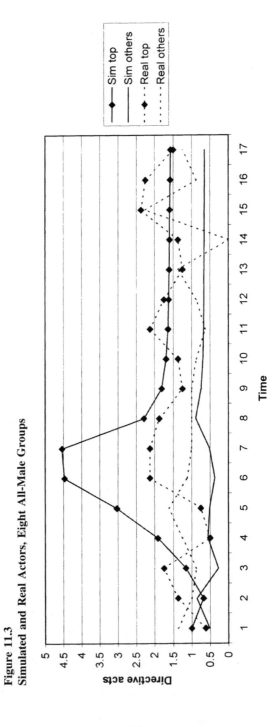

Figure 11.4
Simulated and Real Actors, Four All-Female or Mixed Sex Groups

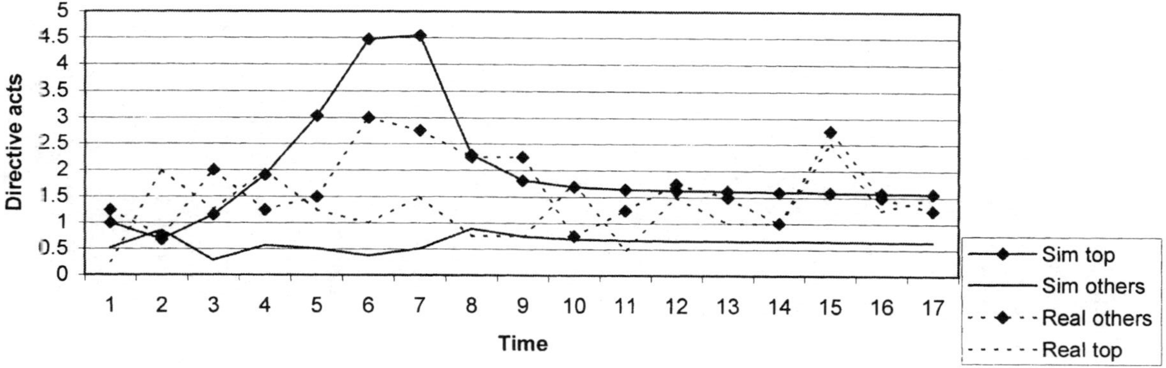

simulation produces data that do not differ by more than chance from the real data.

PHILOSOPHICAL ISSUES

What Are the Conclusions?

We may conclude that the simulation produces a pattern in many respects similar to the phenomenon being modeled. The patterns become most like the phenomenon being modeled, with the additional assumption that social comparison and justice processes modify reactions to one's own and others' acts, and in particular that reactivity (reaction to the other's act) increases as the actor is ahead of the other, that self-response (reaction to one's own act) increases as the actor gets behind the other, and changes based on neither one's own nor others' acts increase as inequality increases in either direction. Furthermore, the results seem to show that by the time the process has stabilized, one actor is paying close attention to reciprocity while the others ignore it.

What is the status of these "results"? They are neither direct empirical tests of propositions, nor are they directly derived from a theory. They have been produced by a computer simulation rather than either by human subjects or mathematical-logical operations (proofs). Furthermore, these results have been produced partly by deduction (following through the consequences of making assumptions) and partly by induction (seeking the form of equations that produces outcomes most similar to those we wish to model). It seems to me that before we can confidently say how to interpret these results and results of other complex computer simulation theories, there are several philosophical questions that need to be addressed. I will discuss especially three: problems of *domain*, of *measurement*, and of *assessment of what constitutes a logical proof*.

Questions about Domain

Domain Question I: Are We All Fish? The *domain* of a scientific theory is the body of phenomena, or items of information about such phenomena, that scientists working in a field recognize as belonging together for purposes of explanation (Shapere 1977). In the history of science, the adequate definition of domain has often been associated with the development of scientific theory (as, for example, the final agreement that different manifestations of electricity, such as lightening and static charges, belong to the same domain, and hence require the same body of theory for explanation). It also may be that some abstract theory must exist for researchers to be able to recognize the underlying similarities of phenomena that may seem quite different.

Definitions of domain are at least partly matters of agreement among researchers, and may of course be targets of political disagreements, turf wars, fashion, prestige, and so on. Some examples in recent sociological research might include the question of whether differences between the behavior of men and women in work groups belong to the domain of gender socialization or of status generalization processes. For a farther-reaching example, consider the debates over sociobiology, which have at the core the question of whether human behavior generally belongs to the domain of phenomena resulting from genetic factors.

In a computer simulation, the domain of the model is completely abstract. Many simulations are developed to model specific social phenomena, for example, collective behavior or mate selection. However, the model, once developed, could easily apply to other phenomena as long as those meet the formal properties of elements of the model (for example, that there are a set of actors, each of whom has a preference for choosing to associate with another actor similar to the self in one or more characteristics). This might, in fact, apply to molecules as well as to human beings.

The Lotka-Volterra model was originally developed to apply to the competition of different species occupying the same ecological niche. Early researchers used data collected from the fishing industry to find applications. In adapting the model to the output of task activities in a small human group, we do not intend to imply that human beings are species of fish. This is a superficial problem of domain, and I am confident that most of my readers are willing to entertain the idea that some abstract properties of species of fish also characterize acts of human beings working on a task. However, it is worth pointing out that as the model applies to both, it cannot quite be called a theory of task acts (or of species of fish).

How do human beings differ from other species? One way is the human propensity to detect and act on emergent features of their social settings (see for example, Gilbert 1996). This requires that simulations of human behavior have complex feedback loops reflecting perception of and attempts to modify the results of previous cycles. In this model, the processes of social comparison and equity are incorporated into our simulation. Most social psychologists would agree that social comparison and equity are fundamental interpersonal processes. However, as I worked on actually incorporating these factors into the model, I realized that theory is ambiguous about precisely how they might work. On the one hand, being behind in a comparison is energizing through a sense of inequity; on the other hand, being ahead may be energizing through an increased level of aspiration.

To return to the question of domain, and making it clear that we are dealing with human behavior, what does characterize the domain of this model? The label *competition* deceived us initially; we had been working with simulations of these processes for some time before we realized how they could describe cooperative settings such as collectively oriented task groups. The abstract properties of species of fish in an ecological niche and task acts in a discussion group are that they occur in a space and time in which a growth process is limited by constraints imposed by one's own and the other's previous productivity. In collectively oriented task groups, these constraints occur *especially* when participants are cooperatively motivated (because they want to pay attention to what others say, and to maintain reciprocity). Thus, the domain may more properly be described as mutual interdependency than competition.

When we look at it this way, we may find other examples of social phenomena that can be modeled in this way. One example is the interdependence of task and affective processes in groups. Another example is allocation of resources within organizations that have multiple purposes or clienteles (as illustrated by debates about the balance between graduate and undergraduate education in contemporary universities). One of the benefits of using complex computer simulation theories is that it encourages us to consider the abstract properties of the phenomena we model.

Conclusion 1. Developers of complex computer simulation models should be aware that they may have models that describe phenomena normally considered to be quite different from the ones they began with. Moreover, the common habit of naming theoretical simulations after a very specific phenomenon may not be the best way to label complex computer simulation models.

Domain Question II: Are We Chaotic Yet? This model shows how very small differences in reaction to own or others' past behavior can result in large differences in outcome: equality vs. differentiation (or even extinction of one actor). Also, both extreme stability and extreme instability can be outcomes of the same equations with only small variations in parameter values or starting conditions. These are the results, however, and not the defining characteristics of items within the domain of the model. That is, it is a model of interdependency of growth processes, *not* of stability or instability, of differentiation or equality.

Mathematical processes such as this one, which are non-linear, go through many iterations of a simple deterministic process, and have dramatically different outcomes for small differences in starting values are the basis of "chaos" models in mathematics. Such models are not really new, as processes with "sensitivity to initial conditions" were known long before chaos theory was developed. However, chaos and the notion of nonlinear dynamics have become very faddish lately and social science "applications" often begin with the assumption that such models have as their domain processes with unpredictable or surprising outcomes, rapid change, instability, and so on. This is not true, nor is it true that such models release the researcher from the constraints of mathematical equations. Nonlinear processes have much promise for sociological theories, and many require complex computer simulation theories. However, we need to avoid the mistake of defining their domain by (some) of their outcomes.

Conclusion 2. The domain of a complex computer simulation should be defined by items that meet the assumptions of the equations, not by the possible outcomes of the simulation.

Domain Question III: Determinism and Choice. The equations of this model are deterministic, not probabilistic. This is quite contrary to most social science computer simulations, which almost universally rely on a random device to move from one state, step, or trial to the next. Is human behavior is inherently probabilistic and hence unsuitable for a deterministic model? In fact, we have used probabilistic models in both the estimation of parameters and assessment of fit for our model, recognizing that in its application to real-world observations, errors will occur.

A philosophical objection to deterministic models is that they do not allow for human variability or choice. Many social scientists find it offensive to violate the assumption of individuals' uniqueness and capacity for choice. As regards variability between humans, we can develop a different set of parameters for each actor, thereby describing many different actors and possibly explaining why different individuals have such different outcomes from what seem to be similar situations. Because small differences in parameters or starting values can make large differences in outcomes, we actually are prepared to acknowledge and describe individual differences more fully than a stochastic model that deals with individual differences by assigning everyone a single probability of action.

The question of choice is trickier. We do take into account the fact that human beings monitor and adjust their behavioral output throughout an interaction, through processes of social comparison and equity. That is, the actors in our model are not passive, but active, in changing the situation. However, it is true that, once in a particular setting, the outcome for a particular pair of actors will always be the same. We need to run each simulation only once, because with a given set of parameters and equations, the outcome will never vary for that pair of actors. If we need to predict variations in outcome, we will need to introduce different parameters or change the equations. Thus, "choice," if one needs it philosophically, comes in the setting of parameters and equations rather than during the process.

One benefit of considering a complex computer simulation theory that allow us to predict variability of behavior and of outcome without a stochastic assumption is that it points out that the concept of choice is often poorly defined theoretically. Including the equivalent of a coin flip as the underlying mechanism in human behavior may be only a way of admitting that the processes are not well understood.

Conclusion 3. In deciding whether a given social phenomenon belongs only to the domain of probabilistic models, one should separate the issue of wanting to describe variability from the issue of wanting a theory based on individual choice.

Measurement Questions

Simulating is believing—unobservable inputs and outcomes. Measurement problems concern the procedures by which observable events or objects are put into a relationship with an abstract classification system. Commonly, measurement questions concern whether the abstract classification can use the real number system (issues of level of measurement) and how many objects are misclassified (issues of reliability, validity, and precision). Sociologists are accustomed to claiming to have measured objects that they have not actually observed. This includes things that are observable but for which we use indirect data (as in self-reports of past behavior) and things that are inherently unobservable (for example, attitudes or self-esteem). There continue to be lively debates about the accuracy of indirect measurement, but decades of systematic work have produced at least some agreement about what these measurements mean and how to interpret results based on them.

Complex computer simulation theories, in contrast, have as yet little systematic work on these issues. Because one of the benefits of complex computer simulation theories is that we can examine different theoretical versions of processes that we cannot actually observe, it seems important to engage in discussion of measurement questions involving them.

In the previous example, some parts of the simulation are observable (number of task acts per unit of time). Moreover, some parts might conceivably be observed or manipulated (for example, the parameter S, representing the amount by which actor's productivity is decreased by own past productivity might be manipulated by increasing the fatigue experienced by the actor). The assumptions about social comparison are more difficult; although social comparison, reciprocity, and judgements of fairness are widely accepted as important processes in human behavior, and we assume these things are happening, either consciously or unconsciously, in people's minds as they interact, direct observation techniques do not exist. Thus, there is all the more reason we should try out different assumptions about how these processes develop using computer simulations. The problem is, how do we interpret the results? How do we make the reverse measurement, from objects and events produced by the simulation to objects or events in the real world? Here are some of the results that might be interpreted.

1. Need for the modification of parameters assumptions: when we simply assume that the parameters R, S, and C are constant (the original species competition model), the results do not resemble the process we want to model; differentiation occurs, but gradually and consistently from the first trial. We wanted to model a process that shows fluctuation of leadership at the beginning and then differentiates. The addition of the process of changing parameter values does produce this pattern. This is reassuringly like the usual theory construction reasoning; a theory including an assumption explains some observable phenomenon and without it does not, which we accept as contributing to the confirmation status of the assumption. Some other results are not so easily assimilated into this framework.

2. Values of parameters as estimated for starting values: we estimated values from the first few trials of a data set. The value of S for example may be interpreted as satiation, fatigue, increasing task difficulty, a personality trait, a gender characteristic, or some sort of learning process, among other interpretations. Unless we know what S "measures," we will not know how to interpret

our results if we should find, for example, that groups of women have different values for S than groups of men,

It seems that what is needed is systematic validation research, comparable to the research that goes into the development of a scale to measure attitudes, values, or self esteem. That is, we need to have parameters estimated from various types of groups, and various types of acts, that are already known to differ in specific ways. After this, we would know more about what the values of the parameters "mean" and how to interpret the results of simulations using different parameter starting values. This would be an expensive research project requiring collection and analysis of new data or reanalysis of data from existing archives.

3. Values of R at equilibrium near 1 for leader and near 0 for the rest of the group: This seems to suggest that the differentiation of observable acts into high actor and low actor is associated with an additional unobservable differentiation of reaction to output of others into high and low reciprocators. I am not sure that this result makes any sociological sense at all; if it does, it is a rather surprising and interesting result, that group leaders pay attention to reciprocity while followers ignore it. There does not seem to be any good way to observe this directly. It is possible that the simulation should be set up so that values of R remain within some range (this could be done easily) but since we do not have a precise meaning for what real phenomenon R measures, it is hard to know whether to place this additional constraint on the model.

Conclusion 4. Adequate interpretation of results of complex computer simulation theories requires attention to problems of measurement, possibly modeled on validation studies of indirect indicators of other unobservable social or psychological phenomena.

Questions about Simulation and Proof

What Is Mathematics, Really? My final set of considerations or dilemmas concerns the relationship between results obtained by computer simulation and those obtained by the traditional mathematical methods of rigorous logical proof. It is a usual supposition that a theory has (at least) two components, a logical component consisting of definitions, axioms, equations, derivations, and so forth and an empirical component consisting of observations that can be compared with predictions derived from the logical component. Each component can be "true" in its own terms: the logical component, by standards of logical consistency, and the empirical, by standards of data collection and analysis. The virtue of rigorous mathematical proof applied to the logical component is that if the results of empirical observation do not correspond with predictions, we know we need to revise one or more of the theoretical assumptions. If the logical component is not rigorously developed, we are not sure where to start if we need to revise.

When we depend on complex computer simulation theories to develop the logical consequences of assumptions, however, we lose some of the virtue of mathematical proof. Some sets of assumptions, such as the ones in the example I have been discussing, cannot be developed by mathematical means alone and must rely on computing. In some areas of mathematics, especially in fields such as chaos and dynamical systems, computers are now used to examine the implications of mathematical assumptions because traditional methods of rigorous logical proof are not available. However, this is controversial among mathematicians at the moment (see for example, Hersh [1997:52–57]; I have, incidentally, borrowed the title of Hersh's book *What Is Mathematics Really?* for the subtitle of this section).

Complex computer simulation theories, then, are a kind of mathematical model but not with the same logical status as more traditional mathematical models. For example, in our model we may note that although we might run our simulation for 1,000 cycles (and we could expand it to run more) and find no change after cycle 150, we cannot say with absolute certainty that the process has stabilized; we do not know whether it might begin to change again after cycle 10,000 or 100,000. We have not given a logical proof that the process is at equilibrium.

Conclusion 5. In developing complex computer simulation theories we need to keep in mind that although they are mathematical models they do not have the same status of rigorous logical proof as more traditional mathematical models.

DISCUSSION AND CONCLUSIONS

The issues I have raised here are philosophically matters of epistemology, that is, the question of how we know what we know. There are three general criteria for claiming that we "know" something: the logical (based on our own reasoning); the empirical (based on our own sensations and perceptions), and the social (based on confidence in the reasoning or observations of others or on social construction processes). A growing theoretical research program mixes elements of all three criteria, and philosophy of science tries to provide guidelines for balancing and integrating them. It is my claim in this chapter that complex computer simulation theories upset the balance among the logical, empirical, and social bases of knowing and require rethinking and, possibly, new answers to some traditional questions.

Chapter 12

Artificial Societies: Laboratories for Theoretical Research

Michael W. Macy and Walter Luke

Mathematical models based on broadly applicable covering laws provide little leverage on social processes, which are rarely well behaved. Agent-based computational models offer a promising "bottom-up" alternative. Although developed in the natural and life sciences, these models are now being applied to social processes in which patterns of interaction suddenly and dramatically change for no apparent reason, as happens in revolutions, market crashes, fads, feeding frenzies, and other cascades. We survey leading sociological applications, including neighborhood segregation, cultural diffusion, and the evolution of cooperation. Concerns about external validity echo those regarding laboratory methods in social psychology. These "artificial societies" simulate, not the "real world," but the controlled environment of the laboratory. They generate hypotheses that can then be empirically tested in the lab and in the field. We conclude by noting that agent-based modeling transcends traditional disciplinary boundaries and defies classification as micro or macro, predictive or interpretive. We see in this method the possibility of a new, generative social science based on experimental methods of theoretical research.

THE SEARCH FOR LAWFUL REGULARITY

The world we encounter is alive with phenomena so richly complex and intricately ordered that it is difficult to comprehend their origin except in the language of mysticism and supernatural design. We marvel at the ability of social insects to maintain elaborate but leaderless social structures. We witness the engineering masterpiece that is the eye and wonder how it could be the creation of a blind watchmaker (Dawkins 1986). We are awed by our own capacity to understand insect society and vision using a small organ made up of trillions of switch-like neurons. Surely there is something more—some intelligent and purposive wizard behind the screen—who is ultimately responsible.

Such complexities inspire metaphysical attributions to the work of "hidden hands," such as the "secret art" that Immanuel Kant (1981:87) believed God invested in nature "so as to enable it to fashion itself out of chaos into a perfect world system." How can there be design without a designer (Paley 1802)? How does the extraordinary complexity of living organisms arise without the intelligence of a supernatural architect?

The triumph of Newtonian physics redirected the search for nature's secrets from metaphysical to physical law. Newton claimed that the world we see is but the manifestation of the behavior of elementary particles guided by a simple set of mathematical equations. The explanatory power of Newton's system established itself as an archetype for scientific endeavor (Coveney and Highfield 1995:23; Harvey 1990:252). In the philosophy of science, this search for a single broadly applicable organizing principle came to be known as the "covering law" model (Hempel 1942). Observed phenomena are explained by showing how they can be mathematically derived from one or more general rules and a set of initial conditions. To explain a natural phenomenon, one must uncover the precise laws by which its constituent parts behave and derive from these a model of the entire system, using the deductive-nomological schema (Coveney and Highfield 1995:11–12). Thus, astronomers came to understand the clockwork motion of the solar system in terms of a neatly defined gravitational force. Similarly, through knowledge of the properties of individual elements, chemists were armed with the building blocks for the systematic discovery of new compounds and reactions.

In contemporary physics, the relentless search for yet more elementary forces and fundamental laws has culminated in the hunt for a "final theory," from which all phenomena can ultimately be derived (Weinberg 1994). Its discovery might well be announced with the proclamation, "God is dead; long live the covering law!"

Meanwhile, the dazzling successes in the natural sciences inspired early efforts to build a parallel "science of society." Borrowing much of the reasoning and conceptual framework of Newtonian mechanics, classical social theorists sought to discover the laws of motion underlying social life. For Karl Marx, it was the contradiction between the forces and relations of production (Marx and Engels 1985 [1888]). For Herbert Spencer it was Lamarckian evolution (Spencer 1902 [1862]). Auguste Comte saw history as a movement from mystical to positivistic reasoning, which would culminate in a world where "sociological priests" would disseminate scientifically correct views throughout society (Ashley and Orenstein 1995:69–102). In searching for "laws of motion" and "driving forces," early sociologists sought to comprehend the social world in much the same way that the physicist understood the clockwork of natural order.

This early optimism was quickly exhausted. The important exception was economics, where the deductive-nomological method offered impressive leverage on the regularities of market equilibrium. These successes continue to inspire sociological applications of models based on elementary principles of rational choice (Coleman 1990) and self-interested social exchange (Homans 1974; Willer 1999). Elsewhere, however, efforts to predict historical development were frustrated by the relentless idiosyncrasies of social life. Eventually, postmodernists came to reject the possibility of a science of society, turning instead to the humanities as the source of more useful and fruitful interpretative methods (Derrida 1991). Others abandoned the search for fundamental causal mechanisms in favor of middle-range theories limited to the identification of covariance structures that underlie sets of observations (Merton 1968). Despite intense conflict between interpretive and predictive approaches to explanation, the so-called "qualitative" and "quantitative" camps agreed that a physics-like science of society was impossible. Social life, it seems, is just not very well behaved.

THE ENIGMA OF COMPLEXITY

But no sooner had a consensus emerged in rejection of the idea of "social physics," something remarkable happened. Scientists began to recognize that physical, chemical, and biological processes are not always all that well behaved either. Turbulence in fluids, the motion of the jet stream, insect foraging, and chemicals in the Belousov-Zhabotinski reaction display the same seemingly idiosyncratic tendencies that sociologists take for granted in the study of social life. The apparent randomness in these dynamical systems could not be captured by a simple and broadly applicable general model.

Fortunately, researchers working on these problems chose not to conclude that they were unsolvable and look for something easier to explain. Instead, they abandoned the covering law approach and turned instead to another possibility: What if highly complex and seemingly random global patterns can be produced by very simple deterministic rules of local interaction?

Consider a flock of geese flying in tight formation. Collectively, they form the image of a giant delta-shaped bird that moves as purposively as if it were a single organism. Yet the flock has no "group mind," nor is there a "leader bird" choreographing the formation (Resnick 1997). Rather, each bird reacts to the movement of its immediate neighbors who in turn react to it. The result is the graceful dance-like movement of the flock whose hypnotic rhythm is clearly patterned, yet also highly nonlinear.

The emergent formation shows how highly complex patterns can self-organize in unexpectedly elegant ways in the absence of global coordination. There are parallels across the sciences, cases in which surprising (and often quite exquisite) global patterns emerge from interactions among relatively simple but interdependent processes, in the absence of central coordination, direction, or planning. From geese flying south to neurons in a vast synaptic network, simple and easily predictable local interactions generate highly intricate—and even inscrutable—global patterns.

These processes are examples of complex systems—dynamic, nonlinear, path-dependent, stochastic global structures that emerge out of a web of local inter-actions. This process of "emergence," where local interactions give rise to structure at the global level, is a defining feature of complex systems and is ultimately responsible for the self-organization we find beneath the apparent chaos of nature (Coveney and Highfield 1995:7). Complexity theorists have identified numerous examples of emergence in nature, such as spiral wave pat-terns produced by molecules with very restricted ranges of motion, or magnetism that emerges from atoms that have no magnetic properties (Resnick 1997). One of the most compelling examples is the emergence of consciousness from tril-lions of neural cells in the brain, none of which is individually conscious. Or consider life itself that emerges from nonliving matter.

"BOIDS" AND BOTTOM-UP EPISTEMOLOGY

From Kant to Paley, intuition tells us that where there is design, there must be a designer. The emergent design of complex systems is an antidote to the attribution of supernatural intelligence. Biological evolution is a celebrated ex-ample of the emergence of unintended "design" in complex systems and is nicely captured by Dawkins' (1986) metaphor of the "blind watchmaker." A very sim-ple process of cumulative selection (building on partial solutions) produces de-signs that far exceed the capabilities of human engineering.

The difficulty believing that such a talented watchmaker might be blind is matched by the incredibility that such complex global structures might emerge from local interactions that are not only clueless but also relatively simple. For example, birds are able to maintain cohesive flight formations without the benefit of leadership or a complex behavioral repertoire, as has been demonstrated using computer programs to simulate their interactions. Craig Reynolds (1987) mod-eled the movement of a population of artificial "boids" based on three simple rules:

- Separation: Do not get too close to any object, including other boids.
- Alignment: Try to match the speed and direction of nearby boids.
- Cohesion: Head for the perceived center of mass of the boids in your immediate neigh-borhood.

Reynold's approach is called "agent-based modeling." Had Reynolds chosen instead to write a top-down program for the global behavior of the flock that captured its elegant dance-like quality, the task would have been vastly more difficult because of the extreme nonlinearity in its movement. By choosing in-stead to model the flock from the bottom up, based on agent-level interaction, he was able to produce highly realistic flight formations using very simple rules that imposed relatively small computational demands.[1]

The startling implication is that we may be able to explain highly non-linear and path-dependent processes even though we cannot predict their outcomes. Rather than trying to model the process at the global level, we should see if we can identify local mechanisms whose behavior is relatively simple and predictable. For example, someday, cognitive scientists may be able to explain consciousness, not by understanding the "mind" as a holistic system, but by producing consciousness on a very powerful computer using a type of artificial neural network.[2]

The epistemological principle was most clearly enunciated by Joshua Epstein and Robert Axtell. "What constitutes an explanation of an observed phenomenon? Perhaps one day people will interpret the question, 'Can you explain it?' as asking 'Can you *grow* it?' " (Epstein and Axtell 1996:20).

LOOKING AT SOCIETY FROM THE BOTTOM UP

This bottom-up method has been successfully applied to the study of fluid dynamics, seismic disturbance, chemical oscillators, avalanches, forest fires, and ecological collapse. These recent successes have led a growing number of social scientists to wonder if perhaps social complexity may be attacked using similar tools. Rather than despairing of a "science of society," maybe we were simply looking at science too narrowly, equating the scientific method with a top-down search for covering laws when instead we should have been looking from the bottom up? Bottom-up self-organization is not limited to the biological and physical worlds. On the contrary, much of social life consists of group processes that are dynamic, nonlinear, path dependent, and self-organizing, in which global (or macro-level) norms, institutions, symbols, identities, meanings and the like emerge unintendedly from the local (or micro) interactions of group members who influence one another in response to the influence they receive. Emergent social patterns can also appear unexpectedly and then just as dramatically transform or disappear, as happens in revolutions, market crashes, fads, and feeding frenzies.

Epstein and Axtell gave the name "artificial societies" to the application of agent-based computational methods to the study of social dynamics. These "toy societies" are intended as laboratories that can be used to search for microprocesses that generate familiar but enigmatic global patterns. Artificial society models are based on three basic assumptions:

- *Decision makers are autonomous. Agents interact with little or no central authority or direction.* Global patterns emerge from the bottom up, determined not by a centralized authority but by local interactions among autonomous decision-makers. Like actors in improvisational theater, these agents generate a story on the fly, with twists and turns that are impossible to predict.

- *Decision-makers are adaptive rather than optimizing*, with decisions based on heuristics, not on calculations of the most efficient action (Holland 1995:43). These heuristics include norms, habits, protocols, rituals, conventions, customs, and routines. They evolve at two levels, the individual and the population. Individual learning alters the probability distribution of rules competing for attention, through processes like reinforcement, Bayesian updating, or the back-propagation of error in artificial neural networks (Rummelhart and McClelland 1988). Population learning alters the frequency distribution of rules competing for reproduction through processes of selection, imitation, and social influence. Genetic algorithms (Holland 1995) are used to model adaptation at the population level.
- *Decision-makers are interdependent.* Strategic interdependence means that the consequences of each agent's decisions depend in part on the choices of others. When interdependent agents are also adaptive, the focal agent's decisions influence the behavior of other agents who in turn influence the focal agent, generating a "complex adaptive system" (Holland 1995:10).

Agent-based models can be classified into three types, based on the type of adaptation they employ. The simplest are ecological models, where agents change states (e.g., alive or dead) or locations (like Reynold's boids), based on the states of other agents. However, agents cannot change the rules that govern their responses. Evolutionary models go further to allow rules to compete for agents who adopt and propagate them. The agents are merely passive carriers of these rules and cannot tailor them to individual experience. Finally, behavioral models allow agents to learn through individual experience and even to make boundedly rational choices.

ECOLOGICAL MODELS

Ecological models sometimes use "cellular automata" (CA), a technique first proposed by Stanislaw Ulam (Coveney and Highfield 1995:94–96). The automata usually live on a checkerboard (either flat or a donut-like torus), and the state of each agent depends on the states of its neighbors. The spatial patterns of ecological adaptation can generate surprising results and lead to unexpected insights.

One of the earliest agent-based models of human social behavior actually predates the personal computer and nicely illustrates the ecological approach. Consider a residential area that is highly segregated, such that the number of neighbors with different cultural markers (such as ethnicity) is at a minimum. If the aggregate pattern were assumed to reflect the attitudes of the constituent individuals, one might conclude from the distribution that the population was highly parochial and intolerant of diversity.

However, a celebrated simulation by Thomas Schelling (1971) shows that this need not be the case. Working without benefit of modern desktop computers, Schelling began by randomly distributing red and blue poker chips, representing different ethnic groups, about a checkerboard. Members of each group were then given a preference regarding the color of immediate neighbors, which dictated whether a given agent would remain settled or move to an adjacent square. For example, residents might be highly intolerant of ethnic diversity, such that they move as soon as the first "outsider" moves in. Alternatively, residents might actually prefer diversity, so long as their own group does not become outnumbered. Common sense tells us what will happen. If we want to prevent residential segregation, we need to persuade people to be more tolerant of ethnic diversity. Why, when the outcome is so obvious, do we need simulation?

We need simulation because common sense is wrong. Indeed, the results surprised Schelling as well. Perfectly segregated neighborhoods form even in a population that is highly tolerant of diversity, a striking example of the principle of emergence. Very small biases proved sufficient to produce sharply segregated neighborhoods. Agents need not prefer an all-blue or all-red neighborhood, only a slightly greater proportion of their own color, for *total* segregation to occur. Decades later, we find that Schelling's results continue to inform scholarly debate over the role of racial prejudice in segregation (e.g., Massey and Denton 1993).

Another example of emergence is provided by Latané's (1996) "social impact model." Like Schelling, Latané also studies a cellular world populated by agents who live on a two-dimensional lattice. However, rather than moving, these agents adapt to those around them, based on a rule to mimic one's neighbors. From a random start, a population of mimics might be expected to converge inexorably on a single profile, leading to the conclusion that cultural diversity is imposed by factors that counteract the effects of conformist tendencies. However, the surprising result was that "the system achieved stable diversity. The minority was able to survive, contrary to the belief that social influence inexorably leads to uniformity" (Latané 1996:294).

More recent applications include cultural diffusion (Axelrod 1984) and the formation of support networks (Hegselmann and Flache 1998). One of the most elaborate and best known CA projects is Epstein and Axtell's (1996) "Sugarscape," in which a territorially distributed population develops a culture, an economy, and a class structure.

Federico Cecconi and Domenico Parisi (1998) employ the "Sugarscape" approach to contrast individual and social survival strategies by modeling two artificial ecologies, one where agents consume all that they find, and one where resources are redistributed to the needy. Agents in Cecconi and Parisi's simulation live on a two-dimensional grid. Each agent receives sensory information about the location of the nearest of many units of food, which are periodically distributed about the grid. Its output nodes encode how the agent should move, given this information. If the agents do not reach food before their energy runs out, they die. After agents eat a certain amount of food, an offspring appears with similar rules for how to forage. While agents do not learn during their lifetimes (they cannot change their rules with individual experience), those who eat more reproduce more frequently, allowing more favorable rules to propagate.

Cecconi and Parisi performed an experiment under three carefully controlled conditions. In the first, one society follows an individual survival strategy, where each agent eats all that it finds, and another follows a specific social survival strategy, where agents contribute some of what they find to a "central store," which redistributes food to those with low energy. With resources relatively plentiful, both strategies produced stable populations. In a second experimental condition, resources became increasingly scarce once each group reached a population of five-hundred agents. Under conditions of scarcity, the individualist society dies out, but the central store provides a safety net that sustains members of the collectivist group through random fluctuations in fortune. Finally, Cecconi and Parisi repeated the previous condition, but endowed agents with a "social gene" that controlled how much individuals should give to the central store. In this condition, *both* societies went extinct when food became scarce. The lesson is that while competition provides more incentive for individual achievement, it also makes it harder to weather hard times. The dilemma is that, in order to survive, each agent must ignore its own self-interests. What is rational for the individual, it turns out, is irrational for the group.

This problem has been formalized as the prisoner's dilemma (PD). PD games are a useful way to explore the effectiveness of individualistic and cooperative strategies under varying conditions. They can also be used to explore the evolution of new strategies that the experimenter may never have anticipated, the problem to which we now turn.

EVOLUTIONARY MODELS

Ecological models study the propagation of agent attributes in social or spatial networks but do not permit the discovery of entirely new solutions to adaptive problems. In evolutionary models, new rules can also emerge. Now Schelling's neighbors might learn to focus on individual traits, rather than cultural markers, in choosing whether to move. Evolutionary models assume that more effective rules flourish at the expense of those that perform poorly.

Political scientist Robert Axelrod is best known for exploring possible solutions to PD. Axelrod (1984) held a series of tournaments where strategies for playing finitely repeated PD were pitted against each other. The best performing strategy, dubbed tit-for-tat (TFT), defected only if its opponent defected in the previous move. Otherwise it cooperated, an ethic Axelrod characterized as reciprocal altruism. It came as a great surprise that the winning strategy was not only so simple but so benevolent! Better yet, Axelrod showed that, once established, a TFT population could not be invaded by mutant predators. But critics noted that Axelrod's results depended on an arbitrary choice of contestants in his computer tournament. Were there other strategies "out there" that might prevail over TFT?

To find out, working with John Holland, Axelrod (1997:14–29) developed a simulation where prisoner's dilemma strategies were evolved using genetic algorithms. Genetic algorithms are strings of computer code that can mate with other strings to produce entirely new and superior programs by building on partial solutions.[3] Each strategy in a population consists of a string of symbols that code behavioral instructions. These symbols are often binary digits (or "bits") with values of 0 or 1. A string of symbols is analogous to a chromosome containing multiple genes. A set of one or more bits that contains a specific instruction is analogous to a single gene. The values of the bits and bit-combinations are analogous to the alleles of the gene. A one-bit gene has two alleles (0 and 1), a two-bit gene has four alleles (00, 01, 10, and 11), and so on.

A strategy's instructions, when followed, produce an outcome (or payoff) that affects the agent's reproductive fitness relative to other players in the computational ecology. In Axelrod's model, fitness was a function of cumulative payoffs in repeated PD games. Relative fitness determines the probability that each strategy will propagate. Propagation occurs when two mated strategies recombine. If two different rules are both effective, but in different ways, recombination allows them to create an entirely new strategy that may integrate the best abilities of each "parent," making the new strategy superior to either contributor. If so, then the new rule may go on to eventually displace both parent rules in the population of strategies. In addition, the new strings may contain random copying errors. These mutations continually refresh the heterogeneity of the population, counteracting selection pressures that tend to reduce it.

Axelrod's results identified a handful of other strategies that performed as well as TFT. However, what is most interesting is that, like TFT, all were relatively "nice," that is, the secret of their success was that they performed well against copies of themselves, which is only possible by finding a way to cooperate. It is reassuring, but also curious, that benevolent strategies can perform well at what is intuitively a "nasty" game.

By evolving strategies to social dilemmas, we can learn much about the problems these present in the real world, and how they might be resolved. What are the evolutionary implications of changes in structural conditions (such as social mobility or organizational hierarchy), cognitive processes (such as group identity or time horizons), or institutional arrangements (such as sanctioning systems)?

To sum up, the models considered so far, from Schelling's checkerboard automata to Cecconi and Parisi's propagators to Axelrod's genetic algorithm, can be viewed as increasingly "adaptive." Schelling's agents could change behavior, but not the underlying rules. The distribution of behaviors could change over time, but not the distribution of rules. Cecconi and Parisi's agents could multiply but their offspring were perfect copies of the parents. The distribution of existing rules could change, but no new rules could appear. Axelrod's genetic algorithms allowed new rules to appear, but these rules remain "hard-wired" in agents who are unable to learn from their own experience. The next step is to relax the assumption that rules are hard-wired and allow agents to learn from their own experience, the approach to which we now turn.

LEARNING MODELS

Axelrold's tit-for-tat strategy has two interesting weaknesses. First, because it refuses to exploit, it can be invaded by naive (unconditional) cooperators who then invite the return of more aggressive and predatory rules. Second, TFT is vulnerable to random miscues that trigger cycles of recrimination when interacting with other reciprocators (known as "echo effects").

Computational studies by Nowak and Sigmund (1993) and by Binmore (1998) have shown that reciprocal altruism is more robust when based on a rule for conditional reciprocity. The strategy, known as "PAVLOV" (a.k.a. "Win-Stay, Lose-Shift," "tat-for-tit," and "SIMPLETON"), is as simple as TFT: "Repeat whatever caused the partner to cooperate, and otherwise switch." Conceptually, TFT and PAVLOV are complements: TFT teaches, while PAVLOV learns. TFT rewards cooperation and punishes defection, as if trying to modify the partner's behavior. Conversely, PAVLOV modifies its own behavior by repeating choices whose outcomes are satisfactory and avoiding those that are not. To avoid blood feuds, PAVLOV stops retaliating if a noncooperative partner is acting defensively rather than aggressively. Unlike TFT, PAVLOV then extends an olive branch, but quickly retracts it if the peace gesture is rebuffed. Although this makes PAVLOV vulnerable to unconditional aggressors, the risk is mitigated by a complementary trait: PAVLOV has no remorse about exploiting naive altruists who unwittingly invite invasion by predators. Hence, PAVLOV stops reciprocating cooperation if a cooperative partner can be exploited. This aggressiveness is clearly not altruistic. Unlike TFT, which never seeks to exploit, PAVLOV reciprocates cooperation only when crime appears not to pay.

PAVLOV is one of the simplest examples of a strategy that learns from its own mistakes. In simple reinforcement, the organism modifies its behavior in response to positive and negative feedback, as predicted by the "law of effect" (Thorndike 1911). Positive outcomes increase the probability that the associated behavior will be repeated, while negative outcomes reduce it. The process closely parallels the replication of rules in evolutionary adaptation, in which positive outcomes increase the rule's chances for survival and reproduction, while negative outcomes reduce it. However, with reinforcement, rules compete *within* the individuals that carry them, not *between* them.

Despite its simplicity, PAVLOV can produce complex and unexpected global patterns when strategically interdependent individuals evolve their relationships by learning how best to interact with others who are trying to do the same. Flache and Macy (1996) used this approach to explore the problem of informal social control against shirking in group-rewarded production teams. Exchange theorists following Homans (1974) have modeled informal social control as exchanges of approval for compliance with group obligations. Accordingly, each agent in their model must make two decisions, whether to work or shirk, and whether to approve of each of the other members of the group. Although the group-payment scheme tempts members to free-ride, agents also depend on others in the group for social approval.

Since Homans, theories of informal social control have assumed that compliance increases with members' dependence on the group for approval. Their experiments with the exchange of approval for compliance confirmed this idea. Agents learned to work as their effort was rewarded with approval from their coworkers.

But then Flache and Macy introduced a small change based on ethnographic studies of "deviant cliques" by Shibutani (1978), Willis (1981), Macleod (1995), and others. These studies suggested that "peer pressure" can also be used to enforce compliance with friendship norms. Thus, they allowed agents to also directly exchange approval for approval as well as approval for compliance with work norms. Now agents could support one another for working hard but also for being supportive in turn. The results were surprising. Dependence on the group for support now backfired, causing social pressures to flow into the enforcement of friendship norms at the expense of group productivity. This led them to identify the "double edge" of social ties. Dependence increases the salience of approval but also reduces the willingness to use approval to enforce prosocial behavior.

An important limitation of their study is that their agents could not learn to use conditional strategies, that is, rules that instruct different behavior under different conditions. One way to implement this ability is with artificial neural networks (or ANN). An ANN is a simple type of self-programmable learning device based on parallel distributed processing (Rummelhart and McClelland 1988). Like genetic algorithms, neural nets have a biological analog, in this case, the nerve systems of living organisms. In elementary form, the device consists of a web of neuron-like units (neurodes) that fire when triggered by impulses of sufficient strength, and in turn stimulate other units when fired. The magnitude of an impulse depends on the strength of the connection ("synapses") between the two neurodes. The network learns by modifying these path coefficients in response to environmental feedback about its performance. Learning only occurs when the response to a given sensory input pattern is unsatisfactory. The paths are then adjusted so as to reduce the probability of repeating the mistake the next time this pattern is encountered.

Deborah Vakas-Duong and Kevin Reilley (1995) used ANN models to demonstrate how associative memory alone is sufficient to precipitate the emergence of status symbols, racial preference, and class division. They built an artificial society of self-programmable agents consisting of a handful of employers and a larger worker population. Workers were given four traits: a fad (easily changed element of appearance), a suit (which can be improved upon the accumulation of wealth), skin color (not changeable), and talent (random).

Each turn, employers dismiss 20 percent of their employees, and then seek replacements. A series of job interviews are conducted, after which the applicant associates its traits with its success, or lack thereof. Likewise, the interviewer learns to associate the traits of past hires with their talent, and makes *intuitive* hiring decisions based on the connotations it has come to associate with the traits exhibited by the applicants.

The simulation results showed that the process was chaotic. Different structures would emerge in different simulations, and small perturbations were sufficient to alter the final outcomes. A bias for expensive suits emerged most easily, as ability to buy one was linked to a history of employment, which was more common among talented agents. Likewise, workers recognized this preference in their employers and sought out expensive suits.

Interestingly, a preference for non–talent-linked traits such as fads and skin color also emerged. All that was necessary was for a few talented or untalented workers with a given trait to be hired for the employer to come to associate the trait with performance. Thus, a few bad apples could sow the seed of racial preference in an employer's mind, which would in turn make it difficult for talented members of the same race to gain employment. This, in turn, would then exacerbate the situation by diminishing that race's access to status symbols. These results are especially interesting because they illustrate how false beliefs may be formed through accident of association, and how these, in turn, can produce system-wide, self-perpetuating changes.

Learning can also be combined with evolutionary processes by allowing individuals to adapt not only to their own experience but to the experience of others through processes like imitation and social influence. For example, Strang and Macy (2001) model fad-like behavior in the business community by assuming that managers evaluate current practice based on their balance sheets, and if dissatisfied, turn to "best practices" for new ideas. They show how this rational decision process can produce the lemming-like bandwagons of adoption and abandonment pilloried by commentators like the "Dilbert" comics' Scott Adams. Local rationality produces a global pattern that causes the individuals to appear to be mindless conformists, even when they are not.

THE NEW SOCIAL SIMULATION AND THE PROBLEM OF VALIDITY

The migration of agent-based modeling to the social sciences has been facilitated by the proliferation of inexpensive, yet powerful, personal computers with graphical user interfaces that have lowered technological and methodological barriers. Most social scientists now have access to machines capable of running very complex and computationally intensive modeling programs. Moreover, graphical interfaces facilitate highly intuitive representations of the results. These technological advances have made computational modeling more accessible to social scientists. While technological barriers have come down, skepticism remains about the validity and robustness of results obtained from social simulation. The criticisms are similar to those directed at laboratory research in sociology: How can experiments under artificial conditions be used to make predictions about behavior outside the lab?

These criticisms reflect a misunderstanding of experimental methodology. Experiments are used to test predictions about outcomes under controlled conditions, not in natural settings where predicted effects are likely to be confounded by the effects of unmeasured conditions. Of course, should the predictions be supported in the lab, it may be useful to apply the theory to real-world conditions that violate its scope. However, the purpose is not to test the theory but to generate intuitions about how the theory might be extended or elaborated.

With agent-based modeling, the misunderstanding may also reflect confusion created by the continued use of the term *simulation*, whose meaning was shaped by earlier generations of computational techniques. *Simulation* means "to feign or mimic." That is the objective in classical simulation models popular in the 1960s (e.g. Cyert and March 1963). These studies used computers to simulate dynamical systems, such as control and feedback processes in organizations, industries, cities, and even global populations. Applications included the flow of raw materials in a factory, inventory control in a warehouse, urban traffic, military supply lines, flight training, demographic changes in a world system, and ecological limits to growth (Forrester 1971; Meadows et al. 1974). These models can properly be characterized as simulations. Their value depends entirely on predictive accuracy and realism.

In contrast, artificial societies are highly abstract "thought experiments."[4] Contrary to the critics, making these models more "realistic" would add complexity that is likely to undermine their usefulness. The priority in building agent-based models is to keep them as simple and abstract as possible.

From this perspective, the artificiality of agent-based models is a virtue, not a vice. When simulation is used to make predictions or for training personnel (e.g., flight simulators), the assumptions need to be highly realistic, which usually means they will also be highly complicated (Axelrod 1997:5). "But if the goal is to deepen our understanding of some fundamental process," Axelrod continues, "then simplicity of the assumptions is important and realistic representation of all the details of a particular setting is not" (1997:5).

This principle extends to the behavioral assumptions about the cognitive complexity of the agents. The principle of emergence suggests that the complexity of social life need not be reducible to the cognitive complexity of individuals. "Human beings," Simon contends, "viewed as behaving systems, are quite simple" (1998:53). We follow rules, in the form of norms, conventions, protocols, moral and social habits, and heuristics. Although the rules may be quite simple, they can produce global patterns that may not be at all obvious and are very difficult to understand. Hence, "the apparent complexity of our behavior is largely a reflection of the complexity of the environment" (1998:53), including the complexity of interactions among strategically interdependent, adaptive agents. The simulation of artificial worlds allows us to explore the complexity of the social environment by removing the cognitive complexity (and idiosyncrasy) of constituent individuals. The intent behind these models is to understand the minimal conditions, the simplest set of assumptions about human behavior required for a given social phenomenon to emerge at a higher level of organization.

In sum, while we continue to use the term *simulation* to include agent-based computational models, we need to be clear about what it is they "simulate." The artificial world these agents inhabit is not the real world inhabited by the researchers, it is the laboratory world inhabited by human subjects whose behavior is studied under controlled conditions. The results of these experiments test only the logical validity of the underlying theory, as a necessary precursor for empirical tests.

WHEN SOCIOLOGY MET COMPLEXITY: A ROMANTIC COMEDY

Curiously, the growing interest in sociological applications has attracted more economists (like Joshua Epstein and Robert Axtell), political scientists (like Robert Axelrod), and psychologists (like Herbert Simon) than sociologists. This may reflect the prejudices of a discipline that sees itself as more "macro" in orientation than the other social sciences. It is thus ironic that the idea of "emergence" was anticipated by one of the founders of the discipline, who established this as a fundamental rule of the sociological method. "The hardness of bronze is not in the cooper, the tin, or the lead, which are its ingredients and which are soft and malleable bodies," Durkheim wrote, "it is in their mixture. Let us apply this principle to sociology," he continued. "[Social facts] reside exclusively in the very society itself which produces them, and not in its parts, i.e., its members" (1986:xlvii).

Durkheim goes too far in concluding that emergent social facts are entirely independent of individual consciousness. Individuals are then little more than the incumbents of structural locations and the carriers of structural imperatives. Macrostructuralists argue that heterogeneity in preferences and beliefs affects only which individuals will fill which "empty slots," whose origin lies in processes that operate at the societal level. For example, differences in the degree of ethnic identity affect who will live where in segregated neighborhoods but are not the cause of neighborhood segregation, which emanates from societal processes like red-lining and patterns of urban development.

The principles of emergence and self-organized complexity correct the hyperstructuralist interpretation of Durkheim by incorporating an essential insight of Joseph Schumpeter's (1909) "methodological individualism," the idea that societal patterns emerge from motivated choices and not from "social facts" external to individuals. Yet microsociologists also go too far when they assume that social facts are merely the aggregations of individual attributes (e.g., residential segregation reflects the preferences of individuals to live among people similar to themselves).

Agent-based models defy classification as either micro or macro and instead provide a theoretical bridge between the two levels. Global patterns emerge from the bottom up, through local interactions, yet emergent phenomena are sui generic, not aggregations of component elements. There is a simple answer to the old methodological conundrum, "Did he *jump* or was he *pushed*?" The answer is both: agents jump when pushed by other agents. Individual choices produce neighborhood segregation, but the segregated pattern need not reflect individual preferences.

Models of artificial society also defy classification as quantitative or qualitative. Quantitative sociologists equate explanation with prediction. The test of explanation is the ability to predict. This method stumbles when confronted with dynamical processes that are highly non-linear, especially when the explanand is not the mean of a distribution but its shape. Meanwhile, qualitative sociologists equate explanation with interpretation: The test of explanation is the plausibility of a narrative. This method stumbles when confronted with processes that are highly counterintuitive, especially when the logical relations are expressed in natural language using terms with highly ambiguous meanings.

Agent-based computational models do not allow for ambiguity of language (otherwise, they will not compile), nor are they limited to linear relationships or comparative statics. They explain empirical patterns by rigorously generating them from a set of initial assumptions that are often counterintuitive. The surprise is theoretical, not empirical; on the contrary, the purpose is to explain familiar but enigmatic global patterns, such as the persistence of residential segregation. The results are often surprising due to the limitations of human intuition based on linear representations of causality.

To sum up, sociology may be the discipline best equipped to develop a methodology that bridges methodological individualism and Durkheim's rules of a nonreductionist method. Bottom-up computational methods promise to transcend old divisions between micro and macro, predictive and interpretive, and mathematical and ethnographic, as well as territorial boundaries between sociology and neighboring disciplines—economics on the one side, and psychology on the other.

CONCLUSION

To be sure, this promise has yet to be realized. The emerging sciences of complexity demonstrate that new methods of theoretical research are needed if we are to understand complex self-organizing systems that confounded traditional deductive-nomological approaches. Even so, two of the early architects of artificial society, Epstein and Axtell (1996:20), see the prospects for far-reaching advances that extend across the social sciences:

Artificial society modeling allows us to "grow" social structures in silico demonstrating that certain sets of microspecifications are sufficient to generate the macrophenomena of interest. And that, after all, is a central aim. As social scientists, we are presented with "already emerged" collective phenomena, and we seek microrules which can generate them. We can, of course, use statistics to test the match between the true, observed structures and the ones we grow. But the ability to grow them—greatly facilitated by modern object-oriented programming—is what is new. Indeed, it holds out the prospect for a new, generative, kind of social science.

Generative social science may seem new to economists seeking physics-like laws of supply and demand, but it should be comfortably familiar to sociologists who abandoned that hope long ago. The generative method models social phenomena as emergent properties of interactions at a lower level of organization, using computational tools that permit physics-like experiments. This method promises to understand social life not in the simplified, deterministic manner of classical physics, but as the intricate, often enigmatic system we have always known it to be.

NOTES

1. Reynold's "boids" were so realistic that they provided the starting point for bat swarms in the movies *Batman Returns* and *Cliffhanger*. You can see the "boids" in action at www.discovery.com/area/science/life/life1.3.html.

2. It might be objected that we would still have no way to know if the computer was "really" conscious or merely behaved as if it were. Need we point out that this same argument can be made about the carbon-based life forms who raise this objection?

3. Recent work in sociology using genetic algorithms includes Egidi and Marengo (1995), Macy and Skvoretz (1998), McCain (1995), Skvoretz and Fararo (1995), and Treuil (1995).

4. For a more detailed overview of the history of social simulation, see Gilbert and Troitzsch (1999).

Chapter 13

The Strength of Weak Power: A Simulation Study of Network Evolution

Phillip Bonacich

It has often been pointed out (Vanberg and Congleton 1992; Orbell and Dawes 1993; Kitcher 1993; Majiski et al. 1997) that the pessimistic inferences about the fate of cooperation in the prisoner's dilemma game may be unwarranted. Unlike the case in prisons, actors can often choose whether or not to interact based on the cooperative histories of their potential partners. The ability to avoid any interaction with likely non-cooperators can give cooperative strategies an evolutionary advantage.

Similarly, I will argue, the scope condition ordinarily assumed in network exchange research—that the exchange network is unchanging—magnifies the degree of inequality present in exchange networks. There are many situations in which dissatisfied and exploited actors can change their positions. As we shall see, the possibility of changing positions may (or may not) reduce the inequality generated by exchange networks. This means that theories designed to predict power in networks are often inapplicable; the outcome is often not, as the theories predict, growing inequality, but rather network change maintaining a high level of equality.

Figure 13.1 illustrates this point. If the network in the upper left forms, the peripheral positions B, C, and D will lose power by competing with one another for inclusion in exchanges with A. Thus, the network in the upper left will become the network in the upper right. On the other hand, if dissatisfied positions can change their positions the network may change into the one in the lower left. In this network no position has a marked power advantage. Which path the network follows will depend on the mutability of the network. Later I will argue that if the network constraints are based on immutable preferences

Figure 13.1
Two Courses of Network Evolution

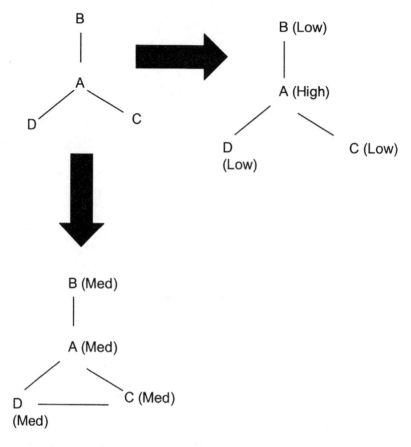

for specific transaction partners by knowledgeable actors, the network will be unalterable and power differences will develop. On the other hand, if the network describes only temporary patterns of ignorance about potential exchange partners, the network is likely to evolve in the other direction, toward equality of power.

In addition to pointing out the limitations of existing theories of network power, this chapter also has a more positive goal, as I attempt to describe the stable forms toward which exchange networks evolve and how this evolution depends on the initial form of the exchange network.

The study of power differences within exchange networks has been an exciting area within social psychology for a number of years (Cook et al. 1983; Markovsky, Willer, and Patton 1988; Markovsky et al. 1993). The excitement of this area is that it is both psychological and structural and thus addresses directly the micro-macro link. A set of actors can engage in a limited number

Figure 13.2
A Hypothetical Network

Andy ———————— Barbara ———————— Charles

Figure 13.3
The Evolution of a Network

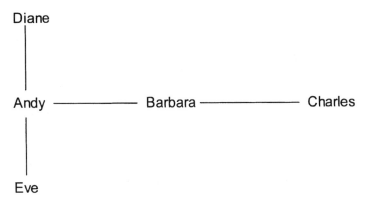

Diane

Andy ———————— Barbara ———————— Charles

Eve

of profitable dyadic transactions, perhaps only one. These theories apply to any situation in which actors must choose with whom to transact from among a fixed set of other actors. Each transaction produces a profit that can be divided between the two participants if they can agree on a division. A network describes the set of dyads that can profitably transact. Some actors have more transaction partners than they can possibly transact with; they must choose some and reject others.

Consider, for example, the following hypothetical situation involving two men, Andy and Charles, who are interested in the same woman, Barbara, and she in them (Figure 13.2).[1] Let us also suppose that one woman dating two men is intolerable to all the participants.

Barbara has a power advantage because of the competition between Andy and Charles to please her. But, suppose that Andy moves and meets two women, Dianne and Eve, with whom he shares mutual attractions. The power distribution for the new network, represented in Figure 13.3, is quite different. Andy, who now enjoys a power advantage over Diane and Eve, no longer has a reason to compete with Charles, and so Barbara's power is reduced.

What happens when such changes are allowed?[2] This chapter will focus on a few key questions:

1. If members of exchange networks migrate when they are dissatisfied with their power, is the result inevitably a network of equal power?
2. What are the characteristics of stable networks?

Figure 13.4
Illustrative Exchange Networks

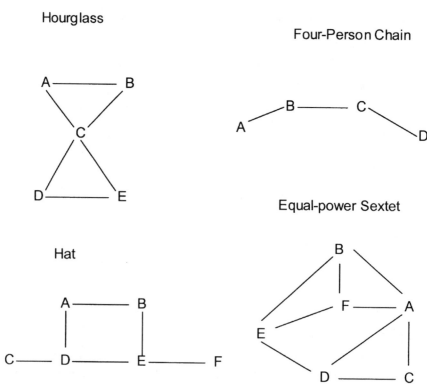

3. How is the outcome of the evolution related to the properties of the starting network?
4. Are there typical stages through which networks evolve?

I will examine these issues using a very simple computer simulation. The simulation mirrors the conditions under which experiments in exchange networks have been conducted and embodies some of the findings from this research. A set of simulated actors has a sequence of opportunities (games) with which to engage in mutually profitable transactions. Pairs of actors may divide fixed numbers of points that constitute their earnings. Actors make offers to those with whom they can transact. Whenever two actors each receive their best offers from each other, they transact, and the process is repeated with the remaining network members until no further transactions are possible.[3] An actor omitted from one game raises his offers to others in the next game. Actors included in exchanges make offers to others in the next game that give themselves the same profit.

Figure 13.4 shows a variety of exchange networks whose emergent distribu-

Figure 13.4 (*continued*)

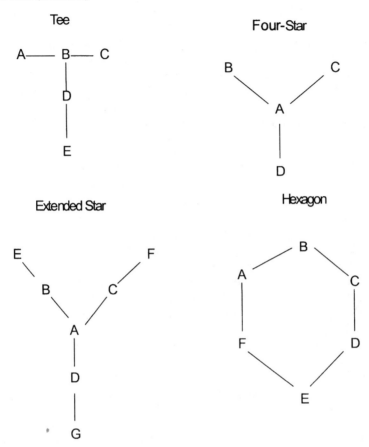

tions of power are well understood, through experiments or computer simulations.

In the Tee network, *B* has power over *A* and *C*, *D* and *E* are equal in power, and *B* and *D* do not exchange. In the Four-Star network, *A* enjoys a large power advantage over the other positions. In the Extended Star network, *B*, *C*, and *D* enjoy a large power advantage over the other positions. In the Hourglass network all exchanges occur, but no position enjoys a power advantage. In the Four-Person Chain network, *B* and *C* rarely exchange with one another but have a small power advantage over their partners, *A* and *D*. In the Hat network *C* trades with *D*, *A* with *B*, and *E* with *F*. There are minor differences in power. In the Hexagon network and in the Equal-Power Sextet network, all positions are equal in power.

I will assume that actors follow a very simple learning model: they do not change their location when they are being rewarded, but if they are not being rewarded, they change their network position in a random way. Actors whose average earnings fall below a minimum change their network connections. This is accomplished in two different ways, with slightly different properties. In one type of simulation, actors are arranged in a two-dimensional surface where neighbors exchange. In this simulation, dissatisfied actors randomly pick a neighboring position and move to it if it is unoccupied. Such moves may expose them to new exchange partners. The second type of simulation, using adjacency matrices, does not assume that exchange partners must be neighbors. In the modern world, only a small proportion of one's network consists of neighbors. An adjacency matrix can be used to represent any network, no matter how widely dispersed. In these simulations the rows and columns of the the adjacency matrix for dissatisfied actors are allowed to change in a random way.

Exchange networks can describe two very different types of constraints on exchange. On the one hand, an exchange network could represent the structure of preferences among a set of actors. For example, the Tee network in Figure 13.4 could represent a set of buyers and sellers of, say, automobiles, where A, C, and D are buyers and B and E are sellers. A connection in the graph would represent those pairs in which a buyer is willing to pay more for the seller's car than the seller's reservation price. In this case, the network is just as immutable as the preferences of the actors. On the other hand, the network could represent a knowledge of others, proximity, or some other historically determined or accidental feature of the situation. In this interpretation, any set of relations among the actors is possible, although only one is currently actualized. Buyers may be aware only of sellers in their neighborhood.[4]

I will be exploring the consequences of this second type of constraint: lack of information reflecting past historical "accidents." This allows the greatest scope for the effects of network change. When there is complete information and the networks reflect preferences the dynamics described in this chapter will not occur.

I am also assuming a very uninsightful actor. This actor does not select the position to which he moves on the basis of its worth; he moves blindly and randomly, quite possibly to a worse position. This is consistent with the assumption that the network of exchange opportunities is a consequence of the limited knowledge of the participants.

TWO REPRESENTATIONS: CA AND ADJACENCY MATRICES

Exchange networks are represented in two different ways in the simulations reported in this chapter: as adjacency matrices and as cellular automata (CA). As the former, an adjacency matrix represents the exchange network. If an actor is dissatisfied with the present rewards, each of his or her connections and nonconnections has a certain probability, p, of changing its value, either from one to zero or from zero to one.[5] Each change is independent. In a latter rep-

Figure 13.5
CA and Adjacency Representations of the Tee Network

0	0	0	0	0	0	0	0
0	0	0	0	0	0	0	0
0	0	0	1	0	1	0	0
0	0	0	0	1	0	0	0
0	0	0	0	1	0	0	0
0	0	0	0	1	0	0	0
0	0	0	0	0	0	0	0
0	0	0	0	0	0	0	0

$$
\begin{pmatrix}
0 & 1 & 0 & 0 & 0 \\
1 & 0 & 1 & 1 & 0 \\
0 & 1 & 0 & 0 & 0 \\
0 & 1 & 0 & 0 & 1 \\
0 & 0 & 0 & 1 & 0
\end{pmatrix}
$$

resentation, neighbors in a two dimensional space (those to the north, northeast, east, southeast, south, southwest, west, and northwest) are potential exchange partners. A dissatisfied position moves to an unoccupied neighboring cell.[6] Thus, the changes in its relations are not all independent. It may gain and lose sets of connections when it moves. Figure 13.5 shows a CA representation and an adjacency matrix representation of the Tee network in Figure 13.4.

This constraint, that connections tend to be gained or lost in bundles, is sometimes a more accurate reflection of reality than the assumption, built into the adjacency representation, that all connections are gained or lost independently. When one changes jobs or neighborhoods one loses and gains sets of connections. Moreover, a cellular automata representation of exchange networks may have empty regions in which actors cannot find partners. This can also be a more accurate representation of social space. Some environments are richer in potential contacts. Also, in the CA representation, exchange networks can shed unwanted members into the empty regions, whereas in the adjacency representation, positions are less likely to be cut off from the whole network. As will become evident, this has implications for the evolution of exchange networks.

TYPES OF POWER IN NETWORKS

Bonacich (1998, 1999) has shown that if actors use the following idealized rules in a repeated network exchange game, only outcomes in the game-theoretic core (Owen 1995:218) are stable:[7]

1. Actors who are excluded from an exchange raise their offers to others in the next game.
2. Actors who are included in an exchange make offers that allow them an unchanged profit.
3. All offers made by actors to others are equal in value (to themselves).
4. An actor leaves a current partner if, and only if, he or she receives a strictly superior offer from another.

This implies that, in the long run, outcomes will be in the core. Moreover, if outcomes are in the core, distributions of rewards can be found through the following procedure.[8] The following definitions will be used.

E = the set of edges in a network.

S = the set of positions in a network.

v = the maximum number of trades possible in the network.

$\{M_i\}$ = the set of maximal trading patterns in the network. All these trading patterns consist of v edges.

$M = \cup\ M_i$, the union of the *maximal* trading patterns. (M is a subset of E).

The set M of edges used in one or more maximal trading patterns will imply a partition of the set S into mutually exclusive sets, where all pairs of positions in the same set are mutually reachable by paths in the set M.

$\{S_i\}$ = the sets of mutually reachable positions. These are disjoint subsets of S. I will call each set along with its relations in M a *component* of the network. There may be one or more than one component.

Consider, for example, the Tee network of Figure 13.3. There are two maximal trading patterns, each with two trades: $M_1 = \{A - B, D - E\}$; and $M_2 = \{B - C, D - E\}$. $M = M_1 \cup M_2 = \{A - B, B - C, D - E\}$. This implies that there are two connected components $S_1 = \{A, B, C\}$ and $S_2 = \{D, E\}$. We will now confine the definitions to *one* component with n positions and m edges. Let v now be the maximum number of trades in this one component. Let A be an $m + 1$ by n matrix in which $a_{ij} = 1$ if edge i contains position j, and $a_{ij} = 0$ otherwise. The last row of A consists entirely of 1's. The column vector w has $m + 1$ elements; $w_i = 1$ for $i \leq m$; $w_{m + 1} = v$.

For example, in the Tee network, for the component consisting of positions A, B, and C, the A and w arrays are:

$$A = \begin{pmatrix} 110 \\ 011 \\ 111 \end{pmatrix}, \; w = \begin{pmatrix} 1 \\ 1 \\ 1 \end{pmatrix}$$

For the second component, consisting of positions D and E, the two arrays are:

$$A = \begin{pmatrix} 11 \\ 11 \end{pmatrix}, \; w = \begin{pmatrix} 1 \\ 1 \end{pmatrix}$$

Exact solutions in the core must satisfy the following equation (Bonacich 1998, 1999):

$$Ax = w$$

Let $\rho(M)$ be the rank of a matrix M. The previous equation has a solution if and only if $\rho(A) = \rho(A|w)$, where the column vector w is adjoined to the matrix A (Basilevsky 1983:125–126). If $\rho(A) = \rho(A|w) = n$, the number of columns of A, then there is a unique solution. If $\rho(A) = \rho(A|w) < n$, then there is an infinity of solutions, and the set of equations is underidentified. Depending on whether these criteria are met, there are only four different types of components.

I. Coreless Components. If $\rho(A) < \rho(A|w)$, the set of equations is inconsistent. This corresponds to the absence of a core in the component.

II. Strong Power Components. If $\rho(A) = \rho(A|w) = n$, there is a unique solution to the set of equations for the component. If the graph corresponding to M, the union of maximal patterns, is bipartite, the component exhibits strong power differences; some positions earn the complete value of the exchange, others nothing (Bonacich 1998, 1999). The solution can be found by solving the matrix equation $Ax = w$.

III. Equal Power Components. If $\rho(A) = \rho(A|w) = n$ and the graph for M is not bipartite, the unique core solution is $x_i = .50$ for all positions in the component. This is the only solution to the equation $Ax = w$.

IV. Indeterminate Power Components. If $\rho(A) = \rho(A|w) < n$, there are an infinite number of solutions. Relations in M do not completely determine power in the component. In some indeterminate components, unused relations between components may affect power in subtle ways. For example, in the Four-person Chain (Figure 13.3), the fact that B and C have each other as potential exchange partners, even if they never exchange, will give them a slight power advantage over A and D, which have no such alternatives. In other Indeterminate components (such as the Hexagon in Figure 13.3), no position enjoys an advantage.

Some approaches to power in networks lump together types I, III, and IV networks into one category, *weak power* (Markovsky et al. 1993). Actually, however, they are quite different. Bonacich and Bienenstock (1995) have demonstrated experimentally that trading patterns are particularly unstable in Coreless (type I) networks. Consider, for example, the Hourglass network (Figure 13.3). Suppose that A trades with B and D with E, with C left out. C will continue to raise his or her offers until he or she is included in an exchange, say with A, leaving B without a partner. Now B will raise his or her offers until it makes better offers than A or C, and so on. If excluded players raise the values of their offers when excluded and accept the best offers made to them there, should be no stability in the exchange patterns of coreless networks. There will be variability in who is left out without any convergence to a stable power distribution.[9]

Even though they may appear to be similar, the type III and IV conditions have different consequences for networks. In the Hexagon (or in an isolated dyad), no position has a *structural* advantage. But unequal outcomes are not inconsistent with the four behavioral assumptions previously described. For example, suppose that in the Hexagon, the exchange pattern is A-B, C-D, and E-F, with A, C, and E earning 60 percent of the profits and B, D, and F, 40 percent. In the next game, A, C, and D offer 40 percent to their potential partners, and the partners accept because that is what they earned in the last game. The outcome is stable but unequal, even though no position has a structural advantage. The initial inequalities, arising, perhaps from the greater aggressiveness or experience of some of the actors are not eliminated by structural features.

Now consider the same starting point in the Equal-power Sextet. In the next game, F's offer of .60 to B is better than A's offer of .40. And B's offer of .60 to F is better than E's offer of .40. So B and F should trade with each other at more equal terms than they enjoyed in the last game. Structural conditions enforce equality. The only stable outcome is when all players earn the same amount.

Table 13.1 lists the component types for the networks in Figure 13.4.

WEAK POWER DIFFERENCES: TWO SOLUTIONS IN SMALL NETWORKS

Approximately equal power exists in two quite different types of networks. In networks of types III—equal power or type IV—indeterminate power all positions exchange and power differences within each exchange are minimal or non-existent. This pattern is illustrated by the Four-Person Chain or Hexagon networks in Figure 13.4. In type I networks, on the other hand, positions are excluded from exchange but exclusion is rotated through all positions so thjat no position enjoys a consistent power advantage.

Both of these types of networks can be the stable equilibrium outcomes of network evolution, but different networks will evolve in different directions. To

Table 13.1
Component Types for the Networks in Figure 13.4

	Component & Type	Component & Type	Component & Type
Tee	{A, B, C} II	{D, E} IV	
Star	{A, B, C, D} II		
Extended Star	{A, B, C, D, E, F, G} II		
Hexagon	{A, B, C, D, E, F} IV		
Hourglass	{A, B, C, D, E} I		
Four-Chain	{A, B} IV	{C, D} IV	
Hat	{A, B} IV	{C, D} IV	{E, F} IV
Equal-Power Sextet	{A, B, C, D, E, F} III		

Figure 13.6
Mean Profits to B Position in Star Network with Movement

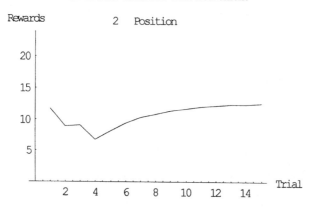

illustrate the difference, consider the evolution of two networks. Figure 13.6 shows the average rewards to one of the peripheral positions, *B*, in the 6-Star network (a central position *A* with five peripheral positions), in a simulation with fifteen games. This and succeeding diagrams show averages of gains in the last four games. To be consistent with the experimental literature, exchanges are worth twenty-four points. All positions start with an average gain of twelve. The diagram shows the average rewards for position *B* when change is allowed. There is a reversal of direction at the fifth game, which corresponds to a change in the network. In the first four games, *B*'s average reward declines because of its competition with *C*, *D*, *E*, and *F*. After the fourth game, a connection was forged between positions *B* and *D*. This new network consists of three components of type IV, {A, F}, {B, D}, and {E, C}. In all pairs the trades are at approximately equal terms.[10]

Now suppose we look at a 5-Star network, with one less peripheral position *F*. Figure 13.7 shows the outcomes for all positions when change in the network is allowed. The pattern is the same as in the 6-Star network; the peripheral positions initially decline in average earnings and then recover, while the central *A* position initially increases his or her earnings and then suffers a decline.

However, this growing equality is accomplished in a different way, as shown in Figure 13.8. The network does not change for the first four games. After the fourth game, low-earning *E* severs the connection with position *A*. After the fifth game, *E* reattaches to *A* (remember that movement is random and uninformed). After the sixth move position, *D* detaches from *A* and *D* and *E* connect. In this new network (the Tee in Figure 13.4), *D* and *E* have escaped exploitation by *A* by forming a component of type IV. However, *B* and *C* are still low in power relative to *A*. After game 8, *B* and *E* form a tie (instigated by *B*). This network is of type I (coreless), and could be a solution. But before the average earnings of the powerless positions can improve enough to prevent further change, the network evolves after game 9 into the last, type I, network in Figure 13.8, which does not change in games 11 through 15. In this network, all positions risk exclusion.

Figure 13.9, on the other hand, shows the evolution of a 6-Star network. Nothing changes for the first four games, while inequality grows. Position *E* is the first to move, attaching itself to *F*. Then *C* moves, attaching itself to *E*. At this point, *A* and *E* are still high-power positions in a single, type-II component. When *B* and *D* form a tie, the network becomes made of three type-IV components: {*B, D*}, {*A, F*}, and {*C, E*}.

The 6-Star and 5-Star networks change in the same direction, from having one high-power position and a number of weak peripheral positions to having equality of power. But the method of producing equality is different. In the 6-Star, the network evolves into three component dyads with approximately equal power within each dyad. The 5-Star network evolves into one coreless (type-I) component in which equality is produced through an unsystematic rotation of exclusion and rewards are approximately equal.

The important difference between the 6-Star and 5-Star networks is that the former has an even number of actors and the latter an odd number. Networks with an odd number of actors cannot avoid having an equilibrium which includes type-I (coreless) components, whereas all type-III and type-IV components have an even number of actors.

TYPES OF EQUILIBRIA IN LARGE NETWORKS

In small networks with just one component, having even or odd numbers of members will be the determining factor. However, in large networks with many components, the evolution networks of even and odd numbers of members will be increasingly alike: both will contain sets of indeterminate and coreless components. The only constraint is that networks with an odd number of positions

Figure 13.7
Average Earnings of Positions in Five-Star Network with Four Peripheral Positions

Position A

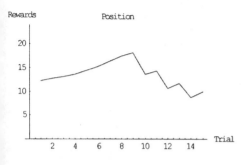

Position B

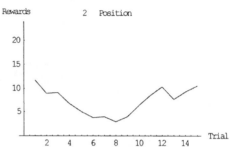

Position C

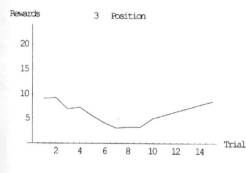

Position D

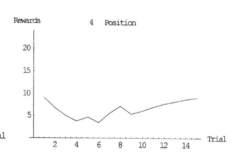

Position E

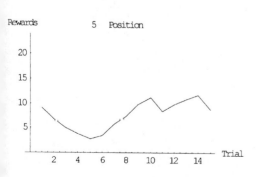

Figure 13.8
Evolution of Star Network with Five Positions

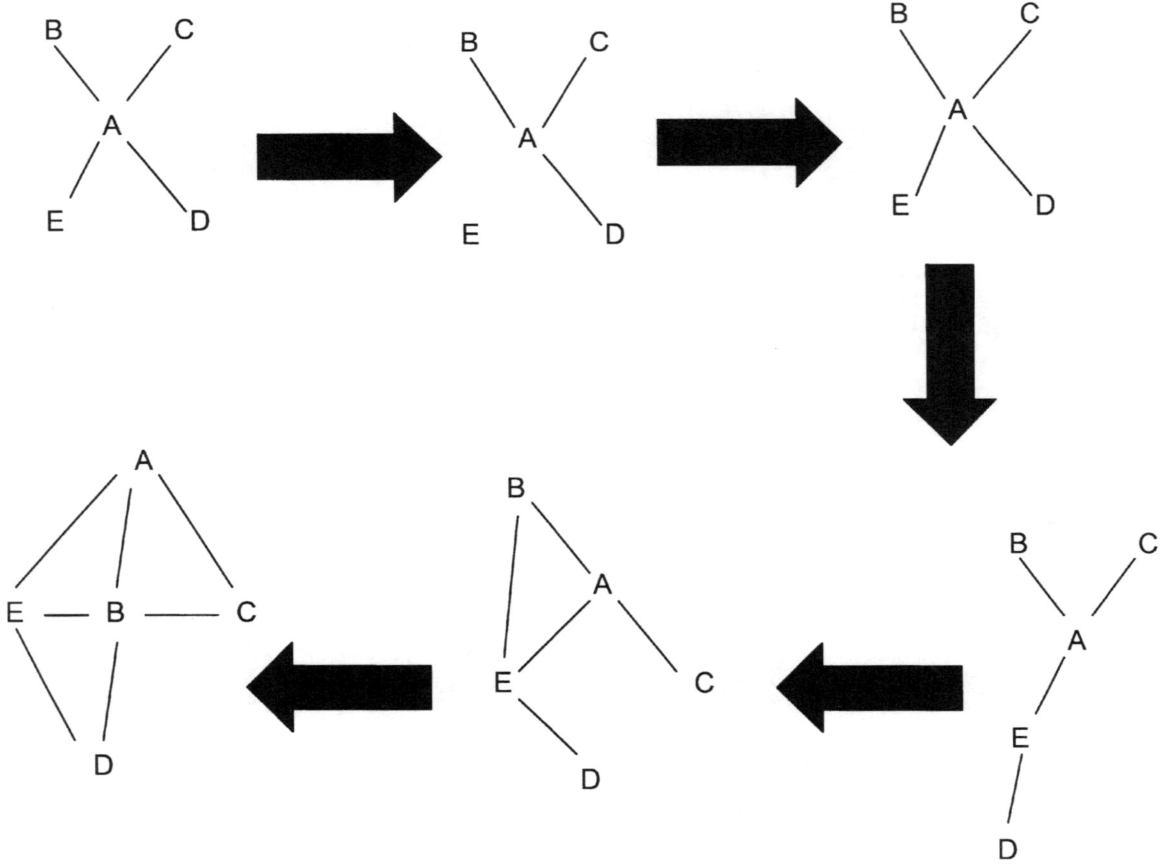

Figure 13.9
Evolution of a Six-Star Network

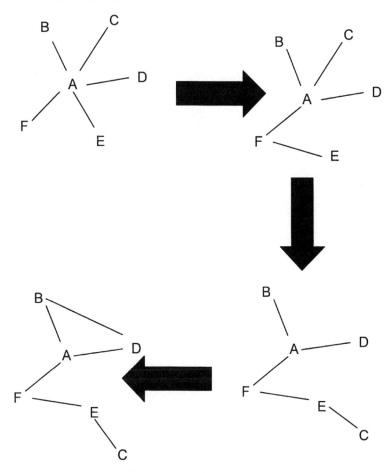

must contain at least one coreless component. Apart from this constraint, the composition of the equilibrium network should be approximately the same for networks with odd and even numbers of positions.

For example, ten simulations for twenty games each of exchange networks with ten positions were run. By the last game, there were more coreless components (seven) than indeterminate components (six), even though simulations in small, even-sized networks produced only indeterminate components. In addition there were two equal-power components.

TYPE III (EQUAL) VERSUS TYPE IV (INDETERMINATE) NETWORKS

Type-III networks can arise whenever there are an even number of actors and no bipartite structure. However, they seem to arise rarely, type-IV networks

Figure 13.10
Network Evolution in CA and Adjacency Matrix Representations

Frequency of Strong   Power
Components in CA Representation

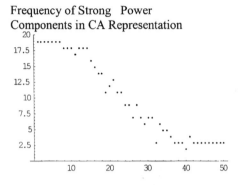

Standard Deviation of Earnings in CA
Representation

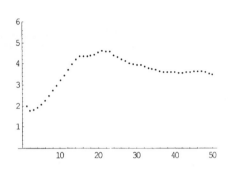

Frequency of Strong Power
Components in Adjacency
Representation

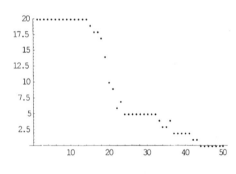

Standard Deviation of Earnings in
Adjacency Representation

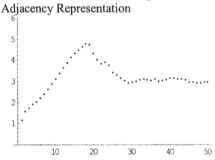

being much more prevalent. For example, when twenty simulations were run, each starting from a 6-Star network (one central position and five peripheral positions), the stable end outcomes had thirty-five type-IV components and only four type-III components. The reason may be that type-III networks are relatively rare. For example, there are sixty-four possible networks with four actors. Thirty-six of these have only type-IV components, but only one is a type-III network.

CELLULAR AUTOMATA VERSUS ADJACENCY MATRIX REPRESENTATIONS

Figures 13.10 and 13.11 compare the evolutions of the Extended Star network (Figure 13.3) using two different representations, a cellular automaton (CA), in which dissatisfied positions can "walk," and an adjacency matrix, whose cells

Figure 13.11

Frequencies of Coreless and Indeterminate Components in CA and Adjacency Representations

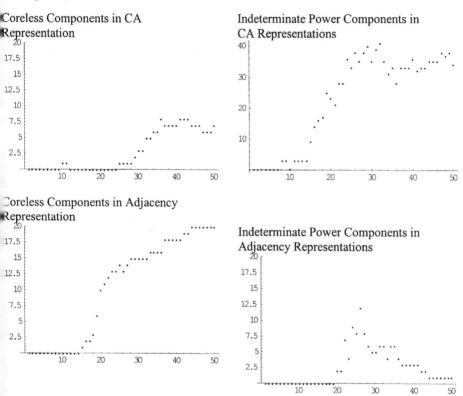

Coreless Components in CA Representation

Indeterminate Power Components in CA Representations

Coreless Components in Adjacency Representation

Indeterminate Power Components in Adjacency Representations

change value independently. The Extended Star network consists of one type-II (strong power) component. Figure 13.10 shows the similarities in the two evolutions, using twenty independent simulations each with fifty games. In both representations the number of strong power components declines from 20 to zero in the adjacency representation and to about 3 in the CA presentation. In both representations the amount of inequality in earnings, as measured by the standard deviation, first increases as powerful positions realize their power and then declines as dissatisfied positions change their network positions.

However, Figure 13.11 shows that the growing equality is accomplished in different ways. In the CA networks the growing equality is accomplished primarily through type IV Indeterminate components, although there are some coreless components as well. In the adjacency representations, equality is accomplished through the creation of single coreless components. The number of indeterminate components peaks at game twenty-five and then declines to zero.

A closer examination shows that in CA networks one of two things happen. Either dyads (type IV) break off from the high power component which itself changes into a coreless (type I) network, or one position breaks off from the high power component, changing it into an Indeterminate component (type IV). The single position then wanders in the empty parts of the CA without successfully reattaching itself. The results of these two processes is many indeterminate and coreless components and some isolates. In the adjacency representation, the network remains as one component until it becomes coreless (type I). The spatial nature of the CA representation produces distinctive evolutionary paths.[11]

BIPARTITE AND NON-BIPARTITE NETWORKS

In graph theory, a bipartite network is one whose vertices can be divided into two disjoint sets where all edges connect members from different sets. Transactions between complementary sets (buyers and sellers, men and women) are represented as bipartite graphs. Not all bipartite graphs, however, need represent exchanges among two complementary sets. For example, if Andy and Charles both want to be Bob's regular racquetball partner, the graph is, technically, bipartite, but there are no underlying complementary sets.

Consider the possibly different evolutionary course of strong power networks with and without underlying categories. Somewhat unconventionally, I will use the term *bipartite* to refer only to networks with two underlying complementary categories. Nonbipartite networks, without underlying complementary categories, can freely evolve into indeterminate or coreless networks. However, if the two categories of a bipartite network are of unequal size, no evolution will eliminate the power disadvantage of the more populous category.

Figure 13.12 shows the evolution of the Extended Star network (adjacency representation) over 50 games in 20 simulations when it is bipartite (with positions B, C, and D in one category and positions A, E, F, and G in the other).[12] The number of strong-power components stayed at about 20; with few exceptions every simulation kept a strong power component throughout the 50 games. (Figure 13.9 also showed a growing number of indeterminate power components. Many of these were unattached dyads temporarily escaping the power of the less frequent category.)

However, if the two categories are of equal size, the outcome of a strong power network will be an Indeterminate network. The outcome cannot be coreless because no bipartite exchange network is coreless (Shubik 1988:198). In Figure 13.13 the starting network consists of two Three-Person Chain components (A-B-C and D-E-F) in which different types of positions predominate in each chain. As can be seen, the number of weak power components increases, the other types disappear (not shown in the figure), and the standard deviation of rewards first increases and then decreases in the expected manner.

Figure 13.12
A Bipartite Network

Frequencies of Strong Power Components

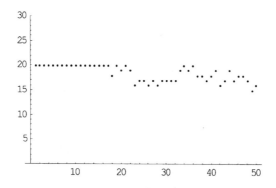

Frequencies of Indeterminate Power Components

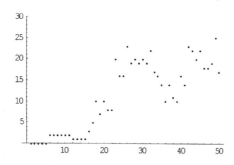

Standard Deviations of Rewards

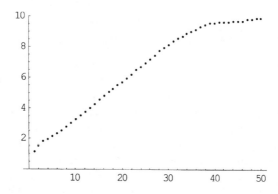

Figure 13.13
Networks with Two Categories of Equal Size

Frequencies of Indeterminate Power Components

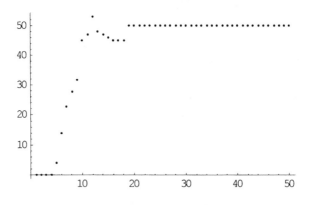

Standard Deviation of Rewards

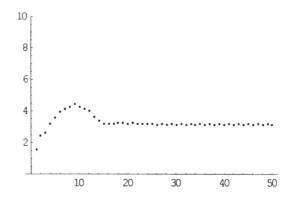

STRATEGY IN BIPARTITE NETWORKS

In bipartite networks in which the numbers in the two categories are unequal, random changes in the network positions of low-earning actors (the higher-frequency category) does not reduce inequality. However, one might ask whether variations in the parameters of the model might allow one actor to improve his or her lot. Would a single member of the more frequent and less powerful category do better with a higher, or a lower, minimum acceptable level before he or she changes networks? The actor might do better if by changing networks (or walking, in the CA simulations) because he or she would be quicker in avoiding undesirable network positions. On the other hand, it is pos- sible that those who waited longer until their competitors had left and their position was less unfavorable might do better. Similar arguments could be made for distinctively high or low values of the probability p of changing relations in the adjacency matrix simulations.

To examine these ideas, simulations were run in which one weak position (in the more frequent category) had either a minimum acceptable profit level higher or lower than 5, the standard value, or, if the minimum profitability was not achieved, had a distinctively high or low probability of changing his relations (instead of the standard probability of .20). None of the variations made a difference. The selected actor did just as badly as his or her compatriots in the more frequent category.

SOCIAL CAPITAL

Social capital can refer to characteristics of the individual or to characteristics of a network. When applied to an individual it refers to the resources that an individual can garner through the members of a personal network. When applied to a network it refers to the *capacity* of a network. A network whose members trust one another has the capacity for some activities that a network with less trustful measures would lack.

A network in which exploited individuals can change their positions potentially has two forms of social capital that more fixed networks may lack. In strong-power networks, such as Star networks, many fewer exchanges occur than could occur if the members were arranged differently. The capacity of the network, as measured by the maximal number of transactions that could occur, is suboptimal. This will be a feature of many, but all, strong-power networks, in which some positions gain power because others are excluded.[13]

For example, consider the evolution of a 6-Star network (one central high power position with five potential exchange partners. The number of exchanges is limited to one. Ten simulations of twenty games each produced a variety of outcomes: three coreless components, three equal power components, and eight indeterminate components. Figure 13.14 shows the increase in the total number of transactions in these networks as power differences decreased.

Equality in a network may also add to its capacity through the promotion of cohesion among the members. The exploitation that occurs in strong-power networks may lead to anger and resentment (Willer, Lovaglia, and Markovsky 1997). Figure 13.15 shows the early increase in inequality in this network, as the powerful central position comes to enjoy the benefits of its privileged position, followed by the decline in inequality, as the network changes its shape.

AN EXPERIMENT FOR THIS MODEL

A simple experiment could be used to examine some of these processes. Subjects are presented with a checkerboard. Each subject controls the movement of one piece on the board. Every move of the game would involve two steps,

Figure 13.14
Increases in Exchanges in the Six-Star Network as It Evolves

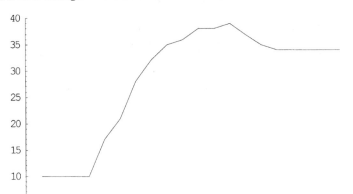

an exchange step and a movement step. In the exchange step each actor can exchange with any of his Moore neighbors, of which he has at most eight. This stage is designed to be as simple as possible and require a minimum of experimenter intervention. Each actor attaches a number from 1 to 23 on his or her piece, representing an offer to others if they exchange with him or her. No player can be involved in more than one exchange. Two players, each of whom makes the highest offer to each other, consummate their exchange on terms that are an average of their offers to each other. The remaining network is then examined for reciprocal highest offers. Ties are settled randomly.

In the second stage, each actor is allowed to move his or her piece to any neighboring unoccupied square. Conflicts occasioned by two or more players wanting to move to the same square are settled randomly. Subjects never communicate verbally with one another. These experiments can alternatively be run with pieces of two colors, where exchanges can occur only between neighboring pieces that are of different colors. As in the simulations, the variables of interest are the evolution of these networks, final equilibrium networks (if they exist), inequalities, and numbers of exchanges.

CONCLUSION

Early in the chapter I raised four questions:

1. If members of exchange networks migrate when they are dissatisfied with their power, is the result inevitably a network of equal power?

The answer is no. In networks with two complementary categories of unequal size the members of the larger category remain weak. In other types of networks, the results are approximately equal power.[14]

Figure 13.15
Standard Deviations of Earnings as the Six-Star Network Evolves

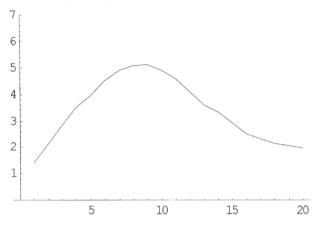

2. What are the characteristics of stable networks?

Stable exchange networks are of two types, either indeterminate, in which all positions are included in exchanges with no or small differences in power, or coreless, in which all positions are subject to exclusion.

3. How is the outcome of the evolution related to the properties of the starting network?

Among nonbipartite networks, the outcome depends on whether there are an even or odd number of actors. With an even number of actors the outcome is indeterminate or equal-power components. Networks with an odd number of actors evolve into coreless networks. Bipartite networks with equal numbers in the two categories evolve into Indeterminate networks. There were also interesting differences between the cellular and adjacency representations of exchange networks. In cellular automata it is easier for the network to split into separate components or to a component plus isolates.

4. Are there typical stages through which networks evolve?

The only transitional stage I detected in network evolution was the temporary appearance of indeterminate components in the adjacency representation of nonbipartite networks with an odd number of actors (Figure 13.8): in the long run, coreless components predominate, but before then indeterminate components appear and then disappear. The reasons for this are unknown.

As stated in the Introduction, there are two thrusts to the chapter. First, there are circumstances in which existing network theories are incorrect; instead of increasing inequality and growing power differences we may see network change without the development of power differences. Which result occurs should depend on the type of constraint described by the exchange network. Suppose, on the one hand, that the exchange network simply reflected which pairs were willing to exchange with one another in a situation of complete information. For example, the *A-B-C* chain could represent a situation in *A* and *C* cannot profitably exchange. The network cannot change as long as individual preferences do not change and *B* should grow more and more powerful if he or she has to choose between *A* and *C*. Suppose, at the other extreme, that all pairs can potentially exchange profitably but that *A* and *C* are simply unaware of one another. One might expect *A* and *C* to search for other alternatives and perhaps find one another, producing another network.

This chapter also has the positive goal of describing the equilibria toward which networks evolve when change is possible. Networks can evolve either toward indeterminate power structures, in which all actors are involved in exchanges and there are small or nonexistent power differences, or networks can become coreless; the positions that are excluded then rotate through the network. The outcome depends on whether there are an even or odd number of actors. The outcome depends on whether the actors are embedded in a social space. Networks embedded in a social space can solve their inequality problems by shedding components or individual actors. Whether there are underlying complementary types of actors has a profound effect: power inequalities may be unavoidable if one category is larger than another.

APPENDIX: DESCRIPTIONS OF TWO SIMULATIONS

Cellular Automata

The dynamics in this cellular automata representation of an exchange network are borrowed from Gaylord and D'Andria (1998). A cellular automaton is created with empty and nonempty cells occupied by actors. The number of rows and columns in the CA are parameters. To eliminate edge effects the CA is a torus. The actors can be placed randomly or according to design. Cells that are Moore neighbors[15] are connected to one another in the exchange network.[16] In each game players begin by making offers to one another on the division of 24 points. Players excluded from exchange in the previous game raise the values of their offers to others by two points. Players included in exchange make offers to others that would give them what they earned in the last game. Two players, each of whom make each other's best offers, conclude a deal, splitting any differences between their offers. The offers of the other players are then examined and further deals concluded until there are no connected pairs remaining. An average gain over the last four games is computed for each player. If this average gain falls below 5 points, the player *walks*, if this is feasible.[17]

Adjacency Matrix

In this simulation the exchange network is represented directly as an adjacency matrix. If the average gain for a player falls below 5 points, every cell in his or her row of the adjacency matrix has a probability of *p* of changing from a one to a zero or from a zero to a one. Because exchange relations are symmetric, his or her column is also changed.

NOTES

1. This situation does not fit the model perfectly. There is no infinitely divisible resource that can be divided between members of a dating dyad. However, the dyads activities could be divided between those favored relatively more by the man or the woman.

2. A recent book edited by Doreian and Stockman (1997) includes many studies of the evolution of social networks. However, none of them involves the evolution of exchange networks.

3. Inconsistent offers in the situation are resolved by "splitting the difference."

4. Most exchange networks undoubtedly reflect both preferences and ignorance.

5. In the reported simulations $p = .20$. Increasing p speeds the rate of change but reduces the model's sensitivity to the effects of single changes in the network.

6. The pattern for the cellular automata simulation is borrowed from the pattern described in a book by Richard J. Gaylord and Louis J. D'Andria (1998).

7. The core is the fundamental solution concept for cooperative games. The core consists of all outcomes in which every subset (coalition) of players earn at least what they can guarantee themselves regardless of the actions of the other players.

8. All transactions are standardized to have a value of 1.00.

9. Not all networks with an odd number of actors lack cores. For example, the Tee and extended Star networks in Figure 13.3 have outcomes in the core.

10. Position A has a slight advantage over C.

11. Watts (1999) finds important differences between what he calls *spatial* and *relational* network models.

12. The adjacency representation was used.

13. A strong power network, like the {A, B, C} component of the Tee network in Figure 13.4, in which only one position is excluded, cannot produce more exchanges under any rearrangement of the positions.

14. Lawler and Yoon (1998) and Kollock (1994) have studied the development of commitment in exchange relations. According to Lawler, commitment is an emotional reaction to frequent and equal power exchange. Kollock finds that uncertainty in exchange increases commitment. Committed actors are less likely to change their exchange partners. However, commitment in exchange relations may slow down the process of achieving equality. Equality in exchange relations is achieved most quickly the more willing actors are to change their networks. There is a sense in which commitment and equality are antithetical.

15. Every position has eight Moore neighbors, those cells to its northwest, north, northeast, west, east, southwest, south, and southeast.

16. When networks consist of two complementary categories, then neighboring positions must also be of different categories to exchange.

17. For the rules governing *walking*, see Gaylord and D'Andria (1998; Ch. 1).

EPILOGUE

Theory, Simulation, and Research: The New Synthesis

Michael J. Lovaglia and Robert B. Willer

If science progresses through the coordination of theory and research, then what role does simulation play in creating scientific knowledge? Computer simulations of social phenomena are not formally derived from existing theories. Although simulations often represent elements of existing theory, they may also incorporate research results as input to make predictions in specific situations. Simulations can also be built with little reference to theory at all, relying instead on a long list of relevant variables associated with some phenomenon. Simulations can be used to model phenomena attempting to accurately predict events and they can be used to represent theory, exploring theoretical ramifications and generating hypotheses. A simulation, then, is neither theory nor empirical research. The output of simulations, however, is similar to empirical research results. What is the proper role of computer simulation in the conduct of science, especially social science?

With computer simulations becoming more prevalent in many areas of science, a new synthesis of scientific method may be emerging in which simulation mediates between theory and research in the practice of modern science. Although computer simulations are a recent development, they are examples of models long used by scientists as aids to theoretical development or accurate prediction.

After describing how scientific theory and research became coordinated during the last hundred years, we examine the development of theoretical research programs in sociology. Then we describe the role of models as mediators between theory and research. Finally, we provide examples of computer simulations as powerful models and show how they contribute to the development of both theory and empirical research in sociology.

COORDINATING THEORY AND RESEARCH

That science creates and cumulates knowledge is not in serious dispute. When the results of scientific research can be used to accomplish other goals, some of them routine, scientific results become generally accepted as fact (Hacking 1983). Arguing about the existence of microwaves, for example, seems pointless when a microwave oven has cooked your baked potato in four minutes. How science works and whether social science can work as effectively as natural science remain undecided.

The expansion of scientific achievement in the twentieth century has been traced to the coordination of theory and empirical research. Before 1900, the link between theory and research had yet to be forged with many researchers taking a largely atheoretical empiricist approach. In the late 1800s, for example, researchers such as Thomas Edison used systematic programs of experimental tinkering, a sort of trial and error empiricism (Israel 1998). Physicists in the early 1900s developed a working strategy that coordinated theory and empirical research. Prior to that time, "the idea of a close coordination in which theory guides experiment and experiment tests theory was not generally understood" (Moore 1989:62). Theory-driven research characterizes twentieth-century science. In the 1930s, the philosopher Karl Popper solidified the relationship between theory and research by proposing that good scientific theories can be falsified (1959). That is, a good theory can be subjected to an empirical test. Developing theories and testing them is now considered to be the hallmark of good science and seems to describe well the basic approach to research of many scientists.

Scientific practice, however, is more complicated than simply developing theories and disproving the invalid ones. Another philosopher, Imre Lakatos (1970), pointed out that whereas Popper was correct to assert that research could never prove the truth of a scientific statement, he was wrong in thinking that research alone could prove a scientific statement false. Whenever test results disagree with predictions derived from a theory, there are at least two possibilities. The theory may be invalid or the test may have been inadequate. Sometimes scientists decide that the theory was invalid and try to develop a better one. Sometimes they decide that the test was inadequate and try to develop a better one. How do scientists decide?

Lakatos (1970) proposed that scientists work within research programs. No one empirical test ever decides the validity of a theory. Rather, a theory is tested repeatedly in a program of research. As the theory develops it suggests new tests and new areas of research. For Lakatos, as long as the research program progresses and the developing theory produces more worthwhile research, the theory is considered valid. Only when the volume of useful research produced by a theory dwindles is the theory eventually discarded.

A marked division of labor characterizes modern scientific research programs. Theoretical physicists may have never conducted an experiment. The daily work of experimental physicists may also have little to do with theory. For science to progress as rapidly as it has, however, experimenters must design some research to test theory and theorists must develop theories that account for the results of research. In sociology too, many researchers devote little time to theory and few theorists collect data. Most sociologists would likely agree, however, that theory should account for the results of research and that the best research is informed by theory.

THEORY AND RESEARCH IN SOCIOLOGY

Theory and research are becoming more closely coordinated in the social sciences as well. Sociological research programs in which theories are developed and tested began in the early 1960s. Status characteristics theory (Berger, Cohen, and Zelditch 1966) and the power-dependence theory of social exchange being prominent early examples (Emerson 1962). Research programs operate through the interplay of theories and empirical research that tests those theories. In the process, research methods become more efficient and theories evolve. Berger and Zelditch (1997) describe five ways that theories develop: (1) *elaboration*, in which a theory is revised to gain analytic power or becomes better established through having passed empirical tests, (2) *proliferation*, in which related theories are created to explain a wider range of phenomena, (3) *variants*, in which new theories explain the same phenomena in different ways, reinforcing the original theory, (4) *competitors*, in which new theories present competing explanations incompatible with the original theory, and (5) *integration*, in which a new theory consolidates the ideas of two theories in a single formulation. Theories grow through relationships with other theories and with empirical tests.

Models in Science

The relationship between a theory and its related research is not simple. Philosopher Nancy Cartwright (1983) points out that a good theory is usually too simple and abstract to apply directly to a specific situation used in an empirical test. Models are constructed to mediate between theories and the results of empirical tests (Morrison and Morgan 1999). Models connect theory to a specific research setting through the use of bridging principles or what sociologists would call scope conditions. Berger and Zelditch (1997) note that constructing a typical theory-based empirical model requires *instantiation* of abstract theoretical elements, *specification* of theoretically relevant special conditions, and *identification* of observational techniques. Thus, a model cannot typically be derived strictly from the theory it is designed to represent. Additional assumptions are needed; some inspired by theory, some based on known empirical parameters, and some added ad hoc to make the model work as its designer intends. Models, then, are partially independent of both theory and empirical results (Morrison and Morgan 1999).

Because models are partially independent of both theory and empirical results and because model building seems messy and sometimes unscientific, it is fair to ask what models do and how they can teach us anything (Cartwright 1999). It is the semiautonomous nature of models—neither derived from theory nor wholly dependent on data—that casts doubt on their scientific status. Berger and Zelditch (1997) suggest that scientists use model building as a working strategy to spur theoretical development. That is, scientists use models to play with theories to get ideas for how to improve them. A scientist's choice of method, however, is often independent of her theoretical orientation (Szmatka and Lovaglia 1996). Often, scientists are drawn to the methods they use for personal reasons that are later justified through theoretical arguments. Models are usually built by people who enjoy the work rather than by people working primarily to develop and test theories, or by people who wish to predict empirical phenomena. Modelers then attempt to justify the value of their labor. Szmatka and Lovaglia's (1996) thesis suggests that in this regard model builders are not different from theorists or empirical researchers who also choose the working methods they prefer and then seek to justify their value. The importance of theory and empirical research to the growth of scientific knowledge, however, is more commonly understood. Thus, the value of models requires demonstration.

A good model has to relate either to theory or to empirical research. Philosophers of science consider the most "interesting"—or scientifically useful— models to be those that relate to both theory and research results (Morrison and Morgan 1999). Useful models may be data driven and used to develop theory or they may represent theory in ways that predict research results. In philosophical terms, a model may be categorized as primarily *representative* of a theory or *phenomenological*, predicting a physical or social phenomenon (Cartwright 1999). A model may be useful in predicting a certain phenomenon without attempting a full explanation. Models can also represent theory, providing a picture of the theory in action. Thus, models promote learning, both as they are built and as they are used (Morrison and Morgan 1999).

A specific discipline may place more emphasis on phenomenological or representative aspects of models. Models proposed by economists are usually phenomenological, emphasizing the statistical modeling of data. In contrast, the models proposed by physicists emphasize the representational aspects of models, their relationship to theories. In both economics and physics, however, models are both representational and phenomenological. For example, economic models belong to two broad types: (1) models based on theory and mathematics, and (2) models based on statistics and empirical research (Morrison and Morgan 1999). The most scientifically useful models contain aspects of both types but are partially independent of both theory and research.

One reason that models are independent of both theory and research results is that model builders make creative use of current technology. Thus in the seventeenth century, the pendulum that was used to investigate Newtonian mechanics (Giere 1988) and the air pump that was used to create a vacuum (Shapin and Schaffer 1985) represented high technology at the time. Mathematical models use the mathematics available to explore the implications of theories. Current models increasingly use computer simulation.

Computer simulations are particularly powerful and flexible models having the potential to teach us a lot as well as to mislead. How do simulations represent a theory? How do they predict empirical phenomena? The boundary problem in the sociology of science becomes relevant (Gieryn 1999). That is, what is it about the use of simulations that makes them scientific?

SIMULATIONS AS AIDS TO THEORY AND RESEARCH

Interesting simulations in sociology that relate to both theory and empirical research are easy to find. We will provide two examples to describe the ways in which sociological simulations use and contribute to theory and research. Less common in sociology are simulations that philosophers would call phenomenological—that is, primarily developed to predict events rather than to provide an understanding of relationships among them. Simulations that accurately model events, however, are powerful tools, accurate prediction being one of the hallmarks of good science. Perhaps by comparing examples of familiar phenomenological simulations in other fields with examples of the simulations developed to represent theory that are common in sociology, we can explain the scarcity of phenomenological simulations in sociology.

Using Simulations to Predict Events

We have all watched the value of models to predict events steadily increase. Simulations of the weather and the economy are perhaps the most striking examples. Predicting the weather and the economy are such difficult problems that recent successes can seem almost miraculous. Economic models allow adjustment of the economy through interest rates, an intervention strategy credited with the longest economic expansion in U.S. history. Computer simulations of the weather now produce useful forecasts up to seven days in advance and strikingly accurate forecasts of weather for the next twenty-four hours.

Weather models are largely phenomenological, they predict the weather in one area based on previous weather in other areas using data from satellite images. The huge increase in daily weather data made possible by satellite images, combined with a huge increase in computing power, has led to accurate weather prediction (at least in the short term), a problem once considered impossible. Thus, phenomenological models progress and become most useful when a constant stream of high-quality data can be used effectively to revise them.

Phenomenological models can be extremely accurate predictors without giving the sense that they explain or represent phenomena in the way that representative, theory-based models do. Builders of weather models may be unable to render a satisfying explanation of how the weather works. Phenomenological computer simulations are so complex that describing how and why they work becomes problematic. They may make accurate predictions but fail to provide a satisfying story explaining why. The role of representative models in the development and testing of theories is more complicated.

Using Simulations to Develop Theory

Simulation in sociology is most often used in conjunction with theory rather than to model events. The raw data used by sociologists comes in a different form from weather data or economic data. Weather and economic data stream in constantly, providing new opportunities to compare simulation with observation. In contrast, the data usually used by sociologists is punctuated and produced to answer specific research questions. Sociologists use surveys, interviews, participant observation, and experiments to collect data. None of these strategies produce streaming data comparable to that produced by weather satellites or the stock market. Public opinion polling has grown to the point where it begins to provide a steady stream of data, which has been used to model the outcome of political elections. Prominent simulations in sociology represent theories. Representative simulations (as opposed to phenomenological simulations) provide a picture that shows how a theory works.

Simulating Theories of Network Exchange

Research on exchange networks has been characterized by cumulative theoretical research programs using experimental research to refine and develop theories. Exchange networks can be studied experimentally by assembling a network in which people can exchange with designated others in the network. The pattern of possible exchange relations constitutes the network. (See Figure 14.1.) When people exchange with each other in the network, their profit can be compared with theoretical predictions. Progress occurs as discrepancies between prediction and observation are resolved by refining experiments and revising theories. As much as any research program in sociology, network exchange research embodies the classic scientific interplay of theory and experiment. Given the effective coordination of theory and experiment, the use of simulation might not seem necessary or warranted. Nonetheless, computer simulations have contributed to exchange research since about 1980 (Cook et al. 1983). Following a brief introduction to the research area, two examples of the

Figure 14.1
Exchange Network Structures

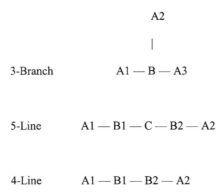

use of simulations in network exchange research show the independent nature of simulations as mediators between theory and research.

Networks of exchange pose an intriguingly simple research problem: Using only our knowledge of network structure and the rules of exchange, can we predict the resources each person will gain when exchanging with each other in a network?

By definition, when exchange occurs, both parties to the exchange profit to some extent.[1] One party, however, may profit more than does the other. Some network positions are at a disadvantage. Suppose several peripheral actors are connected by exchange relations to one central actor. That is, peripheral actors may exchange with the central actor but not with each other. (See the 3-Branch network in Figure 14.1.) Given the 3-Branch structure, suppose also that rules of exchange dictate that actors may exchange with at most one other actor. Thus the central B actor can exchange with only one peripheral A actor. The exchanging actors will profit while those excluded from exchanging will not profit. The result is a bidding war in which peripheral actors compete to offer the central actor more and more profit. If exchange opportunities continue, the central actor will eventually command nearly all the available profit from exchanges. Different network structures confer different relative advantage on positions in the network. How much will each position get after a series of exchange opportunities?

Exchange networks have generated so much research in part because relatively simple networks pose interesting theoretical questions. For example consider a simple network, the five-actor line, in which a person can exchange only with connected positions adjacent to her. (See Figure 14.1.) Early network theories proposed that central positions would have an advantage. However, Cook et al. (1983) argued and demonstrated that the off-center positions (B1 and B2) in the 5-Line network gained the most resources in exchange. Predicting exchange rates in more complex networks poses a theoretical challenge.

Markovsky (1995) describes the development of the X-Net simulator to represent Network Exchange Theory. While setting out to program a simulator that embodied the theoretical axioms and scope conditions of Network Exchange Theory, he soon realized that without auxiliary assumptions, the programmed actors could not "do" anything. Scope conditions are the bridging principles that tie a theory to a specific physical setting capable of testing the theory. For example, "actors consistently excluded from exchanges raise their offers" is a scope condition in network exchange theory. Markovsky programmed actors to decrease offers by one point to those with whom an exchange had been completed and increase offers by one point to those with whom an exchange had not been completed. While consistent with the scope condition, Markovsky chose one-point increases as a way to represent the scope condition from a number of plausible alternatives.

The X-Net simulator reproduces the experimental finding that the off-center actors in the 5-Line network gain the most resources from exchange when actors are allowed to exchange with only one other actor. The flexibility of the simulator also showed that network structure alone was unlikely to determine the outcome of exchanges. By varying the rules of exchange to allow actors to exchange with more than one other actor, the simulator predicted that the advantage held by the off-center actors in the 5-Line would be eliminated or reversed. Thus, the simulation made apparent why early theories of network exchange had failed: exchange rates depend, not only on network structure, but also on the rules of exchange (Markovsky 1995). As a result, network exchange theory was developed to account for exchange rates in network structures under a variety of exchange rules (Markovsky, Willer, and Patton 1988; Markovsky et al. 1993).

The X-Net simulator also contributed to a major development in Network Exchange Theory, the discovery of "weak power." Under the typical "one-exchange" rule, the off-center actors in the 5-Line network eventually garner most of the available profit from exchanges. The 5-Line is considered a *strong-power* network in network exchange theory. In other networks, such as the 4-Line in Figure 14.1, differences in profit between positions are much smaller and seem to stabilize rather than progress (Markovsky et al. 1993). Networks characterized by small, stable profit differences are termed *weak-power* networks in network exchange theory.

It is not apparent, however, from visual inspection or casual analysis that any power differences exist at all among actors in the 4-Line network. One way of analyzing the 4-Line network suggests that the central actors (B1 and B2) may have an exchange advantage because the peripheral actors (A1 and A2) lack alternatives. Another analysis suggests, however, that if the A actors are more compliant exchange partners, then B actors would prefer to exchange with the A actors rather than with each other. The result would be two stable A-B dyads exchanging equally. The original version of network exchange theory predicted no power differences in the 4-Line network. The X-Net simulator, however, predicted a slight power advantage. (If the total available profit from an exchange was 24 points, X-Net simulated an A=B split of 11–13 in the 4-Line network, whereas in the 5-Line network, the A=B difference eventually reached 1–23).

Early experimental results showing small power differences between positions were attributed to experimental artifact or to psychological as opposed to structural conditions (Markovsky 1995). Thus, the development of theory was hampered by small differences in experimental results, which were deemed inconsequential. However, X-Net simulations that also showed small differences between positions motivated theorists to explain the structural basis for them. An extended network exchange theory explaining weak-power differences was then developed and supported by experimental tests (Markovsky et al. 1993). Thus experimental results supporting the existence of weak-power differences in exchange networks were not themselves sufficient to motivate the development of a better theory. Rather, the experimental results were dismissed until a simulation representing the theory also supported their existence. It is a good example of the dictum in physics that observations alone cannot establish a scientific fact. Noted physicist Arthur Eddington is said to have quipped that scientists should never trust an observation until it has been confirmed by theory (Weinberg 1992). The foregoing example makes clear that by mediating between theory and the research results, simulations can speed the process by which theory develops to confirm observations.

The contributions of the X-Net simulator to network exchange theory and research are remarkable because it has never been used to predict the precise amount of resources gained by positions in exchange experiments. For strong-power networks such as the 5-Line, X-Net simulations grossly overstate the differences in resources between positions found in typical experiments, whereas for weak-power networks such as the 4-line, X-net simulations generally understate power differences between positions. Nonetheless, X-Net simulations contributed to major developments described here in network exchange theory and research. A revision of X-Net capable of accounting for known experimental results of exchange in both strong-power and weak-power networks has recently been developed (Lovaglia 2001). It requires additional assumptions, some representing theoretical developments such as the incorporation of the resistance equation from elementary theory used to predict results in weak-power networks (Lovaglia et al. 1995). Other assumptions are ad hoc, calibrating the simulation to known results. For example, elements of both forward-looking and backward-looking actors are programmed into the simulation. In particular, the best results are achieved when simulated actors base their behavior on the outcome of their last three exchange opportunities. Specifying an actor's memory to look backward only to the prior three exchange opportunities is certainly ad hoc. The actor's memory could as easily be longer or shorter. It is unclear, then, how much trust should be placed on predictions of such simulations in networks for which no or little research results exist. It does, however, satisfy the philosophical criterion for the most interesting simulations: those developed to relate both to theory and to research results.[2]

Simulating Collective Action

The collective action problem also attracts simulation work. Like exchange processes in networks, collective action is a fundamental research problem in sociology (Olson 1965). Why do people band together to accomplish a collective good when those who contribute benefit no more than those who do not contribute? Villagers, for example, might work together to dam a stream, providing a reliable source of water for the benefit of all in the village. But if all villagers have access to the water after the dam is built, then there appears to be no incentive for any individual to contribute to building the dam. Might not a rational individual "free-ride" on the contributions of others, contributing nothing but sharing in the collective good? But if too few people contribute, then the dam will not be built. Why does collective action occur?

Unlike network exchange research, collective action is not primarily associated with extensive experimental research. Instead, the difficulties in collecting data relevant to the collective action problem have produced research using a variety of research methods (for recent examples see Barkey 1991; Diani 1996; Gould 1991, 1999; Loveman 1998; Zhao 1998). Observational and historical studies yield rich insights for theorists but lack of control makes deciding among competing theories problematic. Thus, collective action research would appear to have more need of simulation as a theoretical tool than does network exchange research.

Simulation also appears well suited to collective action research because the problem is both fundamental and concerned with how a phenomenon originated. How might collective action originate in a population of selfishly rational individuals? Simulations are well suited for creating populations of rational actors. Then the simulator can flexibly change social conditions and observe which conditions facilitate collective action. The result has been a variety of simulations that focus on different aspects of society proposed to facilitate social action (see, e.g., Chwe 1999; Gould 1993; Granovetter 1978; Heckathorn 1993; Kim and Bearman 1997; Macy 1990, 1991, 1993; Marwell, Oliver, and Prahl 1988; Oliver and Marwell 1988; Oliver, Marwell, and Teixeira 1985).

The proliferation of simulations of collective action has led to concerns about their scientific value. All published simulations propose a plausible social factor capable of generating collective action. They all offer solutions to the collective action problem. Yet more simulations appear. How do we choose a valid simulated representation of collective action? Can we develop a valid theory of collective action from myriad simulations?

Macy's (1990, 1991, 1993, 1995) collective action research illustrates how some simulations come to be preferred over others. We have already noted the philosophical conclusion that the most interesting models relate both to theory and empirical research. One way, then, to decide among competing simulations is to pursue those that generate empirical research in support of the theories they represent.

Macy developed simulations of collective action using research on the less complex problem of cooperation between two rational individuals. The collective action problem is a similar social trap on a larger scale. In social dilemmas, an individual's immediate self interest conflicts with the potential for long-term benefit. The prisoners dilemma in particular has been the subject of extensive experimental research and provides a unique approach to simulation development.

The Prisoner's Dilemma

The prisoner's dilemma is a social trap familiar to viewers of television police dramas.[3] Two suspects are interrogated for committing a crime. A reduced sentence goes to the first one who confesses and implicates his partner who then gets a long prison term. But if neither confesses, they both go free. They would both be better off if they cooperated with each other and kept quiet. Inevitably, however, one confesses. The risk of betrayal is too great for cooperation to regularly occur between suspects. Similar to the collective action problem, the problem of cooperation was stated as a question about the origin of a fundamental social phenomenon (Axelrod 1984). If betrayal avoids the possibility of disaster and offers the possibility of a large reward, then how could cooperation evolve in society?

Axelrod (1984) developed a unique way to answer that question using a computer simulation. Prisoner's dilemma experiments had suggested that if people confront prisoner's dilemmas repeatedly, then they can develop strategies to improve their overall outcomes.[4] Axelrod invited interested researchers to submit possible strategies that people might use when confronted with repeated prisoner's dilemmas. For example, a person might betray the partner every time. Another person might cooperate every time. One strategy that seems to reflect typical human behavior is called tit-for-tat. When using the tit-for-tat strategy, a person chooses the course of action chosen by his partner in the previous round. If my partner betrayed me on the last round, then I will betray my partner on this round. If my partner cooperated with me on the last round, then I will cooperate on this round. Axelrod programmed simulated actors such that some actors used each of the strategies submitted to him by researchers. Then his simulation placed pairs of actors with different strategies in repeated prisoner's dilemmas. His simulated competition among prisoner's dilemma strategies showed which strategies produced the greatest rewards when used against other strategies. In repeated prisoner's dilemmas, tit-for-tat won. Individuals could succeed in repeated social dilemmas by selectively cooperating tit-for-tat.

Macy's Collective Action Research Program

To approach the problem of collective action, Macy (1989) used social learning theory and experimental research on the prisoner's dilemma to develop a simulation of collective action. In doing so, he abandoned the forward-looking "rational calculator" actor featured prominently in collective action theories by Olson (1965) and Oliver, Marwell, and Teixeira (1985). Macy's model assumes that actors in collective action social dilemmas look backward, adjusting their decisions to contribute or not based on evaluations of their outcomes. Macy's model also conformed well with the results of prisoner's dilemma research and reduced the cognitive ability needed for humans to achieve cooperation because people were not assumed to calculate their advantage before acting.

Macy's (1990) simulated actors based their decisions on their previous experience as do those using tit-for-tat, but with an even simpler strategy. Recall that with a successful collective action, everyone benefits whether they contributed or not. But if an insufficient number of people contribute, then the collective action fails and no one benefits. When a collective action is successful, Macy's simulation assumes that people become more likely to choose the same course of action that had previously benefited them. But when a collective action is unsuccessful, people become more likely to choose a different course of action, hoping for more success. For example, if an actor chose not to contribute to collective action and it was successful, the actor would likely again choose not to contribute. An actor who contributed to successful collective action would likely again choose to contribute. In contrast, an actor who chose not to contribute to a collective action that failed would become more likely to contribute next time. And an actor who chose to contribute to a failed collective action would become less likely to contribute next time. It is an elaboration of a strategy used in prisoner's dilemmas called PAVLOV or "win-stay, lose-shift," that can outperform tit-for-tat (Nowak and Sigmund 1993).

Despite using a strategy that successfully promotes cooperation, Macy's (1990) simulation did not regularly produce successful collective action. Unless a critical mass of contributors was achieved early in the simulation, collective action usually failed. The problem was that public goods are never gotten right away, so early on in the simulation there is little reward for contributions causing simulated actors to fly back and forth between contributing and free-riding from one trial to the next. This flip-flopping makes it difficult to reach critical mass and overcome start-up costs. Collective action fails as a result.

To alleviate the problem of contributions failing to reach critical mass needed for successful collective action, Macy (1991) proposed that people have some knowledge of the amount of contributions needed for success and the amount already contributed. Perhaps if people know the contributions necessary for success and about how much has already been contributed, then they will be more likely to contribute themselves. Charities commonly use a related strategy to spur contributions. For example, an annual charity drive in Iowa City uses a large painting of a thermometer filled with red to represent the goal and current contributions. The top of the thermometer represents the goal of half a million dollars with degrees marked off in units of $10,000. As the drive continues, the red rises in the thermometer as thousands of dollars are contributed to the goal. Passersby can easily see how much their neighbors have already contributed and how much is still needed to reach the collective goal. Changes in Macy's (1991) simulation were also straightforward; by making actors' decisions sequential rather than simultaneous, they can be programmed to factor in others' choices. When simulated actors take account of others' contributions, cooperation increases and successful collective action occurs regularly.

Macy's (1989, 1990, 1991) simulations show clear contributions to theoretical development. Macy (1991) presents a cogent theory that explains how successful collective action could regularly occur given plausible initial conditions. Moreover, Macy's research program shows progress; later simulations solve problems arising in earlier simulations. The same, however, can be said of other simulations of collective action, notably that of Oliver and Marwell (1988; Oliver, Marwell, and Teixeira 1985; Marwell, Oliver, and Prahl 1988). Simulations that represent theories can progress only so far unless they generate new empirical research. Otherwise, we cannot accumulate sufficient evidence to judge the validity of the many possible theoretical explanations that can be developed using simulations.

While Macy's (1993) simulation work continues to develop his theory of collective action, he has also completed laboratory experiments testing basic assumptions of his theory. Simulations demonstrate conditions under which a phenomenon can occur. They do not establish that a phenomenon did, in fact, occur. To support the theoretical assumption that collective action occurs because people use a "win-stay, lose-shift" strategy in deciding whether to contribute, it is necessary to demonstrate that real people use the "win-stay, lose-shift" strategy. Macy (1995) developed an experimental setting in which he tested the behavioral assumptions of his learning model. Participants in his experiments engage in a 20-person prisoner's dilemma game, a basic social dilemma analogous to the collective action problem. Each participant interacts with nineteen actors simulated to create a variety of decision contexts. Simulated actors used 4 strategies that have bases in collective action literature and game theory: (1) win-stay, lose shift, (2) a rational calculator of marginal returns for contribution that, in a twenty-person group, amounts to never contributing, (3) tit-for-tat, and (4) a norm-guided, golden-rule follower who always contributes. Macy then calculated which model best fit the participants' actual decision making. The "win-stay, lose-shift" model best described the participants' approach to the collective action problem, though tit for tat also fit the data well. Thus, experimental results provide additional support for the Macy's simulated solution to the collective action problem.

In addition to Macy's (1995) experimental support for the basic assumptions of his theory of collective action, Kanazawa (1998b, 2000) adapted Macy's model to simulate voting behavior. The decision to vote is a form of the collective action problem. Kanazawa then used his model to successfully predict voting behavior in two large, representative data sets, the American National Election Study and the National Opinion Research Center NORC General Social Survey. Support for the model was stronger in elections with only two main candidates. Support was less strong in elections with a strong third-party candidate. The empirical test of the model has detected conditions that might be important for future expansion of the theory. A better model could be developed and tested on data from European elections characterized by multiple parties.

With Kanazawa's contribution to the research program, the theory continues to develop with the help of simulations and has received empirical support for its predictive ability to complement the support for its basic assumptions provided by Macy's experiments. Science is a cumulative collective enterprise rather than an individual one. Good scientific work builds on earlier good scientific work. One strong criterion of a valid theory is that it generates new work, especially new work by other researchers that continues to receive empirical support. Macy's experiments and Kanazawa's theoretical contributions and empirical tests represent ways to judge the scientific value of the simulations that are part of this theoretical research program. Simulations that generate new theoretical development and empirical research grow and become accepted while those that do not are neglected and fade.

Progress in science is commonly acknowledged to result from the interplay of theory and empirical research. In two areas of sociological research, network exchange and collective action, we show the value of simulations to mediate between theory and empirical research, promoting scientific progress.

The New Synthesis: Theory, Simulation and Research

Simulations developed primarily to represent theory have made major contributions in two, quite different, areas of sociological research, network exchange and collective action. Simulations developed primarily to predict events, however, are rare in sociology. Nonetheless, in the two research areas examined here, the most interesting simulations relate to both theoretical development and empirical research. Further, through the synthesis of theory, simulation and empirical research, sociological theory demonstrates progressive growth accompanied by the accumulation of theoretically based empirical knowledge.

Using models to spur theoretical development and make novel predictions about events is not new. Simulations are particularly elaborate and flexible models but researchers have used simpler models for hundreds of years (Morrison and Morgan 1999). Only recently, however, have philosophers and sociologists of science examined the intricate way in which theory, simulations and empirical research coordinate to produce scientific progress (Morrison and Morgan 1999; Berger and Zelditch 1997).

The research areas examined here show how the best simulations relate to

both theory and empirical research but are independent of them. Building simulations and other types of models is an autonomous scientific enterprise as
important as inventing theories or testing them with empirical research. Scientific progress would be problematic without models to mediate between theory
and empirical research. A simulation that slavishly represented theory would do
little to spur theoretical development while a simulation that models events with
no theoretical reference would contribute little to our understanding of those
events. Thus, the ad hoc assumptions and arbitrary parameters used to make
simulations work are not necessary evils but tools that force researchers to think
about the implications of their work. Science is, and has always been, messier
than its public image.

Why are phenomenological models rare in sociology? Models of social processes that make accurate predictions of social behavior would increase sociology's stature as a science. The examples of two very different research areas in
sociology show that the working strategies of sociologists are not fundamentally
different from those of other scientists. Building a phenomenological model to
make accurate predictions is a project that would appeal to many sociologists
in a variety of research areas.

The kinds of sociological data commonly collected may not lend themselves
to the development of phenomenological models built primarily to predict events
rather than to represent theory. If models of the economy and the weather are
prototypical phenomenological simulations, then similarities in the kinds of data
used in those models might indicate why these fields have generated successful
phenomenological simulations. Both weather and economic data are collected
in a stream as the values of key variables are constantly updated. Phenomenological simulators in these areas can use the constant comparison of prediction
and observation to refine their simulations. In contrast, most data in sociology
is collected to answer specific research questions and is updated at long intervals
or not at all. The disconnected quality of sociological data may impede the
development of sociological models capable of accurately predicting social
events.

New sources of data may solve the problem of discontinuous data collection
in sociology. For example, data from supermarket scanners, combined with the
demographic data available from credit and debit cards used by purchasers,
could provide the data stream necessary to model consumer choice behavior.
The Internet presents data collection opportunities as well. Currently, EverQuest,
a popular role-playing game on the Internet, has more than a million subscribers,
and thousands play regularly, often daily. EverQuest creates a virtual society in
which people compete for power and for status-forming networks of relationships with others that will benefit them. Moreover, the human social behavior
of EverQuest society has real consequences. A market has developed for various
abilities acquired by EverQuest inhabitants. Keys to solving problems in
EverQuest are auctioned on Ebay, an Internet marketplace, where computer
codes capable of helping a person rise in EverQuest society have sold for

thousands of dollars. A simulation of EverQuest society could be readily developed because every action of every actor is recorded as it happens. It is a society with virtually perfect record keeping. A researcher could compare the simulation predictions with the observed EverQuest data every day, refining the model until it accurately predicts the human social behavior of EverQuest inhabitants.

Better continuous data may create a new problem for sociology. Sociologists have resisted the allure of empiricism, holding out for a profound understanding of social relationships. We still strive for the *verstehen* (comprehensive understanding) proposed by Max Weber as the ultimate goal of sociology. Better data may allow us to settle for accurate prediction rather than *verstehen*. Can sociology maintain its theoretical traditions as higher-quality streaming data from sources such as the Internet become available?

NOTES

1. See Lovaglia (1999) for a nontechnical description of network exchange theory.

2. Burke (1997) programmed another interesting simulation of network exchange using identity theory to account well for existing research results. In doing so, the simulation motivates theorists to explore the relationship between major theories in sociology.

3. See Poundstone (1992) for an interesting account of the history and development of prisoner's dilemma research.

4. See Poundstone (1992) and Axelrod (1984) for extensive bibliographies of prisoner's dilemma research.

References

Ackoff, Russell L. 1953. *The Design of Social Research*. Chicago: University of Chicago Press.

Aczel, Amir D. 1996. *Fermat's Last Theorem*. New York: Dell Publishing (Bantam Doubleday).

Alcoff, Linda Martin. 2000. "Philosophy Matters: A Review of Recent Work in Feminist Philosophy." *Signs* 25:841–882.

Alexander, Jeffrey C. 1982. *Positivism, Presuppositions, and Current Controversies. Theoretical Logic in Sociology, vol. 1*. Berkeley: University of California Press.

Archibald, Peter W. 1976. "Psychology, Sociology and Social Psychology: Bad Fences Make Bad Neighbors." *British Journal of Sociology* 27:115–129.

Aronson, Elliot, Phoebe C. Ellsworth, J. Merrill Carlsmith, and Marti Hope Gonzales. 1990. *Methods of Research in Social Psychology*. New York: McGraw-Hill.

Arrow, Kenneth J. 1951. *Social Choice and Individual Values*. New York: Wiley (A Cowles Commission Monograph).

Ashby, Ross W. 1963. *An Introduction to Cybernetics*. New York: Wiley.

Ashley, David, and David M. Orenstein. 1995. *Sociological Theory: Classical Statements*. Boston: Allyn and Bacon.

Axelrod, Robert. 1984. *The Evolution of Cooperation*. New York: Basic Books.

Axelrod, Robert. 1997. *The Complexity of Cooperation*. Princeton, NJ: Princeton University Press.

Axten, Nick, and Thomas J. Fararo. 1977. "The Information Processing Representation of Institutionalized Social Action." Pp. 35–77 in *Mathematical Models of Sociology*, edited by P. Krishnan, Sociological Review Monograph 24. Keele, UK. (Reprinted by Rowan and Littlefield, Totowa, NJ, 1979.)

Bak, Per. 1996. *How Nature Works: The Science of Self-Organized Criticality*. New York: Springer-Verlag.

Baker, Wayne E., and Robert R. Faulkner. 1993. "The Social Organization of Conspiracy." *American Sociological Review* 58:837–860.

Bales, Robert F. 1950. "A Set of Categories for the Analysis of Small Group Interaction." *American Sociological Review* 15:257–263.

Bales, Robert F. 1965. "The Equilibrium Problem in Small Groups." Pp. 444–476 in *Small Groups*, rev. ed., edited by A.P. Hare, E.F. Borgatta, and R.F. Bales. New York: Alfred A. Knopf.

Bales, Robert F., Fred L. Strodtbeck, Theodore M. Mills, and Mary E. Roseborough. 1951. "Channels of Communication in Small Groups." *American Sociological Review* 16:461–468.

Balkwell, James W. 1991. "Status Characteristics and Social Interaction." Pp. 135–176 in *Advances in Group Processes, vol. 8*, edited by Edward J. Lawler, Barry Markovsky, Cecilia Ridgeway, and Henry A. Walker. Greenwich, CT: JAI Press.

Balkwell, James W., Joseph Berger, Murray Webster, Jr., Max Nelson-Kilger, and Jacqueline Cashen. 1992. "Processing Status Information: Some Tests of Competing Theoretical Arguments." Pp. 1–20 in *Advances in Group Processes, vol. 9*, edited by Edward J. Lawler, Barry Markovsky, Cecilia Ridgeway, and Henry A. Walker. Greenwich, CT: JAI Press.

Barkey, Karen. 1991. "The State and Peasant Unrest in Early 17th-Century France and the Ottoman Empire." *American Sociological Review* 56:699–715.

Basilevsky, Alexander. 1983. *Applied Matrix Algebra in the Statistical Sciences*. New York: North Holland.

Bavelas, Alexis. 1948. "A Mathematical Model for Group Structures." *Applied Anthropology* 7:16–30.

Bavelas, Alexis. 1950. "Communication Patterns in Task-Oriented Groups." *Journal of the Acoustical Society of America* 22:725–731.

Beck, Lewis White. 1953. "Constructions and Inferred Entities." Pp. 366–381 in *Readings in the Philosophy of Science*, edited by Herbert Feigl and May Brodbeck. New York: Appleton-Century-Crofts.

Becker, Howard S. 1963. *Outsiders*. New York: Free Press.

Bendix, Reinhard, and Seymour M. Lipset. 1966. *Class, Status, and Power*. 2nd ed. New York: Free Press.

Berger, Joseph. 1958. "Relations between Performance, Rewards, and Action-Opportunities in Small Groups." Unpublished Ph.D. dissertation. Department of Social Relations, Harvard University.

Berger, Joseph. 1982 [1974]. "Expectation States Theory: A Theoretical Research Program." Pp. 3–22 in *Expectation States Theory: A Theoretical Research Program*, edited by Joseph Berger, Thomas L. Conner, and M. Hamit Fisek. Cambridge, MA: Winthrop (reprinted, Lanham, MD: University Press of America).

Berger, Joseph, Bernard P. Cohen, J. Laurie Snell, and Morris Zelditch, Jr. 1962. *Types of Formalization in Small Group Research*. Boston: Houghton Mifflin.

Berger, Joseph, Bernard P. Cohen, and Morris Zelditch, Jr. 1966. "Status Characteristics and Expectation States." Pp. 29–46 in *Sociological Theories in Progress, vol. 1*, edited by Joseph Berger, Morris Zelditch, Jr., and Bo Anderson. Boston: Houghton Mifflin.

Berger, Joseph, Bernard P. Cohen, and Morris Zelditch, Jr. 1972. "Status Characteristics and Social Interaction." *American Sociological Review* 37:241–255.

Berger, Joseph, and M. Hamit Fisek. 1970. "Consistent and Inconsistent Status Characteristics and the Determination of Power and Prestige Orders." *Sociometry* 33: 287–304.

Berger, Joseph, M. Hamit Fisek, and Lee Freese. 1976. "Paths of Relevance and the Determination of Power and Prestige Orders." *Pacific Sociological Review* 19: 45–62.

Berger, Joseph, M. Hamit Fisek, and Robert Z. Norman. 1977. "Status Characteristics and Expectation States: A Graph-Theoretic Formulation." Pp. 91–171 in *Status Characteristics and Social Interaction: An Expectation States Approach*, edited by Joseph Berger, M. Hamit Fisek, Robert Z. Norman, and Morris Zelditch, Jr. New York: Elsevier.

Berger, Joseph, M. Hamit Fisek, Robert Z. Norman, and David G. Wagner. 1985. "Formation of Reward Expectations in Status Situations." Pp. 215–261 in *Status, Rewards, and Influence*, edited by Joseph Berger and Morris Zelditch, Jr. San Francisco: Jossey-Bass.

Berger, Joseph, M. Hamit Fisek, Robert Z. Norman, and Morris Zelditch, Jr., eds. 1977. *Status Characteristics and Social Interaction: An Expectation States Approach*. New York: Elsevier.

Berger, Joseph, Cecilia Ridgeway, M. Hamit Fisek, and Robert Z. Norman. 1998. "The Legitimation and Delegitimation of Power and Prestige Orders." *American Sociological Review*. 63:379–405.

Berger, Joseph., Susan J. Rosenholtz, and Morris Zelditch, Jr. 1980. "Status Organizing Processes." *Annual Review of Sociology* 6:479–508.

Berger, Joseph, David G. Wagner, and Morris Zelditch, Jr. 1985. "Introduction: Expectation States Theory: Review and Assessment." Pp. 1–72 in *Status, Rewards, and Influence: How Expectations Organize Behavior*, edited by Joseph Berger and Morris Zelditch, Jr. San Francisco, Jossey-Bass.

Berger, Joseph, David G. Wagner, and Morris Zelditch, Jr. 1989. "Theory Growth, Social Processes, and Metatheory." Pp. 19–42 in *Theory Building in Sociology: Assessing Theoretical Accumulation*, edited by Jonathan H. Turner. Newbury Park, CA: Sage.

Berger, Joseph, David G. Wagner, and Morris Zelditch, Jr. 1992. "A Working Strategy for Constructing Theories: State Organizing Processes." Pp. 107–123 in *Metatheorizing: Key Issues in Sociological Theory, vol. 6*, edited by George Ritzer. Newbury Park, CA: Sage.

Berger, Joseph, Murray Webster, Jr., Cecilia L. Ridgeway, and Susan J. Rosenholtz. 1986. "Status Cues, Expectations, and Behavior." Pp. 1–22 in *Advances in Group Processes, vol. 3*, edited by Edward J. Lawler. Greenwich, CT: JAI Press.

Berger, Joseph, and Morris Zelditch, Jr. 1977. "Status Characteristics and Social Interaction: The Status-Organizing Process." Pp. 3–81 in *Status Characteristics and Social Interaction: An Expectation States Approach*, edited by Joseph Berger, M. Hamit Fisek, Robert Z. Norman, and Morris Zelditch, Jr. New York: Elsevier.

Berger, Joseph, and Morris Zelditch, Jr. 1993a. "Orienting Strategies and Theory Growth." Pp. 3–19 in *Theoretical Research Programs: Studies in Theory Growth*, edited by Joseph Berger and Morris Zelditch, Jr. Stanford, CA: Stanford University Press.

Berger, Joseph, and Morris Zelditch, Jr. 1993b. "Strategies, Theories, and Models: The Case of Expectation States Theory." Paper presented at the 31st Congress of International Institute of Sociology, the Sorbonne, Paris, France.

Berger, Joseph, and Morris Zelditch, Jr., eds. 1993c. *Theoretical Research Programs: Studies in Theory Growth*. Stanford, CA: Stanford University Press.

Berger, Joseph, and Morris Zelditch, Jr. 1997. "Theoretical Research Programs: A Reformulation." Pp. 29–46 in *Status, Network, and Structure: Theory Development in Group Processes*, edited by Jacek Szmatka, John Skvoretz, and Joseph Berger. Stanford, CA: Stanford University Press.

Berger, Joseph, and Morris Zelditch, Jr., eds. 1998. *Status, Power and Legitimacy: Strategies and Theories*. New Brunswick, NJ: Transaction.

Berger, Joseph, Morris Zelditch, and Bo Anderson, eds. 1966. *Sociological Theories in Progress, vol. 1*. Boston: Houghton Mifflin.

Berger, Joseph, Morris Zelditch, Jr., and Bo Anderson. 1972a. "Historical and Generalizing Orientations in Sociology." Pp. ix-xxi in *Sociological Theories in Progress, vol. 2*, edited by Joseph Berger, Morris Zelditch, Jr., and Bo Anderson. Boston: Houghton Mifflin.

Berger, Joseph, Morris Zelditch, Jr., and Bo Anderson, eds. 1972b. *Sociological Theories in Progress, vol. 2*. Boston: Houghton Mifflin.

Berger, Peter, and Thomas Luckmann. 1966. *The Social Construction of Reality*. New York: Doubleday.

Bergmann, Gustav. 1953. "Outline of an Empiricist Philosophy of Physics." Pp. 262–287 in *Readings in the Philosophy of Science*, edited by Herbert Feigl and May Brodbeck. New York: Appleton-Century-Crofts.

Bienenstock, Elisa Jayne, and Phillip Bonacich. 1992. "The Core as a Solution to Exclusionary Networks." *Social Networks* 14:231–243.

Binmore, K. 1998. "Axelrod's The Complexity of Cooperation." *The Journal of Artificial Societies and Social Simulation* 1:1.

Blalock, Hubert M., Jr., and Ann B. Blalock. 1968. *Methodology in Social Research*, 2nd ed. New York: McGraw-Hill.

Blau, Peter. 1964. *Exchange and Power in Social Life*. New York: Wiley.

Blau, Peter. 1970. "A Formal Theory of Differentiation in Organizations." *American Sociological Review* 35:201–218.

Blau, Peter. 1994. *Structural Context of Opportunities*. Chicago: Chicago University Press.

Boden, Margaret. 1980. *Jean Piaget*. New York: Penguin.

Bonacich, Phillip. 1987. "Power and Centrality: A Family of Measures." *American Journal of Sociology* 92:1170–1182.

Bonacich, Phillip. 1998. "A Behavioral Foundation for a Structural Theory of Power in Exchange Networks." *Social Psychological Quarterly* 61:185–198.

Bonacich, Phillip. 1999. "An Algebraic Theory of Strong Power in Negatively Connected Exchange Networks." *Journal of Mathematical Sociology* 23:203–224.

Bonacich, Phillip, and Elisa Jayne Bienenstock. 1995. "When Rationality Fails: Unstable Exchange Networks with Empty Cores." *Rationality and Society* 7:293–320.

Boutilier, Robert G., J. Christian Roed, and Ann C. Svendsen. 1980. "Crises in the Two Social Psychologies: A Critical Comparison." *Social Psychology Quarterly* 43:5–17.

Boyce, William E., and Richard C. Diprima. 1986. *Elementary Differential Equations and Boundary Value Problems*. New York: Wiley.

Brown, Harold I. 1977. *Perception, Theory and Commitment: The New Philosophy of Science*. Chicago: Precedent Publishing.

Burke, Peter J. 1991. "Identity Processes and Social Stress." *American Sociological Review* 56:836–849.

Burke, Peter J. 1997. "An Identity Model for Network Exchange." *American Sociological Review* 62:134–150.

Cartwright, Dorwin, and Frank Harary. 1956. "Structural Balance: A Generalization of Heider's Theory." *Psychological Review* 63:277–293.

Cartwright, Nancy. 1983. *How the Laws of Physics Lie*. Oxford: Oxford University Press.

Cartwright, Nancy. 1999. "Models and the Limits of Theory: Quantum Hamiltonians and the BCS Model of Superconductivity." Pp. 241–281 in *Models as Mediators*, edited by Mary S. Morgan and Margaret Morrison. Cambridge: Cambridge University Press.

Cast, Alicia D., Jan E. Stets, and Peter J. Burke. 1999. "Does the Self Conform to the Views of Others?" *Social Psychology Quarterly* 62:68–82.

Cecconi, Federico, and Domenico Parisi. 1998. "Individual Versus Social Survival Strategies." *Journal of Artificial Societies and Social Simulation* 1(2). Available online at http://www.soc.surrey.ac.uk/JASSS/1/2/1.html.

Chafetz, Janet S. 1978. *A Primer on the Construction and Testing of Theories in Sociology*. Itasca, IL: F.E. Peacock Publishers.

Chase, Ivan D. 1980. "Social Process and Hierarchy Formation in Small Groups: A Comparative Perspective." *American Sociological Review* 45:905–924.

Chomsky, Noam. 1957. *Syntactic Structures*. The Hague: Mouton.

Chomsky, Noam. 1965. *Aspects of the Theory of Syntax*. Cambridge, MA: MIT Press.

Chomsky, Noam, and George A. Miller. 1963. "An Introduction to the Formal Analysis of Natural Languages." Pp. 269–321 in *The Handbook of Mathematical Psychology, vol. 2*, edited by R.D. Luce, R.R. Bush, and E. Galanter. New York: Wiley.

Christensen, Larry. 1997. *Experimental Methodology*. Boston: Allyn and Bacon.

Chwe, Michael S.Y. 1999. "Structure and Strategy of Collective Action." *American Journal of Sociology* 105:128–156.

Cohen, Bernard P. 1988. "A New Experimental Situation Using Microcomputers." Pp. 383–398 in *Status Generalization: New Theory and Research*, edited by Murray Webster, Jr., and Martha Foschi. Stanford, CA: Stanford University Press.

Cohen, Bernard P. 1989. *Developing Sociological Knowledge: Theory and Method*. Chicago: Nelson-Hall.

Cohen, Bernard P. 1994. "Sociological Theory: The Half-full Cup." Pp. 66–83 in *Formal Theory in Sociology: Opportunity or Pitfall?* edited by J. Hage. Albany: State University of New York Press.

Cohen, Bernard P. 1997. "Beyond Experimental Inference: A Decent Burial for J.S. Mill and R.A. Fisher." Pp. 71–86 in *Status, Network, and Structure: Theory Development in Group Processes*, edited by Jacek Szmatka, John Skvoretz, and Joseph Berger. Stanford, CA: Stanford University Press.

Cohen, Elizabeth G. 1971, January. "Interracial Interaction Disability." *Urban Education*. 336–356.

Cohen, Elizabeth G. 1972. "Interracial Interaction Disability." *Human Relations* 25:9–24.

Cohen, Elizabeth G., M. Katz, and Mark R. Lohman. 1976. "Center for Interracial Cooperation: A Field Experiment." *Sociology of Education* 49:47–58.

Cohen, Elizabeth G., Rachel Lotan, and C. Leechor. 1989. "Can Classrooms Learn?" *Sociology of Education* 62:75–94.

Cole, Stephen. 1994. "Why Sociology Doesn't Make Progress like the Natural Sciences." *Sociological Forum* 9:133–154.

Coleman, James S. 1964. *Introduction to Mathematical Sociology*. New York: Free Press.

Coleman, James S. 1990. *Foundations of Social Theory*. Cambridge, MA: Belknap Press of Harvard University Press.

Collins, Randall. 1988. *Theoretical Sociology*. San Diego, CA: Harcourt Brace Jovanovich.

Collins, Randall. 1990. "Stratification, Emotional Energy, and the Transient Emotions." Pp. 27–57 In *Research Agendas in the Sociology of Emotions*, edited by Theodore D. Kemper. New York: State University of New York Press.

Collins, Randall. 1994. "Why the Social Sciences Won't Become High-Consensus, Rapid-Discovery Science." *Sociological Forum* 9:155–177.

Comte, Auguste. 1830. *System of Positive Philosophy*. Paris: Bachelier.

Cook, Karen, Ruth Cronkite, and David Wagner. 1974. Laboratory for Social Research Manual for Experimenters in Expectation States Theory. Unpublished Manuscript, Stanford University, Laboratory for Social Research, Stanford, California.

Cook, Karen S., and Richard M. Emerson. 1978. "Power, Equity and Commitment in Exchange Networks." *American Sociological Review* 43:721–739.

Cook, Karen S., Richard M. Emerson, Mary R. Gillmore, and Toshio Yamagishi. 1983. "The Distribution of Power in Exchange Networks: Theory and Experimental Results." *American Journal of Sociology* 89:275–305.

Cook, Karen S., Linda Molm, and Toshio Yamagishi. 1993. "Exchange Relations and Exchange Networks: Recent Developments in Social Exchange Theory." Pp. 296–322 in *Theoretical Research Programs: Studies in Theory Growth*, edited by Joseph Berger and Morris Zelditch, Jr. Stanford, CA: Stanford University Press.

Cooley, Charles H. 1902. *Human Nature and the Social Order*. New York: Scribner's.

Copi, Irving M. 1954. *Symbolic Logic*. New York: Macmillan.

Cosmides, L. 1989. "The Logic of Social Exchange: Has Natural Selection Shaped How Humans Reason?" *Cognition* 31:187–276.

Coveney, Peter, and Roger Highfield. 1995. *Frontiers of Complexity*. New York: Fawcett Columbine.

Crews, Frederick. 1986, 29 May "In the Big House of Theory: The Return of Grand Theory in the Human Sciences." *New York Review of Books* 33(9):36–42.

Cyert, R., and J.G. March. 1963. *A Behavioral Theory of the Firm*. Englewood Cliffs, NJ: Prentice-Hall.

Davis, James A. 1967. "Clustering and Structural Balance in Graphs." *Human Relations* 20:181–187.

Davis, James A. 1994. "What's Wrong with Sociology?" *Sociological Forum* 9:179–197.

Davis, James A., and Tom W. Smith. 1993. *General Social Surveys, 1972–1993: Cumulative Codebook*. Chicago: National Opinion Research Center.

Davis, Kingsley, and Wilbert E. Moore. 1945. "Some Principles of Stratification." *American Sociological Review* 10:242–249.

Dawkins, Richard. 1986. *The Blind Watchmaker*. New York: Norton.

Dawson, John W., Jr. 1997. *Logical Dilemmas, The Life and Work of Kurt Godel*. Wellesley, MA: A.K. Peters.

Derrida, Jacques. 1991. *Acts of Literature*. New York: Routledge.

Diani, Mario. 1996. "Linking Mobilization Frames and Political Opportunities: Insights from Regional Populism in Italy." *American Sociological Review* 61:1053–1069.

Diestel, Reinhard. 1997. *Graph Theory*. New York: Springer.

Dixon, Keith. 1973. *Sociological Theory: Pretense or Possibility*. London: Routledge.

Doreian, Patrick, and Frans Stockman, eds. 1997. *Evolution of Social Networks*. Amsterdam: Gordon and Beach Publishers.

Driskell, James E., and Murray Webster, Jr. 1997. "Status and Sentiment in Task Groups." Pp. 179–200 in *Status, Network, and Structure: Theory Development in Group Processes*, edited by Jacek Szmatka, John Skvoretz, and Joseph Berger. Stanford, CA. Stanford University Press.

Durkheim, Emile. 1954 [1912]. *The Elementary Forms of Religious Life*. New York: Free Press.

Durkheim, Emile. 1986. *The Rules of the Sociological Method*. New York: Free Press.

Egidi, Massimo, and Luigi Marengo. 1995. "Division of Labour and Social Co-ordination Modes: A Simple Simulation Model." Pp. 40–58 in *Artificial Societies: The Computer Simulation of Social Life*, edited by Nigel Gilbert and Rosaria Conte. London: University College London Press.

Emerson, Richard M. 1962. "Power-Dependence Relations." *American Sociological Review* 27:31–41.

Emerson, Richard M. 1972a. "Exchange Theory, Part I: A Psychological Basis for Social Exchange." in *Sociological Theories in Progress, vol. 2.*, edited by Joseph Berger, Morris Zelditch, Jr., and Bo Anderson. Boston: Houghton Mifflin.

Emerson, Richard M. 1972b. "Exchange Theory, Part II: Exchange Relations and Network Structures." in *Sociological Theories in Progress, vol. 2*, edited by Joseph Berger, Morris Zelditch, Jr., and Bo Anderson. Boston: Houghton Mifflin.

Epstein, Joshua M. and Robert L. Axtell. 1996. *Growing Artificial Societies: Social Science from the Bottom Up*. Cambridge, MA: MIT Press.

Etzioni, Amitai. 1959. "The Functional Differentiation of Elites in the Kibbutz." *American Journal of Sociology* 64:476–487.

Fararo, Thomas J. 1969a. "The Nature of Mathematical Sociology." *Social Research* 36: 75–92.

Fararo, Thomas J. 1969b. "Stochastic Processes." Pp. 245–260 in *Sociological Methodology*, edited by E.F. Borgatta. San Francisco: Jossey-Bass.

Fararo, Thomas J. 1973. *Mathematical Sociology: An Introduction to Fundamentals*. New York: Wiley.

Fararo, Thomas J. 1984. "Neoclassical Theorizing and Formalization in Sociology." *Journal of Mathematical Sociology* 10:361–394.

Fararo, Thomas J. 1989. *The Meaning of General Theoretical Sociology: Tradition and Formalization*. Cambridge/New York: Cambridge University Press.

Fararo, Thomas J., and John Skvoretz. 1984. "Institutions as Production Systems." *Journal of Mathematical Sociology* 10:117–181.

Fararo, Thomas J., and John Skvoretz. 1986. "E-State Structuralism: A Theoretical Method." *American Sociological Review* 51:591–602.

Fararo, Thomas J., and John Skvoretz. 1987. "Unification Research Programs: Integrating Two Structural Theories." *American Journal of Sociology* 92:1183–1209.

Fararo, Thomas J., and John Skvoretz. 1988. "Dynamics of the Formation of Stable Dominance Structures." Pp. 327–350 in *Status Generalization: New Theory and*

Research, edited by M. Webster and M. Foschi. Palo Alto, CA: Stanford University Press.

Fararo, Thomas J., John Skvoretz, and Kenji Kosaka. 1994. "Advances in E-state Structuralism: Further Studies in Dominance Structure Formation." *Social Networks* 16:233–265.

Feather, Leonard. 1993. Liner notes for *Miles* and *Quincy Live at Montreux*. Burbank, CA: Warner Brothers Records, Inc.

Feigl, Herbert. 1969. "The Origin and Spirit of Logical Positivism." Pp. 3–24 in *The Legacy of Logical Positivism*, edited by Peter Achinstein and Stephen F. Barker. Baltimore, MD: Johns Hopkins University Press.

Feigl, Herbert, and May Brodbeck. 1953. *Readings in the Philosophy of Science*. New York: Appleton-Century-Crofts.

Feigl, Herbert, and Grover Maxwell, eds. 1961. *Current Issues in the Philosophy of Science*. New York: Holt, Rinehart and Winston.

Feldmesser, R.A. 1953. "The Persistence of Status Advantages in Soviet Russia." *American Journal of Sociology* 59:19–27.

Festinger, Leon. 1949. "The Analysis of Sociograms Using Matrix Analysis." *Human Relations*, 2:153–158.

Feyerabend, Paul K. 1961. "Comment on Hanson's 'Is There a Logic of Scientific Discovery?'" In *Current Issues in the Philosophy of Science*, edited by H. Feigl and G. Maxwell. New York: Holt, Rinehart and Winston.

Feyerabend, Paul K. 1975. *Against Method*. London: New Left Books.

Feyerabend, Paul K. 1981. *Realism, Rationalism and Scientific Method*. Cambridge: Cambridge University Press.

Fiedler, Fred. 1967. *A Theory of Leadership Effectiveness*. New York: McGraw-Hill.

Fischer, Claude. 1975. "Toward a Subcultural Theory of Urbanism." *American Journal of Sociology* 80:1319–1341.

Fisek, M. Hamit. 1974. "A Model for the Evolution of Status Structures in Task-oriented Discussion Groups." Pp. 53–83 in *Expectation States Theory: A Theoretical Research Program*, edited by J. Berger, T.L. Conner, and M.H. Fisek. Cambridge, MA: Winthrop.

Fisek, M. Hamit, Joseph Berger, and Robert Z. Norman. 1991. "Participation in Homogeneous and Heterogeneous Groups: A Theoretical Integration." *American Journal of Sociology* 97:114–142.

Fisek, M. Hamit, Joseph Berger, and Robert Z. Norman. 1995. "Evaluations and the Formation of Expectations." *American Journal of Sociology* 101:721–746.

Fisek, M. Hamit, Robert Z. Norman, and Max Nelson-Kilger. 1992. "Status Characteristics and Expectation States Theory: A Priori Model Parameters and Test." *Journal of Mathematical Sociology* 16:285–303.

Fiske, A.P. 1991. *Structures of Social Life: The Forms of Human Relations*. New York: Free Press.

Flache, Andreas, and Michael W. Macy. 1996. "The Weakness of Strong Ties: Collective Action Failure in a Highly Cohesive Group." *Journal of Mathematical Sociology* 21:3–28.

Forrester, J.W. 1971. *World Dynamics*. Cambridge, MA: MIT Press.

Foschi, Martha. 1996. "Double Standards in the Evaluation of Men and Women." *Social Psychology Quarterly* 59:237–254.

Foschi, Martha. 1997. "On Scope Conditions." *Small Group Research* 28:535–555.

Foschi, Martha, and Margaret Foddy. 1988. "Standards, Performances, and the Formation of Self-Other Expectations." Pp. 248–260 in *Status Generalization: New Theory and Research*, edited by Murray Webster, Jr., and Martha Foschi. Stanford, CA: Stanford University Press.

Foschi, Martha, Larissa Lai, and Kirsten Sigerson. 1994. "Gender and Double Standards in the Assessment of Job Applicants." *Social Psychology Quarterly* 57:326–339.

Fox, John, and James C. Moore. 1979. "Status Characteristics and Expectation States: Fitting and Testing a Recent Model." *Social Psychology Quarterly* 42:126–134.

Frank, Philipp, ed. 1956. *The Validation of Scientific Theories*. Boston: Beacon Press.

Franzosi, Roberto. 1995. *The Puzzle of Strikes*. Cambridge: Cambridge University Press.

Freese, Lee. 1980a. "Formal Theorizing." Pp. 187–212 in *Annual Review of Sociology, vol. 6*, Palo Alto, CA: Annual Reviews.

Freese, Lee. 1980b. "Introduction." Pp. 1–12 in *Theoretical Methods in Sociology. Seven Essays*, edited by Lee Freese. Pittsburgh, PA: University of Pittsburgh Press.

Freese, Lee, and Jane Sell. 1980. "Constructing Axiomatic Theories in Sociology: Part 1." Pp. 263–309 in *Theoretical Methods in Sociology*, edited by L. Freese. Pittsburgh, PA: University of Pittsburgh Press.

Freud, Sigmund. 1953 [1900]. *The Interpretation of Dreams*. Vol 4 of *The Complete Psychological Works of Sigmund Freud*. London: Hogarth Press.

Friedkin, Noah E. 1992. "An Expected Value Model of Social Power: Predictions for Selected Exchange Networks." *Social Networks* 14:213–229.

Friedkin, Noah E. 1998. *A Structural Theory of Social Influence*. New York: Cambridge University Press.

Friedkin, Noah. 1999. "Choice Shift and Group Polarization." *American Sociological Review* 64:856–875.

Friedkin, Noah E., and Eugene C. Johnsen. 1999. "Social Influence Networks and Opinion Change." Pp. 1–29 in *Advances in Group Processes, vol. 16*, edited by S.R. Thye, E.J. Lawler, M.M. Macy, and H.A. Walker. Stamford, CT: JAI Press.

Friedman, Debra, Michael Hechter, and Satoshi Kanazawa. 1994. "A Theory of the Value of Children." *Demography* 31:375–401.

Friedman, Milton. 1953. *Essays in Positive Economics*. Chicago: University of Chicago Press.

Garfinkel, Harold. 1967. *Studies in Ethnomethodology*. Englewood Cliffs, NJ: Prentice Hall.

Gaylord, Richard, and Louis J. D'Andria. 1998. *Simulating Society: A Mathematica Toolkit and Modeling Socioeconomic Behavior*. New York: Springer-Verlag.

Gergen, Kenneth J. 1973. "Social Psychology as History." *Journal of Personality and Social Psychology* 26:309–320.

Gibbs, Jack P. 1972. *Sociological Theory Construction*. Hinsdale, IL: Dryden Press.

Gibbs, Jack P. 1994. "Resistance in Sociology to Formal Theory Construction." Pp. 90–104 in *Formal Theory in Sociology: Opportunity or Pitfall?* edited by J. Hage. Albany: State University of New York Press.

Giddens, Anthony. 1974. "Introduction." Pp. 1–22 in *Positivism and Sociology*, edited by Anthony Giddens. London: Heinemann.

Giddens, Anthony. 1978. "Positivism and Its Critics." Pp. 237–286 in *A History of Sociological Analysis*, edited by Tom Bottomore and Robert Nisbet. London: Heinemann.

Giddens, Anthony. 1984. *The Constitution of Society: Outline of the Theory of Structuration*. Berkeley: University of California Press.

Giedymin, Jerzy. 1975. "Antypositivism in Contemporary Philosophy of Social Science and Humanities." *British Journal of Philosophy of Science* 26:275–301.

Giere, Ronald. 1988. *Explaining Science: A Cognitive Approach*. Chicago: University of Chicago Press.

Gieryn, Thomas F. 1999. *Cultural Boundaries of Science: Credibility on the Line*. Chicago: University of Chicago Press.

Gilbert, Nigel G. 1996. "Holism, Individualism and Emergent Properties: An Approach from the Perspective of Simulation." Pp. 1–12 in *Modelling and Simulation in the Social Sciences from the Philosophy of Science Point of View*, edited by R. Hegselmann, U. Meuller, and K.G. Troitzch. Dordrecht, the Netherlands: Kluwer Academic Publishers.

Gilbert, N. and K. Troitzsch. 1999. Simulation for the Social Scientist. Buckingham: Open University Press.

Goetsch, G.G., and David D. McFarland. 1980. "Models of the Distribution of Acts in Small Discussion Groups." *Social Psychology Quarterly* 43:173–183.

Goffman, Erving. 1967. *Interaction Ritual*. Garden City, NY: Doubleday.

Goffman, Erving. 1974. *Frame Analysis: An Essay on the Organization of Experience*. New York: Harper and Row.

Goldstone, Jack A. 2000. "The Rise of the West—Or Not? A Revision to Socio-economic History." *Sociological Theory* 18(2):175–194.

Goodman, Walter. 2000, August 19. "Sociologists to the Barricades." *New York Times*. Available on-line at http://www.nytimes.com/library/arts/081900sociology-convention.html.

Gould, Roger V. 1991. "Multiple Networks and Mobilization in the Paris Commune, 1871." *American Sociological Review* 56:716–729.

Gould, Roger V. 1993. "Collective Action and Network Structure." *American Sociological Review* 58:182–196.

Gould, Roger V. 1999. "Collective Violence and Group Solidarity: Evidence from a Feuding Society." *American Sociological Review* 64:356–380.

Gouldner, Alvin W. 1954. *Wildcat Strike*. Yellow Springs, OH: Antioch Press.

Gouldner, Alvin W. 1970. *The Coming Crisis of Western Sociology*. New York: Basic Books.

Granovetter, Mark. 1973. "The Strength of Weak Ties." *American Journal of Sociology* 78:1360–1380.

Granovetter, Mark. 1978. "Threshold Models of Collective Behavior." *American Journal of Sociology* 83:1420–1443.

Guttentag, Marcia, and Paul F. Secord. 1983. *Too Many Women? The Sex Ratio Question*. Beverly Hills, CA: Sage.

Habermas, Jurgen. 1988. *On the Logic of the Social Sciences*. Cambridge, MA: MIT Press.

Hacking, Ian. 1983. *Representing and Intervening: Introductory Topics in the Philosophy of Natural Science*. Cambridge: Cambridge University Press.

Hage, Jerald, ed. 1994. *Formal Theory in Sociology: Opportunity or Pitfall?* Albany: State University of New York Press.

Halfpenny, Peter. 1982. *Positivism and Sociology: Explaining Social Life*. London: Allen and Unwin.

Hall, A.D., and R.E. Fagen. 1968. "Definition of System." Pp. 81–92 in *Modern Systems Research in the Behavioral Sciences*, edited by W. Buckley. Chicago: Aldine.

Harary, Frank. 1969. *Graph Theory*. Reading, MA: Addison-Wesley.

Harary, Frank, Robert Z. Norman, and Dorwin Cartwright. 1965. *Structural Models: An Introduction to the Theory of Directed Graphs*. New York: Wiley.

Harvey, David. 1990. *The Condition of Postmodernity*. Oxford, UK: Blackwell.

Haugeland, John. 1985. *Artificial Intelligence: The Very Idea*. Cambridge, MA: MIT Press.

Hawking, Stephen. 1993. *Black Holes and Baby Universes and Other Essays*. New York: Bantam Books.

Hechter, Michael. 1987. *Principles of Group Solidarity*. Berkeley: University of California Press.

Heckathorn, Douglas D. 1993. "Collective Action and Group Heterogeneity." *American Sociological Review* 58:329–350.

Hegselmann, Rainer, and Andreas Flache. 1998. "Understanding Complex Social Dynamics: A Plea for Cellular Automata Based Modelling." *Journal of Artificial Societies and Social Simulation* 1(3). Available on-line at http://www.soc.surrey.ac.uk/jasss/1/3/1.html.

Hegselmann, Rainer, Ulrich Mueller, and Klaus G. Troitzch. 1996. *Modelling and Simulation in the Social Sciences from the Philosophy of Science Point of View*. Dordrecht, the Netherlands: Kluwer Academic Publishers.

Heider, Fritz. 1946. "Attitudes and Cognitive Organization." *Journal of Psychology* 2: 107–112.

Heider, Fritz. 1958. *Psychology of Interpersonal Relations*. New York: Wiley.

Heimer, Karen, and Ross L. Matsueda. 1994. "Role Taking, Role Commitment, and Delinquency: A Theory of Differential Social Control." *American Sociological Review* 59:365–390.

Heise, David. 1979. *Understanding Events: Affect and the Construction of Social Action*. New York: Cambridge University Press.

Hempel, Carl. 1942. "The Function of General Laws in History." *The Journal of Philosophy* 39:35–48.

Hempel, Carl G. 1965. *Aspects of Scientific Explanation*. New York: Free Press.

Hempel, Carl G., and Paul Oppenheim. 1953. "The Logic of Explanation." Pp. 319–352 in *Readings in the Philosophy of Science*, edited by Herbert Feigl and May Brodbeck. New York: Appleton-Century-Crofts.

Hersh, Reuben. 1997. *What Is Mathematics, Really?* New York: Oxford University Press.

Hindess, Barry. 1977. "Positivism: Fact and Theory." Pp. 113–141 in *Philosophy and Methodology in the Social Sciences*. Hassocks, UK: Harvester Press.

Holland, J. 1995. *Hidden Order: How Adaptation Builds Complexity*. Reading, MA: Perseus.

Homans, George C. 1961. *Social Behavior: Its Elementary Forms*. New York: Harcourt, Brace and World.

Homans, George C. 1974. *Social Behavior: Its Elementary Forms*. New York: Harcourt, Brace and Jovanovich.

Horvath, W.J. 1964. "A Mathematical Model of Participation in Small Groups." *Behavioral Science* 10:164–166.

House, James S. 1977. "The Three Faces of Social Psychology." *Sociometry* 40:161–171.

Houser, Jeffrey Alan. 1997. "Stigma, Spread and Status: The Impact of Physical Disability on Social Interaction." Unpublished Ph.D. dissertation. Department of Sociology, The University of Iowa, Iowa City.

Housman, A. E. 1994. *The Works of A.E. Housman*. Ware, UK: Wordsworth Editions.

Huaco, George A. 1963. "A Logical Analysis of the Davis-Moore Theory of Stratification." *American Sociological Review* 28:801–804.

Hubbell, Charles H. 1965. "An Input-Output Approach to Clique Identification." *Sociometry* 28:377–399.

Huckfeldt, R. Robert, C.W. Kohfeld, and Thomas W. Likens. 1982. *Dynamic Modeling: An Introduction*. Sage Quantitative Applications in the Social Sciences, vol. 27. Newbury Park, CA: Sage.

Hume, David. 1962 [1748]. *Enquiry Concerning the Human Understanding*. Oxford, UK: Clarendon Press.

Inkeles, Alex. 1950. "Social Stratification and Mobility in the Soviet Union: 1940–1950. *American Sociological Review* 16:766–774.

Israel, Paul. 1998. *Edison: A Life of Invention*. New York: John Wiley and Sons.

Janis, Irving L. 1982. *Groupthink: Psychological Studies of Policy Decisions and Fiascoes*. Boston: Houghton Mifflin.

Jasso, Guillermina. 1978. "On the Justice of Earnings: A New Specification of the Justice Evaluation Function." *American Journal of Sociology* 83:1398–1419.

Jasso, Guillermina. 1980. "A New Theory of Distributive Justice." *American Sociological Review* 45:3–32.

Jasso, Guillermina. 1983. "Fairness of Individual Rewards and Fairness of the Reward Distribution: Specifying the Inconsistency between the Micro and Macro Principles of Justice." *Social Psychology Quarterly* 46:185–199.

Jasso, Guillermina. 1988. "Principles of Theoretical Analysis." *Sociological Theory* 6:1–21.

Jasso, Guillermina. 1997. "Derivation of Predictions in Comparison Theory: Foundations of the Macromodel Approach." Pp. 241–70 in *Status, Network, and Structure: Theory Development in Group Processes*, edited by Jacek Szmatka, John Skvoretz and John Berger. Stanford, CA: Stanford University Press.

Jasso, Guillermina. 2000. "How I Became a Theorist." *Sociological Theory* 18:490–497.

Jasso, Guillermina, and Murray Webster, Jr. 1999. "The Gender Gap in Just Earnings and Its Underlying Mechanisms." *Social Psychology Quarterly* 62:367–380.

Jasso, Guillermina, and Bernd Wegener. 1997. "Methods for Empirical Justice Analysis: Part I. Framework, Models, and Quantities." *Social Justice Research* 10:393–430.

Johnson, Cathryn. 1993. "Gender and Formal Authority." *Social Psychology Quarterly* 56:193–210.

Kadane, J.B., and Gordon Lewis. 1969. "The Distribution of Participation in Group Discussions: An Empirical and Theoretical Reappraisal." *American Sociological Review* 34:710–722.

Kaku, Michio, and Jennifer Thompson. 1995. *Beyond Einstein: The Cosmic Quest for the Theory of the Universe*. New York: Anchor Books.

Kanazawa, Satoshi. 1998a. "In Defense of Unrealistic Assumptions." *Sociological Theory* 16:193–204.

Kanazawa, Satoshi. 1998b. "A Possible Solution to the Paradox of Voter Turnout." *Journal of Politics* 60:974–975.

Kanazawa, Satoshi. 2000. "A New Solution to the Collective Action Problem: The Paradox of Voter Turnout." *American Sociological Review* 65:433–442.

Kant, Immanuel. 1981. *Universal Natural History and the Theory of the Heavens*. Edinburgh: Scottish American Press.

Kemeny, John G., J. Laurie Snell, Gerald L. Thompson. 1956. *An Introduction to Finite Mathematics*. Englewood Cliffs, NJ: Prentice-Hall.

Kendall, Patricia L., and Paul F. Lazarsfeld. 1950. "Problems in Survey Analysis." Pp. 133–196 in *Continuities in Social Research*, edited by Robert K. Merton and Paul F. Lazarsfeld. Glencoe, IL: The Free Press.

Kim, Hyojoung, and Peter S. Bearman. 1997. "The Structure and Dynamics of Movement Participation." *American Sociological Review* 62:70–93.

Kiser, Edgar, and Michael Hechter. 1991. "The Role of General Theory in Comparative-Historical Sociology." *American Journal of Sociology* 97:1–30.

Kitcher. P. 1993. "The Evolution of Human Altruism." *Journal of Philosophy* 10:497–516.

Kohn, Melvin L., and Kazimierz M. Slomczynski. 1990. *Social Structure and Self-Direction: A Comparative Analysis of the United States and Poland*. Cambridge: Basil Blackwell.

Kolakowski, Leszek. 1972. *Positivist Philosophy: From Hume to the Vienna Circle*. Harmondsworth, UK: Penguin.

Kollock, Peter. 1993. "An Eye for an Eye Leaves Everyone Blind: Cooperation and Accounting Systems." *American Sociological Review* 58:768–786.

Kollock, Peter. 1994. "The Emergence of Exchange Structures: An Experimental Study of Uncertainly, Commitment, and Trust." *American Journal of Sociology* 100: 315–345.

Kuhn, Thomas S. 1957. *Copernicus Revolution*. Cambridge, MA: Harvard University Press.

Kuhn, Thomas S. 1970. *The Structure of Scientific Revolutions*. Chicago: University of Chicago Press.

Lakatos, Imre. 1968. *The Problem of Inductive Logic*. Amsterdam: North Holland Publishing Company.

Lakatos, Imre. 1970. "Falsification and the Methodology of Scientific Research Programs." Pp. 91–195 in *Criticism and the Growth of Knowledge*, edited by Imre Lakatos and Alan Musgrave. Cambridge, MA: Cambridge University Press.

Lakatos, Imre. 1976. *Proofs and Refutations: The Logic of Mathematical Discovery*. Edited by John Worrall and Elie Zahar. New York: Cambridge University Press.

Lakatos, Imre. 1978. *The Methodology of Scientific Research Programs*. Cambridge, MA: Cambridge University Press.

Lakatos, Imre, and Alan Musgrave. 1970. *Criticism and the Growth of Knowledge*. Cambridge, MA: Cambridge University Press.

Lane, Michael, ed. 1970. *An Introduction to Structuralism*. New York: Basic Books.

Latané, B. 1996. "Dynamic Social Impact: Robust Predictions from Simple Theory." Pp. 287–310 in *Modeling and Simulation in the Social Sciences from a Philosophy of Science Point of View*, edited by R. Hegselmann, U. Mueller, and K. Troitzsch. Boston: Kluwer Dorderecht.

Laudan, Larry. 1977. *Progress and Its Problems: Toward a Theory of Scientific Growth*. Berkeley: University of California Press.

Laudan, Larry. 1990. *Science and Relativism*. Chicago: University of Chicago Press.

Laudan, Larry. 1996. *Beyond Positivism and Relativism: Theory, Method, and Evidence.* Boulder, CO: Westview Press.

Lawler, Edward, and Jeonkoo Yoon. 1998. "Network Structure and Emotion in Exchange Relations." *American Sociological Review* 63:871–894.

Lazarsfeld, Paul F. 1950. "The Logical and Mathematical Foundation of Latent Structure Analysis," and "The Interpretation and Computation of Some Latent Structures." Pp. 362–412 and 413–472 in *The American Soldier: Measurement and Prediction, vol. 4,* edited by Samuel Stouffer, Louis Guttman, Edward A. Suchman, Paul F. Lazarsfeld, Shirley A. Star, and John A. Clausen. Princeton, NJ: Princeton University Press.

Lederman, Leon, with Dick Teresi. 1993. *The God Particle: If the Universe Is the Answer, What is the Question?* New York: Delta.

Lee, Margaret T., and Richard Ofshe. 1981. "The Impact of Behavioral Style and Status Characteristics on Social Influence: A Test of Two Competing Theories." *Social Psychology Quarterly* 44:73–82.

Leik, Robert K. 1967. "The Distribution of Acts in Small Groups." *Sociometry* 30:280–299.

Leik, Robert K., and Barbara F. Meeker. 1975. *Mathematical Sociology.* Englewood Cliffs, NJ: Prentice-Hall.

Leik, Robert K., and Barbara F. Meeker. 1995. "Computer Simulation for Exploring Theories." *Sociological Perspectives* 38:463–482.

Lichter, Daniel T., Diane K. McLaughlin, and David C. Ribar. 1997. "Welfare and the Rise in Female-Headed Families." *American Journal of Sociology* 103:112–143.

Locke, John. 1964 [1690]. *An Essay Concerning Human Understanding.* London: Collins.

Lockheed, Marlaine E., and Katherine P. Hall. 1976. "Conceptualizing Sex as a Status Characteristic: Applications to Leadership Training Strategies." *Journal of Social Issues* 32:111–124.

Lotka, A. J. 1932. "The Growth of Mixed Populations: Two Species Competing for the Common Food Supply." *Journal of the Washington Academy of Sciences* 21:461–469.

Lovaglia, Michael J. 1995. "Power and Status: Exchange, Attribution and Expectation States." *Small Group Research* 26:400–426.

Lovaglia, Michael J. 1999. "Understanding Network Exchange Theory." Pp. 31–59 in *Advances in Group Processes, vol. 16,* edited by S.R. Thye, E.J. Lawler, M.M. Macy, and H.A. Walker. Stamford, CT: JAI Press.

Lovaglia, Michael J. 2001. "A Simulator to Represent Network Exchange Theory and Predict Experimental Results." Unpublished manuscript, University of Iowa, Iowa City, IA.

Lovaglia, Michael J., and Jeffrey A. Houser. 1996. "Emotional Reactions and Status in Groups." *American Sociological Review* 61:867–883.

Lovaglia, Michael J., Jeffrey W. Lucas, Jeffrey A. Houser, Shane R. Thye, and Barry Markovsky. 1998. "Status Processes and Mental Ability Test Scores." *American Journal of Sociology* 104:195–228.

Lovaglia, Michael J., John Skvoretz, David Willer, and Barry Markovsky. 1995. "Negotiated Exchanges in Social Networks." *Social Forces* 74:123–155.

Loveman, Mara. 1998. "High-Risk Collective Action: Defending Human Rights in Chile, Uruguay, and Argentina." *American Journal of Sociology* 104:477–525.

Luce, R. Duncan. 1950. "Connectivity and Generalized Cliques in Sociometric Group Structure." *Psychometrika* 15:169–190.

Luce, R. Duncan, and Howard Raiffa. 1957. *Games and Decisions*. New York: Wiley.

Luce, R. Duncan, and Albert D. Perry. 1949. "A Method of Matrix Analysis of Group Structure." *Psychometrika* 14:94–116.

MacCorquodale, Kenneth, and Paul E. Meehl. 1953. "Hypothetical Constructs and Intervening Variables." Pp. 596–611 in *Readings in the Philosophy of Science*, edited by Herbert Feigl and May Brodbeck. New York: Appleton-Century-Crofts.

MacKinnon, Richard Clark. 1992. "Searching for Leviathan in Usenet." Unpublished M.S. thesis, Department of Political Science, San Jose State University, San Jose, CA. Available on-line at: http://www.virtualschool.edu/mon/Economics/ MacKinnonLeviathanUsenet.html.

MacKinnon, Neil J., and David R. Heise. 1993. "Affect Control Theory: Delineation and Development." Pp. 64–103 in *Theoretical Research Programs: Studies in the Growth of Theory*, edited by Joseph Berger and Morris Zelditch, Jr. Stanford, CA: Stanford University Press.

Mac Lane, Saunders. *Categories for the Working Mathematician*. New York: Springer-Verlag, 1988.

Macleod, Jay. 1995. *Ain't No Makin It: Aspirations and Attainment in a Low Income Neighborhood*. Boulder, CO: Westview Press.

Macy, Michael W. 1989. "Walking Out of Social Traps: A Stochastic Learning Model for the Prisoner's Dilemma." *Rationality and Society* 1:197–219.

Macy, Michael W. 1990. "Learning Theory and the Logic of the Critical Mass." *American Sociological Review* 55:809–826.

Macy, Michael W. 1991. "Chains of Cooperation: Threshold Effects in Collective Action." *American Sociological Review* 56:730–747.

Macy, Michael W. 1993. "Backward-Looking Social Control." *American Sociological Review* 58:819–836.

Macy, Michael W. 1995. "PAVLOV and the Evolution of Cooperation: An Experimental Test." *Social Psychology Quarterly* 58:74–87.

Macy, Michael W., and J. Skvoretz. 1998. "The Evolution of Trust and Cooperation Between Strangers: A Computational Model." *American Sociological Review* 63: 638–660.

Majiski, Stephen, Greg Linden, Corina Linden, and Aaron Spitzer. 1997. "A Spacial Iterated Prisoner's Dilemma Game Simulation with Movement." Pp. 161–167 in *Simulating Social Phenomena*, edited by Rosaria Conte, Rainer Hegselmann, and Pietro Terna. Berlin: Springer.

Manzo, John F. 1996. "Taking Turns and Taking Sides: Opening Scenes from Two Jury Deliberations." *Social Psychology Quarterly* 59:107–125.

Margenau, Henry. 1950. *The Nature of Physical Reality*. New York: McGraw-Hill.

Markovsky, Barry. 1987. "Toward Multilevel Sociological Theories: Simulations of Actor and Network Effects." *Sociological Theory* 5:101–117.

Markovsky, Barry. 1994. "The Structure of Theories." Pp. 3–24 in *Group Processes: Sociological Analyses*, edited by M. Foschi and Edward. J. Lawler. Chicago: Nelson-Hall.

Markovsky, Barry. 1995. "Developing an Exchange Network Simulator." *Sociological Perspectives* 38:519–545.

Markovsky, Barry. 1997. "Building and Testing Multilevel Theories." Pp. 13–28 in *Status, Network, and Structure: Theory Development in Group Processes*, edited by Jacek Szmatka, John Skvoretz and Joseph Berger. Stanford, CA: Stanford University Press.

Markovsky, Barry, John Skvoretz, David Willer, Michael J. Lovaglia, and Jeffrey Erger. 1993. "The Seeds of Weak Power: An Extension of Network Exchange Theory." *American Sociological Review* 58:197–209.

Markovsky, Barry, David Willer, and Travis Patton. 1988. "Power Relations in Exchange Networks." *American Sociological Review* 53:220–236.

Marwell, Gerald, Pamela E. Oliver, and Ralph Prahl. 1988. "Social Networks and Collective Action: A Theory of the Critical Mass III." *American Journal of Sociology* 94:502–534.

Marx, Karl. 1964 [1932]. *The Economic and Philosophical Manuscripts of 1844*. New York: International Publishers.

Marx, Karl, and Friedrich Engels. 1985 [1888]. *The Communist Manifesto*. London: Penguin.

Massey, Douglas, and Nancy Denton. 1993. *American Apartheid: Segregation and the Making of the Underclass*. Cambridge, MA: Harvard University Press.

McCain, Roger. 1995. "Genetic Algorithms, Teleological Conservatism, and the Emergence of Optimal Demand Relations: The Case of Learning by Consuming." Pp. 126–142 in *Artificial Societies: The Computer Simulation of Social Life*, edited by Nigel Gilbert and Rosario Conte. London: University College London Press.

McCall, G.P., and J.L. Simmons. 1978. *Identities and Interactions*. New York: Basic Books.

McMahon, Anne M. 1984. "The Two Social Psychologies: Postcrises Directions." *Annual Review of Sociology* 10:121–140.

Mead, George H. 1934. *Mind, Self, and Society*. Chicago: University of Chicago Press.

Meadows, D.L., W.W. Behrens III, D.H. Meadows, R.F. Naill, J. Randers, and E.K. Zahn. 1974. *The Dynamics of Growth in a Finite World*. Cambridge, MA: MIT Press.

Meeker, Barbara F. 1981. "Expectation States and Interpersonal Behavior" Pp. 290–319 in *Social Psychology: Sociological Perspectives*, edited by M. Rosenberg and R. Turner. New York: Basic Books.

Meeker, Barbara F., and Robert K. Leik. 1997. "Uses of Computer Simulation for Theory Development: An Evolving Component of Theoretical Research Programs." Pp. 47–70 in *Status, Network, and Structure: Theory Development in Group Processes*, edited by Jacek Szmatka, John Skvoretz, and Joseph Berger. Stanford, CA: Stanford University Press.

Menger, Carl. 1996 [1883]. *Investigations into the Method of the Social Sciences*. Grove City, PA: Libertarian Press.

Merton, Robert K. 1967. *On Theoretical Sociology: Five Essays, Old and New*. New York: Free Press.

Merton, Robert K. 1968. *Social Theory and Social Structure*. New York: Free Press.

Molm, Linda D. 1997. *Coercive Power in Social Exchange*. New York: Cambridge University Press.

Molm, Linda D., Gretchen Peterson, and Noboyuki Takahashi. 1999. "Power in Negotiated and Reciprocal Exchange." *American Sociological Review* 64:876–890.

Moore, James C. 1968. "Status and Influence in Small Group Interactions." *Sociometry* 31:47–63.

Moore, James C. 1985. "Role Enactment and Self-Identity." Pp. 262–316 in *Status,*

Rewards and Influence, edited by Joseph Berger and Morris Zelditch, Jr. San Francisco: Jossey-Bass.

Moore, Walter. 1989. *Schrodinger: Life and Thought*. New York: Cambridge University Press.

Morrison, Margaret, and Mary S. Morgan. 1999. "Models as Mediating Instruments." Pp. 10–37 in *Models as Mediators*, edited by Mary S. Morgan and Margaret Morrison. Cambridge: Cambridge University Press.

Nadel, S.F. 1951. *The Foundations of Social Anthropology*. New York: Free Press.

Nagel, Ernest. 1961. *The Structure of Science: Problems in the Logic of Scientific Explanation*. New York: Harcourt, Brace and World.

Neurath, Otto, H. Hahn, and R. Carnap. 1973. "The Scientific Conception of the World: The Vienna Circle." Pp. 299–318 in *Empiricism and Sociology*, edited by Marie Neurath and Robert S. Cohen. Dordrecht, the Netherlands: Reidel.

Newcomb, Theodore M. 1953. "An Approach to the Study of Communicative Acts." *Psychological Review* 60:393–404.

Newell, Alan, and Herbert A. Simon. 1972. *Human Problem Solving*. Englewood Cliffs, NJ: Prentice-Hall.

Neyman, Jerzy, and Egon S. Pearson. 1933. "On the Problem of the Most Efficient Tests of Statistical Hypotheses." *Philosophical Transactions of the Royal Society*, Series A:289–337.

Neyman, Jerzy, and Egon S. Pearson. 1936–1938. "Contributions to the Theory of Testing Statistical Hypotheses," parts 1 and 2. *Statistical Research Memories*.

Nowak, M., and K. Sigmund. 1993. "A Strategy of Win-Stay, Lose-Shift That Outperforms Tit-for-Tat in the Prisoner's Dilemma." *Nature* 364:56–58.

Oliver, Pamela E., Gerald Marwell, and Ruy Teixeira. 1985. "A Theory of the Critical Mass I: Interdependence, Group Heterogeneity, and the Production of Collective Action." *American Journal of Sociology* 91:522–556.

Oliver, Pamela E., and Gerald Marwell. 1988. "The Paradox of Group Size in Collective Action: A Theory of the Critical Mass II." *American Sociological Review* 53:1–8.

Olson, Mancur. 1965. *The Logic of Collective Action*. Cambridge, MA: Harvard University Press.

Opp, Karl-Dieter. 1999. *Methodologie der Sozialwissenschaften*. Opladen and Wiesbaden, Germany: Westdeutscher Verlag.

Orbell, John M., and Robyn M. Dawes. 1993. "Social Welfare, Cooperator's Advantage, and the Option of Not Playing the Game." *American Sociological Review* 58: 787–800.

Owen, Guillermo. 1995. *Game Theory*. 3rd ed. San Diego, CA: Academic Press.

Paley, William. 1802. *Natural Theology*. Philadelphia: H. Maxwell.

Pareto, Vilfredo. 1935. *Treatise on General Sociology*. New York: Harcourt Brace Jovanovich.

Parsons, Talcott. 1951. *The Social System*. Glencoe, IL: Free Press.

Parsons, Talcott. 1968 [1937]. *The Structure of Social Action*. New York: Free Press.

Parsons, Talcott, and Edward A. Shils. 1951. *Toward a General Theory of Action*. Cambridge, MA: Harvard University Press.

Popper, Karl. 1935. *Logik der Forschung: Zur Erkenntnistheorie der modernen Naturwissenschaft*. Vienna: Julius Springer.

Popper, Karl R. 1957. *The Poverty of Historicism*. London: Routledge and Kegan Paul.

Popper, Karl R. 1959. *The Logic of Scientific Discovery*. New York. Basic Books.

Popper, Karl R. 1963. *Conjectures and Refutations: The Growth of Scientific Knowledge*. London: Routledge and Kegan Paul.

Popper, Karl R. 1969. "Science: Conjectures and Refutations." Pp. 33–59 in *Conjectures and Refutations: The Growth of Scientific Knowledge*. London: Routledge and Kegan Paul.

Popper, Karl R. 1972. *Objective Knowledge: An Evolutionary Approach*. Oxford, UK: Clarendon Press.

Poundstone, William. 1992. *Prisoner's Dilemma: John Von Neumann, Game Theory, and the Puzzle of the Bomb*. New York: Doubleday.

Powers, William T. 1973. *Behavior: The Control of Perception*. Chicago: Aldine.

Quine, W.V.O. 1960. *Word and Object*. Cambridge, MA: MIT Press.

Quine, W.V.O. 1963. *From a Logical Point of View*. New York: Harper and Row.

Rapoport, Anatol. 1966. *Two-Person Game Theory*. Ann Arbor: University of Michigan Press.

Rashotte, Lisa Slattery and Lynn Smith-Lovin. 1997. "Who Benefits from Being Bold: The Interactive Effects of Task Cues and Status Characteristics on Influence in Mock Jury Groups." Pp. 235–255 in *Advances in Group Processes, vol. 14*, edited by S.R. Thye, E.J. Lawler, M.M. Macy, and H.A. Walker. Stamford, CT: JAI Press.

Reichenbach, Hans. 1951. *The Rise of Scientific Philosophy*. Berkeley: University of California Press.

Resnick, Mitchell. 1997. *Termites, Turtles and Traffic Jams*. Cambridge, MA: MIT Press.

Reynolds, Craig W. 1987. "Flocks, Herds, and Schools: A Distributed Behavioral Model." *Computer Graphics* 21:25–34.

Richardson, Lewis F. 1960. *Arms and Insecurity*. Pittsburgh, PA: Boxwood.

Ridgeway, Cecilia. 1987. "Nonverbal Behavior, Dominance, and the Basis of Status in Task Groups." *American Sociological Review* 52:683–694.

Ridgeway, Cecilia. 1991. "The Social Construction of Status Value: Gender and Other Nominal Characteristics." *Social Forces* 70:367–386.

Ridgeway, Cecilia. 1997. "Where Do Status Value Beliefs Come From? New Developments." Pp. 137–158 in *Status, Network, and Structure: Theory Development in Group Processes*, edited by Jacek Szmatka, John Skvoretz and Joseph Berger. Stanford, CA: Stanford University Press.

Ridgeway, Cecilia L., Elizabeth H. Boyle, Kathy J. Kuipers, and Dawn T. Robinson. 1998. "How do Status Beliefs Develop? The Role of Resources and Interactional Experience." *American Sociological Review* 63:331–350.

Ridgeway, Cecilia L., and Henry A. Walker. 1995. "Status Structures." Pp. 281–310 in *Sociological Perspectives on Social Psychology*, edited by Karen S. Cook, Gary Fine, and James S. House. Needham Heights, MA: Allyn and Bacon.

Ritzer, George. 1991. *Metatheorizing in Sociology*. Lexington, MA: Lexington Books.

Robertson, Neil, and Paul D. Seymour. 1983–1997. "Graph Minors I, IV–VII, IX–XII, XIV–XX," *Journal of Combinatorial Theory*, Series B, 35, 41, 45, 48, 49.

Robinson, Dawn T., and James W. Balkwell. 1995. "Density, Transitivity, and Diffuse Status in Task-Oriented Groups." *Social Psychology Quarterly* 58:241–254.

Rosser, Barkley. 1939. "An Informal Exposition of Proofs of Godel's Theorems and of Church's Theorem." *Journal of Symbolic Logic* 4: 53–60.

Rule, James B. 1997. *Theory and Progress in Social Science.* Cambridge: Cambridge University Press.

Rummelhart, D., and J. McClelland. 1988. *Parallel Distributed Processing: Explorations in the Microstructure of Cognition.* Cambridge, MA: MIT Press.

Sayer, Andrew. 1994. *The Method in Social Science: A Realist Approach.* London: Routledge.

Scheff, Thomas. 1988. "Shame and Conformity: The Deference-Emotion System." *American Sociological Review* 53:395–406.

Schelling, Thomas. 1971. "Dynamic Models of Segregation." *Journal of Mathematical Sociology* 1:143–186.

Schumpeter, Joseph. 1909. "On the Concept of Social Value." *Journal of Economics* 23: 213–232.

Schutz, Alfred. 1967 [1932]. *The Phenomenology of the Social World.* Evanston, IL: Northwestern University Press.

Schutz, Alfred. 1973. *Collected Papers I: The Problem of Social Reality.* The Hague: Nyhoff.

Scudo, Francesco M., and James R. Zeigler. 1978. *The Golden Age of Theoretical Ecology: 1923–1940.* Lecture Notes in Biomathematics No. 22. New York: Springer-Verlag.

Searle, John. 1984. *Minds, Brains and Science.* Cambridge, MA: Harvard University Press.

Sell, Jane, and Michael W. Martin. 1983. "An Acultural Perspective on Experimental Social Psychology." *Personality and Social Psychology* 9:345–350.

Shapere, Dudley, 1977. "Scientific Theories and Their Domains" Pp. 518–566 in *The Structure of Scientific Theories,* edited by F. Suppe. Urbana: University of Illinois Press.

Shapin, Steven, and Simon Schaffer. 1985. *Leviathan and the Airpump: Hobbes, Boyle, and the Experimental Life.* Princeton, NJ: Princeton University Press.

Shelly, Robert K. 1993. "How Sentiments Organize Interaction." Pp. 113–132 in *Advances in Group Processes, vol. 10,* edited by Edward J. Lawler, Barry Markovsky, Karen Heimer, and Jodi O'Brien. Greenwich, CT: JAI Press.

Shelly, Robert K. 1998. "Some Developments in Expectation States Theory: Graduated Expectation?" Pp. 41–57 in *Advances in Group Processes, vol. 15,* edited by John Skvoretz and Jacek Szmatka. Stamford, CT: JAI Press.

Shibutani, Tamotsu. 1978. *The Derelicts of Company K: A Study of Demoralization.* Berkeley: University of California Press.

Shubik, Martin. 1975. *Games for Society, Business and War: Toward a Theory of Gaming.* New York: Elsevier.

Shubik, Martin. 1988. *A Game-Theoretic Approach to Political Economy.* Cambridge, MA: MIT Press.

Simon, H. 1998. *The Sciences of the Artificial.* Cambridge, MA: MIT Press.

Singh, Simon. 1997. *Fermat's Enigma.* New York: Anchor Books.

Skocpol, Theda. 1979. *States and Social Revolutions.* Cambridge: Cambridge University Press.

Skvoretz, John V. 1988. "Models of Participation in Status Differentiated Groups." *Social Psychology Quarterly* 51:43–57.

Skvoretz, John. 1998. "Theoretical Models: Sociology's Missing Links." Pp. 238–252 in

What Is Social Theory? The Philosophical Debates, edited by Alan Sica. Malden, MA: Blackwell Publishers.

Skvoretz, John, and Thomas J. Fararo. 1995. "The Evolution of Systems of Social Interaction." *Current Perspectives in Social Theory* 15:275–299.

Skvoretz, John, and Thomas J. Fararo. 1996a. "Generating Symbolic Interaction: Production System Models." *Sociological Methods and Research* 25:60–102.

Skvoretz, John, and Thomas J. Fararo. 1996b. "Status and Participation in Task Groups: A Dynamic Network Model." *American Journal of Sociology* 101:1366–1414.

Skvoretz, John, Thomas J. Fararo, and Nick Axten. 1980. "Role-Programme Models and the Analysis of Institutional Structure." *Sociology* 14:49–67.

Skvoretz, John, and Michael J. Lovaglia. 1995. "Who Exchanges with Whom: Structural Determinants of Exchange Frequency in Negotiated Exchange Networks." *Social Psychology Quarterly* 58:163–177.

Skvoretz, John, Murray Webster, Jr., and Joseph M. Whitmeyer. 1999. "Status Orders in Task Discussion Groups." Pp. 199–218 in *Advances in Group Processes, vol. 16*, edited by S.R. Thye, E.J. Lawler, M.M. Macy, and H.A. Walker. Stamford, CT: JAI Press.

Skvoretz, John, and Pidi Zhang. 1997. "Actors' Responses to Outcomes in Exchange Networks: The Process of Power Development." *Sociological Perspectives* 40: 183–197.

Smith-Lovin, Lynn, and Charles Brody. 1989. "Interruptions in Group Discussions: The Effects of Gender and Group Composition." *American Sociological Review* 54: 424–435.

Smith-Lovin, Lynn, and David R. Heise, eds. 1988. *Analyzing Social Interaction: Research Advances in Affect Control Theory*. New York: Gordon and Breach.

Smith-Lovin, Lynn, John V. Skvoretz, and Charlotte Hudson. 1986. "Status and Participation in Six-Person Groups: a Test of Skvoretz's Comparative Status Model." *Social Forces* 64:992–1005.

Sozanski, Tadeusz. 1995. "Co to Jest Nauka? [What is science?]." Pp. 23–50 in *Nauka, Tozsamosc i Tradycja* [Science, identity, and tradition], edited by J. Gockowski and S. Marmuszewski. Krakow: Universitas.

Spencer, Herbert. 1902 [1862]. *First Principles*. New York: P.F. Collier and Son.

Spiro, M.E. 1956. *Kibbutz: Venture in Utopia*. Cambridge, MA: Harvard University Press.

Stephan, F., and E.G. Mishler. 1952. "The Distribution of Participation in Small Groups: An Exponential Approximation." *American Sociological Review* 17:598–608.

Stinchcombe, Arthur L. 1963. "Some Empirical Consequences of the Davis-Moore Theory of Stratification." *American Sociological Review* 28:805–808.

Stinchcombe, Arthur L. 1968. *Constructing Social Theories*. New York: Harcourt, Brace and World.

Stinchcombe, Arthur L. 1991. "The Conditions of Fruitfulness of Theorizing about Mechanisms in Social Science." *Philosophy of Social Sciences* 21:367–388.

Stinchcombe, Arthur L., and T. Robert Harris. 1969. "Interdependence and Inequality: A Specification of the Davis-Moore Theory." *Sociometry* 32:13–23.

Stone, Rob. 1996. *Sociological Reasoning: Towards a Past-modern Sociology*. New York: St. Martin's Press.

Strang, David, and Michael Macy. 2001. "'In Search of Excellence': Fads, Success Stories, and Adaptive Emulation." *American Journal of Sociology* 107:147–183.

Stryker, Sheldon. 1977. "Developments in 'Two Social Psychologies': Toward an Appreciation of Mutual Relevance." *Sociometry* 40:145–160.

Stryker, Sheldon. 1980. *Symbolic Interactionism: A Structural Version.* Menlo Park, CA: Benjamin/Cummings.

Stryker, Sheldon, and Peter J. Burke. 2000. "The Past, Present, and Future of an Identity Theory." *Social Psychology Quarterly* 63:284–297.

Suppe, Frederick. 1973. "The Search for Philosophic Understanding of Scientific Theories." Pp. 3–232 in *The Structure of Scientific Theories,* edited by F. Suppe. Urbana: University of Illinois Press.

Suppes, Patrick. 1957. *An Introduction to Logic.* Princeton, NJ: D. Van Nostrand Co.

Suppes, Patrick. 1984. *Probabilistic Metaphysics.* New York: Blackwell.

Suppes, Patrick, and Richard C. Atkinson. 1960. *Markov Learning Models of Multiperson Interactions.* Stanford, CA: Stanford University Press.

Szmatka, Jacek. 1997. "Testing Elementary Theory for Universality." Pp. 87–109 in *Status, Network, and Structure: Theory Development in Group Processes,* edited by Jacek Szmatka, John Skvoretz, and Joseph Berger. Stanford, CA: Stanford University Press.

Szmatka, Jacek, and Michael J. Lovaglia. 1996. "The Significance of Method." *Sociological Perspectives* 39:393–415.

Szmatka, Jacek, and Joanna Mazur. 1998. "Power Distribution in Conflict Networks: An Extension of Elementary Theory to Conflict Networks." Pp. 187–211 in *Advances in Group Processes, vol. 15,* edited by John Skvoretz and Jacek Szmatka. Greenwich, CT: JAI Press.

Talmon-Garber, Y., and Z. Talmon-Garber. 1956. "Differentiation in Collective Settlements." Pp. 153–178 in *Scripta Hierosolymitana.* Jerusalem: Hebrew University.

Tarrow, Sidney. 1998. *Power in Movement.* Cambridge: Cambridge University Press.

Thomassen, Carsten. 1995. "Embeddings and Minors." Pp. 301–49 in *Handbook of Combinatorics,* edited by R.L. Graham, M. Grotschel, L. Lovasz. New York: Elsevier.

Thorndike, Edward L. 1911. *Animal Intelligence: Experimental Studies.* New York: Macmillan.

Thye, Shane R. 2000. "A Status Value Theory of Power in Exchange Relations." *American Sociological Review* 65:407–432.

Tootell, Geoffrey, Alison Bianchi, and Paul T. Munroe. 1998. "Understanding the Nature of Scope Conditions: Some Considerations and Consequences, Including Hybrid Theories as a Step Forward." Pp. 213–235 in *Advances in Group Processes, vol. 15,* edited by John Skvoretz and Jacek Szmatka. Stamford, CT: JAI Press.

Toulmin, Steven. 1953. *The Philosophy of Science.* London: Hutchinson.

Treuil, Jean. 1995. "Emergence of Kinship Structures: A Multi-agent Approach." Pp. 59–85 in *Artificial Societies: The Computer Simulation of Social Life,* edited by N. Gilbert and R. Conte. London: University College London Press.

Troyer, Lisa. 1999. "MacSES, v. 5.0." Unpublished software manual.

Troyer, Lisa. 2000. "MacSES, v. 7.0." Unpublished software manual.

Troyer, Lisa. 2001. "Effects of Protocol Differences on the Study of Status and Social Influence." *Current Research in Social Psychology.* Available on-line at http://www.uiowa.edu/~grpproc.

Troyer, Lisa, and C. Wesley Younts. 1997. "Whose Expectations Matter? The Relative Power of First-Order and Second-Order Expectations in Determining Social Influence." *American Journal of Sociology* 103:692–732.

Tumin, Melvin M. 1953. "Some Principles of Stratification: A Critical Analysis." *American Sociological Review* 18:387–394.

Turner, Jonathan H. 1985. "In Defense of Positivism." *Sociological Theory* 3:24–30.

Turner, Jonathan H. 1987. "Toward a Sociological Theory of Motivation." *American Sociological Review* 52:15–27.

Turner, Jonathan H. 1988. *A Theory of Social Interaction.* Stanford, CA: Stanford University Press.

Turner, Jonathan H. 1992a. "Positivism." Pp. 1509–1512 in *Encyclopedia of Sociology,* edited by Edgar F. Borgatta and Marie L. Borgatta. New York: Macmillan.

Turner, Jonathan H. 1992b. "The Promise of Positivism." Pp. 156–178 in *Postmodernism and Social Theory,* edited by Steven Seidman and David G. Wagner. Cambridge: Basil Blackwell.

Turner, Jonathan H. 1994. "A General Theory of Emotion in Human Interaction." *Osterreichische Zeitschrift fur Soziologie* 8:20–35.

Turner, Jonathan H. 1998. "Must Sociological Theory and Sociological Practice Be So Far Apart? A Polemical Answer." *Sociological Perspectives* 41:243–258.

Turner, Jonathan H. 1999. "Toward a General Sociological Theory of Emotions." *Journal for the Theory of Social Behavior* 29:109–162.

Turner, Jonathan H. 2000. "A Theory of Embedded Encounters." *Advances in Group Processes* 17:283–320.

Turner, Jonathan H. 2002. *Face-to-Face: Toward a Sociological Theory of Interpersonal Behavior.* Stanford, CA: Stanford University Press.

Turner, Ralph H. 1962. "Role Taking: Process vs. Conformity." Pp. 20–40 in *Human Behavior and Social Processes,* edited by Arnold Rose. Boston: Houghton Mifflin.

Turner, Stephen. 1989. "Jasso's Principle." *Sociological Theory* 7:130–134.

Vakas-Duong, Deborah, and Kevin Reilley. 1995. "A System of IAC Neural Networks as the Basis for Self-Organization in a Sociological Dynamical System Simulation." *Behavioral Science* 40:275–303.

Vallier, I. 1962. "Structural Differentiation, Productive Imperatives, and Communal Norms: The Kibbutz in Crisis." *Social Forces* 40:233–242.

Vanberg, Victor J., and Roger D. Congleton. 1992. "Rationality, Morality, and Exit." *American Political Science Review* 86:418–431.

Volterra, V. 1931. *Leçon sur la Theorie Mathematique de la Lutte pour la Vie.* Paris: Gautheir-Villars.

von Neumann, John, and Oscar Morgenstern. 1947. *The Theory of Games and Economic Behavior.* Princeton, NJ: Princeton University Press.

Wacquant, Loic J.D. 1994. "Positivism." Pp. 495–498 in *The Blackwell Dictionary of Twentieth-Century Social Thought,* edited by William Outhwaite and Tom Bottomore. Cambridge, MA: Blackwell.

Wagner, David G. 1984. *The Growth of Sociological Theories.* Beverly Hills, CA: Sage.

Wagner, David G. 2000. "On Irrationality of Rejecting Falsified Theories." *Sociological Focus* 33:27–39.

Wagner, David G., and Joseph Berger. 1985. "Do Sociological Theories Grow?" *American Journal of Sociology* 90:697–728.

Wagner, David G., and Joseph Berger. 1986. "Programs, Theory, and Metatheory." *American Journal of Sociology* 92:168–182.

Wagner, David G., and Joseph Berger. 1993. "Status Characteristics Theory: The Growth of a Program." Pp. 23–63 in *Theoretical Research Programs: Studies in the Growth of Theory*, edited by Joseph Berger and Morris Zelditch, Jr. Stanford, CA: Stanford University Press.

Wagner, David G., Rebecca S. Ford, and Thomas W. Ford. 1986. "Can Gender Inequalities Be Reduced?" *American Sociological Review* 51:47–61.

Walder, Andrew. 1992. "Property Rights and Stratification in Socialist Redistributive Economies." *American Sociological Review* 57:524–539.

Walker, Henry A. 2000. "Three Faces of Explanation: Rethinking the Theory Project." *Sociological Focus* 33:41–56.

Walker, Henry A., and Bernard P. Cohen. 1985. "Scope Statements: Imperatives for Evaluating Theory." *American Sociological Review* 50:288–301.

Walker, Henry A., Shane R. Thyne, Brent Simpson, Michael J. Lovaglia, and David Willer. 2000. "Network Exchange Theory: Recent Developments and New Directions." *Social Psychology Quarterly* 63:324–337.

Wallace, Walter L. 1988. "Toward a Disciplinary Matrix in Sociology." Pp. 23–76 in *The Handbook of Sociology*, edited by Neil J. Smelser. Beverly Hills, CA: Sage.

Wallace, Walter L. 1995. "Why Sociology Doesn't Make Progress." *Sociological Forum* 10:313–318.

Wartofsky, Max W. 1982. "Positivism and Politics: The Vienna Circle as a Social Movement" *Grazer Philosophische Studien* 16:79–101.

Wattenberg, Ben. 2000, August 18. "Committing Sociology." *Jewish World Review*. Available on-line at http://www.jewishworldreview.com/cols/wattenberg1.asp.

Watts, Duncan J. 1999. *Small Worlds: The Dynamics of Networks between Order and Randomness*. Princeton, NJ: Princeton University Press.

Weber, Max. 1949. *The Methodology of the Social Sciences*. Glencoe, IL: Free Press.

Weber, Max. 1978 [1921]. *Economy and Society. Part 1: Conceptual Exposition*. Berkeley: University of California Press.

Webster, Murrray, Jr. 1977. "Equating Characteristics and Social Interaction: Two Experiments." *Sociometry* 40:41–50.

Webster, Murray, Jr., and James E. Driskell, Jr. 1983. "Beauty as Status." *American Journal of Sociology* 89:140–165.

Webster, Murray, Jr., and Martha Foschi, eds. 1988. *Status Generalization: New Theory and Research*. Stanford, CA: Stanford University Press.

Webster, Murray, Jr., and Stuart J. Hysom. 1998. "Creating Status Characteristics." *American Sociological Review* 63:351–378.

Webster, Murray, Jr., and John B. Kervin. 1971. "Artificiality in Experimental Sociology." *Canadian Review of Sociology and Anthropology* 8:263–272.

Webster, Murray, Jr., and Barbara Sobieszek. 1974. *Sources of Self-Evaluation*. New York: Wiley-Interscience.

Webster, Murray, Jr., and Joseph M. Whitmeyer. 1999. "A Theory of Second-Order Expectations and Behavior." *Social Psychology Quarterly* 62:17–31.

Webster, Murray, Jr., and Joseph M. Whitmeyer. 2001. "Applications of Theories of Group Processes." *Sociological Theory*. 19:250–270.

Weinberg, Steven. 1992. *Dreams of a Final Theory*. New York: Pantheon Books.

Weinberg, Steven. 1994. *Dreams of a Final Theory*. New York: Vintage Books.

Wesolowski, Wlodzimierz. 1962. "Some Notes on the Functional Theory of Stratification." *The Polish Sociological Bulletin* 3–4:28–38.

Wesolowski, Wlodzimierz, and Bogdan Mach. 1986. "Unfulfilled Systemic Functions of Social Mobility I: A Theoretical Scheme." *International Sociology* 1:19–35.

White, Harrison C. 1963. *An Anatomy of Kinships*. Englewood Cliffs, NJ: Prentice-Hall.

Whitmeyer, Joseph M. 1994. "Why Actor Models Are Integral to Structural Analysis." *Sociological Theory* 12(2):153–165.

Whitmeyer, Joseph M. 1997. "Applying General Equilibrium Analysis and Game Theory to Exchange Networks." *Current Research in Social Psychology* 2:13–23. Available on-line at http://www.uiowa.edu/~grpproc.

Whitmeyer, Joseph M. 1999a. "Convex Preferences and Power Inequality in Exchange Networks: An Experimental Study." *Rationality and Society* 11:367–390.

Whitmeyer, Joseph M. 1999b. "Interest-Network Structures in Exchange Networks." *Sociological Perspectives* 42:23–47.

Whitmeyer, Joseph M. 2001. "Measuring Power in Exchange Networks." *Sociological Perspectives* 44:141–162.

Whyte, William Foote. 1982. "Social Inventions for Solving Human Problems." *American Sociological Review* 47:1–13.

Wiles, Andrew. 1993. *Fermat's Last Theorem: The Theorem and its Proof; an Exploration of Issues*. (videotape) Berkeley CA: Mathematical Sciences Research Institute.

Willer, David. 1987. *Theory and Experimental Investigation of Social Structures*. New York: Gordon and Breach.

Willer, David. 1992. "Predicting Power in Exchange Networks: A Brief History and Introduction to the Issues." *Social Networks* 14:187–211.

Willer, David. 1996. "The Prominence of Formal Theory in Sociology." *Sociological Forum* 11:319–331.

Willer, David. 1999. *Network Exchange Theory*. Westport, CT: Praeger.

Willer, David, and Bo Anderson, eds. 1981. *Networks, Exchange and Coercion*. New York: Elsevier.

Willer, David, Michael J. Lovaglia, and Barry Markovsky. 1997. "Power and Influence: A Theoretical Bridge." *Social Forces* 76:571–603.

Willer, David, and Barry Markovsky. 1993. "The Theory of Elementary Relations: Its Development and Research Program." Pp. 323–363 in *Theoretical Research Programs: Studies in Theory Growth*, edited by Joseph Berger and Morris Zelditch, Jr. Stanford, CA: Stanford University Press.

Willer, David, and John Skvoretz. 1997. "Games and Structures II." *Rationality and Society* 9:5–35.

Willer, David, and Murray Webster. 1970. "Theoretical Concepts and Observables." *American Sociological Review* 35:748–757.

Willis, Paul. 1981. *Learning to Labor*. New York: Columbia University Press.

Wirth, Louis. 1938. "Urbanism as a Way of Life." *American Journal of Sociology* 44: 3–24.

Wojcicki, Ryszard. 1974. *Formal Methodology of Empirical Sciences* (in Polish). Wroclaw, Warszawa, Kraków, and Gdansk: Ossolineum.

Wolenski, Jan. 1986. "A Moderate Defense of Scientism" (in Polish). *Studia Filozoficzne* 9(250):63–80.

Yamagishi, Toshio. 1998. *The Structure of Trust*. Tokyo: Tokyo University Press.

Yamagishi, Toshio, and Karen S. Cook. 1993. "Generalized Exchange and Social Dilemmas." *Social Psychology Quarterly* 56:235–248.

Yamagishi, Toshio, Karen S. Cook, and Motobi Watabe. 1998. "Uncertainty, Trust and Commitment Formation in the United States and Japan." *American Journal of Sociology* 104:165–194.

Yamaguchi, Kazuo. 1996. "Power in Networks of Substitutable and Complementary Exchange Relations: A Rational-Choice Model and an Analysis of Power Centralization." *American Sociological Review* 61:308–332.

Zelditch, Morris, Jr. 1991. "Levels of Specificity within Theoretical Strategies." *Sociological Perspectives* 34:303–312.

Zelditch, Morris, Jr. 1992. "Problems and Progress in Sociological Theory." *Sociological Perspectives* 35:415–431.

Zelditch, Morris, Jr. 1999. "Memorandum on the Davis-Moore theory of stratification." Unpublished manuscript, Department of Sociology, Stanford University, Stanford, CA.

Zelditch, Morris Jr., William A. Harris, George M. Thomas, and Henry A. Walker. 1983. "Decisions, Nondecisions, and Metadecisions." Pp. 1–32 in *Research in Social Movements, Conflicts and Change, vol. 5*, edited by Louis Kriesberg. Greenwich, CT: JAI Press.

Zetterberg, Hans L. 1965. *On Theory and Verification in Sociology*. New York: Bedminster Press.

Zhao, Dingxin. 1998. "Ecologies of Social Movements: Student Mobilization during the 1989 Prodemocracy Movement in Beijing." *American Journal of Sociology* 103: 1493–1529.

Zhao, Shanyang. 1996. "The Beginning of the End or the End of the Beginning? The Theory Construction Movement Revisited." *Sociological Forum* 11:305–318.

Index

About the Editors and Contributors

This volume brings together top sociologists as they work to create a truly social science in group processes research. Together the chapters in this volume draw a blueprint for the successful conduct of social science.

ALISON J. BIANCHI is Assistant Professor of Sociology at Kent State University. She received her first master's degree from Stanford University, her second from San Jose State University, and her Ph.D. from Stanford. Her research interests include group processes, mathematical sociology, and the new field of developmental social psychology, specifically as it pertains to adolescent behavior.

PHILLIP BONACICH is Professor of Sociology at the University of California, Los Angeles. He is interested in mathematical models of social networks and applications of game theory to sociology. His articles have appeared in such journals as *Social Psychology Quarterly, Social Networks, Journal of Mathematical Sociology*, and *Rationality and Society*.

DAVID E. BOYNS is the managing editor of *Sociological Theory* and a doctoral candidate and research fellow for the School Improvement Research Group at the University of California at Riverside. His sociological interests include theories of self and identity, emotions, mass media and semiotics, urban sociology, and postmodernism. His theoretical publications have been directed toward the development of theories of self and emotion, as well as the resolution of the micro-macro debate in sociological theory.

THOMAS J. FARARO is Distinguished Service Professor of Sociology at the University of Pittsburgh. He has a Ph.D. in sociology from Syracuse University, was awarded a three-year National Institutes of Mental Health (NIMH) fellowship for the study of mathematics in the social sciences at Stanford University, and joined the Department of Sociology at the University of Pittsburgh in 1967. The early phase of his teaching and research dealt with formal and mathematical methods, including a research monograph, *A Study of a Biased Friendship Net* (coauthored with M. Sunshine) published in 1964, and *Mathematical Sociology*, a text first published in 1973. His most recent book-length work is *Social Action Systems: Foundation and Synthesis in Sociological Theory*, published by Praeger in 2001.

MICHAEL J. LOVAGLIA is Associate Professor of Sociology at the University of Iowa. His work focuses on two fundamental social processes, status and power, and their application in society. A recent project examined the social roots of the racial gap in standardized test scores (1998, "Status Processes and Mental Ability Test Scores," *American Journal of Sociology* 104). In 1995 he helped found the Internet journal, *Current Research in Social Psychology* (http://www.uiowa.edu/~grpproc), and continues as its editor. His recent book, *Knowing People: The Personal Use of Social Psychology*, brings social psychological research to a broad readership.

WALTER LUKE is a graduate student at Cornell University. His research interests include social order and collective action, agent-based social simulation, and the sociology of knowledge.

MICHAEL W. MACY is Professor of Sociology at Cornell University. He is best known for introducing "backward-looking rationality" as a sociological alternative to forward-looking models of *homo economicus*. He uses agent-based computational experiments and laboratory experiments with human subjects to look for elementary principles of organization that may yield clues about the emergence of "everyday cooperation" based on informal norms, habits, rituals, routines, heuristics, or moral rules. His work has appeared in *Annual Review of Sociology, Computational and Mathematical Organization Theory, Social Psychology Quarterly*, and *American Sociological Review*.

BARBARA F. MEEKER is Professor of Sociology at the University of Maryland, College Park. She has both an M.A. and a Ph.D. in Sociology from Stanford University. Before coming to the University of Maryland in 1971, she taught at the University of California, Irvine, and the University of Washington in Seattle and worked as a staff associate at the National Academy of Sciences in Washington, D.C.

PAUL T. MUNROE is Assistant Professor of Sociology at Towson State University. He received his M.A. and Ph.D. from Stanford University and is interested in the effects of social structure on people's behavior, attitudes, and awareness of others and self.

ROBERT K. SHELLY is Professor of Sociology at Ohio University, Athens. For much of his career, he has worked on the activation and emergence of inequality in task groups. Reports of this work appeared recently in *Sociological Perspectives, Social Psychology Quarterly, Current Research in Social Psychology*, and *Small Group Research*. He is currently collaborating with Lisa Troyer on studies of the activation and emergence of inequality in open interaction task groups.

JACEK SZMATKA was Professor of Sociology at Jagiellonian University, Krakow, Poland, and Adjunct Professor of Sociology at the University of South Carolina. He published more than sixty articles, wrote two books, and edited and co-edited eight. His work, published in Polish, includes *Individual and Society: On the Dependency of Individual Phenomena on Social Phenomena* and *Small Social Structures: Introduction to Structural Microsociology*. His coedited publications include *Structure, Exchange, and Power: Studies in Theoretical Sociology, Contemporary Social Exchange Theories*, and, recently, *Status, Network, and Structure. Theory Development in Group Processes* (1997). His major areas of interest included general methodology, investigations of social structures, and group processes; especially in the latter, he had unique contributions. After he established the Group Processes Laboratory in Krakow (the first lab of its kind in Europe), he actively participated in the development of Elementary Theory. His "cross-national experiments" on network exchange structures and investigations on compound networks are very important inputs to our knowledge about structurally determined power. However, his most original idea involved conflict relations and conflict networks. Constructing a new model of conflict relations and conflict networks that consists of conflict relations, Jacek developed an entirely new branch within the scope of the Elementary Theory Research Program. He successfully completed extensive empirical tests of the new Conflict Network Theory and was working on extending the model to include various types of negative sanctions available to actors. Jacek also contributed to the knowledge of mechanisms of theory growth in sociology. The interesting conception and analysis of three genera of sociological theories added to our understanding of methodological progress in the social sciences.

GEOFFREY TOOTELL is Professor of Sociology at San Jose State University. From 1945 through 1946, he toured with the U.S. Army, European Theater, and later received his M.A. and Ph.D. in Sociology from Columbia University. After several years working in industry, he joined the Department of Sociology at San Jose State University, California. His principal research interests include theory and research methods, with applications to organizations and industry; group processes and social psychology, including norms and legitimation, status characteristics theory; and network exchange theory. His theoretical focus is on mathematical sociology and its uses. Other scholarly interests include metaphysics, epistemology, and ethics.

LISA TROYER, Associate Professor of Sociology at the University of Iowa, received her master's and doctoral degrees from Stanford University. Her research, funded through multiple grants from the National Science Foundation and University of Iowa, focuses on social influence, work design, and individual and collective outcomes. Accounts of her research have appeared in *American Journal of Sociology, Social Psychology Quarterly, Work and Occupations, Advances in Interdisciplinary Studies of Work Teams*, and *Advances in Group Processes.*

JONATHAN H. TURNER is Distinguished Professor of Sociology at the University of California at Riverside. He is the author of more than 120 articles and twenty-five books, including *On the Origins of Human Emotions* (2000) and *The Structure of Sociological Theory* (1998).

HENRY A. WALKER is Professor of Sociology at the University of Arizona. He received his M.A. from the University of Missouri, Kansas City, and his Ph.D. from Stanford in 1979. His current research combines ideas from status characteristics theory, legitimation theory and network exchange theory.

JOSEPH M. WHITMEYER is Associate Professor of Sociology at the University of North Carolina, Charlotte. He currently studies second-order expectations with Murray Webster and Lisa Slattery Rashotte. He is also working on analyzing different mechanisms of social power, the mathematics of trust, modeling close friendship networks, and learning the Rachmaninov Preludes. His articles have appeared in such journals as *Sociological Theory, Current Research in Social Psychology, Rationality and Society*, and *Sociological Perspectives.*

ROBERT B. WILLER is a graduate student in Sociology at Cornell University. His undergraduate studies at the University of Iowa included training in social psychology, formal theory, and experimental methods. His current research is threefold: He is pursuing connections between power and status processes; developing experimental tests of criminology theories; and working on agent-based modeling projects.

KINGA WYSIENSKA is an instructor and Ph.D. candidate in Sociology at Jagiellonian University, Krakow, Poland. Her research interests include structural social psychology, the philosophy of science, theory construction, and experimental methods. Her recent work has appeared in *Encyclopedia of Sociology, Sociological Focus*, and *Studia Socjologiczne*.

PIDI ZHANG is Assistant Professor of Sociology at Georgia Southern University. His research interests include the economic performance of different ethnic groups, modeling, theory construction, and network exchange theories.